PSYCHOLINGUISTIC PHENOMENA IN MARKETING COMMUNICATIONS

PSYCHOLINGUISTIC PHENOMENA IN MARKETING COMMUNICATIONS

Edited by

Tina M. Lowrey
University of Texas at San Antonio

Psychology Press
Taylor & Francis Group

NEW YORK AND HOVE

First published by
Lawrence Erlbaum Associates, Inc., Publishers
10 Industrial Avenue
Mahwah, New Jersey 07430

This edition published 2013 by Psychology Press

711 Third Avenue	27 Church Road
New York	Hove
NY 10017	East Sussex, BN3 2FA

Psychology Press is an imprint of the Taylor & Francis Group, an informa business

First issued in paperback 2013

Cover design by Tomai Maridou

Library of Congress Cataloging-in-Publication Data

Psycholinguistic phenomena in marketing communications / Tina M. Lowrey,
editor

p. cm.

Includes bibliographical references and index.
ISBN 978-0-8058-5690-3 — 0-8058-5690-0 (cloth : alk. paper)
ISBN 978-1-4106-1504-6 — 1-4106-1504-9 (e book)
ISBN 978-0-415-65113-4 (pb)

1. Psycholinguistics. 2. Advertising—Language. 3. Semantics I. Lowrey, Tina M.
P37.P7548   2007
401'.9—dc22   2006007564
                                                                     CIP

I would like to dedicate this book to the memory of my parents, George and Mary, who instilled in me the love of words.

And always, to L. J., for everything.

Contents

Preface

It's been a goal of mine to put together a book of this sort for some time. I first became fascinated with words and language when I watched my Mom converse in signs with my deaf aunt. Later, as I watched my Dad fill in his beloved crossword puzzles with carefully sharpened pencils, the fascination only deepened. I remember a particularly selfish Christmas gift I gave my Dad one year—*A Pleasure in Words* (1981) by Eugene T. Maleska (the crossword editor of *The New York Times* from 1977–1993); it was selfish because I also wanted to read it myself. This fascination with language was further sparked in graduate school, when I was fortunate to take a course on psycholinguistics from William F. Brewer at the University of Illinois. This was during the 1980s, when the application of psycholinguistic theory to advertising and other marketing communications was fairly popular. The chance to combine a topic that had fascinated me for years with my advanced studies was immediately evident to me, and so I began pursuing my research.

Unfortunately, after my dissertation was completed, the popularity of the area seemed to wane, and I felt as if I was the only one interested in such issues. Those who had done some of the earliest work had moved on to other topics, perhaps in part due to complicated methodological issues and other difficulties that confront any scholar with a desire to design controlled experiments that will also yield some external validity (a conundrum at all times, but particularly daunting, it seems, when doing research on language).

In recent years, however, it has been very encouraging to see a resurgence of interest and investigations from scholars covering an incredible array of language-based topics that apply psycholinguistic theories to various types of marketing communications. It seems timely, then, to provide a thorough overview of the current work being done in this area, with the express purpose of encouraging others who might be interested in doing similar types of research. Although many of the current scholars doing such work are housed in departments of marketing, I am pleased that this volume has gone beyond these narrow confines to include authors from other disciplines. I hope that the audience for this book will include students and scholars in advertising, anthropology, cognitive psychology, communications, linguistics, marketing, social psychology, and sociology, to name a few.

This volume is designed to demonstrate the diversity of the field, not only in terms of contributing disciplines, but also in terms of relevant topics and methodological approaches. Chapters include both empirical and conceptual treatments, and the empirical pieces use a variety of methodologies. The book is divided into four parts along a continuum: The first part is devoted to words (or, actually, even smaller units—see chaps. 1 and 3), the second part to sentences, the third to larger bodies of text, and the fourth to a comprehensive wrap-up of what we've learned from the research and conceptual discussions that have been included in the book. In truth, the chapters could have been organized along a number of conceptual dimensions. Do not be misled by the existing framework to conclude that chapters in one part have nothing in common with chapters in other parts of the book. For example, both chapter 4 (in part I) and chapter 12 (in part III) will be of great use to those interested in bilingual processing of advertising and other marketing communications. In a similar manner, chapters across all three parts share theoretical underpinnings and/or methodologies. I encourage readers to look for their own comparisons and contrasts in addition to those I've pointed out.

Part I is devoted to the smallest units of linguistic measurement, beginning with single letters and moving on to entire words (in the form of brand names). Chapter 1, by Hoegg and Alba, is a fascinating investigation into the effects of a single letter label on perceptions of taste and brand preference (literally, with each brand being labeled either Brand A or Brand B). They find that brands sharing the same label are judged to be more similar to one another than brands with different labels (even when they are not, actually, more similar). Thus, they provide evidence beyond a "mere labeling" effect.

Gontijo and Zhang's chapter (chap. 2) provides evidence that brand names are processed differently than either common nouns or proper names (the two of which, of course, have been shown to be processed differently from one another). That is, brand names are not processed in the same manner as proper names or common nouns, perhaps due to their hybrid nature. This suggests, as they argue, that brand names are indeed in a class by themselves.

Chapter 3 (Shrum & Lowrey) investigates the effects of phonetic symbolism in brand names both across product categories and within the same category when attributes vary. We find that changing a single letter (and, hence, a single sound) has implications for brand name preferences, depending on the attributes deemed desirable for a particular product. Note the similarity to chapter 1 (in terms of a single letter causing attitudinal differences).

Zhang and Schmitt's chapter (chap. 4) takes the analysis of brand name effects into a dual language scenario, looking at English and Chinese brand names, to uncover what the processing of translations can tell us about underlying cognitive processes. Investigating both the phonetic and semantic properties of brand names (in both phonographic and logographic writing systems), they offer a new bilingual access model.

Chapter 5, by Lerman, is a comprehensive review of previous linguistic research on brand names (and words), as well as the first four chapters of this volume, in order to provide an overarching framework for the psycholinguistic study of brand names. Her chapter weaves together findings from research in phonology, morphology, and semantics to provide a better understanding of the relations between these factors at various levels of processing. The chapter is specifically designed to encourage future work in the complex area of brand name linguistics.

Part II moves on to apply psycholinguistic theory to the study of entire sentences within marketing communications, primarily in the realm of headlines and body copy. Meeds and Bradley (chap. 6) provide evidence that the application of a sentence-based copytesting tool (i.e., sentence importance ratings) might assist copywriters in their quest for impactful and communicative copy. They argue that the rating of sentence importance offers unique insights into copy effectiveness not obtainable through standard readability indices, such as Gunning or Flesch.

Chapter 7 (Dimofte & Yalch) argues that polysemy can enhance advertising's effects, but if used improperly, the effects instead may backfire. In fact, they discuss a moderating variable based on an individual's access to multiple interpretations. Their focus is on how consumers process ambiguous language, and their results suggest that communicators should consider the implicit (as well as explicit) effects when assessing the effectiveness of polysemous slogans.

Phillips and McQuarrie (chap. 8) offer an intriguing methodology for studying the usage of metaphors in advertising. They show how competing metaphors in a specific arena (exercise) are more or less successful. Despite the domain-specificity in the chapter, their conceptualization can be applied to any domain. Indeed, their chapter provides ample description of the method they used to uncover competing metaphors. Note that all three chapters in part II provide novel methodological tools and/or methodologies that should help other scholars interested in doing research in this area.

Part III looks at the largest unit of measurement—entire textual narratives. Chapter 9 (Escalas & Stern) provides empirical evidence for the importance of emotional responses to plot elements in ad narratives, focusing on the positive responses of empathy and sympathy. Well-written ad narratives that evoke positive emotions are more effective across a variety of measures. An intriguing future question given their findings is what the effects might be of well-written ad narratives that evoke negative emotions.

Adaval (chap. 10) provides a thorough conceptualization of how psychological theories can help explain the power of myth in advertising. She investigates how language and images combined can create advertising myths. These myths have implications for how we perceive the world. Basing her argument on cognitive processing theories, she argues that myths can influence our behavior unconsciously.

Chapter 11, by Levi and Pisoni, looks at the importance of specific speech properties in determining the success of voiceovers used in broadcast advertising. In doing so, they go beyond traditional symbolic linguistics to investigate paralinguistic
information (also known as extralinguistic or indexical information). They argue
that such factors as familiarity (e.g., a celebrity voiceover), accent, and speaking
rate have important implications for the success of broadcast advertising and the
retention of spoken materials.

Last (but definitely not least), Carroll, Luna, and Peracchio (chap. 12) investigate the dual language processing of advertising texts, focusing on fluent bilingual
speakers. In a major conceptual contribution, they classify extant research on dual
language processing into three distinct categories: unique language processing, bilingual language processing, and bilingual-bicultural language processing (all of
which are important in better understanding how bilinguals process marketing
communications).

Part IV concludes the book with an afterword by Wyer, who provides an overarching theoretical framework to which each of the preceding chapters can apply.
He offers seven postulates regarding both spontaneous and deliberative comprehension processes. In doing so, he positions each of the chapters within the framework, and also provides ideas for future research in all of these areas. All of us are
grateful for the comprehensive manner in which he pulled our chapters together in a
meaningful way.

This is the first book of its kind to draw together the latest research from a diverse
group of scholars that applies psycholinguistic theories to marketing communications phenomena. I hope it will provide not only a broad overview of what is currently being studied, but also spark additional interest in the study of language in a
marketing communications context. Despite its inherent difficulties, the topic is
fascinating and full of research opportunity.

ACKNOWLEDGMENTS

I would like to acknowledge all of those who helped put this volume together, including the authors (who served as internal reviewers on one another's chapters). I
would also like to thank the anonymous proposal reviewers (all of whom are indi-
rectly responsible for the inclusion of chapters not in the original proposal that have
greatly enhanced the volume) and Chandra Kalapatapu, who assisted with the Author Index. Finally, many thanks to Anne Duffy, Rebecca Larsen, and Tanya
Policht, all three of Lawrence Erlbaum Associates, who provided guidance
throughout the entire process.

About the Contributors

Rashmi Adaval (PhD, University of Illinois) is Associate Professor of Marketing at the Hong Kong University of Science and Technology. Her main research interests include the role played by affect in consumer information processing, the impact of narratives and visual imagery on memory and judgments, and the automatic responses to contextual stimuli. Dr. Adaval's work has appeared in the *Journal of Consumer Research*, *Journal of Consumer Psychology*, *Journal of Experimental Social Psychology*, and *Advances in Experimental Social Psychology*. Her publications include chapters in *Blurring the Lines Between Entertainment and Persuasion: The Psychology of Entertainment Media* and the *Handbook of Communication and Social Interaction Skills*. She is on the editorial boards of the *Journal of Consumer Research* and the *Journal of Consumer Psychology*.

Joseph W. Alba (PhD, Temple University) is Distinguished Professor of Marketing at the University of Florida. His research has appeared in the *Journal of Consumer Research*, *Journal of Marketing Research*, *Journal of Marketing*, *Journal of Consumer Psychology*, *Psychological Bulletin*, *Journal of Experimental Psychology*, and *Organizational Behavior and Human Decision Processes*. He serves on the editorial boards of the *Journal of Consumer Research*, *Journal of Marketing Research*, *Journal of Marketing*, *Journal of Consumer Psychology*, *International Journal of Research in Marketing*, and *Journal of Behavioral Decision Making*. He is past President of the Association for Consumer Research and a Fellow of both the Society for Consumer Psychology and the American Psychological Association.

Samuel D. Bradley (PhD, Indiana University) is Assistant Professor of Advertising at the College of Mass Communications at Texas Tech University. His primary research interests involve cognitive processing of mediated messages, psychophysiological responding to mediated messages, and formal computational modeling of underlying cognitive processes. His work has appeared in *Media Psy-*

chology, Journal of Consumer Psychology, Psychology & Marketing, Journal of Broadcasting & Electronic Media, and *Human Communication Research.*

Ryall Carroll is a marketing PhD candidate at Baruch College. Prior to entering the PhD program, he earned his MS in marketing research from the University of Texas in Arlington and a BA in economics from the University of Rochester. His work experience includes positions at NOP Market Research Company and Ralston Purina Company. His theoretical research interests are in the area of cognitive representations of information and their influence over consumer processing and decision making. In particular, Mr. Carroll is interested in the effects of linguistic, social, and cultural orientations on consumer processing and decision making. His paper on *Marketing in a Multilingual Environment* appeared in the Society for Consumer Psychology (2006) conference proceedings.

Claudiu V. Dimofte (PhD, University of Washington) is Assistant Professor of Marketing at Georgetown University in Washington, DC. His main research interests address unconscious consumer responses to marketing variables. His work has appeared in the *Journal of Consumer Research, Journal of Consumer Psychology,* and *Journal of Advertising.* He has also published a chapter in *Applying Social Cognition to Consumer-Focused Strategy.*

Jennifer Edson Escalas (PhD, Duke University) is Associate Professor at the Owen Graduate School of Management at Vanderbilt University. Her research applies the concept of narrative processing to the study of how advertising affects consumers and how consumers use brands to express themselves. Her work has been published in the *Journal of Consumer Research, Journal of Consumer Psychology, Journal of Advertising,* and *Journal of Public Policy and Marketing.* She is a member of the *Journal of Consumer Research* and *Journal of Consumer Psychology* editorial boards, and is involved in the Association for Consumer Research Advisory Council and the Society for Consumer Psychology Membership Committee.

Possidonia F. D. Gontijo (PhD, University of Edinburgh, Scotland, UK) is a postdoctoral researcher at the Psychology Department of the University of California, Los Angeles, where she has specialized in the study of brain lateralization. Her primary research interests are in language processing and marketing communication. She is particularly interested in the organization of the mental lexicon and how it impacts our language abilities. Her work has appeared in peer-reviewed journals such as *Brain and Language* and *Behavior Research Methods, Instruments & Computers.*

JoAndrea Hoegg (PhD, University of Florida) is Assistant Professor of Marketing at the University of British Columbia. Her research interests include the influence of semantic labels on sensory perception and the effects of product appearance on information processing. Her work has been published in the *Journal of Consumer Research.* She has also authored a chapter on product aesthetics in the *Handbook of Consumer Psychology.*

Dawn B. Lerman (PhD, Baruch College, City University of New York) is Associate Professor of Marketing at Fordham University. Her main research interests include psycholinguistic, sociolinguistic, and cross-cultural aspects of consumer behavior, advertising, and branding. Her work has appeared in journals such as the *Journal of Consumer Research, Journal of Advertising Research, Psychology & Marketing*, and *European Journal of Marketing*. She has authored chapters in *Managing Tourism Firms, Best Practices in International Marketing, European Perspectives in Marketing*, and *Cross-Cultural Marketing: Contexts, Concepts, and Practices*. She is a member of the editorial board for the *Journal of Business Research*.

Susannah V. Levi (PhD, University of Washington) is an NIH postdoctoral fellow in the Speech Research Laboratory in the Department of Psychological and Brain Sciences at Indiana University. She is currently working on the interaction of voice and linguistic effects in the perception of bilingual speakers. Her other specialization is in Turkish phonology. Her work has appeared in the *Journal of the Acoustical Society of America* and *Journal of the International Phonetics Association*.

Tina M. Lowrey (PhD, University of Illinois) is Professor of Marketing at the University of Texas at San Antonio. Her main research interests include psycholinguistic analyses of advertising, gift-giving, and ritualistic consumption. Her work has appeared in numerous journals, including the *Journal of Consumer Research, Journal of Consumer Psychology*, and *Journal of Advertising*. She has authored chapters in *Contemporary Consumption Rituals: A Research Anthology* (which she co-edited with Cele C. Otnes); *Marketing Communication: New Approaches, Technologies, and Styles*; *Gender Issues and Consumer Behavior*; *Gift Giving: A Research Anthology*; and *New Developments and Approaches in Consumer Behavior Research*. She serves on the editorial boards of the *Journal of Advertising, Media Psychology*, and *Psychology & Marketing*.

David Luna (PhD, University of Wisconsin–Milwaukee) is Associate Professor of Marketing at Baruch College (City University of New York). His main research interest is language and information processing in the context of marketing communications. Other interests include imagery processing, mental representations, and the role of automatic processes on judgment formation. His work has been published in the *Journal of Consumer Research, Journal of Consumer Psychology, Journal of the Academy of Marketing Science*, and *Journal of Advertising*, among others. Dr. Luna's research has also appeared in several edited books, including chapters in *Diversity in Advertising*; *Online Consumer Psychology: Understanding and Influencing Behavior in the Virtual World*, and *Persuasive Imagery: A Consumer Response Perspective*. His papers appear regularly in the proceedings of national and international conferences, such as the *Society for Consumer Research* and the *Association for Consumer Research* proceedings.

Edward F. McQuarrie (PhD, University of Cincinnati) is Professor of Marketing at the Leavey School of Business, Santa Clara University. His research interests include qualitative research techniques and market research appropriate to technology products, on the one hand, and advertising research, rhetoric, and semiotics on the other. He has written two books, *Customer Visits: Building a Better Market Focus*, and *The Market Research Toolbox: A Concise Guide for Beginners*, and has published articles in the *Journal of Consumer Research, Journal of Consumer Psychology, Journal of the Market Research Society, Journal of Advertising Research, Journal of Advertising, Marketing Theory*, and elsewhere. He serves on the editorial board of the *Journal of Consumer Research*.

Robert Meeds (PhD, University of Missouri) is Associate Professor and Associate Director for Graduate Studies and Research at the A. Q. Miller School of Journalism and Mass Communications at Kansas State University. His primary research interest lies in applying psycholinguistic models of text comprehension to advertising and persuasive texts. His work has appeared in the *Journal of Consumer Psychology, Psychology and Marketing, International Journal of Advertising, Newspaper Research Journal, Web Journal of Mass Communication Research, and Journal of Advertising Education*.

Laura A. Peracchio (PhD, Northwestern University) is Professor of Marketing at the University of Wisconsin–Milwaukee. Her areas of research interest are visual persuasion, language and culture, and food and nutrition issues. Her work has appeared in the *Journal of Consumer Research, Journal of Consumer Psychology*, and *Journal of Advertising*. Dr. Peracchio is an Associate Editor of the *Journal of Consumer Research* and President of the Society for Consumer Psychology, an international organization composed of marketing and psychology scholars and a division of the American Psychological Association.

Barbara J. Phillips (PhD, University of Texas at Austin) is Professor of Marketing at the University of Saskatchewan, where she has been awarded several College and University teaching awards. Dr. Phillips' research program focuses on visual images in advertising and their influence on consumer response. She has published more than 15 articles in peer-reviewed journals, books, and conference proceedings, such as the *Journal of Advertising* and *Marketing Theory*. Along with Edward McQuarrie, she has received the "Best Article" award in the *Journal of Advertising* (2002, 2005) and the Dunn Award (2004) for "excellence in advertising research." Dr. Phillips currently serves on the editorial boards of the *Journal of Advertising* and *Journal of Current Issues and Research in Advertising*; she has received the "Outstanding Reviewer" award at the *Journal of Advertising* twice (2000, 2004).

David B. Pisoni (PhD, University of Michigan) is a Chancellor's Professor of Psychology and Cognitive Science at Indiana University. He carries out basic and clinical research on speech perception, spoken word recognition, language comprehension, and perceptual development. For the last 15 years, he has been working at the IU School of Medicine on several clinical problems associated with hearing impairment in deaf children and adults who use cochlear implants. He was also an NIH postdoctoral fellow in the speech group at the Research Laboratory of Electronics at MIT from 1975–1976 and was awarded a Guggenhiem Fellowship in 1978.

Bernd H. Schmitt (PhD, Cornell University) is the Robert D. Calkins Professor of International Business at Columbia Business School in New York. His research interests include cross-cultural language processing, as well as research on customer experience and innovation. His articles have appeared in leading consumer behavior, marketing, and psychology journals. In addition, he has published six books that have been translated into 15 languages.

L. J. Shrum (PhD, University of Illinois) is Professor of Marketing at the University of Texas at San Antonio. His research investigates the psychological processes underlying media effects, particularly the role of media information in the construction of values, attitudes, and beliefs. This work has appeared in journals such as the *Journal of Consumer Research, Journal of Consumer Psychology, Media Psychology, Personality and Social Psychology Bulletin, Public Opinion Quarterly, Journal of Advertising, Human Communication Research*, and *Communication Research*, as well as in numerous edited books. He recently edited *The Psychology of Entertainment Media: Blurring the Lines Between Entertainment and Persuasion* (2004, Lawrence Erlbaum Associates). He currently serves on the editorial boards of *Journal of Consumer Research, Human Communication Research, Journal of Communication, Journal of Broadcasting & Electronic Media*, and *Communication Monographs*.

Barbara B. Stern (PhD, City University of New York) is Professor II of Marketing at Rutgers Business School. Her research focuses on the meaning of texts in consumer behavior, and she uses textual analysis adapted from literary theory to examine the effects of stimuli, including ads, marketing communications, and product placements in television programs on consumer responses such as attitudes to ads and verbal protocols. Her research has appeared in the *Journal of Consumer Research, Journal of Marketing, Journal of Advertising, International Journal of Electronic Commerce, Journal of the Academy of Marketing Science*, and other publications. She is the founding coeditor of the journal *Marketing Theory*, which she continues to coedit, and the editor of *Representing Consumers: Voices, Views, Visions*. She has served on more than a dozen editorial boards including the *Journal of Consumer Research, Journal of Marketing, Journal of Advertising*, and *American Behavioral Scientist*, and has won awards such as "Best Reviewer" from the *Journal of Consumer Research*. She received the American Advertising Association Award for Outstanding Contribution to Research in 1997, the Leavey Award for Excellence in Private Enterprise Education, and the Women's Institute for Freedom of the Press Award. She has been actively involved in service to ACR in the capacity of treasurer, member of the Advisory Council, and ACR representative to the Research Industry Coalition; to AAA as Chair of the Publications Committee; and to AMA as cochair of the 1995 Educators' Conference.

Robert S. Wyer, Jr. (PhD, University of Colorado) is Professor of Marketing at the Hong Kong University of Science and Technology (HKUST). His background lies in social cognitive psychology, and he spent most of his career at the University of

Illinois before moving to HKUST. His research interests focus on several aspects of information processing. Dr. Wyer has published numerous books and journal articles in both psychology and consumer behavior, and he is a former editor of both the *Journal of Experimental Psychology* and the *Journal of Consumer Psychology*. He is a recipient of the Alexandr von Humboldt Special Research Prize for Distinguished Scientists and the Thomas M. Ostrom Award for distinguished contributions to person memory and social cognition.

Richard F. Yalch (PhD, Northwestern University) is Professor of Marketing at the University of Washington, Seattle campus. His research focuses on understanding consumers' responses to communications, including advertising, rumors, and infomercials. His work has appeared in the *Journal of Consumer Research, Journal of Consumer Psychology,* and *Journal of Applied Psychology*. He also has coedited a book on *Online Consumer Psychology* and has authored a chapter in *Applying Social Cognition to Consumer-Focused Strategy*. A former associate editor of the *Journal of Consumer Research*, he is also a member of the *Journal of Consumer Psychology* editorial board.

Shi Zhang (PhD, Columbia University) is Associate Professor of Marketing at UCLA's Anderson Graduate School of Management. He conducts experimental research on consumer behavior, judgment, and decision making, particularly in the area of using comparison and feature alignability to form strategies for market entry and marketing communications, as well as in the area of brand naming and positioning in the international market. He is a frequent speaker at professional conferences and seminars and has published articles in journals of marketing and consumer research, including the *Journal of Consumer Psychology, Journal of Consumer Research* and *Journal of Marketing Research*, and in psychology and decision making, including the *Journal of Experimental Psychology: Applied*, and *Organizational Behavioral and Human Decision Processing*.

PART I

The Impact of Mere Words—
Their Meanings and Sounds

CHAPTER 1

Linguistic Framing of Sensory Experience: There Is Some Accounting for Taste

JoAndrea Hoegg
University of British Columbia

Joseph W. Alba
University of Florida

An enduring question in psychology and anthropology concerns whether or not language influences perception and thought (Whorf, 1956). The question is important to consumer researchers because brand and attribute identifiers are ubiquitous, laden with meaning, and frequently used by consumers to identify and evaluate products. This chapter reviews prior research and reports original data that speak to the potential influence of brand, category, and attribute labels on sensory perception.

A focus on experiential consumer behavior addresses activities that are common within the universe of consumption but rarely investigated from a cognitive or linguistic perspective. In the consumption of products such as music, wines, or perfumes, purely perceptual information may be ambiguous, discrimination may be difficult, and verbal identifiers may therefore loom large. It is relatively uncontroversial to argue that decision making can be driven by verbal cues in such situations. The more vexing issue historically has been whether or not these labels actually alter the perceptual experience.

THE WHORFIAN PERSPECTIVE

Whorf proposed that thought was largely dependent on language, arguing specifically that the grammatical background of people's native tongue influences the way they "… dissect nature and break up the flux of experience into objects and entities to construct propositions about" (p. 239). That is, humans do not perceive the world identically, but rather view a world that has been organized by the linguistic system they use.

Interpretation of Whorf's controversial hypothesis has not been monolithic. The strongest version argues that linguistic coding of objects is necessary in all mental

3

operations; in essence, language determines thought. The weaker form is relativistic and suggests that language does not alter perception or thought, but rather makes certain objects easier to code, thereby shaping what people contemplate and remember (Bruner, 1983; Hunt & Agnoli, 1991). Some believe that neither view may be totally accurate because both assume a dichotomy between language and thought, which Whorf may not have intended (Cameron, 1999; Lee, 1996).

Conclusive evidence has proved elusive (Hunt & Agnoli, 1991). Early tests of the hypothesis appeared supportive, but by the 1970's the notion had fallen out of favor (Berlin & Kay, 1969; Clark & Clark, 1977; Heider & Oliver, 1972), replaced by a belief in linguistic universals. More recently, the Whorfian hypothesis has witnessed a resurgence, and reports of support, at least for its weaker form, have become more common (e.g., Hunt & Agnoli, 1991; Roberson, Davidoff, & Shapiro, 2002; Roberson, Davies, & Davidoff, 2000; Schmitt & Zhang, 1998).

Most latter-day tests of Whorf's views have focused on differences in color or shape perception across cultures (e.g., Davies, Sowden, Jerrett, Jerrett, & Corbett, 1998; Kay & Kempton, 1984; Roberson et al., 2000; Roberson, Davidoff, Davies, & Shapiro, 2005; Rosch, 1973). For example, Kay and Kempton (1984) examined perception of the colors green and blue among speakers of English and speakers of Taruhumara, a Uto-Aztecan language that has only one term for both hues. Participants were shown triads of colors from a blue-green continuum and were asked to identify which of the three differed most from the other two. As predicted by the Whorfian hypothesis, English speakers perceived colors falling at the green-blue boundary to be more distinct than did Taruhumara speakers. This effect appeared to result from an unconscious naming strategy in which participants surreptitiously named the colors and then judged the different "named" chip as most different. When the use of such a strategy was made impossible in a second study, the cross-boundary exaggeration disappeared. In contrast, a more recent study comparing speakers of two languages with different numbers of basic color terms (English's 11 vs. Setswana's 5) found that judged similarity of colors was uninfluenced by the degree of linguistic detail (Davies et al., 1998).

The few studies conducted within the consumer context have a similar cross-cultural flavor but a substantive focus outside of color perception. For example, Graham (1981) investigated the perception of time across cultures, distinguishing between linear time, circular time, and procedural time. Linear time is characterized as discrete and possessive of a forward-looking orientation. Accordingly, time is referenced in a manner similar to money; that is, it possesses measurable value that can be "spent" and "wasted." In contrast, these notions are illogical within the circular and procedural perspectives, which lack a future-based orientation. An activity simply takes as long as it takes, and there is little sense of hastening or deadlines. These differences in worldview are accompanied by differences in the language used to describe time, which in turn have interesting implications for marketers. Slogans such as "How much is your time worth?" have little resonance in cultures with either of these time perspectives. Language used to describe entire product categories, such as fast food, would be anomalous. Even the decision-making process, typically investigated within consumer research from a linear perspective, might vary across cultures possessing different time perspectives. Graham argues that these differences in time perspectives are reflected in language differences. However, it would be a dangerous leap to conclude that different cultures perceive the passage of time uniquely. Indeed, Graham notes that people are capable of multiple perspectives, which allows them to interact and conduct business with people from cultures with other time perspectives. This line of reasoning suggests at least a degree of universality in time perception and leaves the Whorfian question of whether language does actually influence perception largely unresolved.

More recently, Schmitt and Zhang (1998; also see Zhang & Schmitt, chap. 4 in this volume) examined the question of whether language influences categorical perception. A series of experiments compared similarity judgments made by native speakers of English, Chinese, and Japanese. The Chinese and Japanese languages have "classifier" words that help to categorize objects. For example, "ba" in Chinese indicates that the object is one that can be grasped with the hand. The word accompanies nouns such as "umbrella" as a category classifier. Schmitt and Zhang found that the presence of such classifiers influences perceptions of similarity. For speakers of Chinese vis-à-vis speakers of English, objects that share a classifier are perceived as more similar than objects that do not share a classifier. The existence of classifiers in the language also influences recall of objects, such that speakers of languages with classifiers appear to possess "classifier-related schematic cluster[s]" that guide expectations regarding attributes and influence choice. Thus, in contrast to the notion of linguistic universals, it appears that the mere presence of a classifier in a language can alter similarity and quality judgments.

Based solely on this limited evidence, it may be argued that linguistic labels assigned to stimuli may influence perceptual response, but the effect occurs primarily at the category boundaries rather than across the continuum. However, even if the phenomenon is limited in this manner, it remains important in the marketing realm, inasmuch as a great deal of the action occurs at the boundaries. A firm may spend substantial sums of money developing its brand image—often using language in its many forms (e.g., brand name, slogan, ad copy)—to maximize the perceived difference between its brand and those of its competitors. It is therefore unfortunate that little consumer research has considered the role of language in sensory discrimination.

LABELS AND EVALUATION: MORE THAN A MATTER OF TASTE

The work of Schmitt and Zhang demonstrates how linguistic differences can influence product perceptions and choice, consistent with the Whorfian perspective. Although centered on cross-cultural effects, it is also consistent with a larger body of within-culture consumer research that has examined the way in which category or brand labels can influence categorization and evaluation. In particular, consumer research has investigated the effects of brand equity on perception, the role of a category label in categorization and choice, and the influence of attribute vocabulary on product evaluation. Although not designed specifically to test the Whorfian hypothesis, it nonetheless examines the effects of verbal identifiers on preference and, in doing so, offers an indirect test.

Brand Equity

Research has provided robust evidence that well-known brand names can influence and even overwhelm taste perception in preference tasks. For example, Allison and Uhl (1964) demonstrated how people's preferences for beer differed dramatically depending on the presence or absence of a brand label. More recently, Hoyer and Brown (1990) found that participants rated peanut butter attributed to a nationally recognized brand as higher in quality than generically labeled peanut butter, even when the product and label were mismatched. Although it is clear that brand equity has a powerful effect on preference, the causal mechanism has not been firmly established. In the present context, the question concerns whether taste perceptions are truly altered as a function of the label. We attempt to shed light on this question in research reported here.

New Product Categorization and Evaluation

Marketers must ensure that consumers understand the positioning of their products. Prior research on categorization has demonstrated that people tend to cluster items based on feature similarity. However, recent work suggests that if sufficiently diagnostic, a category label may be weighted more heavily than feature similarity in categorization and inference tasks (Yamauchi & Markman, 2000) and may influence how a product is evaluated (Moreau, Markman, & Lehman, 2001; see also Gregan-Paxton, Hoeffler, & Zhao, 2005).

When a new product is labeled as a member of a particular product category, beliefs about that category may be transferred to the target product, and attention paid to the product's attributes may vary as a function of the fit between the attribute and the category into which it is placed (Murphy & Ross, 1994). Moreau et al. (2001) demonstrated how categorization of a "really" new product could be influenced by labeling. Providing consumers with a category label influenced not only categorization, but also expectations of performance and preference. One of their most interesting findings involved a large order effect, that is, the category label that was provided first was the one thought to be most appropriate. Thus, it appears people quickly make a label–item association that not only drives evaluation, but also is somewhat resistant to change.

Product labels may influence evaluation even when the labels themselves are ambiguous (Miller & Kahn, 2005). Consistent with Grice's theory of conversational implicature (Grice, 1975), consumers may assume that firms communicate useful product information. When labels are ambiguous, consumers may search for meaning, perhaps inferring more from the label than is appropriate (Gruenfeld & Wyer, 1992; Harris & Monaco, 1987; Miller & Kahn, 2005).

Attribute Labels

A more common use of language to alter product perception involves the framing of a brand's attributes. For example, the real estate industry is legendary for its ability to cast a home in the most positive light (e.g., when a cramped space is described as "cozy"). The limited amount of formal research on such tactics demonstrates that they can be quite effective, altering not only distal ratings but also firsthand perceptions (e.g., Levin & Gaeth, 1988).

In less devious applications, attribute labels provide consumers with a consumption vocabulary that can have more salutary outcomes. West, Brown, and Hoch (1996) found that provision of a consumption vocabulary for quilts caused preferences to become more refined and consistent, perhaps by prompting more analytic processing and directing attention to particular details at the expense of others. Goldstone (1998) argued that, with training, "(p)eople often shift from perceiving stimuli in terms of holistic, overall aspects to analytically decomposing objects into separate dimensions" (p. 600). Such a change may benefit consumers by helping them to distinguish among products, perhaps enabling them to become adept at understanding what features they prefer. Intuition suggests that such outcomes are especially likely in categories known for their subtle complexity, such as wine. Other research points more directly to improvements in choice quality. Shapiro and Spence (2002) demonstrated that consumers who were provided with a vocabulary to describe stereo sound quality exhibited superior memory for the stimuli and were less susceptible to misleading advertising information.

These brand and attribute labeling effects can be dramatic. However, it is not clear from the research whether the effects on preference are due to actual changes in perception or to an independent and more cognitive cause. Firms know quite well that preferences can be driven by much more than product experience and, consequently, any labeling effect observed in a preference task may not coincide with results obtained from a perceptual discrimination task. Prior sensory research in the consumer context has been insensitive to this distinction, with the default assumption that the effect of labels on preference reflects more fundamental effects on perception. However, recent research suggests a dissociation between the two responses (Hoegg & Alba, in press), an outcome consistent with results from neuroscience showing that the effects of the Coke® brand name on taste are not due to changes in perception but rather to high-level thoughts (Thompson, 2003).

The brevity of this discussion reflects the sparseness of consumer-related psycholinguistic research. Although the limited evidence is enticing, the strength and extent of language's effect on product perception remains an open question.

Fortunately, research conducted beyond the consumer context has a richer history and may help inform the central issue at hand.

Labels and Memory

Psychologists have long known that labels can influence perceptual memory. The classic study by Carmichael, Hogan, and Walter (1932) showed that when an ambiguous shape was associated with a particular label, recall of the shape was biased in the direction of the label. On the positive side, Ellis and Muller (1964) found that recognition memory for geometric figures was enhanced by assignment of labels. In a similar vein, Santa and Baker (1975) indicated that when geometric shapes were associated with arbitrary category labels (e.g., animals, furniture, etc.), recall was clustered by category. That is, verbal labels influenced the organization of nonverbal shapes in memory.

Particularly powerful and relevant evidence of the effect of language on memory comes from the *verbal-overshadowing* effect (Schooler & Engstler-Schooler, 1990). Verbal overshadowing refers to the situation in which the act of describing a (typically) nonverbal stimulus (e.g., someone's face, a color, or a wine) impairs its subsequent recognition (see Schooler, 2002; Schooler, Fiore, & Brandimonte, 1997, for reviews).

Verbal overshadowing appears especially likely when perceptual knowledge of the stimulus exceeds the perceiver's verbal ability to describe it. The attempt to assign verbal labels to nonverbal dimensions creates a mismatch between the original perceptual memory and the verbal description, which consequently impairs recognition. It follows, however, that true experts, who may have a highly developed vocabulary, should be immune to the effect. Supportive evidence comes from the wine category. Casual wine drinkers generally lack the vocabulary needed to describe the individual features of a wine; indeed, even when dimensions are pointed out, they may still experience difficulty discerning distinct elements. Wine experts, however, generally have a highly developed verbal repertoire to describe the subtleties of wine. Results reported by Melcher and Schooler (1996) show verbal overshadowing among the former, but not the latter, group.

Labels and Social Perception

Although the effects of language on memory have been well established across numerous domains, other paradigms have considered the more powerful question of whether the labels associated with a range of stimuli influence perception in a stimulus-based environment. In particular, social psychologists have long recognized the importance and influence of verbal labels in social perception (e.g., Allport, 1954). Results from studies on stereotype formation and intergroup differentiation consistently show that between-group differences are overestimated, as is the degree of within-group homogeneity. Even when there are no strong a priori group differences and groups are assigned randomly, in-group–out-group differences can arise (e.g., Allen & Wilder, 1975).

Perceptual Discrimination.   Tajfel (1959) suggested that such grouping effects represent a perceptual rather than a social phenomenon. His accentuation theory argued that the mere application of group labels to sets of stimuli changes the way the stimuli are perceived, such that people minimize differences between stimuli within the same category and exaggerate differences between stimuli in different categories. Consider, for example, his original perceptual accentuation study (Tajfel & Wilkes, 1963). Arbitrary labels (A and B) were assigned to lines of increasing length such that shorter lines were labeled "A" and longer lines were labeled "B." After learning this association, participants were asked to estimate the lengths of test lines. Results indicated that participants exaggerated the gap between the longest "A" and the shortest "B." However, in contrast to the accentuation theory hypothesis and findings in social perception, minimization of differences between lines with the same label was not observed. Thus, consistent with the color research conducted in pursuit of Whorf's hypothesis, the results suggest that labels might influence perception at the boundaries but not necessarily within a category. Tajfel and Wilkes argued that the effect was perceptual but could not definitively rule out a conceptual process. As noted by Rothbart, Davis-Stitt, and Hill (1997), it is exceedingly difficult to separate the pure effect of labeling, per se, from the meaning carried by the label, inasmuch as the typical function of a label is to imbue objects with meaning.

Subsequent research has been largely supportive of the original findings (e.g., Goldstone, 1994, 1995; Krueger, Rothbart, & Sriram, 1989; but see Livingston, Andrews, & Harnard, 1998). In a different perceptual-grouping task, Goldstone (1994) trained participants on a dimension, either the size or brightness of a square, causing them to learn both the boundary of the dimension and the range of stimuli that fell within its boundaries. As in the Tajfel and Wilkes (1963) study, participants exaggerated differences across categories but did not minimize differences within categories along the learned boundary, again suggesting that within-category minimization does not occur in perceptual tasks. In fact, Goldstone observed a degree of enhancement of within-category discrimination. It should be noted, however, that this pattern may be peculiar to single-dimension perceptual studies. Research involving multidimensional stimuli has found support for the minimization of within-category differences (e.g., Corneille & Judd, 1999; Goldstone & Steyvers, 2001; Livingston et al., 1998).

Accentuation and Memory.   Stepping away from the traditional stimulus-based perceptual paradigm, evidence for both across-boundary exaggeration and within-category minimization has been found with single-dimension stimuli in paradigms involving a memory component. In particular, Krueger and Clement (1994) tapped prior knowledge for temperature estimates across different days of the year. Despite the arbitrariness of monthly boundaries, people rated days within a single month as being more similar to one another and days across months as being more distinct. Unlike the aforementioned studies, it would be difficult to characterize these results in terms of perceptual discrimination. It is more likely that the labels for the months tapped associations regarding temperature and these associations led to inferences consistent with the predictions of accentuation theory.

Task Parameters.   Most accentuation-related studies employ some form of learning as part of the paradigm. Either the category labels are learned in a training phase, as in the Tajfel and Wilkes (1963) study, or they are known from prior experience, as in the Krueger and Clement (1994) study. However, the role played by learning has not directly been investigated. Similarly, some basic questions regarding category structure have been ignored. For example, in most previous research, category learning involved precise boundaries that did not overlap; thus, it is unclear what would have happened if boundaries were allowed to overlap (see Livingston et al., 1998, for an exception). Moreover, in previous work, the learned categories consisted of a distribution of stimuli. It is unclear if accentuation will arise in the absence of within-category variance. These issues are important in consumer applications because consumers may form strong priors in the absence of direct experience and quality control will determine the extent to which the distribution of outcome quality varies across and within brand categories. In the research reported next, we address these questions while also testing the symmetric predictions of original accentuation theory, that is, across-category accentuation and within-category minimization.

TASTE DISCRIMINATION: A COMMON CONSUMER TASK

One translation of accentuation to the idiom of consumer psychology is that consumers will perceive more variation in samples from different sources than from samples produced by the same source. The applied context of consumer behavior also raises a question not salient in basic research involving the nature of the category label. That is, are the semantics of the label important or is the simple presence of a differentiating cue sufficient (i.e., the arbitrary "A" versus "B" labels of Tajfel and Wilkes)?

To address these questions, we conducted an experiment involving a simple taste discrimination task. Participants tasted and rated the similarity of beverages that either had the same label or had different labels. Two kinds of labels were used in the label conditions: "brand" labels (which indicated to participants that items differentiated by labels represented different brands on the market) and arbitrary labels (which conveyed no particular meaning). The arbitrary labels were used as a conceptual replication of prior accentuation research and to provide a comparison for brand label effects. A primary objective of our experiment was to test for the existence of accentuation in a taste discrimination setting that used consumer-relevant category markers. To this end, we viewed brand labels as most appropriate. However, when using brand markers to test the pure effects of labeling, it is critical to avoid the confounding effects of prior beliefs that underlie traditional branding phenomena. Consequently, the study employed fictitious brand labels (i.e., A and B) that had no inherent meaning to our respondents. The question was whether the mere concept of a brand, rather than knowledge of a particular brand, would influence taste perception. We considered this to be a conservative test of labeling effects and speculate that any accentuation observed under such conditions would be amplified in the natural environment of familiar brands.

A second objective was to test the importance of prior category learning. Previous research has relied on category training to induce accentuation effects, but no work has directly investigated its role. If labels serve to identify group members, then accentuation may obtain whenever labels are applied to different objects. However, labels may interact with experience such that perceivers must first associate group members with a general location along the to-be-judged scale. We considered the role of learning in accentuation by manipulating the presence of a learning phase. In addition, unlike most previous accentuation studies, we used overlapping distributions during the learning phase.

Most investigations of perceptual categorization have been conducted in the realms of vision, with particular emphasis on color discrimination (e.g., Bornstein & Korda, 1984; Goldstone, 1994, 1995; Roberson & Davidoff, 2000), and hearing, with emphasis on phoneme discrimination (e.g., Bornstein & Korda, 1984; Hanson, 1977; McMurray, Tanenhaus, & Aslin, 2003). The use of a taste paradigm provided a further extension in a common marketing context.

Predictions

As a result of ubiquitous marketing attempts to distinguish products on the basis of brand identity, consumers are likely to expect differences across brands. Moreover, prior research on accentuation has consistently demonstrated intercategory accentuation of differences. Thus, we expect exaggeration across category boundaries. Within-label results, however, are more difficult to predict. Due to present-day quality control, consumers presumably do not anticipate wide variation within a brand and may not notice differences that do exist. However, if expectations of taste uniformity are strong, then it is possible that deviations from expectation would be particularly salient. Research on perceptual discrimination has shown no minimization in unidimensional studies, but experiments involving conceptual categories, such as social stereotypes or monthly temperatures, have produced a conflicting outcome. Because consumers are highly familiar with the concept of branding, results consistent with the latter would not be entirely unexpected. However, inasmuch as the brands are unfamiliar, it is not unreasonable to expect a pattern that is limited to across-boundary exaggeration.

The role of learning is also difficult to predict. On the one hand, prior accentuation research has routinely incorporated a learning phase into the procedure for obvious reasons. Participants must first understand that different categories exist and each category is associated with a particular level of the dimension of interest. A learning phase achieves these goals without the introduction of direct but demand-laden instructions. On the other hand, branding research suggests that brand effects are very strong. Perhaps the notion of a brand is sufficiently powerful to lead to accentuation in the absence of a learning phase.

Method

Participants and Design.   Three hundred undergraduate participants completed the study in exchange for partial course credit. The experiment employed a 3 (label: No Label, Arbitrary Label, Brand Label) × 2 (learning phase: present–absent) × 2 (stimulus pairs) mixed design in which label and learning were manipulated between subjects and stimuli were manipulated within subject. The stimulus pairs comprising the within-subject factor were the two ratings made by each participant: the perceived difference between two orange juice samples with the same taste but with different labels (STDL) and the perceived difference between samples with a different taste but with the same label (DTSL). This factor is confounded because "same taste" is always paired with "different label" and "different taste" is always paired with "same label." However, additional factor levels were not examined, because the corresponding ratings of different taste–different label or same taste–same label that would be included in a full-factorial design are relatively intuitive and not of particular interest to the research questions.

Stimuli.   Tropicana® pure, pulp-free orange juice served as the base product. The juice was manipulated to create just noticeable differences across three taste levels: (a) low sweet, which was the pure orange juice; (b) medium sweet, which was a mixture of 2 grams of Equal® sweetener per 800 ml of pure orange juice; and (c) high sweet, which was a mixture of 6 grams of Equal sweetener per 800 ml of pure orange juice. The juice was served in 1.25-ounce styrofoam cups, filled to the 1-ounce level. In addition, all participants were given a cracker and 5 ounces of water to cleanse their palates between taste opportunities.

Procedure.   For participants in the learning conditions, the study consisted of two phases, a learning phase and a testing phase. The learning phase provided exposure to the labels and an opportunity for participants to learn the taste range of the stimuli.

During the first portion of the learning phase, participants were presented with three cups of orange juice, all labeled "A" (or unlabeled for the control group); a cracker; a cup of 5 ounces of water; and a napkin. The labels were counterbalanced so that for half the participants Brand A was sweeter and for the remaining participants Brand B was sweeter (see Fig. 1.1). The three samples consisted of two samples of low sweet (or high depending on counterbalance) and one sample of medium sweet juice. The three samples were presented on the desk in random or-

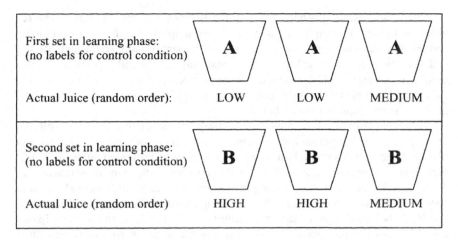

Figure 1.1.   Learning phase stimuli (with sweetness counterbalanced across labels).

der. To avoid hypothesis guessing, it was important that participants not realize the goal of the learning phase; thus, a cover story about palette preparation was provided. Participants in the Brands condition saw the following instructions:

> You will be tasting and rating two brands of orange juice. These brands are well known to you, but we cannot disclose their names. Because what you ate or drank before tasting can significantly impact your taste buds and your ability to differentiate, you will have practice samples before the actual taste test. Research has shown that six ounces of orange juice is the minimum necessary for taste buds to become accustomed to orange juice flavors, so you will have six one-ounce practice samples. However, because research has also shown that the taste buds cannot process more than three flavors at one time, you will taste the practice samples one brand at a time.

> Please follow the instructions below:

> 1. Taste all the samples of Brand A until you feel comfortable with the taste. Sip water and take a bite of a cracker after tasting the samples to cleanse your palate. You do not have to taste them in order, and you may go back and forth between samples as much as you like.
> 2. Raise your hand when you have finished tasting. The administrator will bring you the samples of Brand B.
> 3. Taste all the samples of Brand B until you feel comfortable with the taste. Sip water and take a bite of a cracker after tasting the samples to cleanse your palate. You do not have to taste them in order, and you may go back and forth between samples as much as you like.
> 4. When you have finished tasting, leave the cups on the desk and move to the station on the other side of the room. Take a pencil or pen with you. You will find instructions on the desk. Follow them carefully.

When participants finished Step 2 in the instructions, the "A" cups were replaced with the "B" samples, consisting of two samples of high (low) sweet juice
and one sample of medium sweet juice, and participants continued through Steps 3
and 4. Participants in the category label condition had virtually identical instructions, except they were not informed that the samples were brands. Those in the No
Label condition also had similar instructions, except there was no mention of "A"
or "B," and the cups were not labeled.

After completing the learning phase, participants moved to a different station to
participate in the test phase. For participants in the no learning conditions, the experiment began at this point. Four samples of juice were presented on the desk. For
participants in the Arbitrary and Brand Label conditions, the cups were labeled A_1,
A_2, B_1, and B_2 (see Fig. 1.2). One sample of A and one sample of B were identical in
taste (both medium sweet). The other two samples were high sweet and low sweet.
For No Label participants, cups were simply labeled 1, 2, 3, and 4. Participants
tasted all four samples prior to answering any questions. Participants were then
asked to provide difference ratings for three critical pairs: A_1 versus A_2, A_2 versus
B_1, and B_1 versus B_2. They were permitted to taste the samples again while making
their ratings. Questions 1 and 3 were counterbalanced versions of the same question; thus, after confirming there were no differences between the two ratings
(paired t-test, p's n.s.) the variables were collapsed to create the two dependent
measures comprising the within-subjects factor, STDL and DTSL.

Results

Figures 1.3 and 1.4 present the key dependent measures: perceived difference between samples with the same taste but different labels (STDL) and between samples
with different tastes and the same label (DTSL). A 2 (stimuli: same taste, different label–different taste, same label) × 2 (learning: present–absent) × 3 (label: No La-

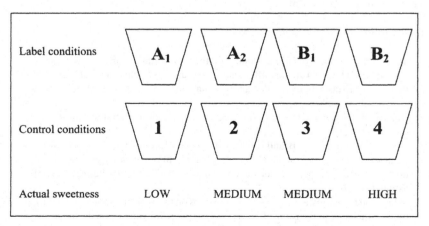

Figure 1.2.   Test phase (no learning groups begin experiment at this point).

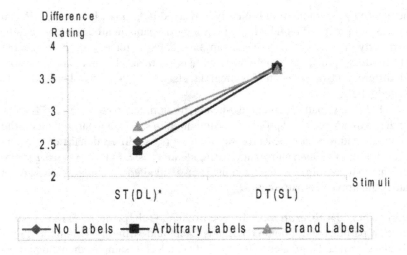

Figure 1.3. Results without learning phase.

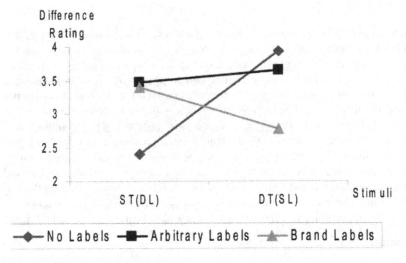

Figure 1.4. Results with learning phase.
Note: "DL" (Different Label) and "SL" (Same Label) apply to the Arbitrary Labels and Brand Labels conditions. For participants in the No-Labels conditions, the cups were simply numbered 1, 2, 3, and 4.

bel–Arbitrary Label–Brands) mixed analysis of variance (ANOVA) revealed a significant three-way interaction of stimuli, label, and learning, $F(2, 297) = 6.01, p < .01$. We also observed a main effect of stimuli, $F(1, 297) = 41.34, p < .001$, a stimuli by learning interaction, $F(1, 297) = 10.44, p < .01$, a stimuli by label interaction, $F(2, 297) = 9.83, p < .01$, and a label by learning interaction, $F(2, 297) = 3.07, p < .05$.

The nature of the interaction is clearly portrayed in Figures 1.3 and 1.4. When testing was not preceded by a learning phase, participants in all three label conditions properly discriminated between samples. Pairs of juice that possessed the same taste (despite different labels) were rated as more similar than pairs that possessed different tastes (despite identical labels; all p's $< .05$). That is, taste dominated labels.

A much different pattern emerged when learning preceded testing. The No Label condition again exhibited proper discrimination ($p < .01$), but participants in the Brand Label condition showed a reversal. Juice pairs that differed in taste were perceived as more similar than pairs that were identical in taste, $F(1, 49) = 4.16, p < .05$. Participants in the Arbitrary Label condition also failed to discriminate, showing a flat rather than reversed pattern ($F < 1$).

Intercategory Exaggeration.   In accordance with prior research, results showed that participants in both the Brands Label and Arbitrary Label conditions perceived a significantly greater difference between STDL samples than did participants in the No Label condition, both p's $< .01$, indicating accentuation of across-category differences.

Intracategory Minimization.   As noted earlier, within-category homogenization has been more elusive than across-category accentuation. To understand the extent to which within-category homogenization obtained with category training, we conducted comparisons across label groups for the learning participants only. Relative to the No Label condition, participants receiving arbitrary labels did not minimize the differences between distinct items with the same label, $F(1, 99) = 1.19, p > .25$. Interestingly, however, participants in the Brand Label condition perceived less difference between DTSL stimuli than did participants in the No Label control condition, $F(1, 99) = 25.18, p < .001$, suggesting a minimization of within-category differences. This result is unique in single-dimension perceptual discrimination research and suggests an incremental brand effect over an effect of mere labeling. The result is particularly noteworthy in light of the fact that participants had the opportunity to learn in Phase 1 that within-brand variance could exist.

Discussion

The results speak to the phenomenon of accentuation in several ways. It is important, however, to dismiss uninteresting interpretations of the labeling effect. First, a simple demand explanation can be ruled out via the divergent results obtained across learning conditions. In particular, participants in the Brand Label conditions showed opposite patterns depending on learning condition. This result is important in the context of some claims that the basic accentuation paradigm suffers from threats of experimental demand (Andrews & Livingston, 2000). To our knowledge, no previous study has been able to refute a demand explanation in the manner of the present experiment. Second, failure to perform proper discrimination in the learning conditions cannot be attributed to impaired taste buds resulting from the learning phase. Participants in the No Label condition who received initial learning performed identically to their counterparts who bypassed the learning phase.

Two results are particularly interesting from a consumer perspective. The first pertains to the accuracy of the brands group in the no learning condition. Despite believing that they were sampling two different brands, participants were not affected by the presence of the label. Thus, learning may be a prerequisite for accentuation. In one sense, this result deviates from the Whorfian view, but in another sense it is consonant. Whorf proposed that language colors our perceptual experiences. In the no learning condition, participants possessed only half the requisite knowledge. They had knowledge of brands, which should have led to accentuation, but they had no opportunity to learn the meaning of those brand labels; hence, the language did not influence perception. If no prior association is made, then presumptions about differences between objects in different categories should vary with prior beliefs about the existence of differences. In the present case, orange juice from a common growing region may be viewed as a commodity. Indeed, a brief follow-up survey indicated that 70% of 17 independent participants believed that there was "little" or "no" difference across brands that were "100% fresh-squeezed from Florida." Once a difference is learned, however, subsequent experience is biased by expectations of difference across categories and homogeneity within category.

The second consumer-relevant result is the dominance of the label over taste in the brand learning group. Despite opportunities to learn that within-brand samples could vary and between-brand samples could be identical, the labels overwhelmed taste perception. Perhaps due to prior expectations regarding quality control and brand differences, we observed both interbrand exaggeration and intrabrand minimization. This result has not been reported in prior perceptual studies and suggests an additive effect of perceptual groups and conceptual labels.

One issue pertaining to generalizability merits attention. Accentuation and minimization were observed only in the learning conditions. However, the learning phase not only enabled participants to associate labels with particular levels of sweetness (i.e., one category was generally sweeter than the other), but also conveyed the possibility that samples sharing the same label could also differ. We have no basis on which to make broad statements about the true level of quality control across firms that produce edible products, but informal evidence suggests that real-world within-brand variance is less than depicted in the experiment. Thus, to enhance generalizability, a modified replication of the learning conditions was conducted with 61 participants. The within-brand variance in the learning phase was eliminated such that Brand A consisted of all low-sweet samples and Brand B consisted of all medium-sweet samples (counterbalanced). The design was further simplified to focus only on the Brand Label and No Label conditions. The experimental procedure was held constant. Results from a 2 (No Label vs. Brand Label) × 2 (STDL vs. DTSL) ANOVA revealed a significant interaction, $F(1, 59) = 4.16, p <$

.05. No other effects were significant. The No Label group conformed to the pattern observed in the main experiment, accurately perceiving greater difference between different samples than between identical samples, $F(1, 30) = 7.40$, $p < .05$. Participants receiving brand labels failed to discriminate, although the pattern was flat rather than reversed ($F < 1$). Overall, there is little reason to believe that the results of the main experiment are limited to instances in which there is perceptible within-category variance.

Accentuation research is not typically cast in terms of the Whorfian hypothesis, but both traditions address the potential influence that language can exert on perception. The questions shared by both paradigms involve the extent to which labels influence perceptual discrimination and the conditions under which such influence is most likely to be observed. The results of our research shed some light on these questions, suggesting that labels can indeed overwhelm discrimination but that the effect is sensitive to the nature of the labels and product experience.

CONCLUSIONS AND FUTURE RESEARCH

Most consumer research on the effects of labels on sensory perception has understandably focused on brand preference. We argue that brand discrimination is a largely ignored topic that is no less important both for marketers and consumers. Marketers expend substantial resources to distinguish their products from the competition and to ensure quality control; consumers routinely make choices, but the extent to which those choices are driven by accurate perceptions versus social and cognitive forces is an open question.

Whorf proposed that the language used to label objects influences how we perceive the world. Although the assertion that language wholly determines thought may be viewed skeptically, there is mounting evidence that language can influence stimulus discrimination. Across color, shape, product, and brand boundaries, the labels that people assign to stimuli appear to influence perceptions of similarity. However, such effects are not ubiquitous. An important task for consumer researchers is to explore the many parameters of the phenomenon.

For example, stimulus complexity represents an untapped area of investigation. Most experiments within the sensory domain, including our own, have focused on single dimensions. Efficient markets are characterized by much greater complexity, with multiple trade-offs required across dimensions. Thus, even the prior research examining multiple dimensions is not informative because it has employed correlated dimensions (e.g., Corneille & Judd, 1999; Goldstone & Steyvers, 2001).

Future research could also examine the effects of labeling in the context of entirely different dependent measures. For example, it is not unreasonable to anticipate a labeling effect on product identification, such that identification is hindered in the absence of a label and perceived prototypicality of the stimulus is biased by the label.

Finally, the interaction of perception and language remains a potentially profitable target of inquiry. Despite the disappointing results from initial tests of the

Whorfian hypothesis, there is ample justification for the emergence of a psycholinguistic arm of consumer research. A sizable amount of consumption is sensory in nature, and labels clearly assert some influence on consumer response. The extent of that influence and the way it should be parsed into perceptual, social, and cognitive effects remain largely unknown.

REFERENCES

Allen, V. L., & Wilder, D. A. (1975). Categorization, belief similarity, and intergroup discrimination. *Journal of Personality and Social Psychology, 32,* 971–977.

Allison, R. I., & Uhl, K. P. (1964). Influence of beer brand identification on taste perception. *Journal of Marketing Research, 1,* 36–39.

Allport, G. W. (1954). *The nature of prejudice.* New York: Addison-Wesley.

Andrews, J. K., &. Livingston, K. R. (2000). Accentuation of category differences: Revisiting a classic study. In L. R. Gleitman & A. K. Joshi (Eds.), *Proceedings of the 22nd annual conference of the Cognitive Science Society* (p. 1015). Mahwah, NJ: Lawrence Erlbaum Associates.

Berlin, B., & Kay, P. (1969). *Basic color terms: Their universality and evolution.* Berkeley: University of California Press.

Bornstein, M. H., & Korda, N. O. (1984). Discrimination and matching within and between hues measured by reaction times: Some implications for categorical perception and levels of information processing. *Psychological Research, 46,* 207–222.

Bruner, J. S. (1983). *In search of mind.* New York: Harper & Row.

Cameron, D. (1999). Linguistic relativity: Benjamin Lee Whorf and the return of the repressed. *Critical Quarterly, 41,* 153–156.

Carmichael, L., Hogan, H. P., & Walter, A. A. (1932). An experimental study of the effect of language on the reproduction of visually perceived form. *Journal of Experimental Psychology, 15,* 73–86.

Clark, H. H., & Clark, E. V. (1977). *Psychology and language: An introduction to psycholinguistics.* San Diego: Harcourt Brace Jovanovich.

Corneille, O., & Judd, C. M. (1999). Accentuation and sensitization effects in the categorization of multifaceted stimuli. *Journal of Personality and Social Psychology, 77,* 927–941.

Davies, I. R. L., Sowden, P. T., Jerrett, D. T., Jerrett, T., & Corbett, G. G. (1998). A cross-cultural study of English and Setswana speakers on a colour triads task: A test of the Sapir–Whorf hypothesis. *British Journal of Psychology, 89,* 1–15.

Ellis, H. C., & Muller, D. G. (1964). Transfer in perceptual learning following stimulus predifferentiation. *Journal of Experimental Psychology, 68,* 388–395.

Goldstone, R. L. (1994). Influences of categorization on perceptual discrimination. *Journal of Experimental Psychology: General, 123,* 178–200.

Goldstone, R. L. (1995). Effects of categorization on color perception. *Psychological Science, 6,* 298–304.

Goldstone, R. L. (1998). Perceptual learning. *Annual Review of Psychology, 49,* 585–612.

Goldstone, R. L., & Steyvers, M. (2001). The sensitization and differentiation of dimensions during category learning. *Journal of Experimental Psychology: General, 130,* 116–139.

Graham, R. J. (1981). The role of perception of time in consumer research. *Journal of Consumer Research, 7,* 335–342.

Gregan-Paxton, J., Hoeffler, S., & Zhao, M. (2005). When categorization is ambiguous: Factors that facilitate the use of a multiple category inference strategy. *Journal of Consumer Psychology, 15,* 127–140.

Grice, H. P. (1975). Logic and conversation. In P. Cole & J. L. Morgan (Eds.), *Syntax and semantics III: Speech acts* (pp. 41–58). New York: Academic Press.

Gruenfeld, D. H., & Wyer, R. S. (1992). Semantics and pragmatics of social influence: How affirmations and denials affect beliefs in referent propositions. *Journal of Personality and Social Psychology, 62*, 38–49.

Hanson, V. L. (1977). Within-category discriminations in speech perception. *Perception and Psychophysics, 21*, 423–430.

Harris, R. J., &. Monaco, G. E. (1978). Psychology of pragmatic implication: Information processing between the lines. *Journal of Experimental Psychology: General, 107*, 1–22.

Heider, E. R., & Oliver, D. C. (1972). The structure of the color space in naming and memory for two languages. *Cognitive Psychology, 3*, 337–354.

Hoegg, J., & Alba, J. W. (in press). Taste perception: More (and less) than meets the tongue. *Journal of Consumer Research.*

Hoyer, W. D., & Brown, S. P. (1990). Effects of brand awareness on choice for a common, re-peat-purchase product. *Journal of Consumer Research, 17*, 141–148.

Hunt, E., & Agnoli, F. (1991). The Whorfian hypothesis: A cognitive psychology perspective. *Psychological Review, 98*, 377–389.

Kay, P., & Kempton, W. (1984). What is the Sapir–Whorf hypothesis? *American Anthropologist, 86*, 65–79.

Krueger, J., & Clement, R. W. (1994). Memory-based judgments about multiple categories: A revision and extension of Tajfel's accentuation theory. *Journal of Personality and Social Psychology, 67*, 35–47.

Krueger, J., Rothbart, M., & Sriram, N. (1989). Category learning and change: Differences in sensitivity to information that enhances or reduces intercategory distinctions. *Journal of Personality and Social Psychology, 56*, 866–875.

Lee, P. (1996). *The Whorf theory complex: A critical reconstruction.* Philadelphia: Benjamins.

Levin, I. P., & Gaeth, G. J. (1988). How consumers are affected by the framing of attribute information before and after consuming the product. *Journal of Consumer Research, 15*, 374–378.

Livingston, K. R., Andrews, J. K., & Harnad, S. (1998). Categorical perception effects induced by category learning. *Journal of Experimental Psychology: Learning, Memory and Cognition, 24*, 732–753.

McMurray, B., Tanenhaus, M. K., & Aslin, R. N. (2002). Gradient effects of within-category phonetic variation on lexical access. *Cognition, 86*, B33–B42.

Melcher, J. M., & Schooler, J. W. (1996). The misremembrance of wines past: Verbal and perceptual expertise differentially mediate verbal overshadowing of taste memory. *Journal of Memory and Language, 35*, 231–245.

Miller, E. G., & Kahn, B. E. (2005). Shades of meaning: The effect of color and flavor names on consumer choice. *Journal of Consumer Research, 32*, 86–92.

Moreau, C. P., Markman, A. B., & Lehmann, D. R. (2001). "What is it?" Categorization flexibility and consumers' responses to really new products. *Journal of Consumer Research, 27*, 489–498.

Murphy, G. L., & Ross, B. H. (1994). Prediction from uncertain categorizations. *Cognitive Psychology, 27*, 148–193.

Roberson, D., & Davidoff, J. (2000). The categorical perception of colors and facial expressions: The effect of verbal interference. *Memory and Cognition, 28*, 977–986.

Roberson, D., Davidoff, J., Davies, I. R. L., & Shapiro, L. R. (2005). Color categories: Evidence for the cultural relativity hypothesis. *Cognitive Psychology, 50*, 378–411.

Roberson, D., Davidoff, J., & Shapiro, L. R. (2002). Squaring the circle: The cultural relativity of "good" shape. *Journal of Cognition and Culture, 2*, 29–51.

Roberson, D., Davies, I. R. L., & Davidoff, J. (2000). Color categories are not universal: Replications and new evidence from a stone-age culture. *Journal of Experimental Psychology: General, 129*, 369–398.

Rosch, E. (1973). On the internal structure of perceptual and semantic categories. In T. E. Moore (Ed.), *Cognitive development and the acquisition of language* (pp. 111–144). Oxford, England: Academic Press.

Rothbart, M., Davis-Stitt, C., & Hill, J. (1997). Effects of arbitrarily placed category boundaries on similarity judgments. *Journal of Experimental Social Psychology, 33*, 122–145.

Santa, J. L., & Baker. L. (1975). Linguistic influences on visual memory. *Memory and Cognition, 3*, 445–450.

Schmitt, B. H., & Zhang, S. (1998). Language structure and categorization: A study of classifiers in consumer cognition, judgment, and choice. *Journal of Consumer Research, 25*, 108–122.

Schooler, J. W. (2002). Verbalization produces a transfer inappropriate processing shift. *Applied Cognitive Psychology, 16*, 989–997.

Schooler, J. W., & Engstler-Schooler, T. Y. (1990). Verbal overshadowing of visual memories: Some things are better left unsaid. *Cognitive Psychology, 22*, 36–71.

Schooler, J. W., Fiore, S. M., & Brandimonte, M. A. (1997). At a loss from words: Verbal overshadowing of perceptual memories. In D. L. Medin (Ed.), *The psychology of learning and motivation: Advances in research and theory* (Vol. 37, pp. 291–340). San Diego: Academic Press.

Shapiro, S., & Spence, M. T. (2002). Factors affecting encoding, retrieval, and alignment of sensory attributes in a memory-based brand choice task. *Journal of Consumer Research, 28*, 603–617.

Tajfel, H. (1959). Quantitative judgment in social perception. *British Journal of Psychology, 50*, 16–29.

Tajfel, H., & Wilkes, A. L. (1963). Classification and quantitative judgement. *British Journal of Psychology, 54*, 101–114.

Thompson, C. (2003, October 26). There's a sucker born in every medial prefrontal cortex. *New York Times*, Section 6, p. 54.

West, P. M., Brown, C. L., & Hoch, S. J. (1996). Consumption vocabulary and preference formation. *Journal of Consumer Research, 23*, 120–135.

Whorf, B. L. (1956). *Language, thought and reality: Selected writings* (J. B. Carroll, Ed.). Boston: Cambridge Technology Press.

Yamauchi, T., & Markman, A. B. (2000). Inference using categories. *Journal of Experimental Psychology: Learning, Memory, and Cognition, 26*, 776–795.

CHAPTER 2

The Mental Representation of Brand Names: Are Brand Names a Class by Themselves?

Possidonia F. D. Gontijo
University of California, Los Angeles

Shi Zhang
UCLA Anderson Graduate School of Management

What are brand names? This question has fascinated marketers and researchers for decades and has been addressed from various perspectives. There is the marketing view that brand names are part of the actual product and services (e.g., Javed, 1993); there is the branding view that brand names are linguistic symbols associated with a set of new meanings (Aaker, 1991; Keller, 1998); there is the social psychological view that brand names can be emotion-laden identities (e.g., Mehrabian, 1992), and so on.

This chapter investigates brand names from a new perspective. Attention is focused on brand names' linguistic attributes, such as differences in name types (e.g., existing items vs. newly coined items), and their rich array of inherent perceptual features, such as case, color, size, fonts, and so forth. One unique aspect of our method resides in the use of the laterality framework as our experimental paradigm, which enables us to investigate the hemispheric processing and neuropsychological status of brand names by measuring participants' accuracy and reaction times in lexical decision tasks, as well as participants' memory of the brand names. Interestingly, brand names as a class of words have been relatively unexplored by cognitive neuroscientists, which might be due to the implicit assumption that they are a subset of proper names. We suggest that brand names have a special neuropsychological status, but one that is different from proper names. This chapter is structured in the following way: First, it offers a brief background on the neuropsychological status of proper names and brand names. Next, it reports some research results. Finally, there is a discussion of the implications of the results for marketing and psycholinguistics.

23

BACKGROUND

The Neuropsychology of Proper Names

Proper names have been found to behave differently than common nouns, not only in patterns of breakdown (see Semenza, 1997, for a review; i.e., on how the brain is affected by injury), but also in how much more difficult they are to recall normally and how particularly vulnerable they are to the effects of aging (Cohen & Burke, 1993; Cohen & Faulkner, 1986; McWeeny, Young, Hay, & Ellis, 1997). An intriguing report by Saffran, Schwartz, and Marin (1976) documents some paralexic errors committed by two dyslexic patients with acquired deep dyslexia. They could read aloud lexical items that were part of a proper name more accurately than they could read the same item presented as a single word. For example, "olive" was read as "black" and "robin" as "bird," but "Robin Kelly" and "Olive Cooper" were read correctly.

Convergent evidence for the "special status" of proper names can also be found in hemispheric studies, where proper names were found to be less lateralized than other categories of words. Saffran, Bogyo, Schwartz, and Marin (1980), using a lexical decision task (LDT), examined laterality differences across several lexical categories and found that proper names were a class of relatively low frequency words that deep dyslexics were selectively able to identify. They also found that normal subjects' accuracy of written responses of lateralized first names was equal in the two fields, whereas performance was superior for right visual field (RVF) presentations of all other word categories tested. Using a matching task, Bradshaw, Gates, and Patterson (1976) also found some evidence that proper names are represented in the right hemisphere (RH) lexical system. The clinical literature (Damasio, Grabowski, Tranel, Hichwa, & Damasio, 1996; Fukatsu, Fujii, Tsukiura, Yamadori, & Otsuki, 1999), as well as recent imaging studies (from both event related potentials, Proverbio, Lilli, Semenza, & Zani, 2001; and functional magnetic resonance imaging, Tempini et al., 1998), suggest a selective role of the anterior temporal lobe in production of proper names. However, the perception of proper names may be more bilaterally represented.

More subtle differences between processing proper names and common nouns can be found in studies investigating orthographic representation, such as those on the role of word shape in reading. Baron (1977), for example, detected a familiarity effect related to the capitalization of the initial letter of proper names when he asked subjects to name a list of 30 names of three letters or less, in a familiar form (Al, Abe, Dan) and in an unfamiliar form (al, abe, dan). In English, proper names are printed with their initial letter capitalized almost universally. In two experiments manipulating the capitalization of the initial letter of nonwords, Gontijo (1998) found that subjects produced fewer pronunciations for centrally presented nonwords with an initially capitalized letter than for noncapitalized nonwords. She argued that capitalization of the first letter influences word recognition by working as a clue to which category the word to be recognized belongs.

When put together, these findings have led researchers to suggest that proper names attain a "special status" and they may be processed differently from other word categories. Brand names also have unique features that deserve to be explored in the context of representational issues. We propose that brand names possess a distinct neuropsychological status that is different from that of proper names. The next section reports evidence from existing studies as well as evidence from our own empirical studies.

The Neuropsychology of Brand Names

Understanding how we recognize a printed brand name could significantly contribute to our understanding of how semantic knowledge is organized in the brain. This is because brand names appear to have a special psycholinguistic status, intermediate between common nouns and personal names. A brand name's references are narrower than those of common nouns but wider than those of personal names. Furthermore, brand names have prominent emotional and graphic representations that are central to their meanings. It has been argued that brand names, as well as personal names, have a finer grained degree of conceptual organization than previously suspected. Further, Crutch and Warrington (2004) propose that the organization of a category of names in psychological space is reflected in its neural organization. However, there are no cognitive models, so far as we are aware, that directly address the recognition of brand names. Such knowledge would also be of great applied interest to marketers who have long recognized the strategic importance and the complex role of brand names in building brand equity. It has been suggested, for example, that brand names are perhaps one of the most valuable of the intangible assets a company possesses (Aaker, 1991, 1996). The reason is very simple: A product's name is the main interface between a product and the prospect's mind. Thus, the choice of a brand name requires the utmost care because it is going to be the most common medium through which consumers will relate to the product.

Brand Names' Shape. Brand names are pervasive. We are continuously reminded of their existence either by the presence of the products themselves or by powerful advertising campaigns. Intuitively, the power of brands partly stems from this relentless presence that engenders familiarity. And familiarity, psychologists found, engenders preference. Brands are therefore carefully nurtured. One of the main vehicles used to enhance brand awareness and loyalty is the printed word.

Two intriguing features of the visual representation of brand names is the dazzling variety of graphical designs used and the zealous consistency with which most brands are represented. We rarely find, for example, advertising material containing powerful brand names (e.g., "SONY®," "GUCCI®," or "IBM®") where these names are not printed in their elected familiar uppercase letters. In an environment that has become so cluttered, it surely makes good sense to use a name that is graphically distinct and also repeatedly represented in the same format in order to facilitate its recognition.

Gontijo (1998) used a self-paced LDT and found a word shape familiarity effect for brand names that are normally represented only in an uppercase format. Participants were faster in recognizing brand names in their familiar uppercase format compared to the unfamiliar lowercase one. No difference was found between the upper- and lowercase common word stimuli. Similar earlier findings had been found for abbreviations. Henderson and Chard (1976) report a same–different matching task experiment where they found that the word superiority effect (WSE) for abbreviations was confined to the visually familiar case [e.g., RT (FBI) < RT (IBF) but RT (fbi) = RT (ibf)].

The capitalization effect has been further demonstrated despite different sets of materials and methodologies used (Gontijo, Rayman, Zhang, & Zaidel, 2002). Undergraduate subjects were found to be faster and more accurate in recognizing brand names when the names were printed in their familiar format (i.e., uppercase letters) than when they were printed in an unfamiliar format (i.e., lowercase letters). Common words, used as control, were also presented in upper case and lower case, but no difference in response time and accuracy were observed between the cases. (See Fig. 2.1.)

Baron (1977) found that participants named names with the initial letter capitalized faster than they did for those without initial capitals. We suggest that proper names and brand names are sensitive to capitalization in a way that common nouns are not. This is likely so because classes of words such as proper names and brands

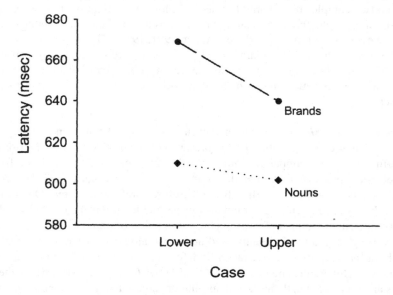

Figure 2.1.   Interaction between word-type and case for latencies.

have a consistent visual representation. For example, proper names are conventionally and invariably seen as initially capitalized; brand names have a consistent orthographic representation because of marketing communications strategies. Thus, unlike common nouns, brands do not switch between upper and lower case depending on contexts. For example, in English, words must have an initial capital letter at the beginning of a sentence; when seen in isolation, presumably both capitalization of the initial letter and lower case are acceptable. The visual features are clues to the lexical categories to which a word belongs. Thus, we claim that people's cognition about linguistic representations of brands, proper names, abbreviations, and those words that are deeply entrenched in the surrounding environments may have been incorporated into people's processing strategies that aid the retrieval of these items. It is very likely that further experiments, now in progress, will find similar results for other types of visual features, such as color, style, shape, and so on. We suggest that in the case of brand names, visual features become an intrinsic part of their identity and have been incorporated into people's processing strategies that aid their retrieval.

Brand Names and the Cerebral Hemispheres.   The human brain presents a fundamental duality, that is, it is comprised by two structures: the left and the right cerebral hemispheres, which are entirely separate except for the cerebral commissures connecting them. The corpus callosum, the major commissure, is estimated to be composed of 200 million axons and is responsible for transferring information between the two hemispheres. The left hemisphere (LH) and the right hemisphere (RH) are similar in appearance; however, there are major functional and anatomical asymmetries between them. Functionally, control of the body's basic movements and sensations is evenly divided between the two cerebral hemispheres. This control occurs in a crossed fashion: The LH controls the right side of the body and the RH controls the left side of the body. These functional differences are commonly referred to as lateralization of function.

When fixating on a point, each eye sees both visual fields but sends information about the RVF only to the LH and the information about the left visual field (LVF) only to the RH. The crossover and the split is a result of the manner in which the nerve fibers leading from the retina divide at the back of each eye. The visual areas of the left and right hemisphere normally communicate through the corpus callosum. Visual information is also transmitted in a cross fashion through the optic chiasm. Myers and Sperry (1953) took advantage of how the visual system is organized and completely severed the corpus callosum and the optic chiasm of cats. In doing so, they completely blocked the transferring of information from one eye to the contralateral hemisphere and after a series of experiments they concluded that a major function of the corpus callosum is to transfer learned information from one hemisphere to the other. Further, they concluded that, when the corpus callosum is cut, each hemisphere is able to function independently.

Their series of experiments opened the door to one of the most fascinating chapters in medical history, namely, the split-brain phenomenon. Inspired by the work of Myers and Sperry, two neurosurgeons, Vogel and Bogen, initiated the procedure of severing the corpus callosum of patients with intractable epilepsy. These became known as the split-brain patients. Among the different techniques developed for neuropsychologically testing split-brain patients is the so-called hemi-field tachistoscopic paradigm. This technique consists of asking the subject to fixate on the center of a screen while visual stimuli are shown either on the left or the right side of the screen for the duration of approximately 0.15 seconds. This brief exposure is normally long enough for subjects to perceive the stimuli, but also sufficiently short to preclude confounding effects of eye movements. As a consequence, all stimuli presented to the LVF goes to the right visual cortex and the stimuli presented to the RVF goes to the left visual cortex. The results are frequently measured in terms of the accuracy with which the subjects perceive the stimuli and the time they take to react to the stimuli, which is known as reaction time, or latency.

Language has proven to be a highly lateralized function and one that is predominantly located in the LH. However, evidence suggests that proper names are represented in the lexical system of both hemispheres (Safran et al., 1980). There is also evidence that the RH is selectively involved in processing proper names (Semenza, 1997; Van Lancker & Klein, 1990; but see Damasio et al., 1996, and Fukatsu et al., 1999).

It turns out that brand names may also be processed by distinct brain regions. By employing the hemi-field tachistoscopic paradigm, Gontijo et al. (2002) were able to demonstrate a larger RH involvement in the processing of brand names than of common words. (See Fig. 2.2.)

The repository of all the information readers or listeners have attained about words of their language is known as "the mental lexicon" (Coltheart, Davelaar, Jonasson, & Besner, 1977; Treisman, 1960, 1961). To read a word is to extract information from a set of printed marks and then to use that information as a means of reaching the word's lexical entries in the mental lexicon. This process is known as *lexical access*. Texts are normally composed by familiar and unfamiliar words, and even the most skilled readers find from time to time a word that they have never seen before. Psycholinguists use the technical name "nonword" to refer to them. A great deal can be learned about how our brain processes reading by experimentally testing letter strings that present different degrees of familiarity and/or different degrees in the frequency with which they appear in the language. One example is the measurement of the speed and accuracy with which we are able to process words and nonwords. Two of the most reliable effects in word recognition studies are: the *frequency effect*, that is, the speed and the accuracy with which a word is processed is dependent on its frequency. The higher the frequency, the faster and more accurately a word is processed (all else being equal); and the so-called *lexicality effect*, that is, the finding that words are processed faster and more accurately than nonwords (Coltheart, 1978; Foster & Chambers, 1973; Rubenstein, Lewis, & Rubenstein,

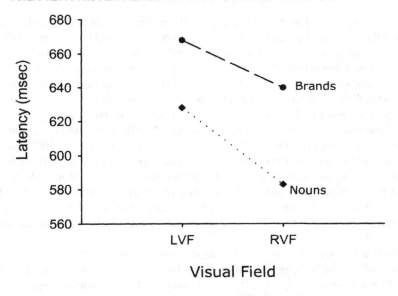

Figure 2.2. Interaction between wordness and visual field for latencies.

1971). Subjects, for example, take longer on average to respond to the string "lece" compared to "lace."

We have constructed two different types of nonwords according to an algorithm developed by Gontijo (1998). Half of the nonwords are orthographically close to the English language, that is, normal nonwords (e.g., seid) and the other half differ orthographically from the English language, that is, the weird nonwords (e.g., nioth). In our studies, we have always found a lexicality effect, with faster reaction times and more accurate performance for common nouns and brand names compared to nonwords (Gontijo, 1998; Gontijo et al., 2002). This result suggests that brand names share with common nouns their *word status*. Nevertheless, when compared to each other directly, common nouns and brand names exhibit distinct patterns of behavior with regard to their hemispheric status. Gontijo et al. (2002) have found that the lateralization pattern of brand names is closer to that of the normal nonwords as compared to the common words. It is common in hemispheric studies to find that nonwords are less lateralized than common words (Iacoboni & Zaidel, 1996; Measso & Zaidel, 1990). This difference, we suggest, can be used as a criterion for testing how brand names differ from words.

Why should we care about where and how brands are processed in the brain? Answers to this question may help us to explain brand name effects on consumers and to leverage our ability to increase a brand name's power of persuasion.

Brand Names' Different Linguistic Make-Ups. Brand names come in a variety of linguistic forms, which essentially can be reduced to two types: names that are also common words or composed of common words (CBs), and names that are the so-called coined brand names. Coined or invented brand names (IBs), which, for the most part, do not resemble directly any word from the lexicon, have been built with the sole function to be a brand name. Due to the explosion of new products and services over the past decade, all in need of a name, it has become increasingly difficult to find appropriate words to be trademarked. Thus, out of necessity, the use of IBs has increased considerably. However, there is a considerable debate over the advantages and disadvantages of using both types of names when naming products. CBs have the advantage of being descriptive of the product and its benefits, thus allowing for immediate recognition from consumers. Also, the strong semantic links of common words are useful in making the brand name memorable and facilitating the prospect's identification with the product. However, the use of suggestive brand names can be detrimental to product extensions or when there is a need for changing the way the product has been positioned.

IBs do not have the advantages of being descriptive or suggestive, but everything can be built in and in the process allow room for future positioning change. Also, they do not have to compete with a large number of words for recognition and memory.

We used the laterality framework to investigate these two types of brand names. The experiment consisted of a lateralized LDT. Participants were asked to sit in front of a computer screen and fixate their gaze at a small cross located at the center of the screen and indicate by pressing buttons on a bottom box whether or not a string of letters randomly displayed to the right or to the left side of the cross was a word. Presentation was done bilaterally in black on a gray background for 165 msec. Different letter strings appeared in each visual field, one as a target and the other one as a distractor. The distractor was composed of a string of "Xs" matching in length the target's number of letters. The target was underlined. The reason for using distractors is that they are known to enhance visual field effects (Iacoboni & Zaidel, 1996). The innermost edge of the letter string appeared 1.5 degrees of visual angle from fixation. The brief visual presentation combined with the visual angle of display are crucial to the hemi-field paradigm. Together they make possible for information presented on a particular visual field to be initially sent exclusively to one hemisphere. Central fixation is normally monitored before each trial by the experimenter, who watches the participant's eyes, in order to ascertain that they do not move their eyes from the fixation cross.

Participants, at the start of the experiment, were given instructions to decide as quickly and as accurately as possible whether or not each of the strings appearing on the screen was a real word by pressing the appropriate button on the response box. It was emphasized to participants that brand names were to be counted as real words.

The brand names were chosen from a list of 282 brand names, compiled from a wide variety of sources (magazines, billboards, product packages, Internet, newspapers, etc.) and 22 UCLA undergraduates were asked to perform the following three tasks in this order: (a) rate the brand names in terms of familiarity by using a 1–7 point scale (1—not familiar at all, 7— very familiar), (b) choose from 15 different product categories those that better fit each of the brand names (e.g., HONDA® = automobile, HEINZ® = food, SONY® = electronics, etc.), and (c) categorize the brand names according to their linguistic type (i.e., as a real word, an invented letter string, a proper name, or a foreign name). Afterward, only those brand names considered to be highly familiar were selected (i.e., only those that achieved an overall rating over 5 points). Each brand name was assigned to the linguistic type in which agreement among participants was the highest in terms of percentages (e.g., 91% of participants agreed on ADIDAS® being an invented brand name, 5% perceived it as a foreign name, and only 4% perceived it as being derived from a proper name). In reality, ADIDAS is a personal name, but for the purpose of our experiments what mattered was how participants perceive the brand names. Only the brand names that participants correctly matched to their product category were chosen. This method helped us to discard generic brand names, that is, those names that have become so familiar to us that they can be considered to be common words in our lexicon. Also, preference was given to familiar brand names composed of common words of lower frequencies in the CELEX[1] database (e.g., PUMA familiarity = 5.9 and frequency = 37).

The common words were selected from the CELEX database and they had frequencies between 100 and 160 occurrences per million according to the CELEX database (Baayen, Pipenbrock, & Gulikers, 1995). Each list was rated for familiarity by two different groups of 16 UCLA students (volunteers). A 1–7 point scale (1—not familiar at all, 7—very familiar) was used. The lists were randomized. Only familiar common words that matched the brand names in familiarity were selected (i.e., only those that achieved an overall rating over 5 points were chosen as experimental material). Further, an effort was made to use only concrete and imageable items (i.e., items that can be pictured in our minds), according to the Paivio, Yuille, and Madigan (1968) norms.

The nonwords were constructed according to an algorithm developed by Gontijo (1998). Orthographically, they have a monosyllabic structure: onset, nucleus, and coda. Only onsets and codas, which have a high frequency of appearance in the CELEX database, were used here to compose the nonwords.

Interestingly, brand names that are actual words in the lexicon (CBs) were the only type of brand names that did not exhibit a laterality effect—that is, they were equally processed by both brain hemispheres. A possible explanation for this finding is that CBs' orthographical familiarity, which results in them functioning in the lexicon also as a common word, facilitates the use of a visual processing strategy by the RH. It has been previously demonstrated that the RH does not use a phonological strategy due to

---

[1]CELEX Lexical Database of English (Version 2.5). Dutch Centre for Lexical Information, Nijmegen.

lacking this type of information. This explanation is consistent with our findings regarding IBs, which are often composed of orthographically and phonologically challenging novel letter strings. IBs showed the longest reaction times and the poorest accuracy results. We argue that the superior performance of CBs over IBs is due to CBs' dual lexical status (i.e., they are both a familiar word in the lexicon, as well as a familiar brand name). (See Figs. 2.3 and 2.4.)

Memory for Brand Names.   Memory is one of the most fundamental and also complex cognitive capacities with which we are endowed. The consumer's ability to recognize and recall a brand name is perhaps one of the best predictors of how successful a brand name performs in the marketplace. This belief has been the motivation behind our next set of studies where we tried to answer the question of how the hemispheric differences found in our other studies would translate into memory performance. Is it the case that CBs, which were faster recognized than coined brand names and were also equally processed by both hemispheres, would also be better retrieved from memory?

We carried out two studies using two different experimental paradigms, namely, a recognition memory task and a recall task. The recognition memory experiment was self-paced and followed a lateralized LDT, where different types of brand names, common words, and nonwords were briefly and randomly presented into each hemi-field. CBs and IBs were among the presented stimuli and participants had to decide, by pressing *yes* or *no* in a button box, if they had seen them or not dur-

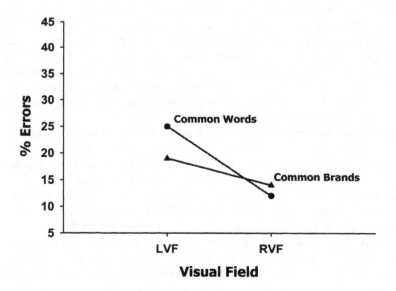

Figure 2.3.   Interaction between brandness (common brands × common words) and visual field for accuracy.

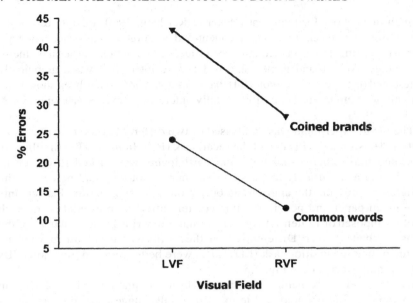

Figure 2.4.   Interaction between brandness (coined brands × common words) and visual field for accuracy.

ing the LDT. In the memory recognition task, brand names were recognized faster and more accurately than common words independently from the initial visual field of presentation. However, the common words originally presented into the RVF were processed more accurately compared to those presented into the LVF. These results give further support to our hypothesis that brand names are a lexical category on their own and entail special processing strategies.

Particularly telling was our finding that CBs were distinctly processed from common words. We interpret this finding as a result of brand names possessing more restricted and well-defined sets of positive semantic associations compared to common words, which is probably achieved through the well-orchestrated advertising campaigns purposefully conducted by marketers in their sustained and consistent communication efforts.

An insistent feature of these campaigns is their appeal to the emotional components of human cognition. In striving for creating brands with strong positive semantic associations, these campaigns aim at arousing in the consumer positive feelings that are believed to strengthen the bonds between consumers and the advertised brand. For example, it has been shown that brand preference is higher for names that generate appropriate feelings. Emotional arousal at the time of an experience may play a critical role in influencing memory strength (Bower, 1992). Findings of many experimental studies of human as well as animal memory suggest that the emotional arousal induced by an experience is an important determinant of the strength of memory for the event (Heuer & Reisberg, 1990; Revelle & Loftus, 1992). Moreover, recent findings have identified neurobiological systems that appear to play critical roles in mediating the influence of emotional arousal on memory storage. Also, brand names tend to be more interesting when graphically represented (e.g., being more colorful) than common words. It has been shown that recognition memory is better for visually interesting objects (Humphreys & Riddoch, 1987).

The recall experiment was comprised of two different tasks, namely, a perception decision task (PDT) and the recall task (RT). In the PDT, stimuli were presented into either visual field and participants were asked to decide as quickly and as accurately as possible whether or not they had perceived the stimulus by pressing the appropriate button on the response box. Participants were given paper and pencil and immediately after the presentation of each block, composed of 12 items, they had 2 minutes to write down the names of the items they had just seen. Differently from the results we have obtained when using the online recognition task (LDT), IBs were better recalled than both CBs and common words. (See Fig. 2.5.)

IBs, by their very nature, are distinct from common words and CBs in orthographical and phonological terms. Our results suggest that distinctiveness played a positive role in the recall of coined brand names. The distinctiveness of a word—its novelty and uniqueness as a construct—has been demonstrated to influence both encoding and retrieval (Eysenck, 1979; Gregg, 1976). Similar to semantics, distinctiveness has been claimed to promote more in-depth processing

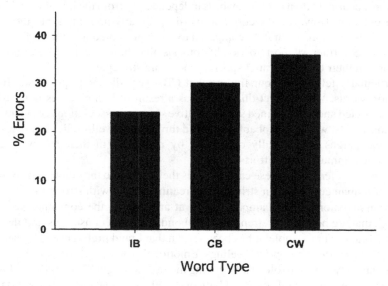

Figure 2.5.   Main effect of recognition memory for accuracy.

(Berlyne, 1971; Craik & Lockhart, 1972) and in this manner enhance recall (Lowrey, Shrum, & Dubitsky, 2003).

Further, we hypothesize that although both semantic processing and distinctiveness prompt deeper levels of processing, less complex computations are involved in registering distinctiveness than in processing semantic associations. Our results reflect the processing demands of the laterality paradigm caused by participants' very brief exposure to the stimulus. Moreover, an inherent feature of the laterality paradigm is that stimuli are initially sent to only one of the hemispheres and have to be transferred to the other one. This takes processing resources and thus it is natural under such conditions that the brain chooses the more economical processing strategy, if that is available.

CONCLUSIONS

This research took a different approach to brand names and investigated how they are represented and processed in the mind and brain. It studied the hemispheric representation of brands as a clue to their special neuropsychological status. We looked into how coined brand names and common word brand names are recognized in terms of latency and accuracy relative to each other, and relative to the control categories (i.e., common nouns and invented words). We did so using three different experimental paradigms: an LDT and two different types of memory tasks. Further, in all our experiments, we have used the lateralized framework. Our results suggest that brand names are not only distinct entities from other categories, but also that these two types of brand names are treated differently. This is possibly a consequence of people's frequent exposures to brands and marketing communications. The significance of testing stimuli using the brief presentations required by laterality techniques and measuring reaction time becomes evident in the presence of the big shifts that are happening in the marketplace due to the fast expansion of Internet trade.

One recent significant development in marketing communications is the concerted effort to figure out how to make brand advertising work online. For example, Google, the most highly prized media company, is reinventing online advertising with targeted, classified-like text links that we now begin to see everywhere. In this regard, increasingly close attention is being paid to the importance of the relationships built between consumers and brands. The approach we are suggesting here studies brand name cognition and its possible behavior consequences. Thus, it is important to explore and understand the automatic processes governing our reactions to brands, brand displays, and brand associations, all of which are often represented and symbolized in an encompassing linguistic entity—the brand name.

ACKNOWLEDGMENTS

This research was carried out in Professor Eran Zaidel's laboratory at the UCLA Psychology Department.

REFERENCES

Aaker, D. A. (1991). *Managing brand equity.* New York: The Free Press.

Aaker, D. A. (1996). *Building strong brands.* New York: The Free Press.

Baayen, R. H., Pipenbrock, R., & Gulikers, L. (1995). *The CELEX lexical database* (CD-ROM). Linguistic Data Consortium, University of Pensylvania, Philadelphia, PA.

Baron, J. (1977). Mechanisms for pronouncing printed words: Use and acquisition. In D. Laberge & S. J. Samuels (Eds.), *Basic processes in reading: Perception and comprehension* (pp. 207–208). London: Lawrence Erlbaum Associates.

Berlyne, D. E. (1971). *Aesthetics and pychobiology.* New York: Appleton-Century-Crofts.

Bower, G. (1992). How might emotions affect language? In S. A. Christianson (Ed.), *The handbook of emotion and memory* (pp. 3–32). Hillsdale, NJ: Lawrence Erlbaum Associates.

Bradshaw, J. L., Gates, A., & Patterson, K. (1976). Hemispheric differences in processing visual patterns. *Quarterly Journal of Experimental Psychology, 28,* 667–681.

Cohen, G., & Burke, D. M. (1993). Memory for proper names: A review. *Memory, 1*(4), 249–263.

Cohen, G., & Faulkner, D. (1986). Memory for proper names: Age differences in retrieval. *British Journal of Development Psychology, 4,* 187–197.

Coltheart, M. (1978). Lexical access in simple reading tasks. In G. Underwood (Ed.), *Strategies of information processing* (pp. 151–216). London: Academic Press.

Coltheart, M., Davelaar, E., Jonasson, J., & Besner, D. (1977). Access to the internal lexicon. In S. Doric (Ed.), *Attention and performance* (Vol. 6, pp. 535–555). Hillsdale, NJ: Lawrence Erlbaum Associates.

Craik, F. I. M., & Lockhart, R. S. (1972). Levels of processing: A framework for memory research. *Journal of Verbal Learning and Verbal Behavior, 11,* 671–684.

Crutch, S. J., & Warrington, E. K. (2004). The semantic organization of proper nouns: The case of people and brand names. *Neuropsychologia, 42,* 584–596.

Damasio, H., Grabowski, T. J., Tranel, D., Hichwa, R. D., & Damasio, A. R. (1996). A neural basis for lexical retrieval. *Nature, 380,* 499–505.

Eysenck, M. W. (1979). Depth, elaboration, and distinctiveness. In L. S. Cermak & F. I. M. Craik (Eds.), *Levels of processing in human memory* (pp. 89–118). Hillsdale, NJ: Lawrence Erlbaum Associates.

Foster, K. I., & Chambers, S. M. (1973). Lexical access and naming time. *Journal of Verbal Learning and Behaviour, 12,* 627–635.

Fukatsu, R., Fujii, T., Tsukiura, T., Yamadori, A., & Otsuki, T. (1999). Proper name anomia after left temporal lobectomy: A patient study. *Neurology, 52,* 1096–1099.

Gontijo, P. F. D. (1998). *Familiarity effects in visual word recognition.* Unpublished doctoral thesis, University of Edinburgh, Scotland, UK.

Gontijo, P. F. D., Rayman, J., Zhang, S., & Zaidel, E. (2002). How brand names are special: Brands, words and hemispheres. *Brain and Language, 82,* 327–343.

Gregg, V. H. (1976). Word frequency, recognition and recall. In J. Brown (Ed.), *Recall and recognition* (pp. 183–216). London: Wiley.

Henderson, L., & Chard, J. (1976). On the nature of the facilitation of visual comparisons by lexical membership. *Bulletin of the Psychonomic Society, 7*(5), 432–434.

Heuer, F., & Reisberg, D. (1990). Vivid memories of emotional events: The accuracy of remembered minutiae. *Memory and Cognition, 18,* 496–506.

Humphreys, G. W., & Riddoch, M. J. (1987). *To see but not to see: A case study of visual agnosia.* London: Lawrence Erlbaum Associates.

Iacoboni, M., & Zaidel, E. (1996). Hemispheric independence in word recognition: Evidence from unilateral and bilateral presentations. *Brain and Language, 53,* 121–140.

Javed, N. (1993). *Naming for power: Creating successful names for the business world.* New York: Linkbridge Publishing.

Keller, K. V. (1998). *Strategic brand management: Building, measuring and managing brand equity.* Englewood Cliffs, NJ: Prentice-Hall.

Lowrey, T. M., Shrum, L. J., & Dubitsky, T. M. (2003). The relation between brand name linguistic characteristics and brand name memory. *Journal of Advertising, 32,* 7–17.

McWeeny, K. H., Young, A., Hay, D. C., & Ellis, A. W. (1987). Putting names to faces. *British Journal of Psychology, 78,* 143–144.

Measso, G., & Zaidel, E. (1990). Effects of response programming on hemispheric differences in lexical decisions. *Neurospsychologia, 28,* 635–646.

Mehrabian, A. (1992). Interrelationships among name desirability, name uniqueness, emotion characteristics connoted by names, and temperament. *Journal of Applied Social Psychology, 78,* 143–144.

Myers, R. E., & Sperry, R. W. (1953). Interocular transfer of a visual form discrimination habit in cats after section of the optic chiasma and corpus callosum. *American Association of Anatomists: Abstract of papers from platform,* p. 351.

Paivio, A., Yuille, J. C., & Madigan, S. A. (1968). Concreteness, imagery, and meaningfulness values for 925 nouns. *Journal of Experimental Monographs, 76*(1, Pt. 2), 1–25.

Proverbio, A. M., Lilli, S., Semenza, C., & Zani, A. (2001). ERP indexes of functional differences in brain activation during proper and common names retrieval. *Neuropsychologia, 39,* 815–827.

Revelle, W., & Loftus, D. (1992). The implications of arousal effects for the study of affect and memory. In S. A. Christianson (Ed.), *The handbook of emotion and memory* (pp. 113–150). Hillsdale, NJ: Lawrence Erlbaum Associates.

Rubenstein, H., Lewis, S. S., & Rubenstein, M. A. (1971). Evidence for phonemic recoding in visual word recognition. *Journal of Verbal Learning and Verbal Behaviour, 10,* 645–658.

Saffran, E. M., Bogyo, L. C., Schwartz, M. F., & Marin, O. S. M. (1980). Does deep dyslexia reflect right-hemisphere reading? In M. Coltheart, K. Patterson, & J. Marshall (Eds.), *Deep dyslexia* (pp. 381–406). London: Routledge & Kegan Paul.

Saffran, E. M., Schwartz, M. F., & Marin, O. S. M. (1976). Semantic mechanisms in paralexia. *Brain and Language, 3,* 255–265.

Semenza, C. (1997). Proper-name-specific aphasias. In H. Goodglass & A. Wingfield (Eds.), *Anomia: Neuroanatomical and cognitive correlates* (pp. 115–135). San Diego: Academic Press.

Tempini, M. L. G., Price, C. J., Josephs, O., Vandenberghe, R., Cappa, S. F., Kapur, N., & Frackowiak, R. S. J. (1998). The neural systems sustaining face and proper name processing. *Brain, 121,* 2103–2118.

Treisman, R. (1960). Contextual cues in selective listening. *Quarterly Journal of Experimental Psychology, 12,* 242–248.

Treisman, R. (1961). *Attention and speech.* Unpublished doctoral dissertation, Oxford University.

Van Lancker, D., & Klein, K. (1990). Preserved recognition of familiar personal names in global aphasia. *Brain and Language, 39,* 511–529.

CHAPTER 3

Sounds Convey Meaning: The Implications of Phonetic Symbolism for Brand Name Construction

L. J. Shrum
Tina M. Lowrey
University of Texas at San Antonio

When brand managers are confronted with the task of constructing brand names for new products, they undoubtedly face a complex and difficult task. Few would disagree that a brand's name can have a huge impact on the success of the brand. In fact, in one notable example (the Ford *Edsel*), the general pervasive dislike for the brand name has been suggested as a major reason for the product's failure (Hartley, 1992; Klink, 2000). It is thus no surprise that brand name construction and testing is itself a big business (Kohli & LaBahn, 1997) and few companies would choose a brand name these days without extensive testing.

But how does a brand manager get started in both generating and choosing among brand names? One obvious way is a semantic approach that looks at the meaning of particular words or syllables (for a review, see Lerman, chap. 5 in this volume). This strategy attempts to create meaningful brand names by choosing those that say something about the product category (e.g., *Newsweek*, Juicy Juice®) or about attributes that the product possesses (e.g., Mop & Glo®, Eveready®). These techniques have been shown to influence marketing and advertising effectiveness measures such as brand name recall and product preference (Keller, Heckler, & Houston, 1998; Lowrey, Shrum, & Dubitsky, 2003; Meyers-Levy, Louie, & Curren, 1994). It seems reasonable to suppose that brand managers would likely focus on just such techniques.

There are also quite a number of nonobvious, nonsemantic ways in which words can convey both meaning and distinctiveness. Some examples include phonetic devices such as rhyming, vowel repetition, and alliteration, orthographic devices such as unusual spellings or abbreviations, and morphological devices such as the compounding or blending of words (see Vanden Bergh, Adler, & Oliver, 1987, for a comprehensive list and brand name examples). This chapter focuses on one of those nonobvious and nonsemantic devices, *phonetic symbolism*. Phonetic symbolism refers to the notion that the mere sound of a word, apart from its semantic connotation, conveys meaning. This notion has been speculated on and debated at least as far back as Plato. Empirical research on phonetic symbolism also has a long history and has itself generated quite a bit of controversy and debate, whether it be in terms of demonstrating the presence of the effect in a language, the generalizability of the effect across languages, or the underlying origin and mechanisms of the effect. In recent years, this research has been extended to the application of phonetic symbolism in constructing brand names.

The purpose of this chapter is twofold. First, it reviews in depth the research on phonetic symbolism, focusing on the different types of perceptions induced by various sounds, the nature of the evidence for and against these effects, and the generalizability of the effect. A thorough knowledge and understanding of previous research should be useful for researchers interested in applying these principles to marketing situations. Second, it extends this discussion to cover research that has specifically looked at phonetic symbolism and its implications in a marketing context. We discuss in detail previous empirical work that has looked at the effects of phonetic symbolism on brand name preference.

EMPIRICAL EVIDENCE FOR PHONETIC SYMBOLISM

Phonetic symbolism is simply the notion that phonemes can convey meaning on their own, apart from their configuration in words. Phonemes are the smallest unit of sound (e.g., the sound of the letter *t*) and form the basic building blocks of language. Phonetic symbolism might be best understood in terms of its opposite, that the sounds of words are arbitrary conventions. This debate has its origin at least from 400 B.C. In Plato's dialogue, *Cratylus* (Plato, 1892), Hermogenes asks Socrates if the sound of a word is merely arbitrary (Hermogenes believes that it is) or if the relation between a word's sound and its meaning is, well, meaningful. Socrates argues that, although the relation between the sound and meaning of some words may indeed be arbitrary, *good* words are those in which their sounds fit with their meaning (see also Fitch, 1994; Klink, 2000). This debate reemerges in the works of de Saussure (1916), who argues for the arbitrary relation, and Jespersen (1922), who argues for a meaningful relation.[1]

There are, of course, clear instances in which sound does convey meaning (and even Saussure would agree, but consider it to be an aberrant case), such as words

---

[1] In an amusing application of another linguistic device—metaphor—the debate between arbitrariness and meaningfulness of the sound–meaning relationship has been termed a conflict between the Juliet Principle (from Shakespeare's *Romeo and Juliet*, "that which we call a rose, by any other name would smell as sweet") and the Joyce Principle (in reference to James Joyce's frequent use of phonetic symbolism in his works; see Collins, 1977).

that are likely purposely constructed to convey that relation (e.g., cockadoodledoo, kerplunk, hiss). These words that imitate sounds are referred to as onomatopoeia. Apart from these obvious (and intended) relations, as Saussure believed, it seems unlikely, if not farfetched, that languages could develop such systematic nuance. Yet, the empirical research on the topic, although not without its share of controversy, tends to suggest otherwise. As we detail in the following sections, although all of the specific causal mechanisms have yet to be uncovered, the demonstrations of phonetic symbolism, both within and across languages, have been impressive.

The research on phonetic symbolism takes a variety of forms, differing on dimensions such as experimental control, universality of effects, and types of sounds or phonemes that are investigated. In fact, these dimensions are often constantly overlapping, making categorization somewhat difficult. Nevertheless, there are some general classifications that may be useful.

Vowels and Consonants

One convenient distinction for phonetic symbolism research is vowels versus consonants. By far the most research has focused on vowels, perhaps because the small number (relative to consonants) is more manageable. Vowels are generally categorized on a front versus back distinction. This distinction refers to the position of the tongue during pronunciation. For example, the highest position of the tongue is more toward the front of the mouth for *bee* than for *bin*, and more toward the back for *boot* than for *bin* (Klink, 2000).

Evidence for phonetic symbolism is provided by studies that have shown that the front–back distinction is consistently related to a variety of spacial dimensions. In what appears to be one of the first controlled demonstration of this effect, Sapir (1929) gave participants nonsense (artificial) words in the form of consonant-vowel-consonant that differed only in the middle vowel (e.g., *mil* vs. *mal*). He then gave participants an arbitrary referent ("these are tables") and asked them to indicate which was large and which was small. The participants showed over 80% agreement across a large number of word pairs in their association of the back vowel sound (e.g., *mal*) with a large table and the front vowel sound (e.g., *mil*) with a small table. The results were consistent regardless of whether the participants were children (ages 11–18), university students, American adults, or Chinese speakers. In a second experiment, he found similar results on judgments of size and speed.

Following Sapir's (1929) study, other research extended the range of the front–back distinction to include more vowels. Sapir's student, Stanley Newman (1933), was able to show that the vowel sounds could be ordered along a continuum of implied size (e.g., the sounds $[\bar{e}]^2$, [i], [ô], as in beat, hit, posh). As the vowel sounds move from front to back, perceptions of size increase. He also found similar

---

[2]The symbols used to denote sounds come from Webster's New World Dictionary (3rd college ed.).

results on judgments of brightness (front vowels are associated with greater bright-ness than back vowels). Both Birch and Erickson (1958) and Becker and Fisher (1988) extended this research using semantic differential scales (rather than choice). Numerous other studies have since shown that the front–back distinction is related to judgments of many different dimensions (e.g., hard–soft, angular–round, fast–slow, light–heavy, with front vowels more associated with the first word in each pair; for a review, see French, 1977). One caveat is worth noting, however. The results appear to hold only when participants are directed toward particular dimen-sions (which is larger, which is faster, etc.). When participants are given nonsense words varying in their sound and asked to spontaneously provide the first thing that comes to mind, evidence for phonetic symbolism is not observed (Bentley & Varon, 1933).

Although more research has focused on vowels, studies have also investigated the phonetic symbolism associated with various consonant sounds. Consonants, like vowels, can be classified on the front–back distinction. Studies of sounds re-lated to consonants tend to show the same pattern of effects as vowels. For example, Miron (1961) found that both front vowels and consonants appearing in nonsense words tended to be associated with evaluations of "weak" and "pleasant," whereas back vowels and consonants were "unpleasant" and "strong." Folkins and Lenrow (1966) found similar results on the pleasant–unpleasant dimension.

Although the front–back distinction has been used for consonants, a classifi-cation based on a different articulatory position is actually more common. Con-sonants are typically categorized as either fricatives (spirants) or stops. Fricatives are formed by allowing air to flow past the articulators (lips, teeth, tongue), which creates friction. Examples of fricatives are *s*, *f*, and *z*. Stops, however, are formed from the complete closure of the articulators, which im-pedes air flow. Examples include *p*, *k*, *t*, *b*. In addition, consonants are also fur-ther categorized as either voiced or voiceless. Voiced consonants are produced with the vocal cords vibrating (*b*, *d*) and voiceless consonants are pronounced without vocal cord vibration (*p*, *t*). Note that the two dimensions (stop–frica-tive, voiced–voiceless) are orthogonal, and thus one has voiced and voiceless fricatives and voiced and voiceless stops. This somewhat lengthy explanation of categorization leads to a less lengthy observation: Voiceless consonants tend to be perceived as smaller (Klink, 2000; Newman, 1933), less potent (Folkins & Lenrow, 1966), and lighter and sharper (Klink, 2000) than voiced consonants, and fricatives tend to be perceived as smaller, faster, and lighter than stops (Klink, 2000). However, this categorization is not completely clear, as Klink (2000) did not manipulate the two dimensions orthogonally. Moreover, some variation within the stop consonants appears to exist. Taylor and Taylor (1962) found that *t* and *p* were perceived by English speakers to be small sounds, and *g* and *k* were perceived as large sounds; Greenberg and Jenkins (1966) found dif-ferences between voiced and voiceless consonants, and between stops and fricatives, for some dimensions but not others.

Artificial or Natural Language?

Another way in which research on phonetic symbolism can be divided is based on whether the studies use artificial, or nonsense, words or natural language. The use of artificial words has obvious merits in that it can control for semantic meaning associated with those words. Such studies, many reviewed in the previous sections, generally find that there is a high level of agreement between participants on the connotation of words with certain types of vowels (i.e., back vowels are associated with bigger size). However, for the most part, these studies investigated the effects within one language, usually English.

To provide confidence that phonetic symbolism is a real phenomenon, it seems reasonable to expect there to be some evidence in real language. But, obtaining this evidence in a rigorous manner poses some important threats to internal validity. For example, examination of certain types of words suggests a relation between sound and meaning. As noted by Jespersen (1922), back vowels such as the [u] sound in *dull* are very often found in words expressing disgust or dislike: "blunder, bungle, bung, clumsy ... sloven, muck, muddle ..." (p. 26). Words beginning with *fl* are often found in words expressing movement (e.g., flutter, flap, flit, flicker) and words beginning with *sl* often have a negative connotation (slouch, slut, slovenly, slime; Fitch, 1994; Jespersen, 1922). The same exercise can be undertaken to suggest a shared effect of phonetic symbolism across languages and cultures. Words for *little* in other languages are *kleine* (German), *mikros* (Greek), *petite* (French), *piccola* (Italian). Diminutives in English are made by adding *ie*, in Spanish *ico* and *ito*, in Italian *ino* (Brown, 1958).

Of course, these words or endings may simply be the ones that come most quickly to mind but do not necessarily indicate actual frequency biases, and there are always counterexamples (e.g., *big*). But, other studies have provided more rigor in testing these hypotheses. Newman (1933) took words from *Roget's Thesaurus* with meanings associated with size and compared the counts in terms of their relation to vowel sounds. Although Newman's initial conclusion was that there was little systematic relation between the meaning and the vowel sounds, a reanalysis of the data (Johnson, 1967) showed that the size words not only differed greatly when the farthest back and farthest front vowels were compared (by about a 2:1 margin) but that the order was similar to those found in Newman's experiments with nonsense words. Johnson (1967) replicated this effect, but this time had participants write down all the words they could think relating to either smallness or largeness. He then compared the frequency of words with their vowel sounds. The same order as previous studies emerged, and the differences between vowel sounds were even more dramatic than Newman's. Other studies have shown that there does appear to be a more than arbitrary relation between the use of particular consonants or consonant pairs. For example, Bolinger (1950) documented that roughly half of all English words that begin with *gl* have a visual connotation (e.g., *glance, glitter, gleam, glow*).

Although these results are suggestive, it is difficult to address the issue in an exhaustive manner. One way to bridge the gap between experimental control and still use natural language is to test whether participants who speak one language agree on the meaning of words in another language when the words differ in their sounds. A number of studies have provided evidence of this effect. Tsuru (1934; see also Tsuru & Fries, 1933) had undergraduates who were native English language speakers read a list of Japanese language antonym pairs that had been translated into Roman characters (the words were also read out loud by a native Japanese speaker), and match the pairs to English equivalent pairs. The results showed that not only did the participants show very high agreement in their choices, but their level of translation accuracy was also remarkably high (69%). The same results have been replicated frequently (e.g., Brown, Black, & Horowitz, 1955; Weiss, 1963, 1966) in languages that are closely related (e.g., Indo-European languages such as English and German) and in languages that are historically unrelated (English and Japanese, English and Korean, English and Hindi, etc.). The results have also been replicated across all ages, including children as young as age 4 (Roper, Dixon, Ahern, & Gibson, 1976). However, for certain languages, the supportive results have not been obtained (e.g., Navajo: Atzet & Gerard, 1965; Hawaiian: Roper et al., 1976). Finally, the results have been replicated using native speakers other than English (e.g., Japanese, Chinese, Thai: Huang, Pratoomraj, & Johnson, 1969) and across numerous dimensions (Becker & Fisher, 1988). However, it is worth noting that this effect tends to be observed only when one of the pairs of antonyms is in the participant's native language. When participants must indicate which of two foreign word pairs (e.g., Japanese and Croatian) are similar, they perform no better than chance (Maltzman, Morrisett, & Brooks, 1956). The findings make sense in light of the Bentley and Varon (1933) findings that people do not spontaneously provide perceptions of dimensions. Rather, some understandable anchor is needed (e.g., same language).

Culture-Specific or Universal Effect?

Quite a bit of debate has been generated on whether phonetic symbolism is culture-specific or a universal effect across languages. It is an important debate because it has implications for the underlying mechanisms, which we discuss in the next section. Evidence for at least a culture-specific phonetic symbolism is very strong. The high level of agreement for within-culture participants on dimensions such as size, speed, hardness, and so forth, suggests that a particular language seems to have recognizable associations between sound and meaning. So too do the studies that show that same-language participants agree highly with the meaning of foreign words. The studies show that this effect can be obtained in most (but not all) languages.

What is particularly intriguing for the universality hypothesis is the results showing that not only do participants show a high level of agreement on what words in other languages mean (when prompted with appropriate dimensional guides), but they are also almost always correct at a rate better than chance. Recall that in the Tsuru (1934) study, English language participants guessed the meaning of Japanese words 69% of the time, and in Brown et al. (1955) they were correct on Hindi and Chinese words almost 60% of the time. A culture-specific hypothesis has difficulty accounting for such results. In addition, this type of evidence for phonetic symbolism has been shown across a large number of languages, regardless of whether the languages are historically related. However, as noted earlier, there are some instances (Hawaiian, Navajo) in which no effects were found. Although this calls into question the complete universality of the effect, such negative findings may be useful in understanding how the effect occurs.

A number of studies have shown that the same sound–meaning relations noted in the English lexicon also tend to appear in a vast number of languages. Fitch (1994) selected a language from each of the major language phyla (but excluding Indo-European), for a total of 16 languages. He then consulted sources of vocabularies (e.g., dictionaries) to obtain word pairs pertaining to size (e.g., big–small, huge–tiny) and noted whether the words for big versus small conformed to the front–back distinction (he called them short vs. long vocal tracts). He found support for phonetic symbolism in 11 of the 16 languages, with the results of the remaining 5 languages being inconclusive. Thus, put differently, in no instance did he find support contradicting the pattern of phonetic symbolism noted by Sapir (1929) and so many others. Other studies have found similar results (Jespersen, 1933; Nichols, 1971). In a more comprehensive study, Ultan (1978) surveyed 136 languages for evidence of the relation between vowel sounds and size. Although some of the languages did not show any conclusive phonetic symbolism for size, for those that did, 83% were consistent with the front–small, back–large relation. Finally, in a study that looked specifically at ethnozoological nouns (as opposed to the more typical adjectives in the studies previously mentioned), Berlin (1994) analyzed a Jivaroan language, Huambisa, and found that smaller birds and fish tend to be named with higher frequency (front) vowel sounds and larger fish and birds named with lower frequency (back) vowel sounds.

Underlying Mechanisms

So what can explain the phenomenon of phonetic symbolism? On the one hand, it is a somewhat difficult concept to grasp. It might be thought of as a form of synesthesia, which refers to cross-modal sensory associations such as hearing in colors. In the case of sound symbolism, the sense of sound might imply another sense or perception (size, brightness, etc.). However, it is unclear how certain degrees within a sense would necessarily become associated with certain degrees within another sense. On the other hand, perhaps it is not that difficult to grasp at all. Onomatopoeia—sound imitating sound—is straightforward and uncontroversial. Perhaps sound symbolism is a more subtle extension of this relation in which sound is used to represent nonacoustic perceptions. Ullmann (1966) calls this "secondary onomatopoeia." Some scholars have echoed Socrates' argument that these learned associations essentially make for "good words" and thus tend to get selected for as a language evolves, thereby moving our language to greater and greater use of symbolic words (Brown et al., 1955; Jakobson & Waugh, 1979; Jespersen, 1922).

Although this general explanation provides a framework for understanding why phonetic symbolism might exist, it does not tell how the association comes about. This question has also generated a number of speculations. Unfortunately, many of these explanations are difficult to untangle. Consider the most consistent finding in the literature: The [i] vowel sound in *mil* connotes smallness relative to the [a] sound in *mal*, which is more associated with largeness. Both Sapir (1929) and Newman (1933) suggest that this relation might be due to the fact that the "volume" of certain vowel sounds is greater than others (Sapir, 1929, p. 235). For higher front vowels, in which the tongue is higher and at the front of the mouth, the resonant cavity is small relative to back vowels, in which the tongue is lower and toward the back of the mouth (Pinker, 1994). But this difference in resonant cavity itself produces differences in amplification of frequencies (front vowels produce small cavities, which produce higher formant frequencies).

From these two explanations only, it is unclear whether it is a physiological effect or an acoustical effect. Some research seems to suggest that it is likely a frequency (acoustical) effect. This research has looked at the effects of varying either the formant frequencies of pronounced words or varying pure tones that participants hear. The findings from this extensive program of research show that higher frequencies exhibit consistently different associations than lower frequencies, and these differences are similar to those found with front versus back vowels. For example, lower frequencies are generally associated with larger, rounder figures, and higher frequencies associated with smaller, angular features (O'Boyle & Tarte, 1980; see also Tarte, 1982), and this pattern has been found for speakers of Urdu as well as speakers of English (O'Boyle, Miller, & Rahmani, 1987).

A recent investigation of the formant frequency hypothesis posed another possibility: Differential perceptions of size associated with the front and back vowels may be evolutionary. Fitch (1994) was interested in investigating the connections between vocal tract length, formant dispersion, and perceived body size. He reasoned that perhaps it is not frequency per se, but the size of the vocal tract (which is positively correlated with formant dispersion) that predicts body size. He provided supportive data for this hypothesis by showing that vocal tract length correlates with body size in rhesus macaques (Fitch, 1997). In experiments with humans, using synthesized vowel sounds and independently varying formant frequency and dispersion, he had participants estimate the body size of the "person" speaking the vowel sound (the sounds were actually synthesized sounds that approximated a human voice). In the first experiment, he found that human participants used vocal tract length (formant dispersion) and formant frequency to estimate body size. In the second experiment, he made the connection to phonetic symbolism by showing that lengthening the vocal tract while producing the sound of [oo] (as in *boot*) versus [ē] as in *beet* ncreased perceptions of body size by human participants (for reviews, see Fitch, 1994; Fitch & Hauser, 2002). These results suggest that, over time, humans used formant dispersion as a cue to body size. Moreover, because of this attribution, animals also learned to manipulate vocal tract length, and therefore formant dispersion, to increase perceptions of size in listeners when it was advantageous (e.g., during encounters with an enemy). Fitch (1994) supported this reasoning by showing that saki monkeys use lip protrusion (which elongates the vocal tract) during aggressive interactions. Ironically, this method of attempting to appear bigger to others is referred to as lack of "truth in advertising" (Fitch, 1994).

PHONETIC SYMBOLISM AND BRAND NAMES

The implications of the research on phonetic symbolism just reviewed seem very straightforward. If the sounds of words do in fact convey meaning, then that meaning should not only be conveyed by a particular brand name, but may also have implications for the evaluation of the product itself. A number of studies have shown that the congruency or "fit" between a brand name and the product category can increase important marketing variables such as recall, preference, and inference (Chisnall, 1974; Lowrey et al., 2003; Meyers-Levy et al., 1994; Peterson & Ross, 1972). Other research suggests that consumers have a general (but ill-defined and poorly articulated) notion that certain brand names and products fit together (Zinkhan & Martin, 1987). Thus, it seems reasonable to think that if word sounds (apart from their direct semantic associations) induce particular inferences regarding attributes, some word sounds may be more preferable than others for specific products.

Despite the logic of the relation between phonetic symbolism and brand names, it remains an empirical question as to whether or not such effects exist, and if they do, whether or not they are important. In fact, there are ample reasons to think that phonetic symbolism might have little or nothing to do with brand name perceptions. For one, firms spend quite a bit of time and energy in developing brand names (Chisnall, 1974; Kohli & LaBahn, 1997). Because the "suggestiveness" or "meaningfulness" of a brand name has an important impact on memory and perception (Childers & Houston, 1984; Keller et al., 1998; Lutz & Lutz, 1977; Saegert & Young, 1983), names tend to be used that provide direct (e.g., Easy-Off®, Picture Perfect) or indirect (e.g., Lexus being related to luxurious because of the orthographic relatedness of the two words) connections between the brand and its attributes. In such cases, subtle effects of simple sounds may be overwhelmed by other features of the brand names. A second issue is whether the possibly subtle effects of phonetic symbolism get transferred from perceptions that the word or name engenders to perceptions of the product itself and, in turn, whether these perceptions get transferred to marketing variables such as product or brand name preference.

Fortunately, there are a number of studies that provide answers to these empirical questions. Like the basic research in phonetic symbolism, these studies vary from general ones that look at the features of actual brand names in the marketplace, to correlational studies relating frequency of usage and phonetic characteristics, to controlled laboratory studies using artificial and nonsense brand names.

Phonetics in Brand Names

Perhaps one of the first to discuss phonetic symbolism in the context of brand names was Collins (1977), who coined the terms *Joyce Principle* and *Juliet Principle* (noted earlier) to describe the pro- and anti-phonetic symbolism arguments, respectively. In fact, Collins discusses in detail the early findings of Sapir (1929) and Newman (1933) and speculates on their implications for brand name perceptions. Other researchers have focused on the peculiar nature of certain consonants and, in particular, the letter k. Schloss (1981) noted that certain letters appear to occur more often in brand names than one would expect given their base rate of occurrence in all words in the English language. He compiled a list of the top 200 brands of 1979 and found that 54% of the names began with the letters c, p, or k, but only 19% of words in the English language start with those letters. For k in particular, 6% of brand names began with k, but only 1% of English language words begin with k. Vanden Bergh (1990) replicated these findings in a later and larger set of brand names, and Vanden Bergh, Collins, Schultz, and Adler (1984) showed that nonsense words beginning with stop consonants (also called "initial plosives") are better recalled than words that do not start with initial stop consonants.

Although these findings are interesting, they provide little help in understanding why these effects occur or whether or not they have anything to do with phonetic symbolism. It may be that a letter such as k simply looks funny, either because of its odd, angular shape, or simply because it doesn't occur that often in the English language. The latter example might cause it to be distinctively encoded (Eysenck, 1979). Indeed, word frequency has been shown to induce such processing (Lockhart, Craik, & Jacoby, 1976) and to enhance the memory of brand names (Meyers-Levy, 1989). In this case, it would be an orthographic rather than a phonetic linguistic device that causes the effect. In a similar manner, the letter k is considered a "versatile" letter in that it is infrequently used in the English language but nevertheless is more easily combined with other common consonants than are the other infrequently used letters such as j, q, x, y, and z. Moreover, because it has the same sound as a "hard" c, it provides the opportunity for unusual spellings (e.g., Kool-Aid®), which have been shown to enhance brand name recall and recognition (Lowrey et al., 2003).

Phonetic Symbolism and Perceptions of Product Attributes

Recent research has attempted to address the relation between phonetic symbolism and brand names in a more systematic and controlled manner and, in particular, to look at how phonetic symbolism may impact the perceptions of a brand's attributes. These studies have borrowed heavily from the concepts and methods employed in the initial Sapir and Newman studies in an effort to tease out and isolate particular effects. One of the first was conducted by Heath, Chatterjee, and France (1990). They systematically varied single-syllable, artificial words on whether the initial consonants were hard (stops) or soft (fricatives), and whether the vowel sounds were high (front) or low (back; e.g., Sige, Suge, Kige, Kuge). They had participants indicate their perceptions of hardness, brand attitudes, and purchase intentions. The results showed a general (although sometimes only marginally significant) effect for both the consonant and vowel sounds. The presence of both stop consonants and front vowels caused the product to be judged as harsher than either fricatives or back vowels. However, these perceptions did not appear to translate into brand attitudes or purchase intentions in any meaningful way.

A more comprehensive study of vowel and consonant effects was conducted by Klink (2000). He constructed 124 nonsense word pairs that varied only on one phonetic dimension, either they began with a stop or a fricative consonant (e.g., kobal vs. fobal), or they had either a front or back vowel in the first syllable (e.g., geleve, goleve). He also coded whether the stops and fricatives were voiced or voiceless, allowing for a comparison within each consonant category. Klink then had participants judge the words on a variety of different dimensions within particular product category (e.g., "Which ketchup seems thicker?"). As expected, he found that words with front vowel sounds were considered smaller, lighter (in color), milder, thinner, softer, faster, colder, less bitter, more feminine, lighter (in weight), and prettier than words with back vowel sounds. He found similar results with the stops versus fricatives. Words with initial stops were perceived to be smaller, faster, lighter, and more feminine than words with fricatives (but contrary to predictions, not sharper or harder). Within the voiced versus voiceless contrasts, words beginning with voiceless stops were perceived as smaller, faster, lighter, and sharper than words beginning with voiced stops, and likewise, words beginning with voiceless fricatives were perceived as smaller, softer, and more feminine than words beginning with voiced fricatives.

Phonetic Symbolism and Product Preference

The Klink (2000) studies demonstrated that the same types of phonetic symbolism effects noted in early studies manifest themselves in perceptions of product attributes. In particular, the meaning created by the *sound* of the brand names appears to be used to form impressions of the attributes of that brand. However, it is unclear whether the attribute impressions created through this phonetic symbolism translate into product preference. On the one hand, it is reasonable to think that it might, given that the fit between a brand name and product attributes has been shown to influence product preference (Meyers-Levy et al., 1994). On the other hand, the effects may be so subtle that no such transfer takes place.

Three particular sets of studies since then have attempted to address this very issue. The first is Klink (2003). Two studies addressed the relation between sound symbolism, shape of the brand mark (i.e., logo), and brand liking. In the first study, Klink found that front vowels in brand names tended to be more associated with lighter colors than did back vowels. The same pattern was also noted with fricatives and stops, respectively. Moreover, he found that front vowels and fricatives in brand names tended to be more associated with smaller and more angular shapes compared to back vowels and stops. In the second study, Klink showed that the effects of sound symbolism on perceptions of size, shape, and color exhibited an effect on brand liking and perceptions of taste. For ratings of beer, liking and strength of taste was greatest when the effects of size, shape, and color were consistent. That is, the beer was perceived to be stronger, darker, heavier, and was liked better when the name used a back vowel and the logo was more rounded, darker, and larger.

A second set of studies was conducted by Yorkston and Menon (2004) to specifically address whether sound symbolism translates to brand liking and under what conditions. They constructed two fictitious brand names for ice cream, Frish and Frosh, which differed only on the vowel sound. The [i] sound in Frish is more of a high, front sound than the [ä] sound in Frosh. They reasoned that because the [ä] sound has been shown to be associated with things being bigger, heavier, duller, and slower (compared to more high, front vowel sounds; e.g., Newman, 1933), then the Frosh brand may be more likely to be perceived as smoother, richer, and creamier than the Frish brand name. If so, because these are positive attributes of ice cream, ice cream with the brand name Frosh should also be preferred over ice cream with the brand name Frish.

Their results supported these hypotheses. Frosh was indeed perceived to be smoother, richer, and creamier than Frish, and it was also evaluated more favorably. Moreover, Yorkston and Menon were able to make some inferences about the underlying processes, given their experimental design. Along with the sounds of the brand names, they also manipulated the perceived diagnosticity of the brand names (by telling some participants the name was real and others that the name was just a test name), the timing of the diagnosticity information (presented at the same time as the brand name or after the presentation of the brand name), and the cognitive capacity available for processing (having some participants pay attention to the mention of a specific number by the experimenter). Their results suggest that phonetic symbolism is a relatively automatic process but that people can correct for its use when it is not diagnostic (e.g., in the test condition rather than real condition), but then only if they are presented with the diagnostic information at the time they form the initial impression. If they receive information that the brand name is not diagnostic after they form the initial perception based on phonetic symbolism, then they do not go back and correct for that initial impression.

Finally, in a third set of studies (Lowrey & Shrum, 2005), we attempted to build on the Yorkston and Menon (2004) findings and to address some potential ambiguities. For example, the Yorkston and Menon studies used only one brand name pair,

Frish and Frosh. One problem with these names is that structurally they are closely related to real words and thus may bring to mind the semantic meaning of those words. Frish is similar to fish; Frosh is similar to frost or frosty. Both might have implications for naming a product such as ice cream (e.g., negative for Frish, positive for Frosh). Another potential problem lies in the ambiguity of the attributes for the product category. Note that previous research on phonetic symbolism did not look at the attributes of creamy, rich, or smooth, and thus there is no systematic confirmation of this perception. In addition, previous research has shown that the high front vowel in Frish is associated with coldness, which might be considered a positive attribute for ice cream.

Although the pattern of the Yorkston and Menon results suggest that these ambiguities did not present problems for the interpretation of their results, we thought it would be useful to test the same general notion—that phonetic symbolism not only affects perceptions of product attributes, but can also translate into brand name preference—in a more systematic manner. We were also interested in testing another hypothesis relating to sounds associated with disgust or dislike. As discussed earlier, linguistic scholars have noted the link between certain back vowel sounds (e.g., the [u] sounds in *blunder, bungle, muck, yuck*) and words of disgust (Jespersen, 1922; see also Jakobson & Waugh, 1979). To our knowledge, only one empirical study has looked at the implications of this relation. Smith (1998) investigated the effect of name sounds on political elections. He coded the names of candidates on various linguistic dimensions, which he combined to form a "comfort factor." This comfort factor consisted of positive (e.g., stressed middle vowel, two syllables, initial stress) and negative (e.g., stressed high back vowel as in *yuck, phooey*, initial fricative) linguistic signifiers. Thus, *Jackson* would receive a fairly high score and *Hughes* would receive a fairly low score. When he used this analytical technique for all U. S. presidents in races from 1824 (i.e., when popular votes were first recorded) to the present, he found that 35 of 42 (83%) of the winning last names had more positive comfort scores. He also used the technique to analyze the 1995 local elections in Spokane County, Washington, and found that 73% of the winning candidates had more positive comfort scores than their opponents.

To test the general front–back hypothesis and the "disgust" hypothesis, we created two sets of brand name pairs using artificial words. One set was designed to test the same front–back vowel distinction addressed by Yorkston and Menon (i.e., [i] vs. [ä]). A second set was constructed to test a particular sound often associated with disgust, the [yo͞o] sound (as in *puke*). The first set consisted of six different word pairs (e.g., *nillen* vs. *nallen, gimmel* vs. *gommel*). The second set consisted of four word pairs (e.g., *fewtip* vs. *fawtip, mewlad* vs. *mawlad*). Note that the back vowel [ä] sound in *mawlad* is identical to the back vowel [ä] sound in *nallen*.

Next, we constructed a study that would allow for a within-subjects design but not create worry about participant anticipation of the purpose of the study. In the first study, we presented all participants with the two sets of word pairs just described (10 word pairs total; order was counterbalanced) and asked them to choose which they preferred as a brand name for a particular product category. The important part of the design was that product category was manipulated such that in some cases the attributes implied by a front vowel sound would be positive, but in other cases would be negative. Conversely, the attributes implied by a back vowel sound would be positive for one product category but negative for another.

Recall that front vowel sounds tend to be perceived as smaller, faster, sharper, whereas back vowel sounds tend to be perceived as bigger, slower, duller. Given this, we chose the product categories of SUV, two-seater convertible, hammer, and knife, and manipulated them between groups. Thus, we had a mixed design in which phonetic sound was a within-subjects variable and product category was between subjects. For the front–back vowel contrast, we expected a sound by product category interaction in which back vowel sounds would be preferred as a brand name when the categories were SUV or hammer, and front vowel sounds would be preferred for brand names when the categories were convertible and knife. However, for the words that we expected to have generally negative connotations (e.g., *fewtip* less preferred than *fawtip*), we expected a main effect for vowel sound: Regardless of product categories, the back vowel sound [ä] would be preferred over the sound of [yōo], which is often associated with sounds of disgust. Note that this implies that the association with sounds of disgust would generally override the symbolism of back vowel sounds in the other word pair set. That is, the [yōo] sound is actually more of a front vowel than [ä], and thus should be preferred over [ä] for two-seater convertible or knife, if it did not carry the extra "baggage" of association with disgust.

The results of this experiment were consistent with our expectations. First, with respect to the front–back distinction and perceptions, participants perceived the back vowel sounds to differ from the front vowel sounds in the expected ways (thicker, heavier, stronger, duller, etc.). Second, the expected interaction between vowel sound and product category was observed. Brand names with front vowel sounds were preferred over names with back vowel sounds, by roughly a 2 to 1 margin, for the categories of convertible and knife. However, the pattern was reversed when the product categories were SUV or hammer. Brand names with back vowel sounds were preferred over names with front vowel sounds, again by over a 2 to 1 margin. In addition, the pattern of results for the [yōo] versus [ä] distinction also supported our reasoning. Regardless of product category, the [ä]-sounding words were preferred over [yōo]-sounding words, again by roughly a 2 to 1 margin.

These results provide further evidence of the effects of phonetic symbolism, and also show that the effect sizes can at times be substantial. We conducted an additional experiment to further extend these findings. In the previous experiment, we varied the product category and its associated attributes, and showed that names in which the attributes implied by the vowel sounds (e.g., front vowel = sharp) were a positive fit for a product (e.g., knife) were preferred over names with sounds that implied a poor fit (e.g., back vowel = dull). To provide an even more stringent test, we conducted a second experiment in which we held the product category constant but manipulated the attributes associated with the product. We chose beer because it has positive attributes associated with both front vowel sounds (cold, clean, crisp) and back vowel sounds (smooth, mellow, rich). We expected that brand names with front vowel sounds would be preferred over names with back vowel sounds when the product was described as a cool, clean, crisp-tasting beer, but the opposite would be true when the product was described as a smooth, mellow, rich-tasting beer (attributes similar to those used in Yorkston and Menon, 2004). Thus, we expected an interaction between vowel sound and product attribute. However, as in Experiment 1, we expected to see only a main effect when the choice involved [yo͞o] versus [ä] words, such that [ä] words would be preferred over [yo͞o] words regardless of product attributes.

Again, the findings supported our hypotheses. Front vowel sounds were preferred over back vowel sounds for a cool, clean, crisp-tasting beer, but back vowel sounds were preferred over front vowel sounds for a smooth, mellow, rich-tasting beer. In contrast, just as in Experiment 1, the [ä] sound was preferred over the [yo͞o] sound regardless of the attributes of the beer. In addition, manipulation checks indicated that relative to the front vowel sound, the back vowel sound was perceived in the manner expected on 15 relevant dimensions. However, the front vowels did not differ from back vowels in ratings of bad–good or pleasant–unpleasant. Conversely, the [yo͞o] was rated as more bad and more unpleasant than the [ä], but differed on few other dimensions.

CONCLUSIONS

Based on the body of evidence accumulated to date, it seems evident that phonetic symbolism effects are real and not spurious. Multiple methods have been used to show evidence of the effect: natural occurrence in language, controlled experiments using natural language, controlled experiments using artificial (nonsense) words, studies of multiple languages using those that are both historically related and historically unrelated to each other. Research has also ruled out some alternative explanations, such as the possibility that it is the shape rather than sounds of words that convey meaning (i.e., *mil* might be perceived as more angular than *mal* because of the respective shapes of the vowels), by showing that the phonetic symbolism effects are obtained for hearing participants but not for deaf participants (Johnson, Suzuki, & Olds, 1964). Although any one study often has some limiting flaws, the convergence of the findings provides impressive support for the effects of sound on meaning.

Even if the general notion of phonetic symbolism is a valid one, it is unclear how pervasive or generalizable it is. Clearly, the most evidence has emerged for the relation between front versus back vowels and perceptions of size (and to a lesser degree, brightness). However, as noted earlier, a large number of studies (including two of our own) have shown that the front–back distinction can be extended to perceptions along a number of dimensions. In addition, consonant sounds have also been shown to impart meaning, although the evidence seems to be weaker than for vowels. The relative lack of evidence for consonants may simply be that because they are more numerous than vowel sounds, they are difficult to study systematically. Moreover, one aspect missing from previous research is how the vowel and consonant sounds either offset or interact with each other. For example, English speakers tend to classify the sounds associated with the consonants *g* and *k* as "big" sounds and the sounds associated with the *t* and *n* as small sounds (Taylor, 1963; Taylor & Taylor, 1962). Couple this finding with the frequently documented association between front vowels and smallness, and between back vowels and largeness, and the ambiguity quickly becomes evident. In fact, this "confound" was pointed out by Taylor (1963) in her comments on Newman (1933). As noted earlier, Newman's list of natural words showed little evidence of phonetic symbolism: There appeared to be little relation between the meaning of the words and their front–back distinction (but as noted earlier, see Johnson's, 1967, reanalysis). However, Taylor (1963) points out that there is actually a significant tendency for Newman's words beginning with *t* and *n* to be related to smallness and *g* and *k* to be related to largeness. Thus, it is unclear in situations that mix the vowel and consonant effects which has the bigger effect, which effects get cancelled, and so forth.

The "almost universal" classification of phonetic symbolism effects also receives some support. Again, the size dimension and its relation to front versus back vowels has received the most study, but the effects have also been shown to hold for a number of dimension perceptions. An abundance of evidence shows consistent findings across languages, regardless of whether the languages are historically related or unrelated. This evidence has been shown both experimentally and in studies of naturally occurring language. The seminal work of Fitch (1994), which linked the perceptions of sounds to survival and evolutionary mechanisms (see also, Morton, 1977), provides further support for the universality hypothesis.

However, notwithstanding Fitch's (1994) research on size and its relation to sound, little work has been able to satisfactorily address the underlying mechanisms. What makes research in this area so difficult is that the origins and underlying mechanisms of sound–meaning relationships may differ across different sounds. For example, simply because the front–back distinction has been linked with evolutionary concepts of survival and defense mechanisms is not sufficient reason to conclude that the possible associations between words beginning with *fl* and movement have similar explanations.

A major impediment to believing in the existence of sound symbolism is that clearly not all words possess it. Of course, that is to be expected, given the relatively small number of sounds compared to the size of the lexicon. However, as others have noted, it is not that all words possess sound symbolism, but as Socrates suggests, it is a hallmark of *good* words. Perhaps Jespersen (1922, p. 398) said it best:

> There is no denying, however, that there are words we feel instinctively to be adequate to express the ideas they stand for, and others the sounds of which are felt to be more or less incongruous with their signification.

This notion of *good* words and *bad* words being rooted in part in sound symbolism provides a useful segué into the sound symbolism and naming of brands. In the general use of language, it may make little difference whether a word's sound fits its meaning as long as the communicators agree on its meaning. An exception would be for literary endeavors (e.g., poems) that rely on sense elements to create mood or meaning. However, for naming brands, the fit may be crucial. There is a rapidly accumulating body of research attesting to the fact that people often make quick, if not unconscious, judgments and decisions on a regular basis, and also often have little understanding of why they make them (Hassin, Uleman, & Bargh, 2004; Kahneman, Slovic, & Tversky, 1982). Thus, a simple incongruence between sound-based perceptions and the brand's positive attributes may be enough for consumers to pass on a potential purchase.

The newly emerging research on the relation between sound symbolism and brand name preference suggests that attention to the sound–meaning relation may be useful for marketers. Certainly, no one would suggest that it is the only, or even the main, determinant in forming impressions of a brand, nor would anyone suggest that a brand be renamed simply because its sound symbolism is incongruent with its attributes, or even negative in general. However, if a new brand name is being developed, attending to sound symbolism features would likely be useful. In addition, in the event that a particularly negative name cannot be changed, the perceptions might be addressed through advertising. This was certainly the strategy for Smucker's® jelly and their slogan "With a name like Smucker's, it has to be good."

In conclusion, the research linking sound symbolism and brand name preference has done two things. First, it has given marketers something relatively simple to consider in developing brand names. Companies clearly test a lot during this process, with a focus on some obvious associations (rhymes, close spellings, etc.). However, some less obvious associations may also come to mind, for reasons that are generally not clear to either the marketer or the consumer. Second, the research that links phonetic symbolism to brand name perceptions and preference also adds importantly to the basic body of work in the field. In fact, these studies take phonetic symbolism a clear step further than any research on phonetic symbolism to date. They show that not only does the sound of words convey meaning, but people use this information in forming judgments. Thus, this work not only extends theory and research in phonetic symbolism, it also bolsters the previous research. That is, the brand name research makes it increasingly difficult to argue against the notion that at least some aspects of the sounds of words convey meaning.

REFERENCES

Atzet, J., & Gerard, H. E. (1965). A study of phonetic symbolism among native Navajo speakers. *Journal of Personal and Social Psychology, 1*, 524–527.

Becker, J. A., & Fisher, S. K. (1988). Comparison of associations to vowel speech sounds by English and Spanish speakers. *American Journal of Psychology, 101*, 51–57.

Bentley, M., & Varon, E. J. (1933). An accessory study of "phonetic symbolism." *American Journal of Psychology, 45*, 76–86.

Berlin, B. (1994). Evidence for pervasive synesthetic sound symbolism in ethnozoological nomenclature. In L. Hinton, J. Nichols, & J. J. Ohala (Eds.), *Sound symbolism* (pp. 76–103). Cambridge, England: Cambridge University Press.

Birch, D., & Erickson, M. (1958). Phonetic symbolism with respect to three dimensions from the semantic differential. *Journal of General Psychology, 58*, 291–297.

Bolinger, D. (1950). Rime, assonance, and morpheme analysis. *Word, 6*, 117–136.

Brown, R. (1958). *Words and things.* New York: The Free Press.

Brown, R., Black, A. H., & Horowitz, A. E. (1955). Phonetic symbolism in natural languages. *Journal of Abnormal and Social Psychology, 50*, 388–393.

Childers, T. L., & Houston, M. J. (1984). Conditions for a picture superiority effect on consumer memory. *Journal of Consumer Research, 11*, 551–563.

Chisnall, P. M. (1974). Aluminum household foil in the common market: Research for an effective brand name. *Journal of Management Studies, 11*, 246–255.

Collins, L. (1977). A name to conjure with. *European Journal of Marketing, 11*, 340–363.

Eysenck, M. W. (1979). Depth, evaluation, and distinctiveness. In L. S. Cermak & F. I. M. Craik (Eds.), *Levels of processing in human memory* (pp. 89–123). Hillsdale, NJ: Lawrence Erlbaum Associates.

Fitch, W. T. (1994). *Vocal tract length perception and the evolution of language.* Unpublished doctoral dissertation, Brown University.

Fitch, W. T. (1997). Vocal tract length and formant frequency dispersion correlate with body size in rhesus macaques. *Journal of the Acoustical Society of America, 102*, 1213–1222.

Fitch, W. T., & Hauser, M. D. (2002). Unpacking "honesty": Vertebrate vocal production and the evolution of acoustic signals. In A. Simmons, R. R. Fay, & A. N. Popper (Eds.), *Springer handbook of auditory research* (pp. 65–137). New York: Springer.

Folkins, C., & Lenrow, P. B. (1966). An investigation of the expressive values of graphemes. *The Psychological Record, 16*, 193–200.

French, P. L. (1977). Toward an explanation of phonetic symbolism. *Word, 28*, 305–322.

Greenberg, J. H., & Jenkins, J. J. (1966). Studies in the psychological correlates of the sound system of American English. *Word, 22*, 207–242.

Hartley, R. F. (1992). *Marketing mistakes* (5th ed.). New York: Wiley.

Hassin, R. R., Uleman, J. S., & Bargh, J. A. (Eds.). (2004). *The new unconscious.* New York: Oxford University Press.

Heath, T. B., Chatterjee, S., & France, K. R. (1990). Using the phonemes of brand names to symbolize brand attributes. In W. Bearden & A. Parasuraman (Eds.), *The AMA educator's proceedings: Enhancing knowledge development in marketing* (pp. 38–42). Chicago: American Marketing Association.

Huang, Y. H., Pratoomraj, S., & Johnson, R. C. (1969). Universal magnitude symbolism. *Journal of Verbal Learning and Verbal Behavior, 8*, 155–156.

Jakobson, R., & Waugh, L. (1979). *The sound shape of language.* Bloomington, IN: Indiana University Press.

Jespersen, O. (1922). *Language: Its nature, development and origin.* London: Allen & Unwin.

Jespersen, O. (1933). Symbolic value of the vowel i. In O. Jespersen (Ed.), *Linguistica* (pp. 283–303). Copenhagen: Levin & Munksgaard.

Johnson, R. C. (1967). Magnitude symbolism of English words. *Journal of Verbal Learning and Verbal Behavior, 6*, 508–511.

Johnson, R. C., Suzuki, N. S., & Olds, W. K. (1964). Phonetic symbolism in an artificial language. *Journal of Abnormal and Social Psychology, 69*, 233–236.

Kahneman, D., Slovic, P., & Tversky, A. (Eds.). (1982). *Judgment under uncertainty: Heuristics and biases.* New York: Cambridge University Press.

Keller, K. L., Heckler, S. E., & Houston, M. J. (1998). The effects of brand name suggestiveness on advertising recall. *Journal of Marketing, 62,* 48–57.

Klink, R. R. (2000). Creating brand names with meaning: The use of sound symbolism. *Marketing Letters, 11,* 5–20.

Klink, R. R. (2003). Creating meaningful brands: The relationship between brand name and brand mark. *Marketing Letters, 14,* 143–157.

Kohli, C., & LaBahn, D. W. (1997). Creating effective brand names: A study of the brand naming process. *Journal of Advertising Research, 37,* 67–75.

Lockhart, R. S., Craik, F. I. M., & Jacoby, L. L. (1976). Depth of processing, recognition, and recall: Some aspects of a general memory system. In J. Brown (Ed.), *Recall and recognition* (pp. 107–123). London: Wiley.

Lowrey, T. M., & Shrum, L. J. (2005). *Effects of phonetic symbolism on brand name preference.* Unpublished manuscript, University of Texas at San Antonio.

Lowrey, T. M., Shrum, L. J., & Dubitsky, T. M. (2003). The relation between brand-name linguistic characteristics and brand-name memory. *Journal of Advertising, 32*(3), 7–17.

Lutz, K. A., & Lutz, R. J. (1977). Effects of interactive imagery on learning: Application to advertising. *Journal of Applied Psychology, 62,* 493–498.

Maltzman, I., Morrisett, L., & Brooks, L. O. (1956). An investigation of phonetic symbolism. *Journal of Abnormal and Social Psychology, 53,* 249–251.

Meyers-Levy, J. (1989). The influence of a brand name's association set size and word frequency on brand memory. *Journal of Consumer Research, 16,* 197–207.

Meyers-Levy, J., Louie, T. A., & Curren, M. T. (1994). How does the congruity of brand names affect evaluations of brand name extensions? *Journal of Applied Psychology, 79,* 46–53.

Miron, M. S. (1961). A cross-linguistic investigation of phonetic symbolism. *Journal of Abnormal and Social Psychology, 62,* 623–630.

Morton, E. W. (1977). On the occurrence and significance of motivation-structural rules in some bird and mammal sounds. *American Naturalist, 111,* 855–869.

Newman, S. S. (1933). Further experiments in phonetic symbolism. *American Journal of Psychology, 45,* 53–75.

Nichols, J. (1971). Diminutive consonant symbolism in western North America. *Language, 47,* 826–848.

O'Boyle, M. W., Miller, D. A., & Rahmani, F. (1987). Sound–meaning relationships in speakers of Urdu and English: Evidence for a cross-cultural phonetic symbolism. *Journal of Psycholinguistic Research, 16,* 273–288.

O'Boyle, M. W., & Tarte, R. D. (1980). Implications for phonetic symbolism: The relationship between pure tones and geometric figures. *Journal of Psycholinguistic Research, 9,* 535–544.

Peterson, R. A., & Ross, I. (1972). How to name new brands. *Journal of Advertising Research, 12,* 29–34.

Pinker, S. (1994). *The language instinct.* New York: William Morrow.

Plato (1892). Cratylus. In B. Jowett (Ed.), *The dialogues of Plato* (Vol. 1, pp. 253–289). Oxford, England: Clarendon.

Roper, C. W., Dixon, P. W., Ahern, E. H., & Gibson, V. L. (1976). The effect of language and sex on universal phonetic symbolism. *Language and Speech, 19,* 388–396.

Saegert, J., & Young, R. K. (1983). Levels of processing and memory for advertisements. In L. Percy & A. G. Woodside (Eds.), *Advertising and consumer psychology* (pp. 117–131). Lexington, MA: Lexington Books.

Sapir, E. (1929). A study in phonetic symbolism. *Journal of Experimental Psychology, 12,* 225–239.

Saussure, F. D. (1916). *Course in general linguistics* (W. Baskin, Trans.). New York: McGraw-Hill.

Schloss, I. (1981). Chickens and pickles: Choosing a brand name. *Journal of Advertising Research, 21,* 47–49.

Smith, G. W. (1998). The political impact of name sounds. *Communication Monographs, 65*(2), 154–172.

Tarte, R. D. (1982). The relationship between monosyllables and pure tones: An investigation of phonetic symbolism. *Journal of Verbal Learning and Verbal Behavior, 21,* 352–360.

Taylor, I. K. (1963). Phonetic symbolism re-examined. *Psychological Bulletin, 60,* 200–209.

Taylor, I. K., & Taylor, M. M. (1962). Phonetic symbolism in four unrelated languages. *Canadian Journal of Psychology, 16,* 344–356.

Tsuru, S. (1934). *Sound and meaning.* Unpublished manuscript.

Tsuru, S., & Fries, H. (1933). A problem in meaning. *Journal of General Psychology, 8,* 281–284.

Ullmann, S. (1966). Semantic universals. In J. H. Greenberg (Ed.), *Universals of language* (pp. 217–262). Cambridge, MA: MIT Press.

Ultan, R. (1978). Size–sound symbolism. In J. H. Greenberg, C. A. Ferguson, & E. A. Moravcsik (Eds.), *Universals of human language: Vol. 2. Phonology* (pp. 525–568). Stanford, CA: Stanford University Press.

Vanden Bergh, B. (1990). The rekurring kase of the special k. *Brand Names,* RC9–12.

Vanden Bergh, B., Adler, K., & Oliver, L. (1987). Linguistic distinction among top brand names. *Journal of Advertising Research, 27,* 39–44.

Vanden Bergh, B., Collins, J., Schultz, M., & Adler, K. (1984). Sound advice on brand names. *Journalism Quarterly, 61,* 835–840.

Weiss, J. H. (1963). "Meaningfulness" versus meaning dimension in guessing the meanings of foreign words. *Journal of Abnormal and Social Psychology, 66,* 541–546.

Weiss, J. H. (1966). A study of the ability of English speakers to guess the meanings of nonantonym foreign words. *Journal of General Psychology, 74,* 97–106.

Yorkston, E. A., & Menon, G. (2004). A sound idea: Phonetic effects of brand names on consumer judgments. *Journal of Consumer Research, 31,* 43–51.

Zinkhan, G. M., & Martin, C. R., Jr. (1987). New brand names and inferential beliefs: Some insights on naming new products. *Journal of Business Research, 15,* 157–172.

CHAPTER 4

Phonology and Semantics in International Marketing: What Brand Name Translations Tell Us About Consumer Cognition

Shi Zhang
UCLA Anderson Graduate School of Management

Bernd H. Schmitt
Columbia Business School

Phonology and semantics are fundamental building blocks of a linguistic system. To speak and understand a language means to be familiar with and be able to use its phonology and semantics. In the research reviewed in this chapter, we have explored phonological and semantic properties of different languages by investigating how consumers respond to brand names in an international marketing context. We believe that consumer responses to phonological and semantic properties of a language can tell us a lot about language-related consumer cognition.

As we will show, how consumers respond to a brand name, and particularly a name translation, depends on how the name is presented to them in terms of its phonological and semantic features. Consumer responses are also very sensitive to contextual factors as well as long-term memory effects. Finally, consumers' language proficiency plays a key role: How well consumers speak a language (particularly a foreign one) determines how they process the phonological and semantic features of the name.

Our findings support the well-known Whorfian hypothesis (Whorf, 1956). Whorf proposed that language affects thought, a proposition that has been difficult to prove. In Hunt and Agnoli's (1991) reformulation, the Whorfian hypothesis has been related to the mainstream information-processing paradigm by stating that syntactic and semantic language components affect consumer information processing. In our studies, structural aspects of name translations affect the processing of these names and how consumers judge and evaluate them.

Our research also has important practical implications for marketers and brand managers operating in a global environment. As marketers become more globally oriented, the question of how to best translate a brand name from one language into another has become a key communication decision task (Aaker, 1991; Aaker & Joachimsthaler, 2000; Javed, 1993; Schmitt & Simonson, 1997).

HOW TO TRANSLATE A NAME FROM ENGLISH TO CHINESE

Translations of brand names is one of the key marketing activities in international business. Although name translation often appears to be a straightforward process, in many cases it is not. In fact, rather than speaking of "translation," which often connotes a one-to-one correspondence of a linguistic item in two different languages, it may be more appropriate to use the term "name adaptation." The translation—or adaptation—process is particularly complex when a name or phrase needs to be adapted from one type of linguistic system into another. In our research, we have focused on such complex situations by studying how to adapt a brand name from one writing system to another.

Linguists have distinguished two major types of writing systems: phonographic systems (e.g., English), where written words represent the sound components of the spoken language; and logographic systems (e.g., Chinese), where written "sign" symbols represent both words and concepts (Akmajian, Demers, Farmer, & Harnish, 1992). In short, in phonographic systems like English, it is possible to "sound out" an unknown written word but not possible to guess its meaning, whereas in logographic systems such as Chinese, the reverse is often true. These linguistic differences result in different processing: Phonetic languages are more likely to be processed by sound and represented in a "phonological loop," whereas logographic languages are processed in a visual-semantic way—a difference that we will refer to as the language differential processing hypothesis (Zhang & Schmitt, 2004).

What challenges does this situation present to marketers who wish to translate a brand name from a phonological system into a logographic system? The major challenge is the choice of the "right" translation method (Nida & Tabert, 1969). Consider, for example, possible translation methods from English into Chinese. In the first method, the phonetic method, the Chinese name is created simply on the basis of the sound of the original English name. The Chinese name for Nabisco, for example, sounds similar to its English counterpart. In the second method, the semantic method, the Chinese name is created on the basis of the *meaning* of the English name. The Chinese name for Microsoft®, "wei-ruan," meaning "micro/tiny–soft," was translated in such a way. Finally, in the phono-semantic method, names are created based on some combination of sound plus meaning. For example, the Chinese name for Colgate sounds similar to the original English name and also conveys semantic, or meaningful, information (signifying that the product is "minty" and clean). Many major multinational companies have used at least one of these translation methods; at times, the same company has used different translation methods for different brand names.

Importantly, both the original English name and the translated Chinese name (based on sound, meaning, or sound-plus-meaning) often appear on the packaging of the product, in ads, and on Web sites. That is, the actual brand name is in fact a "dual name." In these dual names, some products emphasize the English component (e.g., with a bold typeface, distinct graphic design, or by placing it above the Chinese), whereas others emphasize the Chinese component. Chinese consumers are quite familiar with this type of "bilingual" dual naming and product packaging.

WHICH TRANSLATION METHOD WORKS BEST?

At first glance, it would appear that phonetic-semantic translations would consistently be the most effective (as they would appear to combine the benefits of both "sound alone" and "meaning alone" translations). In experiments investigating English-Chinese brand name translation, however, we found a more refined pattern of perception and evaluation. Specifically, consumers seem to be quite sensitive to both external and internal contextual linguistic cues: They seem to consider, for example, not only the method of translation but also which name is emphasized and which linguistic cues they have stored in their long-term memories. Moreover, language proficiency—that is, how well they speak a particular language, especially when they are bilingual or multilingual—also affects their perceptions and evaluations. All of this tells us a lot about how consumers process phonetics and semantics in different languages. And it is very useful information for marketers as well.

Let's take a closer look at these experiments and their specific results. The first two studies were originally published in the *Journal of Marketing Research* (Zhang & Schmitt, 2001); the third study focusing on language proficiency was published in the *Journal of Consumer Research* (Zhang & Schmitt, 2004).

First, what effects did we predict? As we just described, because both phonological (English) and logographic (Chinese) representations of the brand name appear on a product sold in China—the former more tied to sound and the latter more tied to meaning—we expected that Chinese consumers would be most inclined to favor phonetic translations if the English name was emphasized but favor semantic translations if the Chinese name was emphasized. This prediction is based on conceptual frameworks that suggest that a phonological language is represented phonologically (or more precisely, in a "phonological loop") and a logographic language is represented visually and semantically (Pan & Schmitt, 1996; Schmitt, Pan, & Tavassoli, 1994). In other words, if the (logographic) Chinese name was the focus, then a consumer might be inclined to favor a Chinese name that conveyed the "meaning" of the product (best approximated by a semantic method). On the other hand, if the (phonological) English name was highlighted, then a consumer might prefer a Chinese name "sounding like," or "matching with," the English name (best approximated by a phonetic translation). In the case of phono-semantic translations, we did not expect to see any differences relating to language emphasis.

We tested these predictions with a sample of 183 native Chinese speakers in Shanghai. All respondents were familiar with the alphabetic writing system; they could read and understand basic English; and they could easily distinguish between phonetic, semantic, and phono-semantic English-Chinese translations. In the first set of studies, we did not measure their language proficiency in detail; in retrospect, we feel we should have, as we will explain later. Participants were asked to evaluate a series of six fictitious Chinese brand names (translated from original English names) that might ultimately be used for real product packaging. The stimuli included fictitious names for products such as shampoo, crackers, and contact lenses. In presenting the names to subjects, we systematically varied both the translation method used for the Chinese name (phonetic, semantic, or phono-semantic) and the language of emphasis (Chinese or English). We then collected three separate measures of name evaluation.

As expected, none of the translation methods was seen consistently as the best. Instead, evaluations of the translated names depended on whether there was an emphasis on the Chinese name or the English name (see Fig. 4.1). Our results indicated that our participants evaluated phonetic translations more favorably when the English name rather than the Chinese name was emphasized. In other words, it seems as if the English emphasis focused participants' attention on phonetic aspects, resulting in a proclivity to favor phonetically translated names. Also as ex-

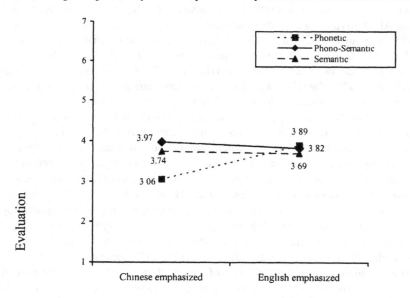

Figure 4.1.   Chinese speakers' evaluations of different types of brand names as a function of language name emphasis.

pected, our participants saw phono-semantic translations as equally good, regardless of whether a product emphasized the Chinese name or the English name. But, contrary to our predictions, we did not find that semantic translations were evaluated significantly better in the case of Chinese emphasis rather than English emphasis. Although this last finding did not confirm our specific predictions, the general pattern that emerged in this study confirmed our overall hypothesis: Chinese speakers favor one type of name translation over another depending on language-related contextual cues (e.g., name emphasis).

HOW ABOUT THE STUFF MEMORIES ARE MADE OF?

Priming effects such as those we expected in the study described have usually been shown to occur in the case of immediate contextual cues (e.g., name emphasis on product packaging). However, priming effects can also occur when long-term memory structures are cued (Bargh, 1989; Fiske & Taylor, 1991; Higgins & King, 1981; Sinclair, Mark, & Shotland, 1987). Consistent with such findings, we proposed that in addition to relatively immediate linguistic cues present in people's environments, long-term linguistic cues—"stuff that memories are made of," to paraphrase Shakespeare—can also affect preferences for different types of name translations. We thus proposed the following hypothesis: When consumers are asked to evaluate fictitious names for a new product, and they know that existing successful products in the same category were created with a given translation method, then they should show a preference for fictitious names that have been created using the same method.

To test this hypothesis, we recruited 120 Shanghai consumers. Participants were told that their opinions were needed in order to help a group of managers decide which Chinese names (presented in a "bilingual" format) to use for different products. In this experiment, we focused only on phonetic and phono-semantic name translations. We told half of our participants that prior successful products had used the phonetic method, and we told the other half that prior successful products had used the phono-semantic method. Additionally, we presented half of our participants with products emphasizing the Chinese name, and the other half with products emphasizing the English name. Participants were then asked to evaluate a series of fictitious names, some created by phonetic translation and others created by phono-semantic translation.

The results of this study strongly supported our overall predictions. As expected, when participants were informed that prior products used phonetic translations, they in turn showed a preference for new phonetic names in the English, compared to the Chinese, emphasis condition. There was no difference between emphasis conditions for phono-semantic translations (see Fig. 4.2a). However, when informed that prior products used phono-semantic translations, on the other hand, they showed a preference for the new phono-semantic names in the Chinese, compared to the English, emphasis condition. There was no difference between emphasis conditions for phonetic translations (see Fig. 4.2b). These results suggested that name translation conventions in a given product category could serve as important cues, setting up cognitive expectations and preferences vis-à-vis new brand names. Importantly, in an additional study that we will not feature here, we ruled out the alternative interpretation that these effects stemmed from foreign "image" rather than linguistic cues.

a. Prior Products Using Phonetic Translation Methods

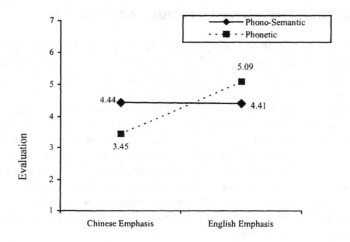

b. Prior Products Using Phono-Semantic Translation Methods

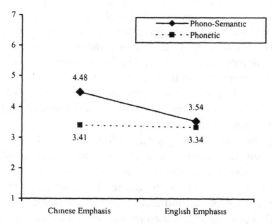

Figure 4.2.   Chinese speakers' evaluations of different types of brand names as a function of prior naming methods: (a) prior products using phonetic translation methods; (b) prior products using phono-semantic translation methods.

THE ROLE OF LANGUAGE PROFICIENCY

Although the prior studies revealed important insight into the processing of phonological and lexical-semantic properties of a language, and the importance of contextual effects, both the studies we discussed thus far excluded an important concept that is at the core of psycholinguistic processing: language proficiency. Language proficiency refers to how well individuals can process a particular language, and if individuals speak several languages, how well they can process any of these languages. Chinese consumers, especially young ones, are usually somewhat proficient in two languages—Chinese and English—as are many youths around the globe. Moreover, because many products are marketed in China using both a Chinese and an English name, the critical issue is how Chinese consumers that differ in language proficiency in English process dual names. Specifically, do consumers who are highly proficient in English respond differently than consumers who are less proficient? Does it matter, again, which language is highlighted? Most important, how can we explain emerging differences on a theoretical level?

Consumer researchers have paid surprisingly little attention to bilingual information processing and decision making in general, and brand names in particular. Instead, research, including most of our own work, has focused largely on how monolingual consumers process and respond to linguistic information (Lowrey 1998; Lowrey, Shrum, & Dubitsky, 2003; Schmitt, Pan, & Tavassoli, 1994; Schmitt & Zhang, 1998; Tavassoli, 1999, 2001; Tavassoli & Han, 2001). There are some noteworthy exceptions, especially in advertising research such as articles on English-Spanish bilinguals by Koslow, Shamdasani, and Touchstone (1994) and Luna and Peracchio (2001), as well as research on dual-language processing (detailed in chap. 12 of this book by Carroll, Luna, & Peracchio). However, there continues to be a real need for bilingual research on brands, and we addressed this need in the following experiment (Zhang & Schmitt, 2004).

A theoretical model was developed that laid out how bilingual consumers process names and other verbal stimuli that are presented in two different languages. Language proficiency was included in that model as a key theoretical construct. Although language proficiency had not been employed in consumer and marketing research, the concept had been included in psycholinguistic research on lexical-semantic access, as well as research on word processing and conceptual memory (Chen, 1990; Chen & Leung, 1989; Dufour & Kroll, 1995; Holm & Dodd, 1996).

Our model included key aspects of the bilingual interactive activation (BIA) model, which is the most prominent model for explaining lexical-semantic access in a bilingual context (Dijkstra & Van Heuven, 1998; Grainger & Dijkstra, 1992; Jared & Kroll, 2001). The model states that words are processed "bottom-up," starting with letter features (e.g., consonant or vowel), moving on to letters, and then to words. For a bilingual speaker, this bottom-up process occurs either for both languages, or for only one, depending on a top-down process that activates both languages or inhibits the nondominant language. For stimuli with words from both languages, inhibition occurs when the dominant language is used for the lexical decision task. In contrast, when the nondominant language is used, there is no inhibition; instead, both languages are activated (Beauvillain & Grainger, 1987; De Groot, Delmaar, & Lupker, 2000; Gerard & Scarborough, 1989).

However, there is one important condition when words from the nondominant language are activated even though lexical decisions are made in the dominant language. This happens when an individual is highly proficient in the nondominant language. In a study by Jared and Kroll (2001), highly and less proficient English-French bilinguals were asked to read English words that were either related to French in spelling or unrelated. Evidence of processing of the words in both languages (slowing down—i.e., interference—of the reading of English words that had related words in the French language) were observed for highly proficient but not for less proficient individuals. Similar results have been obtained for English-Spanish and English-Dutch speakers (Beauvillain & Grainger, 1987; Bijeljac-Babic, Biardeau, & Grainger, 1997; De Groot et al., 2000). Most important, studies focusing on phonological representations by highly proficient bilingual speakers have shown similar effects (Brysbaert, Van Dyck, & Van de Poel, 1999; Dijkstra, Grainger, & Van Heuven, 1999; Gollan, Forster, & Frost, 1997). Based on these findings, the BIA model specifies which language a bilingual speaker will be more likely to activate: Both the dominant and nondominant languages are activated for speakers highly proficient in the nondominant language, whereas primarily the dominant language is activated for less proficient speakers.

Despite the strong support for the model, there is one critical limitation of the BIA model: It does not address translations between two different language systems. In fact, all languages studied were of the same type (so-called "phonetic languages," such as English and French); none of the studies used "logographic languages." The model therefore does not specify whether both phonological and semantic representations of the languages are processed to an equal extent or whether one of them—phonological or semantic—receives priority. This critical issue is important, however, for bilingual environments in which one language is phonetic (e.g., English) and the other logographic (e.g., Chinese)—which is precisely the situation that Chinese consumers face.

In our research, we therefore revised and expanded the BIA model, incorporating the ideas discussed earlier in this chapter, which propose that Chinese and English result in distinct processing. As discussed earlier, the primary mental code for verbal information of phonetic languages such as English is phonological (i.e., sound based). However, the primary code for logographic languages is visual-semantic (i.e., meaning based).

Combining the two models—the bilingual interactive activation (BIA) model and the language differential processing (LDP) model—also seemed to be called for because of the unexpected and unexplained finding in one of the studies discussed earlier. As already described, the first study discussed in this chapter had provided only partial evidence for the differential processing of the names based on language emphasis: When respondents saw sound-based (i.e., phonetic) translations, they preferred the brand names when the emphasis was English rather than Chinese. Surprisingly, for product meaning-based (i.e., semantic) translations, there was no difference in attitudes toward the brand names between the two emphasis conditions.

We speculated: Could it be that we observed this pattern of results because we had not included a key construct in our prior research—namely, language proficiency? That is, perhaps we had observed no difference between the emphasis conditions for product meaning-based names because we had not fully assessed the exact level of language proficiency of our respondents. If correct, then a model focusing only on differential processing of languages, name emphasis, and memory cues alone may not fully address how bilingual consumers respond in a bilingual context. In that case, combining the BIA and the LDP model should lead to better predictions about how bilingual consumers respond in a mixed-language context.

What does a combined model predict for a dual-name situation? How is such a situation being processed by speakers of varying language proficiency? Also, how do people respond to different types of relatedness between the English and Chinese names (e.g., when the words are related by sound or by meaning)?

Consider first highly proficient Chinese-English speakers, processing the dual English-Chinese names. They should activate phonological and semantic representations of both languages and thus attend to both sound relations and meaning relations of the names. Thus, proficient speakers should rely on both sound and meaning relatedness (of the Chinese and English names) in evaluating the brand names.

How about less proficient Chinese-English speakers? Less proficient bilingual speakers should primarily activate phonological and semantic representations of the dominant Chinese language. Because Chinese is primarily visual-semantic and processing English seems to be based on Chinese semantic mediation, dual name processing and evaluations should be largely based on meaning. Consequently, less proficient speakers should rely more on meaning than sound relatedness in evaluating the brand names.

Finally, contextual cues such as language emphasis should direct respondents to place weights on sound and meaning differentially. Highly proficient speakers access both phonological and semantic representations of Chinese and English, following Zhang and Schmitt (2001), so language emphasis should cue either phonological or semantic representations, and thus "sound" or "meaning" relatedness between the English and Chinese names. This cuing effect should be much less pronounced for less proficient individuals because these speakers are more likely to access phonological and semantic representations of Chinese. In sum, high proficiency respondents should be directed to place differential weights of sound and meaning in evaluations, depending on language emphasis, whereas low proficiency respondents should primarily use a uniform meaning processing strategy regardless of language emphasis.

We tested these hypotheses in a study that presented English and Chinese brand names as one compound stimulus and emphasized either the Chinese name or the English name. To determine which type of processing occurs, we created "relations" or "no relations" between the dual names (i.e., the two languages), using methods similar to previous studies of lexical-semantic representations (Jared & Kroll, 2001). Specifically, we created the meaning relations between the Chinese and English names by having the Chinese name depict the specific meaning of brand associations contained in the English name (e.g., the unit "death" in a fictitious name "deathlon" for boxing gloves—one of four product categories besides lotion, tissue, and supermarket store).

How did we measure the key construct of language proficiency? To make sure we had an objective, reliable, and valid measure, we employed the most widely used test in China: the College English Test (CET). Those who had achieved levels 5–6 (equivalent to scoring 550 or above in TOEFL) were classified as having high English proficiency and those who had achieved levels 1–2 (equivalent to scoring 500 or below) were classified as having low English proficiency.

The linguistic details of stimulus construction were also undertaken in a rigorous fashion. To give the reader a sense of the necessity and extent of linguistic examination and pretesting, we will describe our procedures in some detail. The final stimuli and results of the key tests are shown in Table 4.1.

The sound and meaning manipulations were accomplished through stimulus design. A number of fictitious English brand names were created and selected through pretests with native speakers in such a way that these names satisfied linguistic lexical criteria of word formation (e.g., syllabic structure, vowel, and consonant combinations). All selected names fulfilled certain criteria: They were bisyllabic, used a variety of vowels, and different initial consonants across the names contained a specific meaningful unit—a part that can be easily identified with a word. Those that had similar perceived familiarity, similar high likelihood brand name ratings, and similar ease of meaning identification were then used as original English names for Chinese name creations, as shown in column 2 of Table 4.1. In column 2, hyphenation was used in the English name to separate the special meaningful unit from the rest of the name.

More pretests were conducted based on the selected English names. Four types of Chinese names were constructed by a group of language study experts according to a 2 × 2 scheme of sound (related/similar vs. unrelated/dissimilar) and meaning (related/similar vs. unrelated/dissimilar). We defined a mock-up Chinese name as similar in sound if the individual characters making up the Chinese name sounded like the original English name, syllable by syllable, especially in reference to the meaningful unit. A mock-up Chinese name was defined as related in meaning if the individual characters making up the Chinese name suggested brand associations indicated by the meaningful unit of the original English name. For example, in columns 3 and 4 of Table 4.1, the Chinese names were created to sound similar to the English name, the overall name as well as the particular meaningful part; in columns 3 and 5 of Table 4.1, the Chinese names were created to be related in possessing specific meanings suggested by the hyphenated units: "death-," "-rub," "-tons," (for "lots of") and "sof-" (for "soft").

Next, to validate the stimulus construction, bilingual English-Chinese students judged the created names in terms of how similar in sound the Chinese name, character by character, was to the original English name, syllable by syllable, and how related in meaning the Chinese name was to the original name, particularly in reference to the meaningful unit of the original English name. As shown in Table 4.1, names that received a mean 6 or above on a 7-point scale in sound and in meaning scales were kept for the sound-plus-meaning type of names; names that received a mean 6 or above in sound and 2 or below in meaning were kept for the sound-related type of names; names that received a mean 2 or below in sound and 6 or above in meaning were kept for the brand name meaning-related type of names; and, finally, names that received a mean 2 or below for both were kept for the type of names that had no sound or brand name meaning relatedness.

The four types of Chinese names were then tested with Chinese native speakers on familiarity and brand name likelihood. These subjects were randomly assigned to the four types of names. They were asked to rate their familiarity with each Chinese translation and the extent to which they thought the translation was a likely brand name. Based on the test results, four names for each type were selected for the main study, as shown in Table 4.1. There were no significant differences between these selected names regarding familiarity or brand name likelihood in each condition or between conditions.

In the actual experiment, 368 Chinese respondents in Tianjin were shown the "brand names" in a booklet format. At the bottom of each page were three evaluation scales (good–bad, unsatisfactory–satisfactory, dislike–like). All instructions and scales were given in Chinese.

There were various main and interaction effects in the analysis. The key effects were two three-way interactions that we will examine in more detail: a significant three-way interaction of language proficiency by emphasis and by meaning and a three-way interaction of language proficiency by emphasis and by sound. We expected that high language proficiency subjects would focus more on the processing of meaning of the names when Chinese language was emphasized, but more on the processing of sound of the names when English language was emphasized. As shown in Figure 4.3a, when Chinese was emphasized, names related to brand meaning were evaluated more favorably than names unrelated to brand meaning, regardless of whether the sound of the name was similar or dissimilar to the original name. In contrast, when English was emphasized, as shown in Figure 4.3b, names

TABLE 4.1

Stimulus Brand Names and Pretest Means

Products and Measures[a]	English names	Chinese names:[b] Sound: similar Meaning: related	Chinese names:[c] Sound: similar Meaning: not related	Chinese names:[d] Sound: not similar Meaning: related	Chinese names:[e] Sound: not similar Meaning: not related
1. Boxing gloves	Death-lon	De(2)shi(4)yong(3) 得逝勇	De(2)shi(4)long(2) 得师隆	Wei(1)shi(4) 威逝	Dan(1)hui(4) 丹汇
Meaningful unit	6.78	–	–	–	–
Familiarity	2.81	1.93	1.78	1.97	1.68
Likelihood	2.65	2.94	2.66	2.97	2.45
Sound	–	6.42	6.01	1.41	1.57
Meaning	–	6.56	1.54	6.42	1.32
2. Lotion	With-rub	Wei(2)run(4)rou(2) 维润揉	Wei(3)ruo(4)pu(3) 韦若普	Rou(2)shu(1) 揉舒	Hong(2)lang(3) 宏朗
Meaningful unit	6.67	–	–	–	–
Familiarity	2.69	2.06	2.01	1.94	1.89
Likelihood	2.71	3.23	3.41	3.02	2.87
Sound	–	6.14	6.37	1.76	1.49
Meaning	–	6.47	1.36	6.54	1.25

3. Superstore	Pe-tons	Bei(4)duo(1) 贝多	Pai(4)teng(2) 派腾	Duo(1)man(3)le(4) 多满乐	Hao(3)tai(4) 好泰
Meaningful unit	6.12	-	-	-	-
Familiarity	2.78	2.86	2.64	2.88	2.47
Likelihood	2.56	3.34	3.27	3.76	3.04
Sound	-	6.47	6.52	1.65	1.43
Meaning	-	6.58	1.58	6.71	1.61

4. Facial Tissue	Sof-ra	Si(1)ruan(3) 丝软	Si(1)jia(1)ruo(4) 斯佳若	Rou(2)ruan(3) 柔软	Di(2)ya(3) 涤雅
Meaningful unit	6.54	-	-	-	-
Familiarity	2.83	1.97	1.78	2.15	1.72
Likelihood	2.79	3.64	3.44	3.02	3.56
Sound	-	6.36	6.28	1.92	1.48
Meaning	-	6.45	1.29	6.44	1.36

[a] The measures "meaningful unit" (the unit is easily seen as meaningful) are for the created fictitious English brand names only. The measures "sound (sound similarity to the original name) and meaning (meaning similarity to the original name)" are for the created Chinese brand names only. See discussions in the method section. Other measures "familiarity (familiarity with the linguistic name), and likelihood (brand name likelihood)" are for both the English and Chinese names; the measures, however, are used on different samples of subjects. See discussions on all measures in the method section.

[b] For the Chinese brand names, the Pinyin may appear to be the same (e.g., 'shi[4]' in different columns); however, the represented characters are not the same. The literal meanings of the characters are: De(2)shi(4)yong(3) meaning "the knocking-out courage," wei(2)run(4)rou(2) meaning "rubbing on to keep moist," bei(4)duo(1) meaning "tons of good stuff," si(1)run(3) meaning "fine and soft."

[c] De(2)shi(4)long(2) meaning "acquiring, teaching, and thriving," wei(3)ruo(4)pu(3) meaning "the surname of Wei, similar and general," pai(4)teng(2) meaning "dispatch and jump," si(1)jia(1)rou(4) meaning "this, good and similar."

[d] Wei(1)shi(4) meaning "having the power to knock out," rou(2)shu(1) meaning "rub to make comfortable," duo(1)man(3)le(4) meaning "tons and full to make you happy," rou(2)ran(3) "flexible and soft."

[e] Dan(1)hui(4) meaning "redness comes together," hong(2)lang(3) meaning "grand and bright," hao(3)tai(4) meaning "grand and peaceful," di(2)ya(3) meaning "wash to be elegant."

a. Chinese Emphasis

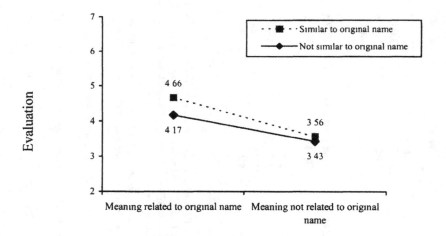

b. English Emphasis

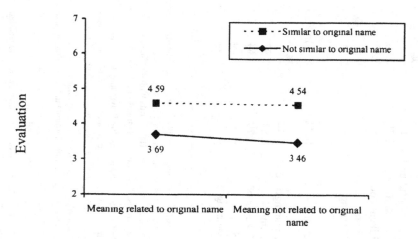

Figure 4.3.   High English proficiency subjects' brand name evaluations as a function of proficiency, name emphasis, sound, and meaning: (a) Chinese emphasis; (b) English emphasis.

similar to the original English were evaluated more favorably than names that were dissimilar, regardless of whether the meaning of the name was related or unrelated to the brand meaning suggested by the original English name.

As for the low language proficiency subjects, as expected, they focused more on the processing of meaning in the Chinese emphasis condition as well as in the English emphasis condition. When Chinese was emphasized, names related to the brand meaning were evaluated more favorably than names unrelated to the brand meaning, regardless of whether the sound of the name was similar or dissimilar to the original name (see Fig. 4.4a). Similar patterns of name evaluations were observed when English was emphasized (see Fig. 4.4b).

The results of the experiment thus indicated that highly proficient Chinese-English speakers activated both lexical-semantic and phonological representations of the dominant (i.e., Chinese) and nondominant (i.e., English) language. Less proficient speakers, in contrast, activated primarily the representations of Chinese. These results provided evidence for our new bilingual access model that incorporated aspects of the BIA model and the LDP model. The BIA part of the model explains how bilingual speakers respond differently in terms of language proficiency, whereas the LDP part of the model addresses processing differences based on type of language. Combining the models, we can explain how bilingual consumers evaluate dual brand names that include a phonetic and logographic language.

The differential pattern of results obtained in the experiment suggests that the lack of distinguishing levels of proficiency may have been a possible confounding source in prior research—namely, the lack of support for predictions that the semantic name should be evaluated better when Chinese was emphasized, and the phono-semantic name should be evaluated equally well for either language emphasis.

SUMMARY

To summarize, our stream of research showed that of the three methods available for translating English names into Chinese names, no one method is always preferable to Chinese speakers. Instead, preferences are apparently contingent on immediate, environment-based linguistic cues, long-term, memory-based linguistic cues, and person-specific characteristics such as language proficiency. Therefore, when marketers make naming decisions—decisions that often entail significant amounts of time and resources—they must pay close attention to the name, the naming context, and the consumer's linguistic abilities.

FROM NAMES TO PHRASES TO NUMBERS

Where do we go from here? One key question is: Does the proposed bilingual access model apply to linguistic units larger than words? Research on phrases and sentences will be discussed in the next section of this book. We invite the reader to read that sec-

a. Chinese Emphasis

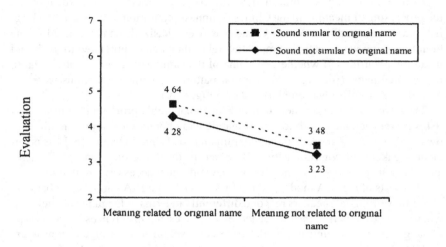

b. English Emphasis

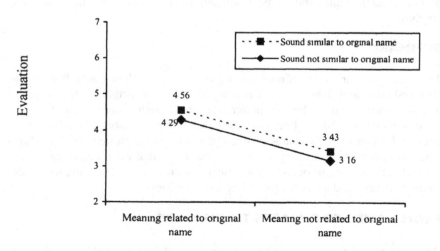

Figure 4.4.   Low English proficiency subjects' brand name evaluations as a function of proficiency, name emphasis, sound, and meaning: (a) Chinese emphasis; (b) English emphasis.

tion, in particular chapter 12 by Carroll, Luna, and Peracchio on dual language advertising, with the following ideas regarding bilingualism in mind. We believe that theories on bilingual phrases and sentence processing require that we supplement our access model with theories that have been designed for phrasal and sentential processing such as script and frame-based models (Kintsch, 1998; Schank & Abelson, 1977). Such models often include, besides linguistic bottom-up and top-down processes of lexical-semantic and phonological information, broader based pragmatic and contextual information. This will be a major theoretical undertaking, especially when we strive to expand such models into bilingual processing of different language systems. We believe researchers should face the challenge and investigate what kind of cross-cultural differences exist in pragmatics and in the processing of sequential (i.e., temporally expanded) action chains. Because it has been shown that phonological encoding results in better encoding of temporal information (Tavassoli, 1999), it is likely that broader linguistic and cognitive factors will interact with phonological and visual-semantic processing.

Another intriguing future research stream that we are currently engaged in concerns how a nonlinguistic system such as numbers is represented linguistically and, in turn, how different linguistic representations in different languages may impact the mental representations and processing of such nonlinguistic systems. For example, some numbers and number concepts are represented differently in one language than another. For example, some languages have different "focal numbers" than others. In English, "100" is a focal number, used to form compounds such as "two hundred," "three hundred," or "hundred thousand." Also, "1,000" and "1,000,000" are other examples. Furthermore, "20" is a focal number in French (but not in English); it is used, for example, as part of a compound that represents "80" (as *quatre-vingt*, i.e., "four [times] twenty"). And, "10,000" is a focal number in Japanese and Chinese, used to represent 100,000. Some numbers are uniquely lexicalized in some languages, not others (e.g., the number "11" in English; in Chinese or Japanese, it is "ten [plus] one"). Finally, the order of representation of individual units in a number compound may differ from one language to another. For example, "51" is *einundfünfzig* (one-plus-fifty) in German but, of course, fifty-one in English.

We are currently conducting experimental studies in three continents to examine these issues. Participants in our research are asked to evaluate various pricing strategies to test hypotheses related to the three key concepts outlined here. For example, to test the number order hypothesis, English and German speakers will be compared in how they evaluate price increases from 51 to 59 (in a hypothetical currency) versus 21 to 91. Whereas both German and English speakers should find the price increase from 21 to 91 more aversive, the key prediction will be that—if language matters and affects mental processes—the price increase from 51 to 59 will be judged as having relatively more disutility for German speakers than English speakers, whereas a price increase from 21 to 91 will have more disutility for English than German speakers. Other experiments will use similar designs and predictions.

Such research will expand the work presented in this chapter by including an examination of consumer cognition of linguistic representations of a tight and precise nonlinguistic system such as numbers. This research is important both from a theoretical and an applied point of view. Theoretically, it provides a test of the classic Whorfian hypothesis ("language influences thought") in its contemporary reformulation—that is, how syntactic and semantic aspects of a language affect consumer information processing as well as choice and evaluations (Hunt & Agnoli, 1991; Lucy, 1992; Whorf, 1956). Practically, this research provides specific guidance on how to consider language as part of pricing decisions in international markets.

REFERENCES

Aaker, D. A. (1991). *Managing brand equity*. New York: The Free Press.

Aaker, D. A., & Joachimsthaler, E. (2000). *Brand leadership*. New York: The Free Press.

Akmajian, A., Demers, R. A., Farmer, A. K., & Harnish, R. M. (1992). *Linguistics: An introduction to language and communication*. Boston: MIT Press.

Bargh, J. A. (1989). Conditional automaticity: Varieties of automatic influence in social perception and cognition. In J. S. Uleman & J. A. Bargh (Eds.), *Unintended thought* (pp. 3–51). New York: Guilford.

Beauvillain, C., & Grainger, J. (1987). Accessing interlexical homographs: Some limitations of a language-selective access. *Journal of Memory and Language, 26*, 658–672.

Bijeljac-Babic, R., Biardeau, A., & Grainger, J. (1997). Masked orthographic priming in bilingual word recognition. *Memory and Cognition, 25*, 447–457.

Brysbaert, M., Van Dyck, G., & Van de Poel, M. (1999). Visual word recognition in bilinguals: Evidence from masked phonological priming. *Journal of Experimental Psychology: Learning, Memory and Cognition, 25*, 137–148.

Chen, H.-C. (1990). Lexical processing in a non-native language: Effects of language proficiency and learning strategy. *Memory and Cognition, 18*, 279–288.

Chen, H.-C., & Leung, Y.-S. (1989). Patterns of lexical processing in a nonnative language. *Journal of Experimental Psychology: Learning, Memory and Cognition, 15*, 316–325.

De Groot, A. M. B., Delmaar, P., & Lupker, S. J. (2000). The processing of interlexical homographs in translation recognition and lexical decisions: Support for non-selective access to bilingual memory. *Quarterly Journal of Experimental Psychology, 53*, 397–428.

Dijkstra, T., Grainger, J., & Van Heuven, W. J. B. (1999). Recognition of cognates and interlingual homographs: The neglected role of phonology. *Journal of Memory and Language, 41*, 496–518.

Dijkstra, T., & Van Heuven, W. J. B. (1998). *The BIA model and bilingual word recognition*. Mahwah, NJ: Lawrence Erlbaum Associates.

Dufour, R., & Kroll, J. F. (1995). Matching words to concepts in two languages: A test of the concept mediation model of bilingual representation. *Memory and Cognition, 23*, 166–180.

Fiske, S., & Taylor, S. (1991). *Social cognition*. New York: McGraw-Hill.

Gerard, L., & Scarborough, D. (1989). Language-specific lexical access of homographs by bilinguals. *Journal of Experimental Psychology: Language, Memory, and Cognition, 15*(2), 305–315.

Gollan, T. H., Forster, K. I., & Frost, R. (1997). Translation priming with different scripts: Masked priming with cognates and noncognates in Hebrew-English bilinguals. *Journal of Experimental Psychology: Learning, Memory, and Cognition, 23,* 1122–1139.

Grainger, J., & Dijkstra, T. (1992). On the representation and use of language information in bilinguals. In R. J. Harris (Ed.), *Advances in psychology: Cognitive processing in bilinguals* (pp. 207–220). Amsterdam: Elsevier.

Higgins, E. T., & King, G. A. (1981). Accessibility and social constructs: Information processing consequences of individual and contextual variability. In N. Cantor & J. F. Kilstrom (Eds.), *Personality, cognition and social interaction* (pp. 75–115). Hillsdale, NJ: Lawrence Erlbaum Associates.

Holm, A., & Dodd, B. (1996). The effect of first written language on the acquisition of English literacy. *Cognition, 59,* 119–147.

Hunt, E., & Agnoli, F. (1991). The Whorfian hypothesis: A cognitive psychology perspective. *Psychological Review, 98,* 377–389.

Jared, D., & Kroll, J. F. (2001). Do bilinguals activate phonological representations in one or both of their languages when naming words? *Journal of Memory and Language, 44,* 2–31.

Javed, N. (1993). *Naming for power.* Ontario: Linkbridge Publishing.

Kintsch, W. (1998). *Comprehension: A program for cognition.* New York: Cambridge University Press.

Koslow, S., Shamdasani, P. N., & Touchstone, E. E. (1994). Exploring language effects in ethnic advertising: A sociolinguistic perspective. *Journal of Consumer Research, 20,* 575–585.

Lowrey, T. M. (1998). The effects of syntactic complexity on advertising persuasiveness. *Journal of Consumer Psychology, 7, 187–206.*

Lowrey, T. M., Shrum, L. J., & Dubitsky, T. M. (2003). The relation between brand-name linguistic characteristics and brand-name memory. *Journal of Advertising, 32*(3), 7–17.

Lucy, J. A. (1992). *Language diversity and thought: A reformulation of the Whorfian hypothesis.* Cambridge, England: Cambridge University Press.

Luna, D., & Peracchio, L. A. (2001). Moderators of language effects in advertising to bilinguals: A psycholinguistic approach. *Journal of Consumer Research, 28,* 284–295.

Nida, E. A., & Tabert, C. R. (1969). *The theory and practice of translation* (E. J. Brill, Ed.). Leiden, Netherlands: United Bible Societies.

Pan, Y., & Schmitt, B. H. (1996). Language and brand attitudes: The impact of script and sound matching in Chinese and English. *Journal of Consumer Psychology, 5,* 263–277.

Schank, R. C., & Abelson, R. P. (1977). *Scripts, plans, goals, and understanding.* Hillsdale, NJ: Lawrence Erlbaum Associates.

Schmitt, B. H., Pan, Y., & Tavassoli, N. T. (1994). Language and consumer memory: The impact of linguistic differences between Chinese and English. *Journal of Consumer Research, 21,* 419–431.

Schmitt, B. H., & Simonson, A. (1997). *Marketing aesthetics: The strategic management of brands, identity and image.* New York: The Free Press.

Schmitt, B. H., & Zhang, S. (1998). Language structure and categorization: A study of classifiers in consumer cognition, judgment and choice. *Journal of Consumer Research, 25,* 108–122.

Sinclair, R. C., Mark, M. M., & Shotland, R. L. (1987). Construct accessibility and generalizability across reponse categories. *Personality and Social Psychology Bulletin, 13,* 239–252.

Tavassoli, N. T. (1999). Temporal and associative memory in Chinese and English. *Journal of Consumer Research, 26,* 170–181.

Tavassoli, N, T. (2001). Color memory and evaluations for alphabetical and logographic brand names. *Journal of Experimental Psychology: Applied, 7,* 104–111.

Tavassoli, N. T., & Han, J. K. (2001). Scripted thought: Processing Korean Hancha and Hangul in a multimedia context. *Journal of Consumer Research, 28,* 482–493.

Whorf, B. (1956). *Language, thought and reality: Selected writings of Benjamin Lee Whorf* (J. B. Carroll, Ed.). Cambridge, MA: MIT Press.

Zhang, S., & Schmitt, B. H. (2001). Creating local brands in multilingual international markets. *Journal of Marketing Research, 38,* 313–325.

Zhang, S., & Schmitt, B. H. (2004). Activating sound and meaning: The role of language proficiency in bilingual consumer environments. *Journal of Consumer Research, 31,* 220–229.

CHAPTER 5

Phonology, Morphology, and Semantics: Toward a Fuller Conceptualization of Brand Name Meaning

Dawn B. Lerman
Fordham Universiy

Consumer understanding of a brand—its image and its meaning—derives, at least initially, from the brand name and the associations it elicits (Aaker, 1991; Kohli & LaBahn, 1997). Brand names play such a key role when they have meanings related to product attributes, imagery, and/or usage. Imbuing a brand name with meaning has a number of advantages because embedded meanings can affect brand evaluations (Klink, 2001; Yorkston & Menon, 2004), memory for ads carrying those brand names (Keller, Heckler, & Houston, 1998), and memory for the brand names themselves (Baker, 2003; Lerman & Garbarino, 2002).

Brand name meaning derives from one or more linguistic sources. These sources are key both to understanding consumer response to brand names and facilitating the often difficult and complex brand naming process (Kohli & LaBahn, 1997; Shipley, Hooley, & Wallace, 1988; Shipley & Howard, 1993). A number of recent consumer studies have investigated phonology and phonetics as one such source (e.g., Klink 2000, 2001, 2003; Vanden Bergh, Collins, Schultz, & Adler, 1984; Yorkston & Menon, 2004; see also Shrum & Lowrey, chap. 3 in this volume). These studies focus on the meaning associated with certain sounds, a phenomenon referred to as sound symbolism or phonetic symbolism. Generally speaking, these studies have found that sound symbolism can convey product-related information and affect attitudes toward brands and brand names.

In addition to sound, brand name meaning may also be derived from morphology and semantics. Although researchers recognize the role of morphology and semantics in brand name creation (e.g., Robertson, 1989), the little work that has been done in this area tends not to be strongly based in the psycholinguistics literature and lacks both an organizing framework and empirical focus. Moreover, only a few studies have examined the impact that these linguistic sources of meaning have on consumer response to brand names and/or the relative effect of semantic or morphemic versus sound-based meaning (e.g., Klink, 2001; Lowrey, Shrum, & Dubitsky, 2003). The result is a fragmented view of brand name meaning.

This chapter seeks to advance our understanding of brand name meaning and of consumer response to brand names in general. It does so by incorporating and applying previous research in psycholinguistics to our understanding of brand name meaning. As such, it encourages a more systematic approach to and holistic view of brand name meaning than currently exists in this area of consumer research. The chapter makes an additional contribution by exploring the relationships among various sources of linguistically based brand name meaning (i.e., phonology, morphology, and semantics), thus further advancing this holistic view and encouraging more integrative research. Finally, the chapter introduces presentation mode as a linguistically based contextual factor relevant for understanding how, when, and what meaning is derived from brand names.

It is important to note that this chapter focuses only on brand names in alphabet-based languages. Clearly, researchers are interested in brand naming in other language systems, namely logographic systems (e.g., Schmitt, Pan, & Tavassoli, 1994; Tavassoli, 1999; Tavassoli & Han, 2002), and have generated some important findings in this area. However, as Zhang and Schmitt point out in their earlier chapter, there are fundamental differences in the structure of alphabetic versus logographic systems and, consequently, in the manner in which brands names from these systems are processed. These differences might very well fill an entire book on their own and are thus beyond the scope of this chapter. This does not mean, however, that this chapter and the research it intends to spawn will not be fruitful for expanding this area of research. Specifically, a more comprehensive and systematic understanding of brand name meaning within alphabet-based language systems should open further avenues for such comparative research (e.g., brand name meaning in alphabetic vs. logographic systems) and may inspire similar attempts at broadening our understanding of brand name meaning in non-alphabet-based language systems.

LEVELS OF UNDERSTANDING

Brand name meaning is derived from a variety of linguistic sources. In this context, the linguistic term most likely to come to mind is semantics. In fact, semantics is often defined as the study of meaning. Meaning in this sense refers to the message conveyed by an utterance, or a series of words (O'Grady, Dobrovolsky, & Aronoff, 1993). That is, together, the meaning of individual words give meaning to an utterance such as a sentence. For example, the meaning of Nike's "Just Do It®" slogan is generated from the combination of words in the slogan. As such, the slogan would communicate something different than it does now if one word, say "just," were missing. "Do It" is semantically different than "Just Do It" because each word brings meaning to the slogan.

Like words, brand names have meaning. However, the meaning embedded in the brand name itself may be derived just as much from the structural components of the name—its phonology and morphology—as it is from semantics. Specifically, it is the combination of phonemes (i.e., sounds) and morphemes (i.e., word components) that create the words and phrases, which by virtue of their meaning are able to enter into a variety of semantic relations with other words and phrases in our language (e.g., the relationship between *Just* and *Do It* in the Nike slogan; O'Grady et al., 1993). Within a branding context, this means that brand names are able to enter a variety of semantic relations with brands as well as with other brand names and their brands. A brand may, for example, be linguistically related to its brand name through semantic appositeness, which is typically defined as the fit between brand name and product attributes, benefits, or function (Keller et al., 1998; Vanden Bergh, Adler, & Oliver, 1987).

Beyond these relationships, semantics may also be relevant to the study of individual words or brand names. O'Grady et al. (1993) point out a number of attempts to understand word meaning from a semantic perspective by focusing on a word's referents, extension, intension, and semantic features. They also point out a whole host of exceptions, limitations, and difficulties arising from this perspective, leading them to declare: "It seems that meaning must be something that exists in the mind and that it must be more abstract than pictures and more complex than features" (p. 217).

This idea that meaning exists in the mind is consistent with recent approaches to branding that focus on mind share (Berry, 2000) and emphasize the consumer's role in defining a brand and what it stands for (Muniz & Shau, 2005). Within this context of consumer-generated meaning, what is the role of various brand elements, including the brand name? The mere presence of a brand name can, in certain circumstances, serve as a perceptual cue that accentuates real or perceived differences between brands (see Hoegg & Alba, chap. 1 in this volume). Expectations as to the particular differences between the brands come, at least in part, from their brand names (Aaker, 1991; Kohli & LaBahn, 1997). A brand name may not be sufficient to define a brand, but it can inspire a certain brand meaning. It does so via relationships with other words or names (i.e., semantics as discussed earlier), as well as via elements of the name itself. These elements are phonology and morphology.

Phonology

Phonology refers to the function of sounds and sound patterns in a language. The study of the sounds themselves is called phonetics. Researcher interest in the sounds and sound patterns of brand names has focused on phonetics or sound symbolism, "a highly controversial subject that continues to provoke empirical study and debate among linguists, anthropologists, and philosophers" (Nuckolls, 1999, p. 226). As Nuckolls (1999, p. 226) explains:

> The problematic nature of sound symbolism arises from its conflict with the structural linguistic axiom that sounds do their work through contrastive relations with other sounds rather than through their intrinsic sound qualities. Consider a pair of words such as "tip" and "dip." We cannot assign semantic responsibility for their different meanings to their contrasting alveolar stops, /d/ and /t/. It is the fact that one is pronounced with vibrating vocal cords and the other with nonvibrating vocal cords that is conventionally understood as significant.

As Nuckolls (1999) goes on to explain, sound symbolism refers to a situation where a sound unit such as a phoneme, syllable, feature, or tone extends beyond its linguistic function as a contrastive, non-meaning-bearing unit, to express a particular meaning (p. 228). More simply put, it refers to a direct relationship between sound and meaning (Hinton, Nichols, & Ohala, 1994). Sound symbolism is not something particular to English or to alphabet-based languages, but rather has been observed across a wide range of languages in a variety of countries (see Hinton et al., 1994).

As Shrum and Lowrey point out in their earlier chapter, sound symbolism is of interest to consumer researchers to the degree that brand names can convey product-related information (Klink, 2000), or that consumers use the sounds in brand names to infer product attributes and benefits. Early research in sound symbolism found that certain vowels and consonants suggest a particular size (e.g., large vs. small; Sapir, 1929) or degree of darkness (Newman, 1933). More recently, Klink (2000, 2003) found evidence that products with brand names containing front vowel sounds, as opposed to back vowel sounds, and those containing certain types of consonants (i.e., stops vs. fricatives) are perceived differently (e.g., smaller, lighter, faster, etc.). In a follow-up study, Klink (2003) found evidence that certain vowel and consonant sounds are also related to brand marks of a particular color, shape, and size. Apparently, consumers are not conscious of the inferences that they make based on these sounds, but rather infer these product attributes as part of a process that Yorkston and Menon (2004) propose to be "uncontrollable, outside of awareness, and effortless, making it automatic" (pp. 43–44). Given the theoretical and managerial implications of processing automaticity, the Yorkston and Menon (2004) hypothesis is worth testing directly.

The power of sound symbolism has not been overlooked in the marketplace. Schloss (1981) found, for example, that names beginning with a particular type of stop called *plosives* (i.e., a non-nasal stop with a release burst, e.g., B, D, G, K, P, and T) accounted for a disproportionate number of top brands sold in the United States from 1975–1979. More recently, Vanden Bergh et al. (1987) found that the use of plosives has been the most common linguistic device used in brand naming, followed by semantic appositeness (i.e., fit between product and name, e.g.,

Bufferin®). From a marketing perspective, the use of plosives in brand naming makes good sense because such names appear to produce higher recall and recognition scores than names that do not begin with a plosive (Vanden Bergh et al., 1984). Moreover, consumers appear to like names using symbolic sounds better than names that do not use such sounds (Klink, 2001). It appears, however, based on studies that Shrum and Lowrey report in their earlier chapter, that this preference depends on the fit between the sound and the product category (e.g., front vowels, which tend to suggest sharpness, are a better fit for a knife than back vowels, which tend to suggest dullness).

Despite these findings and the relative acceptance of sound symbolism in the marketing literature, this area of research remains controversial among linguists. Part of this controversy is conceptual, as explained earlier, and part of it is methodological (Nuckolls, 1999). Some of the methodological issues will be discussed in a later section on the activation of brand name meaning. In the meantime, suffice it to say that sound symbolism remains an area of interest because researchers have uncovered evidence of its existence and it has powerful implications for consumer behavior in the marketplace.

Morphology

Morphology, unlike phonology, has a relatively clear and less controversial semantic focus. Libben and Jarema (2004) define morphology as the "semantic and syntactic substructure of language strings" (p. 3), although other linguists will often define it much more simply as the structure or formation of words. Yet, even this simple definition has semantic implications because words can be broken down into smaller units that each have and bring meaning to the words containing them (e.g., break + fast = breakfast; Plaut & Gonnerman, 2000).

Brand names, like words, are often created using combinations of morphemes (Robertson, 1989). A *morpheme* is defined as the smallest unit of language that carries information about meaning or function (O'Grady et al., 1993).[1] English, for example, contains more than 6,000 morphemes ranging from full words (free morphemes), such as "man," to small parts of words that cannot stand alone (bound morphemes), such as "-ly." These 6,000+ morphemes can and have been combined to form the tens of thousands of words found in today's English language dictionaries.

The lexicon (i.e., the consumer's mental dictionary containing a variety of information about words) includes knowledge of the morphemic structure of a learned language. More specifically, it contains knowledge of the morphemes within a language as well as the rules for combining them (Barsalou, 1992). English speakers know, for example, that the bound morpheme "s" can be added to nouns (to express

---

[1]Researchers studying phonetic symbolism would take issue with this definition, arguing instead that phonemes are the smallest units of language that carry information about meaning.

plurality) and verbs (for proper subject-verb agreement) but not to adjectives or adverbs. They also know, for example, that adding the prefix "non" to a word changes the meaning of that word to its opposite. Thus, in any language, additional words may be formed by generating new morphemic combinations and speakers of the language will be able to draw on their morphemic knowledge to understand the meaning of these newly formed words (Libben & Jarema, 2003). At one time, for example, words like "Americanize" and "globalize" did not exist; yet no English speaker needed a dictionary to understand these new words upon initial exposure. Similarly, if an English-speaking job applicant were told at an interview, "Unfortunately, our company is not at all cyberized," he would understand his interviewer even having never before heard the term *cyberized*.

Brand names composed of morphemic combinations abound in the modern marketplace; the names Vitabath (bath products), Duracraft (household fans), and Hydrovive (shampoo), for example, each represent a combination of two English language morphemes.[2] The morphemic approach to brand naming carries a number of advantages for the marketer. For an English-speaking consumer, for example, the morphemes contained in the names Vitabath®, Duracraft, and Hydrovive are already represented in memory, thus aiding brand name learning. Moreover, because morphemes themselves are meaningful units, their use can result in a name with associations that support the desired brand image (Robertson, 1989). Thus, the name Duracraft suggests that the fans bearing this name are well-made and will last a long time. As such, this name would seem to satisfy at least two important brand name criteria: memorability and elicitation of brand benefits (Kohli & LaBahn, 1997).

Despite the advantages of morphology from a known language, some marketers choose names that consist of non-native morphemes even within their domestic markets. Marketers wanting to elicit a country-of-origin effect, for example, will likely use morphemes that are generally recognized as originating from the language intended as the country-of-origin (e.g., French-sounding Mont Blanc, a German brand; Harris, Strum, Klassen, & Bechtold, 1986), even if consumers do not understand their meaning. However, the use of unfamiliar morphemes goes beyond foreign-sounding names. Even Nike, the all-American brand, has a name consisting of a Greek free morpheme that refers to victory. Although certainly meaningful for the brand, few consumers outside of Greece would ever make this association between the name and the brand unless the company were to make this association explicit, perhaps through advertising. Of course, the company could have chosen a name like "Victory" (or some other name containing the free morpheme "victor"). In this case, however, the name would have likely been less distinctive (Klink, 2003) and distinctiveness is yet another important naming criterion (Kohli & LaBahn, 1997).

As these examples suggest, the morphological choices in brand naming are laden with trade-offs; morphemes (or combinations thereof), when understood and

---

[2]Vanden Bergh et al. (1987) refer to the combination of morphemes as "blending."

processed by the consumer, are likely to aid learning and elicit associations, but may appear less distinctive than unknown or relatively unfamiliar morphemes. This trade-off should be of interest to researchers as novel words appear to capture attention (Johnston, Hawley, Plewe, Elliott, & DeWitt, 1990) and encourage deeper processing (Friedman, 1979; Loftus & Mackworth, 1978) than do familiar or high frequency words.

The Nike example raises a related issue as it suggests that consumers may not process morphemic information even when it is embedded in the name. Perhaps the issue is most clear in the case of foreign-sounding names, because it is often the sound of the morphemes and not the morphemes themselves that convey meaning. Later, I will examine this processing issue in more depth, focusing both on the processing of brand name meaning in general as well as the specific contexts in which certain levels of brand name meaning may be activated. First, however, let us turn to semantics, the area of linguistics that focuses exclusively on meaning.

Semantics

Generally speaking, semantics refers to the study of meaning in human language (O'Grady et al., 1993). Most often, semantics is concerned with the meaning of words. However, semantics also refers to the meaning of the morphemes in a word as well as the meaning of a string of words, such as a sentence. Let us return to an earlier example—Hydrovive—to illustrate the role of semantics, particularly vis-à-vis other linguistic elements of the name, such as morphology. Morphology tells us that this brand name contains two morphemes, *hydro* and *vive*, but it does not tell us what these morphemes mean. This is the role of semantics. Only through semantics do we understand that *hydro* is somehow related to water or moisture and that *vive* refers to life.

The Hydrovive example is also helpful for understanding much of the consumer research conducted to date on the semantics of brand names. The majority of studies tend to focus on the imbedding of existing words or morphemes in a brand name, a phenomenon that has been referred to as semantic appositeness (Klink, 2001; Lowrey et al., 2003). As mentioned earlier, consumer researchers have been interested in semantic embedding to the degree that it can help to convey specific attributes or benefits and encourage particular associations to the brand (Robertson, 1989) and impact positively and/or negatively memory for ad claims that are consistent with the suggested benefit (Keller et al., 1998) or memory for the brand name itself (Lerman & Garbarino, 2002; Lowrey et al., 2003).

Whereas it seems natural that researchers studying brand name meaning would draw on semantics, it should be pointed out that not all meaning is semantic. Some linguistics, for example, restrict semantics to the study of literal meaning. Kearns (2000) offers the following example: Suppose one roommate says to another, "I forgot the paper." Semantics provides the meaning for each word in the sentence, thus, the literal meaning of *I*, *forget*, in past tense, *the*, and *paper*. The hearer, however, likely understands more than just the meanings of these words. Suppose that it is a Sunday morning and the speaker just returned from a local bakeshop. In this context, the hearer understands, among other things, that it was the Sunday paper, she intended to buy it either at or on the way to/from the bakeshop, and she had forgotten to do so, but she remembered upon returning (Kearns, 2000).

This extra understanding—the understanding that goes beyond the literal meaning of "I forgot the paper"—derives from what linguists would call *pragmatic meaning*. Pragmatics considers the context in which an utterance occurs, including the participants' identity, role, and location (Levinson, 1983). Pragmatics is considered by some linguistics as a branch of inquiry separate and distinct from semantics (e.g., Morris, 1938), whereas others classify it as a subfield of semantics (e.g., O'Grady et al., 1993). Despite this disagreement, research in the area of pragmatics has grown exponentially and spawned a variety of new and expanded approaches to studying language, such as discourse analysis and conversation analysis.

Regardless of its classification, pragmatics is quite relevant and has much to offer to consumer research on brand names. In chapter 2, Gontijo and Zhang reviewed literature suggesting that brand names are, at least in some sense, processed differently than common nouns. Of course, in order for these processing differences to occur, consumers must first recognize that a particular letter string is a brand name. Oftentimes, it is the appearance and usage of the letter string in advertising and on packaging that indicates its brand name status. However, as Gontijo and Zhang point out, brand names are also distinguished by linguistically based grammatical features, most notably capitalization, which has been shown to induce unique processing strategies. They also report examining similar effects for other visually based linguistic features such as color, style, and shape. To the degree that these features provide the context in which a letter string is presented and recognized as a brand name, research in this area falls within the realm of pragmatics.

Historically, researchers have indeed been interested in pragmatic effects but have tended to lump them under the general rubric of semantics. For example, although they have been generally described in the brand naming literature as a "semantic device" (e.g., Lowrey et al., 2003, p. 7), metaphors typically fall under pragmatics as they are not intended to be taken literally. Lowrey et al. (2003) offer the brand name Arrid as an example of metaphor in brand naming. The name is not meant to suggest that the antiperspirant with this name is dry, but rather that it will keep the user dry, as dry perhaps, as arid desert land. Whereas semantic approaches to metaphors have yielded interesting insights with respect to consumer memory (Lowrey et al., 2003), pragmatic approaches would be helpful for understanding the process of interpreting metaphors, making inferences, and developing brand attitudes based on those inferences. The pragmatic approach to metaphor has already helped to expand our understanding of advertising (e.g., Callow & Schiffman, 2004; McQuarrie & Phillips, 2005) and buyer–salesperson interaction (e.g., Comstock & Higgins, 1997; Lerman, 2006b) and has served as a backbone to semiotic approaches to marketing (Mick, 1986). It is reasonable to expect, then, that pragmatics would be helpful for expanding on our understanding of metaphors in brand names as well.

More generally speaking, marketers recognize that brand names can take on meaning that is not entirely semantic, a phenomenon that, in some cases, has prompted name changes. The beauty brand Oil of Olay® is a case in point. The word "oil" in Oil of Olay once suggested the moisturizing benefits of the brand, but to young women in the 1990s, it suggested that the product is greasy (Nelson, 2000). The semantics of the word "oil" did not change; English language dictionaries likely defined the word "oil" much in the same way as they did generations ago when the brand got its start. Rather, the environment in which the brand and its name lived—the context—changed. Given that pragmatics is concerned with context, it is worth separating this area of inquiry from semantics in order to provide a richer understanding of brand name meaning. This will be helpful for understanding which meanings may be activated and when.

ACTIVATING BRAND NAME MEANING

As verbal stimuli, brand names contain a variety of features (e.g., letters, sounds, and morphemes) to which the consumer may or may not attend. More specifically, consumers can process any given brand name at a variety of levels. Based on comparative studies of various encoding strategies (e.g., Elias & Perfetti, 1973), semantic processing is considered the deepest level of processing. In semantic processing, the individual focuses on the meaning of the verbal stimulus and typically relates this meaning to the context (e.g., sentence or story; Chaffin, 1997). When semantically processing a meaningful brand name, then, a consumer would relate the meaning of the name to the brand or product (Durgee & Stuart, 1987; Robertson, 1989).

In contrast, a focus on surface features, such as letters and sounds, is typically associated with relatively low levels of processing (Elias & Perfetti, 1973; Hennessey, Bell, & Kwortnik, 2005). Such a low level of processing can be induced by the task as when, for example, a teacher instructs an elementary school student to count the number of vowels present in a particular word. Surface processing, however, may also be induced by the stimulus itself. Chaffin (1997) found, for example, that whereas high-familiarity stimuli tend to elicit semantically based or meaning-based responses, low-familiarity and novel verbal stimuli elicit any of a variety of surface string responses, including same-sound responses (e.g., rhyme), sound-mediated responses (i.e., associates of same-sounding words that act as mediators, e.g., "persimmon" elicited the response "spice" from respondents who thought of "cinnamon," a similar sounding word), similar spelling responses, as well as responses with no identifiable relation to the stimulus. Durso and Shore (1991) obtained similar results with highly unfamiliar stimuli, including words mistaken by respondents to be non-words. More specifically, they found that although respondents may extract meaningful information from highly unfamiliar letter strings, they are often unable or unwilling to use it.

The distinction between semantic and sound-based, or high and low processing raises a number of questions with regard to brand name processing in general and, more specifically, with regard to the relative reliance on phonology (e.g., sound symbolism) versus morphology for making product inferences. If highly unfamiliar stimuli tend *not* to elicit the highly meaningful responses associated with deeper levels of processing (Hennessey et al., 2005), are consumers less likely, on presentation of a novel brand name, to rely on morphology than phonology in deriving some meaning from the name? Moreover, what would be considered a novel brand name? A brand name consisting of morphemes is certainly less novel than a nonmorphemic one (e.g., Häagen Dazs®, an American brand whose name was not derived from recognizable morphemes). But what about a name made up of both morphemic and nonmorphemic components? Moreover, a new brand name may appear novel after the first exposure, but when does that novelty fade? Does it fade after the second exposure? The third exposure? The fourth exposure? Does it only fade after product trial?

A complicating factor in understanding the derivation of meaning from novel brand names is the relationship between sound symbolism and morphology. Bolinger (1950) identified conventional sound-symbolic principles in the structuring of English morphology, stimulating a number of similar analyses (Marchand, 1959; Markel & Hamp, 1960). He points out, for example, that the letters *gl-*, in roughly half of all commonly used English words (e.g., glance, glare, gleam, glimmer, glitter), imply something visual, whereas words with the letters *-ash* (e.g., bash, dash, gash) imply fragmentation, collision, or impact. Could it be, then, that sounds contribute to morphemic meaning?

This is not necessarily the case. Consider the sound /p/, a plosive, a type of consonant that in the marketing literature has been shown to generate high rates of recall and recognition relative to other types of consonants (Vanden Bergh et al., 1987). If /p/ refers to something related to smallness as in *puny, petit, pea,* and *pin,* then how do we account for words like *plenty, partner, pelican,* and *potato*? Perhaps the answer lies in the vowels. For example, the smallness of /p/ might be offset by /o/, which connotes largeness (Jespersen, 1933). Or, in the case of *plenty,* the addition of /l/ to /p/ to form a pl- combination may result in different sound symbolism. Were not that sound symbolism appears to be "automatic" (Yorkston & Menon, 2004), this would all be very confusing to a consumer relying on sounds to learn something about a new brand. It also suggests that relying on sound symbolism may not be, or may not always be, an efficient way of deriving meaning from brand names. It could depend, for example, on the presence or absence of other cues from the brand name itself (e.g., presence of morphemes) and/or the context in which the brand name is presented.

So when do consumers focus on sound and when do they focus on morphemes? A study by Lowrey et al. (2003) may provide some insight. Based on an adapted version of linguistic variables identified by Vanden Bergh et al. (1987), Lowrey et al. (2003) found that linguistic variables are more likely to affect brand name memory when the brand is unfamiliar than when it is familiar. The only exception was in the case of blending (i.e., morphemic combinations such as Aspergum®), which appeared to inhibit memory for brand names. This was an unexpected but interesting result.

The unexpected pattern observed by Lowrey et al. (2003) draws our attention to possible processing differences associated with various types of brand names. When presented with a morphemic brand name (e.g., one using blending in the study by Lowrey et al., 2003), respondents likely focus on the morphemes and their meaning, perhaps at the expense of surface features. Yet, in typical memory tests, including those in the Lowrey et al. (2003) study, respondents are then asked to remember surface features (i.e., letters and sounds) of the name. This test may be a challenge, particularly as such names are not necessarily unique. Instead, there are often many ways to express morphemic meaning, although of course, each has its own subtle meaning. For example, the shampoo brand Hydrovive™ would communicate something very similar if it were called Hydrolife or Moisturevive. In their particular study, the inhibition may also have been related to the fact that presentation was on television, which presumably allowed respondents to focus on the name either auditorally or visually, whereas the memory test was only auditory. Finally, this one unexpected result could have been related to the combination of recall and recognition into a single memory measure, which the authors admit was not ideal. Lerman and Garbarino (2002) found, for example, that memory for brand names depends on both the linguistic features of the name (e.g., word vs. non-word name) and the memory task (i.e., recall vs. recognition).

Let us suppose for a moment that respondents in the Lowrey et al. (2003) study did focus on the morphemes and their meaning at the expense of surface features. Would this suggest that phonology and morphology act independently? In early studies, Sapir (1929) and Newman (1933) uncovered evidence suggesting that sound symbolism may indeed operate independently from, and regardless of, the underlying morphemic meaning in which letters are embedded. Sapir (1929), for example, presented respondents with the letter strings such as *mal* and *mil* and assigned these strings the arbitrary meaning "table." Although he chose these and other letter strings to serve as "meaningless words" (Sapir, 1949, p. 62), they are not necessarily meaningless. *Mal* and *mil*, for example, are both morphemes in English, the first meaning "bad" (e.g., malady, malevolent) and the second meaning "thousand" (e.g., millennium). Yet, despite such meanings, respondents associated letter strings with the vowel "a" with a larger table than those with the vowel "i."

The results obtained by Sapir (1929), Newman (1933), and their contemporaries has led some linguists to question the existence or importance of sound symbolism. These linguists would argue that any evidence for sound symbolism is methodologically driven. Nuckolls (1999) explains that "subjects are highly susceptible to suggestions of the meaningfulness of sounds" (p. 231)—"suggestions" being the key word here. In other words, she argues that the results are a demand artifact and that research subjects would not make these associations (e.g., to size for the vowels "a" and "i") if they were not asked to do so. This raises the question concerning what consumers do when presented with brand names in the marketplace, a situation that is very different than the contexts in which many sound symbolism studies are conducted. It is possible, for example, that the multitude of cues in the marketplace draws their attention away from surface features. This would be especially so if the ad in which a brand is advertised encourages conceptual processing or, perhaps, if the consumer is highly involved in the product category (Howard, Kerin, & Gengler, 2000).

Within the marketing literature, few (if any) studies offer insight into the relationship between or the interaction of phonology and morphology in brand name processing. This is in part because studies of sound symbolism typically use nonmorphemic stimuli (e.g., "Frish" and "Frosh" in Yorkston & Menon, 2004) for purposes of experimental control. As a result, we do not know if the same sound symbolism would exist if consumers were able to derive meaning from some morphemic element of the brand name.

Despite the fact that their research was not designed to address this particular issue, Yorkston and Menon (2004) may offer some preliminary insight. They found that when information regarding the diagnosticity of the brand name is provided at the time the name is encountered, consumers can control whether or not they process any underlying sound symbolism. This suggests that reliance on sound symbolism is strategically contingent and indicates that, perhaps, consumers would not make inferences from sound if they were to have deeper meanings on which to draw, such as the meaning derived from morphemes.

Thus far, the question concerning which linguistic elements of the brand name a consumer will process has focused entirely on the brand name itself. However, it was suggested earlier that the type and depth of brand name processing may also depend on the context in which the name is presented. In consumer research, respondents are most often, if not always, presented brand names visually (e.g., on paper or on a computer screen). Yet, in the marketplace, consumers may be exposed to brand names auditorily (e.g., radio advertising, WOM), visually (e.g,. print advertising), or both auditorily and visually (e.g., television advertising). The next section examines the role that presentation mode plays in brand name processing.

Lexical Access and Presentation Mode

The process by which verbal information accesses the lexicon depends on the manner in which it is presented. It is widely accepted that English speakers rely on sound-based coding, whether acoustic or phonological, for auditorily presented information (Salamé & Baddeley, 1982; Tyler & Frauenfelder, 1987). In other words, upon exposure to an orally presented word, a listener searches his lexicon for matching sounds. If a matching sound or combination of sounds is identified, then the word is recognized. Such recognition may occur before the listener has heard the word completely, particularly if "the word recognition point corresponds to its uniqueness point, where the word's initial [sound] sequence is common to that word and no other" (Harley, 1995, p. 53).

The processing of visually presented information, however, is less well understood and therefore much more widely studied. Based on the results of a variety of experiments (e.g., Meyer, Schvaneveldt, & Ruddy, 1974; Rubenstein, Lewis, & Rubenstein, 1971; Shulman, Hornak, & Sanders, 1978), many researchers originally supported the notion of phonological recoding. According to the phonological recoding hypothesis, readers rely on a learned set of grapheme-to-phoneme correspondence rules "that translate letter patterns into the sound patterns produced by the auditory analysis of spoken words" (Garnham, 1985, p. 57). One attractive feature of this hypothesis is its consistency with language learning. That is, "spoken language is prior to written language—both in the development of the species and of the individual—and learning to read is, at least initially, learning that certain visual patterns correspond in an orderly way to words already in the speaking vocabulary" (Garnham, 1985, p. 57).

A simple example of phonological recoding can be provided by a word that appears in this sentence: the word "phonological." Typically, the grapheme "p" corresponds to the phoneme /p/, as in the word "plant," and the grapheme "h" corresponds to the phoneme /h/, as in the word "house." An English speaker knows, however, that these letters, when appearing consecutively, can correspond to different phonemes under certain circumstances. Such is the case with the word "phonological." Here, a reader must rely on a combination of correspondence rules and word formation rules that together indicate that the graphemes "p" and "h," when appearing consecutively at the beginning of a word, are equivalent in sound to the letter "f." This sound is written phonologically as /f/ and is the same phoneme that appears in the words "foliage," "feather," and "forest."

Despite its appeal, the phonological recoding hypothesis was seriously challenged by an experiment conducted by Kleiman (1975). Having found that sound interferences prevented respondents from classifying orally presented information but not visually presented information, Kleiman (1975) proposed that visually presented words can either gain direct access to the mental lexicon or indirect access via phonological recoding. Despite the popularity of such dual access theories (Garnham, 1985), the circumstances determining access route remain unclear. Noting that children use the grapheme-to-phoneme conversion route by spelling out words letter by letter when they learn to read, Harley (1995) suggests that phonological recoding may only be used for learning new words and pronouncing non-words. In the only study of its kind within the marketing literature, Schmitt et al. (1994) found disconfirming evidence for Harley's theory in that respondents performed better at a visual recognition task than an auditory recognition task when a non-word was visually presented as a brand name.

The results obtained by Schmitt et al. (1994) might be reconciled with past results within the linguistic literature given the latest thinking that reliance on phonology is strategically contingent. In developing the newest models of visual word recognition, researchers have been seeking to account simultaneously for a multiple of potential influences on reading performance, including but not limited to orthography, phonology, morphology, and word frequency (e.g., Coltheart & Rastle, 1994; Jacobs & Grainger, 1994; Massaro & Cohen, 1994; Milota, Widau, McMickell, Juola, & Simpson, 1997). Within these models, "whether phonological information is maintained or suppressed ... depends on its overall usefulness for the task" (Milota et al., 1997, p. 333). In the study performed by Schmitt et al. (1994), then, respondents may have relied on visual encoding because (a) the brand names had multiple pronunciations leading respondents to believe, whether consciously or subconsciously, that visual encoding would result in more accurate memory for those brands or (b) the brand names contained letter strings that are unfamiliar in the native language of the respondents (i.e., non-native morphemes) and therefore potentially difficult to pronounce. In either of these cases, phonological recoding would not necessarily have been "useful for the task."

The distinction between visual and sound-based coding has implications for which elements of a brand name (e.g., phonemes, morphemes) a consumer will process and the timing of that processing. More specifically, access to the lexical representations of written words and their oral equivalents may differ drastically. One difference is the sequential delivery and subsequent interpretation of stimulus information in the auditory domain (Marslen-Wilson, Tyler, Waksler, & Older, 1994). Sequence may not be an issue for the written stimulus, at least to the degree that readers can process entire words without breaking them into their morphological components (Caramazza, Laudanna, & Romani, 1988; Fowler, Napps, & Feldman, 1985; Henderson, 1985). A second difference is the presence of cues to morphological structure in the written versus spoken word. Marslen-Wilson et al. (1994) offer the prefix in *rebuild* as an example. The *re-* pronounced with a full vowel in *rebuild*—as opposed to the shortened vowel in *return*—is a cue to morphological structure (and as a consequence, to the semantics of the word, meaning "to build *again*") that is available to the listener but not to the reader. Thus, Marslen-Wilson et al. (1994, p. 4) conclude that "although the lexical entry itself may be modality independent, different access routes can give different pictures of its properties as well as having different properties itself."

It would appear that from a marketing perspective, access route has the potential to affect consumer perceptions of the brand as well as, perhaps, memory for the brand name. These potential effects may be most evident in cases of a non-word brand name. Upon initial exposure to such a name, the consumer cannot draw on any prior lexical entry for the name regardless of whether the name is morphemic (e.g., Hydrovive) or nonmorphemic (e.g., Häagen Dazs). Thus, if the non-word brand name is presented visually, the consumer may not know how to pronounce it. If the name is then processed visually, rather than phonologically recoded, it is not clear which, if any, sound symbol would be activated. Presumably, this would be less of a concern if the brand name were to be presented auditorily. Here, however, sequence may play a role. After hearing the brand name, the consumer may, for example, focus on an early morpheme, thereby limiting the sound symbolism of any significant but late appearing sound.

In addition to limiting sound symbolism, an inability to pronounce a brand name may inhibit proper encoding of a brand name and then, subsequently, memory for the brand, depending perhaps on the retrieval task. The modern marketplace often requires that consumers retrieve visually presented information auditorily and auditorily presented information visually. A consumer interested in buying a brand that she heard advertised on the radio, for example, must visually recall the brand name in order to include it on her shopping list and then must visually recognize the brand name as it appears on product packaging. Similarly, a customer seeking to purchase a brand that appeared on a billboard may have to auditorily recall the brand name in order to ask for it in a store or recognize the brand name when said aloud by a salesperson. In both of these scenarios, the consumer is exposed to the brand name in one mode but must retrieve it in another.

In either type of mismatch (auditory exposure/visual retrieval or visual exposure/auditory retrieval), two possible scenarios emerge: (a) Upon initial exposure, the consumer encodes the information both visually and auditorily by performing online grapheme-to-phoneme (i.e., letter to sound) or phoneme-to-grapheme (i.e., sound to letter) transcription and then retrieves the requested information directly from memory or (b) the consumer encodes the information either visually or auditorily—whichever mode the name is presented in—and retrieves this same information, performing online transcription in order to present the information in the requested memory mode. Although these scenarios differ in the timing of transcription, they both require that transcription be performed. Proper performance in either case, then, requires knowledge of applicable grapheme-to-phoneme and phoneme-to-grapheme correspondence rules. Exposure/memory mode match does not require such knowledge, because the consumer is asked to retrieve the brand name as it was originally presented.

Given this varying role of correspondence rule knowledge, I have been interested in investigating the impact of matched versus mismatched modes on consumer memory for brand names. In a currently unpublished manuscript (see Lerman, 2006a), I exposed respondents to one of two names (*Plentron*, a morphemically familiar name, or *Imswut*, a morphemically unfamiliar name), either visually or auditorily. Then, after a short delay and regardless of their assigned experimental condition, respondents were tested for both auditory and visual recall as well as auditory and visual recognition. Auditory recall required subjects to say aloud into a microphone the name(s) they remembered. Each of these utterances was then coded as either completely correct, partially correct, or incorrect. The same measure and coding was used for visual recall, except that they wrote the name(s) they remembered. Recognition was measured using a multiple choice item containing four names (the two targets and two fillers) presented across the four experimental conditions. For auditory recognition, subjects listened to the four choices in alphabetical order and were instructed to circle the number(s) corresponding to the name(s) they recognized. The same measure was used for visual recognition with the exception that the names appeared in print.

Based on the findings of previous research (e.g., Durso & Shore, 1991), I expected that respondents would either be unwilling or unable to use their learned correspondence rules to transcribe morphemically unfamiliar names from one mode to another. Thus, instead of novelty aiding recognition as would typically be expected (e.g., Eysenck, 1979), I expected that it would impede it. However, I did not expect that the distinction between matched and mismatched modes would affect recall. Rather, I reasoned that because the components (i.e., morphemes) of a morphemically familiar name are already represented in the lexicon, a morphemically familiar name would be recalled more easily than a morphemically unfamiliar name. I was not expecting that respondents would expend, following a single exposure, the cognitive effort or elaboration necessary for creating a lexical entry for a morphemically unfamiliar name (see Mandler, 1982), thus impeding recall of the name (Meyers-Levy, Louie, & Curren, 1994; Meyers-Levy & Tybout, 1989).

Consistent with my expectations, results from the experiment suggest that the distinction between matched and mismatched modes does indeed affect recognition but not recall. Nonetheless, it appears that an inability or hesitancy to apply correspondence rules may only impede recognition in the case of visual-auditory mismatch. For recall, exposure mode rather than exposure/retrieval match appears to affect which name outperforms the other. Specifically, the morphemically familiar name was better recalled following auditory exposure and the morphemically unfamiliar name was better recalled following visual exposure.

Although the results of this experiment open somewhat of a Pandora's box with respect to previous research, one of the more curious findings is the superior recall of the visually presented morphemically unfamiliar name to the visually presented morphemically familiar name. The latest thinking that phonological recoding may be strategically contingent (see Harley, 1995) and the differential effects of orthographic-to-phonological mapping versus phonological-to-orthographic mapping on recall (Hirschman & Jackson, 1997) may provide a theoretical explanation. I am currently running additional experiments to examine the role of phonological recoding in memory for visually presented brand names. Early results suggest that consumers do use phonological recoding to process morphemically unfamiliar names to a greater degree than they do for morphemically familiar names and that such recoding aids recall even in the case of visual match. Given that both the morphemically familiar and unfamiliar names were new to the respondents in the study, the results suggest that the phonological recoding hypothesis might be refined to account for the degree of non-word novelty.

In the meantime, the processing differences associated with visual versus auditory access routes makes the incorporation of presentation mode in research on brand name meaning an imperative. As a contextual variable, presentation mode should be particularly helpful in specifying the relative role of phonology versus morphology, thereby also assisting researchers in determining if and when results supporting sound symbolism reflect true effects or are methodologically driven. The resulting insights will go a long way in extending consumer theory related to brand name processing.

CONCLUSIONS AND FUTURE RESEARCH

Brand names are complex verbal stimuli with meaning that operates at many different linguistic levels. Having focused predominantly on sound-based meaning, consumer researchers have only scratched the surface in building theory about brand name meaning and consumer processing of brand names. The application of a broader range of psycholinguistic literature should be helpful in both broadening and deepening both our understanding of brand name meaning and the manner and situations in which consumers process that meaning. Toward this end, this chapter distinguishes between three levels of meaning—phonemic, morphemic, and semantic—and considers the relationships between them. In some sense, however, this chapter asks more questions than it answers, an indication, perhaps, of some of the many directions for future research. May these questions inspire consumer researchers to explore new avenues of inquiry in an effort to build theory on brand name meaning and consumer processing of brand names.

In pursuing new avenues, researchers should keep in mind that whereas much of the phonemic, morphemic, and semantic meaning in brand names may be shared by speakers of a language, there may also be subcultural or idiosyncratic influences informing the meaning that any individual consumer derives from a brand name. Such influences have been observed with respect to both brand meaning in general (e.g., Schouten & McAlexander, 1995) and brand name meaning in particular. Reece and Ducoffe (1987), for example, found variations in the meanings consumers derive from brand names, albeit often variations on a theme. This finding suggests the importance of investigating relevant contextual variables or perhaps individual differences and incorporating them into future research. Doing so will serve to build an increasingly comprehensive, integrative, and holistic understanding of consumer response to brand names.

REFERENCES

Aaker, D. A. (1991). *Managing brand equity*, New York: The Free Press.
Baker, W. E. (2003). Does brand name imprinting in memory increase brand information retention? *Psychology and Marketing, 20*, 1119–1135.
Barsalou, L. (1992). *Cognitive psychology: An overview for cognitive scientists*. Hillsdale, NJ: Lawrence Erlbaum Associates.
Berry, L. L. (2000). Cultivating service brand equity. *Journal of the Academy of Marketing Science, 28*, 128–137.

Bolinger, D. (1950). Rime, assonance, and morpheme analysis. *Word, 6,* 117–136.

Callow, M., & Schiffman, L. (2004). Sociocultural meanings in visually standardized print ads. *European Journal of Marketing, 38,* 1113–1128.

Caramazza, A. A., Laudanna, A., & Romani, C. (1988). Lexical access and inflectional morphology. *Cognition, 28,* 297–332.

Chaffin, R. (1997). Associations to unfamiliar words: Learning the meaning of new words. *Memory and Cognition, 25,* 203–226.

Coltheart, M., & Rastle, K. (1994). Serial processing in reading aloud: Evidence for dual-route models of reading. *Journal of Experimental Psychology: Human Perception and Performance, 20,* 1197–1211.

Comstock, J., & Higgins, G. (1997). Appropriate relational messages in direct selling interaction: Should salespeople adapt to buyers' communicator style? *Journal of Business Communication, 34,* 401–418.

Durgee, J. F., & Stuart, R.W. (1987). Advertising symbols and brand names that best represent key product meanings. *Journal of Consumer Marketing, 4,* 15–24.

Durso, F. T., & Shore, W. J. (1991). Partial knowledge of word meanings. *Journal of Experimental Psychology: General, 120,* 190–202.

Elias, C. S., & Perfetti, C. A. (1973). Encoding task and recognition memory: The importance of semantic encoding. *Journal of Experimental Psychology, 99,* 151–156.

Eysenck, M. (1979). Depth, elaboration, and distinctiveness. In L. S. Cermak & F. I. M. Craik (Eds.), *Levels of processing in human memory* (pp. 89–118). Hillsdale, NJ: Lawrence Erlbaum Associates.

Fowler, C. A., Napps, S. E., & Feldman, L. (1985). Relations between regular and irregular morphologically related words in the lexicon as revealed by repetition priming. *Memory and Cognition, 13,* 241–255.

Friedman, A. (1979). Framing pictures: The role of knowledge in automatized encoding and memory for gist. *Journal of Experimental Psychology: General, 108,* 316–355.

Garnham, A. (1985). *Psycholinguistics: Central topics.* Cambridge, England: Cambridge University Press.

Harley, T. A. (1995). *The psychology of language: From data to theory.* East Sussex, United Kingdom: Lawrence Erlbaum Associates/Taylor & Francis.

Harris, R. J., Strum, R. E., Klassen, M. L., & Bechtold, J. I. (1986). Language in advertising: A psycholinguistic approach. *Current Issues and Research in Advertising, 9,* 1–27.

Henderson, L. (1985). Towards a psychology of morphemes. In A. W. Ellis (Ed.), *Progress in the psychology of language* (Vol. 1, pp. 15–72). London: Lawrence Erlbaum Associates.

Hennessey, J. E., Bell, T. S., & Kwortnik, R. J. (2005). Lexical interference in semantic processing of simple words: implications for brand names. *Psychology and Marketing, 22,* 51–69.

Hinton, L., Nichols, H., & Ohala, J. (1994). Introduction: Sound symbolic processes. In L. Hinton, H. Nichols, & J. Ohala (Eds.), *Sound symbolism* (pp. 1–14). Cambridge, England: Cambridge University Press.

Hirschman, E., & Jackson, E. (1997). Distinctive perceptual processing and memory. *Memory and Language, 36*(2), 2–12.

Howard, D. J., Kerin, R. A., & Gengler, C. (2000). The effects of brand name similarity on brand source confusion: Implications for trademark infringement. *Journal of Public Policy and Marketing, 19,* 250–264.

Jacobs, A. M., & Grainger, J. (1994). Models of visual word recognition—sampling the state of the art. *Journal of Experimental Psychology: Human Perception and Performance, 20,* 1311–1334.

Jespersen, O. (1933). Symbolic value of the vowel i. In *Linguistica: Selected papers in English, French, and German* (pp. 283–233). Copenhagen: Levin & Munksgaard.

Johnston, W. A., Hawley, K. J., Plewe, S. H., Elliott, J. M. G., & DeWitt, M. J. (1990). Attention capture by novel stimuli. *Journal of Experimental Psychology: General, 119*, 397–411.

Kearns, K. (2000) *Semantics*. New York: St. Martin's Press.

Keller, K. L., Heckler, S. E., & Houston, M. J. (1998). The effects of brand name suggestiveness on advertising recall. *Journal of Marketing, 62*, 48–57.

Kleiman, G. M. (1975). Speech recoding in reading. *Journal of Verbal Learning and Verbal Behavior, 14*, 323–339.

Klink, R. R. (2000). Creating brand names with meaning: The use of sound symbolism. *Marketing Letters, 11*, 5–20.

Klink, R. R. (2001). Creating meaningful new brand names: A study of semantics and sound symbolism. *Journal of Marketing Theory and Practice, 9*, 27–34.

Klink, R. R. (2003). Creating meaningful brands: The relationship between brand name and brand mark. *Marketing Letters, 14*, 143–157.

Kohli, C., & LaBahn, D. W. (1997). Creating effective brand names: A study of the brand naming process. *Journal of Advertising Research, 37*, 67–75.

Lerman, D. (2006a). *The effect of morphemic familiarity and exposure mode on recall and recognition of novel brand names*. Unpublished manuscript.

Lerman, D. (2006b). The relationship between consumer politeness and complaining behavior. *Journal of Services Marketing, 20*, 92–100.

Lerman, D., & Garbarino, E. (2002). Recall and recognition of brand names: A comparison of word and nonword name types. *Psychology and Marketing, 19*, 621–639.

Levinson, S. (1983). *Pragmatics*. New York: Cambridge University Press.

Libben, G., & Jarema, G. (2004). Conceptions and questions concerning morphological processing. *Brain and Language, 90*, 2–8.

Loftus, G. R., & Mackworth, N. H. (1978). Cognitive determinants of fixation location during picture viewing. *Journal of Experimental Psychology: Human Perception and Performance, 4*, 565–572.

Lowrey, T. M., Shrum, L. J., & Dubitsky, T. M. (2003). The relation between brand-name linguistic characteristics and brand-name memory. *Journal of Advertising, 32*, 7–17.

Mandler, G. (1982). The structure of value: Accounting for taste. In M. S. Clark & S. T. Fiske (Eds.), *Affect and cognition: The 17th annual Carnegie symposium* (pp. 92–102). Hillsdale, NJ: Lawrence Erlbaum Associates.

Marchand, H. (1959). Phonetic symbolism in English word-formation. *Indogermanische Forschungen, 64*, 146–168.

Markel, N. N., & Hamp, E. P. (1960). Connotative meanings of certain phoneme sequences. *Studies in Linguistics, 15*, 47–61.

Marslen-Wilson, W., Tyler, L. K., Waksler, R., & Older, L. (1994). Morphology and meaning in the English mental lexicon. *Psychological Review, 101*, 3–33.

Massaro, D. W., & Cohen, M. M. (1994). Visual, orthographic, phonological and lexical influences in reading. *Journal of Experimental Psychology: Human Perception and Performance, 20*, 1107–1128.

McQuarrie, E., & Phillips, B. (2005). Indirect persuasion in advertising: How consumers process metaphors presented in pictures and words. *Journal of Advertising, 34*, 7–20.

Meyer, D. E., Schvaneveldt, R. W., & Ruddy, M. G. (1974). Functions of graphemic and phonemic codes in visual word recognition. *Memory and Cognition, 2*, 309–321.

Meyers-Levy, J., Louie, T. A., & Curren, M. T. (1994). How does the congruity of brand names affect evaluations of brand name extensions? *Journal of Applied Psychology, 79*, 46–53.

Meyers-Levy, J., & Tybout, A. M. (1989). Schema incongruity as a basis for product evaluation. *Journal of Consumer Research, 16*, 39–54.

Mick, D. (1986). Consumer research and semiotics: Exploring the morphology of signs, symbols and significance. *Journal of Consumer Research, 13*, 196–213.

Milota, V. C., Widau, A. A., McMickell, M. R., Juola, J. F., & Simpson, G. B. (1997). Strategic reliance on phonological mediation in lexical access. *Memory and Cognition, 25,* 333–344.

Morris, C. W. (1938). Foundations of the theory of signs. In O. Neurath, R. Carnap, & C. Morris (Eds.), *International encyclopedia of Unified Science* (pp. 77–138). Chicago: University of Chicago Press.

Muniz, A. M., Jr., & Shau, H. J. (2005). Religiosity in the abandoned Apple Newton brand community. *Journal of Consumer Research, 31,* 737–747.

Nelson, E. (2000, May 16). P & G tries to hide wrinkles in aging beauty fluid—it took the "Oil" out of Oil of Olay; now it hopes young women will buy "cleansing clothes." *Wall Street Journal,* p. B1.

Newman, S. S. (1933). Further experiments in phonetic symbolism. *American Journal of Psychology, 45,* 53–75.

Nuckolls, J. B. (1999). The case for sound symbolism. *Annual Review of Anthropology, 28,* 225–252.

O'Grady, W., Dobrovolsky, M., & Aronoff, M. (1993). *Contemporary linguistics.* New York: St. Martin's Press.

Plaut, D. C., & Gonnerman, L. M. (2000). Are non-semantic morphological effects incompatible with a distributed connectionist approach to lexical processing? *Language and Cognitive Processes, 15,* 445–485.

Reece, B. B., & Ducoffe, R. H. (1987). Deception in brand names. *Journal of Public Policy and Marketing, 6,* 93–104.

Robertson, K. (1989). Strategically desirable brand name characteristics. *Journal of Consumer Marketing, 6,* 61–71.

Rubenstein, H., Lewis, S. S., & Rubenstein, M. E. (1971). Evidence for phonemic recoding in visual word recognition. *Journal of Verbal Learning and Verbal Behavior, 10,* 645–657.

Salamé, P., & Baddeley, A. D. (1982). Disruption of short-term memory by unattended speech: Implications for the structure of working memory. *Journal of Verbal Learning and Verbal Behavior, 21,* 150–164.

Sapir, E. (1929). A study in phonetic symbolism. *Journal of Experimental Psychology, 12,* 225–239.

Sapir, E. (1949). A study in phonetic symbolism. In D. G. Mandelbaum (Ed.), *Selected writings of Edward Sapir in language, culture and personality* (pp. 61–72). Berkeley, CA: University of California Press.

Schloss, I. (1981). Chickens and pickles: Choosing a brand name. *Journal of Advertising Research, 21,* 47–49.

Schmitt, B. H., Pan, Y., & Tavassoli, N. T. (1994). Language and consumer memory: The impact of linguistic differences between Chinese and English. *Journal of Consumer Research, 21,* 419–431.

Schouten, J. W., & McAlexander, J. H. (1995). Subcultures of consumption: An ethnography of the new biker. *Journal of Consumer Research, 22,* 43–61.

Shipley, D., Hooley, G. J., & Wallace, S. (1988). The brand name development process. *International Journal of Advertising, 7,* 253–266.

Shipley, D., & Howard, P. (1993). Brand-naming industrial products. *Industrial Marketing Management, 22,* 59–66.

Shulman, H. G., Hornak, R., & Sanders, E. (1978). The effects of graphemic, phonetic, and semantic relationships on access to lexical structures. *Memory and Cognition, 6,* 115–123.

Tavassoli, N. T. (1999). Temporal and associative memory in Chinese and English. *Journal of Consumer Research, 26,* 170–181.

Tavassoli, N. T., & Han, J. K. (2002). Auditory and visual brand identifiers in Chinese and English. *Journal of International Marketing, 10,* 13–28.

Tyler, L. K., & Frauenfelder, U. H. (1987). The process of spoken word recognition: An introduction. In U. H. Frauenfelder & L. K. Tyler (Eds.), *Spoken word recognition* (pp. 1–20). Cambridge, MA: MIT Press.

Vanden Bergh, B. G., Adler, K., & Oliver, L. (1987). Linguistic distinction among top brand names. *Journal of Advertising Research, 27,* 39–44.

Vanden Bergh, B. G., Collins, J., Schultz, M., & Adler, K. (1984). Sound advice on brand names. *Journalism Quarterly, 61,* 835–840.

Yorkston, E., & Menon, G. (2004). A sound idea: Phonetic effects of brand names on consumer judgments. *Journal of Consumer Research, 31,* 43–51.

PART II

Stringing Words Together—
The Importance of Sentences

CHAPTER 6

The Role of the Sentence and Its Importance in Marketing Communications

Robert Meeds
Kansas State University

Samuel D. Bradley
Texas Tech University

The purpose of this chapter is to present a theoretical justification for reconsidering the role of the sentence as a key persuasive linguistic unit in predicting responses to marketing communications. Consider the headline from a recent print ad for Dermasil® Dry Skin Treatment: "Now your red, rough, painfully dry skin can be the picture of health." There is nothing unusual about how the sentence is constructed or about the problem–solution persuasive technique it employs. Syntactically, the sentence is not complex, following the default noun phrase ("skin")—verb phrase ("can be")—object phrase ("picture of health") construction. If we were to analyze this sentence at the lexical level, we would note that "red," "rough," "painful," and "dry" all carry negative connotations, whereas "health" is the only descriptive word carrying a positive connotation. Yet, the sentence still communicates a primary benefit—a main point the ad seeks to deliver. To understand the persuasive effects of such a proposition, we argue, the sentence itself is the appropriate unit of analysis.

Additionally, we propose the application of sentence importance ratings as a simple yet viable way of analyzing sentence-level effects in marketing communications. Sentence importance ratings adopt a reader-driven technique developed in psycholinguistic research that has previously been used to measure readers' understanding of the propositional structures of written texts (Kieras, 1985). One point that distinguishes sentence importance ratings from traditional copy testing methods is that this technique allows researchers to examine communication points and complexity within a copy block, whereas more traditional measures (e.g., Flesch Reading Ease formula) assess global complexity. Sentence importance ratings have been used for several years in linguistic and composition research as a diagnostic tool to examine the relationships between readers' assessments of what is important in a text and readers' subsequent comprehension of what is traditionally considered a text's macropropositional structure, or gist (Kintsch & van Dijk, 1978).

Why focus on the sentence as a unit of analysis in marketing communications research? In the psycholinguistic hierarchy of language units, the sentence falls somewhere in the middle. The sentence is a narrower approach than looking at ads, copy blocks, or even paragraphs as a whole. The latter domains are appropriate for research analyzing executional styles such as image-oriented versus attribute-oriented (e.g., Malaviya, Kisielius, & Sternthal, 1996), or transformational versus informational ads. These broader approaches are referred to as *global* copy approaches. Conversely, the sentence represents a broader and more complex unit of analysis than, say, the phonemes, morphemes, and psuedowords that act as stimuli in much of the lexical decision and word comprehension research paradigms. Applied to marketing communications research, such microlevel approaches are readily adapted to studies analyzing structural features of language that influence attention, recognition, and recall. These microlevel approaches are represented in much of the empirical work on psycholinguistic effects in marketing communications conducted in the last decade (e.g., Bradley & Meeds, 2002; Chebat, Gelinas-Chebat, Hombourger, & Woodside, 2003; Lowrey, 1998).

THE SENTENCE AS A LINGUISTIC CONCEPT

The mere fact that the middle ground in this hierarchy is occupied by the sentence is not what makes it useful to study, however. We view the sentence as the basic unit of persuasive communication—"the minimal domain into which elementary meanings can be placed and combined" (Townsend & Bever, 2001, p. 1). Despite the fact that recent research on meanings conveyed by brand names focuses on the lexical level as the basic (and often polysemic) unit (e.g., Huang, Schrank & Dubinsky, 2004; Isen, Labroo, & Durlach, 2004; Lowrey, Shrum, & Dubitsky, 2003), we view brand names as a special case due to their repetition and frequent isolation from other advertising copy elements. In fact, many concepts associated with the idea of a generative grammar (e.g., Chomsky, 1959) view the basic noun-verb proposition as the natural level at which the patterns and habits of spoken communication evolve into the grammatical rules that guide both expression and comprehension. Although not all "sentences" in advertising copy contain discrete noun-verb phrases (and, conversely, not all noun-verb phrases form sentences), we adopt the sentence as a general proxy for the noun-verb concept.

Applied to persuasive marketing or advertising texts, the sentence is the place where a product's features may be described or embellished, where a benefit to a consumer may be explicitly stated or implied, where the reader's curiosity piqued by the ambiguity of a visual pun is rewarded, and where emotions or themes are linked to a mental representation of a brand. In the framework outlined here, advertising copy blocks can be considered exemplar texts for the purpose of examining reader reactions to novel ad copy. Consumers' processing of copy blocks in advertising is a complex process. This process, we argue, is affected not only by the global structure of the overall text, such as the average sentence length or the average number of syllables, but also by highly localized factors such as the way in which the text is constructed surrounding the most important product features and benefits.

The assumption of this sentence-focused framework is that, if advertising copy can be written in ways that make the encoding and comprehension of key features and benefits more clear and relevant (i.e., if the sentence construction helps make the most important ideas more salient), then the advertisement can be a more effective source of information during the purchase decision process. Further, if this assumption is correct, then advertising researchers should be able to (with the help of ad readers) identify specific areas of ad copy texts that readers find most helpful and, perhaps more importantly, identify ineffective passages in advertising copy.

The Propositional Paradigm and Sentential Load

Although studies directly examining language's role in advertising encoding, comprehension, memory, and persuasion represent a very small (and, some might add, obscure) portion of advertising and marketing communication research, psycholinguistic studies that manipulate the difficulty of comprehending particular words and phrase combinations in general texts are quite common. And there is much we can learn from this research and apply to marketing communications. Propositional models of text comprehension (e.g., Kintsch, 1988; Kintsch & van Dijk, 1978) posit that comprehension is based initially on a surface level understanding of the words and sentences strung together in a text, followed by a deeper level understanding in which the semantic content is compared to and integrated with readers' previously existing knowledge structures.

Rarely, however, do readers devote the time or effort to give marketing communications a second reading. Yet, evidence is beginning to emerge that even though word meanings are not always fully processed, especially on a first reading, the degree and locus of readers' semantic processing can be readily influenced by directing readers to focus on specific types of words or parts of speech (A. J. Sanford & Sturt, 2002; Sturt, Sanford, Stewart, & Dawdiak, 2004). Intersentential context (i.e., when information from previous sentences influences comprehension of a later sentence) appears to offer a primary cue for readers in "the initial assignment of a meaning" (Townsend & Bever, 2001, p. 332). Similarly, within-sentence cues can affect sentential load, or the amount of cognitive effort required to process and comprehend a sentence. In particular, initial findings suggest that higher sentential loads lead to increased verb-object comprehension problems in embedded clauses (A. J. S. Sanford, Sanford, Filik, & Molle, 2005). As we gain a better understanding of how these cues influence readers' linguistic focus, the natural place to apply these models in marketing communications research is at the propositional or sentence level.

Frequently, psycholinguistic studies of text comprehension attempt to assess how much mental effort is required to understand a text. However, the most frequently used measures of cognitive processing (e.g., secondary task reaction times, reading times, gaze fixation times) are ambiguous in that they provide only an estimation of the *amount* of mental effort dedicated to a task. The *type* of mental effort involved in text comprehension is difficult to gauge using these measures. One technique that does examine differences in the type of mental effort is to study event-related potentials (ERPs), which measure different types of neurological brain activity as an indication of the type of cognitive processing occurring at that time. Raney (1993) found that ERPs for brainwaves associated with lower order reading processes, such as word recognition, were high when readers encountered a text for the first time. As familiarity with a text increased (e.g., on a second reading), cognitive load decreased for these types of processes according to the ERP measurements. But, when ERPs were examined for higher order processes such as comparing the text to one's previous memory representation, cognitive load actually increased during a second reading of a text. Further, although the cognitive load effects from word recognition and syntactic processing appear to operate independently of semantic processing, predicting the precise parts of a text where comprehension will be influenced by syntax is proving to be a complex process (A. J. S. Sanford et al., 2005). Recent studies (e.g., Caplan & Waters, 1999; Fiebach, Schlesewsky, & Friederici, 2001) have further supported the idea that separate neural resources are allocated for parsing syntactic structure and for determining meaning; however, the implications for how these resources may be brought to bear on individual consumers' processing of persuasive communications in noisy environments remains unclear.

HOW SENTENCES ARE PROCESSED

One of the central issues in the psychology of reading involves delineating the processes of how written words are identified and understood (Pollatsek & Rayner, 1989; Rayner & Pollatsek, 1989). Models of word recognition and text comprehension typically begin with readers' identifications of orthographic features (i.e., shapes of letters) of letter strings, followed by a phonological representation of the written information, which is followed by searches of long-term memory for matches to the identified features. When the strongest match is found, recognition occurs and semantic connotations are retrieved (Kintsch, 1988; Van Orden, Johnston, & Hale, 1988). At this point, the new sentences can be integrated with existing knowledge.

Chomsky's (1957, 1959) theory for explaining language comprehension and production was transformational grammar. Chomsky's explanation for how readers process sentences included first a decoding of a sentence's surface structure (which was a function of words, syntax, and phrase structure), followed by a transformation of the sentence into its deep structure, or propositional form. Several aspects of Chomsky's theory did not hold up under later testing, yet his ideas on the propositional nature of sentence processing directly influenced later connectionist and associationist language and memory models (J. R. Anderson, Budiu, & Reder, 2001; Townsend & Bever, 2001).

Recently, models in computational linguistics (e.g., Tabor & Tanenhaus, 1999; Vosse & Kempen, 2000) have provided support for the notion of multiple-route processes in word recognition and text comprehension. These models demonstrate that readers can simultaneously be using both semantic and syntactic cues to parse and comprehend a sentence. In real time, the multiple cues from an advertisement are being pulled together toward some semantic representation in the mind of the reader. Rather than having some symbolic representation of a brand in the brain (i.e., there is no neuron or set of neurons that represents Coca-Cola®, the so-called "grandmother cell" in cognitive science), semantic meaning appears to be stored as distributed representations across different regions of the brain (McClelland & Rogers, 2003). Thus, if a consumer fails to sufficiently understand or appreciate the salient, or important, points of an advertisement, then the meaning that the consumer leaves with is not some arbitrary or unrelated meaning. Instead, the consumer understands the ad in a way that is related to, or correlated with, the intended meaning, but is in some way more vague or less thorough.

Micropropositions, Macropropositions, and Gist

Returning to Kintsch and van Dijk's (1978) conceptualization of text comprehension, if initial comprehension is in some way incomplete, then the deeper understanding that follows from integrating the new material with existing knowledge structures itself will be incomplete, flawed, or altogether nonexistent.

As an analogy, it is as if a text-based advertisement is giving the reader "directions" to a specific mental representation. The better the directions—especially important points—the higher the probability that the reader will end up in the correct place. If important points (e.g., "Turn left on Main Street") are insufficiently encoded (e.g., "Turn left somewhere"), then it follows that the appropriate mental representation will not be achieved. Subsequently, one would expect it to be more difficult to recall a message if it were improperly encoded, and the salient points of an ad can hardly be persuasive if they are not encoded or comprehended. This conceptualization is supported by Kintsch and van Dijk's (1978) theory of text comprehension, Thorson and Snyder's (1984) ad language model that was derived from Kintsch and van Dijk's model, and computational models of semantics that view cognition as patterns of activation across a distributed network of neurons (McClelland & Rogers, 2003).

Adopting the nomenclature from Kintsch and van Dijk's model of text comprehension (1978), most of the psycholinguistic research in marketing communications exploring syntactic effects deals with texts at the micropropositional level. Micropropositions are strung together to form the surface structure of texts, and they represent several kinds of word and morpheme combinations and relationships, including noun-verb phrases, verb-object phrases, verb-adverb relationships, modifier-modified relationships, arguments, predicates, quantifiers, and so on. At the next level of meaning, readers form inferences about important points or themes, which are called macropropositions. Although van Dijk and Kintsch (1983) articulate complex rules for determining macropropositions, they may also generally be indentified by selecting "the most typical sentence in the section" (Kintsch, 2002, p. 166). Finally, readers form a gist (or summary) representation of the text as a whole (van Dijk & Kintsch, 1983).

At the micropropositional level, complex sentences in which the structures of embedded clauses and noun phrases are the same have been shown to result in poorer comprehension than complex sentences in which clause and phrase structures differ (Gordon, Hendrick, & Johnson, 2001). However, textual approaches that register as "fresh" also are less familiar by definition, and prior research has confirmed that passages with unfamiliar words take longer to read (Graesser & Riha, 1984). Other studies have shown that processing time increases whenever readers encounter new nouns (Kintsch, Kozminsky, Streby, McKoon, & Keenan, 1975). Thus, attempts to introduce new information or bend the rules of grammar almost by definition make the ad more difficult to encode and comprehend. Thus, we see that the copywriter is walking a difficult line. Ads with no novelty will be lost in the clutter. Ads with too much novelty will not be encoded.

Returning our focus to global examinations of texts, the complexity or difficulty of the text as a whole, which is related to the number of concepts presented and the repetition of concepts (cf. Luna, 2005), also plays a role in readers' abilities to recall textual information (cf. Kintsch et al., 1975). Difficult texts have also been shown to require more cognitive processing capacity as evidenced by longer secondary reaction times (Inhoff & Fleming, 1989).

The Given–New Framework for Sentence Comprehension and Consumer-Level Variables

In the research already outlined, however, the amount of information readers already knew about a subject did not vary. Yet, an existing knowledge base that can be applied to the understanding of new information appears to be one of the key dimensions of expertise. The lack of such a knowledge base, then, presents a barrier to comprehension of new information for novices. Haviland and Clark (1974) explain that "the listener, in comprehending a sentence, first searches memory for antecedent information that matches the sentence's Given information; he then revises memory by attaching the New information to that antecedent" (p. 512). In

Haviland and Clark's given–new conceptualization, the ability to recall new information is dependent on the presence of related information (or a schema) in long-term memory to which the new information can be attached. If such a structure does not already exist in the reader's memory, however, the new information will either be lost or a new structure must be developed. Further, evidence now suggests the location of given information in a text is also important, with the distance between given information and its referent influencing complexity as well (Warren & Gibson, 2002).

Because existing schemas enhance the reader's ability to retain relevant new information and discard irrelevant information, readers who are essentially in the process of constructing new schemas to handle new information may lack the filtering capability to distinguish between relevant and irrelevant information. Inefficient encoding of information can then result in retrieval difficulties (Kintsch & Vipond, 1979). Thus, we again see a case where individual difference variables among consumers should interact with the syntactic structure and semantic composition of an advertisement to affect how well the ad is processed. We will be better able to predict these interactions if we investigate both global and local features of advertising copy. These interactions, we argue, should be best detected at the sentence level.

WHERE SENTENCE-LEVEL EFFECTS FIT IN MARKETING COMMUNICATIONS RESEARCH

Copy Testing

The goal of copy testing research is to compare the effectiveness of an ad relative to alternative ads or to preestablished criteria for predicting how successful the ad will be prior to placement in media. "One thing that most copy-research professionals agree on is that copy testing works—that it does relate to sales" (Haley & Baldinger, 1991, p. 27). What professionals and academics do not agree on when it comes to copy testing, however, are which techniques and measures are most predictive for testing persuasion or other communication measures. Although copy testing research is often concerned with evaluating an ad as a whole, headline and copy block variations in different versions of individual ads are often tested as well.

Historically, advertising copywriters and researchers have espoused the virtues of simplicity in advertising copy, arguing that simple text is easier to comprehend and therefore more likely to persuade its intended audience (Abruzzini, 1967). Such principles remain commonly accepted. Advertising textbook writers still caution students that advertising "copy should be as easy to understand as possible" and to use "short, familiar words and short sentences" (Wells, Burnett, & Moriarty, 1995, p. 447). And, professionally, copy testing methods such as the Cloze procedure, Starch scores, and the Fog reading index have been used for decades to gauge the readability of advertising texts, with easier texts resulting in "better" scores.

Some of these copy testing methods were originally developed in linguistic and educational psychology research (e.g., The Dale–Chall formula, the Fog index) for evaluating reading skills and school textbooks. Not surprisingly, psycholinguistic research has generally shown that simpler, less complex text passages are better comprehended and more easily recalled than difficult text passages (e.g., Kintsch et al., 1975). Similarly, studies that have manipulated reading difficulty over an entire passage have also indicated that as the overall level of reading difficulty increases in a text, demands on cognitive processing capacity increase as well (Inhoff & Fleming, 1989).

Global Copy Effects and Readability

Yet, some contradictory findings have emerged to indicate that, at least in some situations, simple copy does not always yield the best results. R. E. Anderson and Jolson (1980) manipulated the level of technical language in camera advertisements and in general found that nontechnical ads produced more favorable evaluations from participants low in product knowledge, and technical ads produced more favorable evaluations from participants high in product knowledge. This study is one in a series that has found interesting interactions between linguistic factors in an advertisement and individual difference variables among consumers.

In another seemingly contradictory study, Macklin, Bruvold, and Shea (1985) found no differences in recall, attitudinal judgments, or purchase intent for three different readability versions of a print ad. Results from both these studies should be interpreted with caution, however, because only one stimulus was used in each case. This inconsistency among studies illustrates exactly why it is difficult to make normative assumptions about the simplicity of advertising copy.

Wesson (1989) sought to further examine the "simple" copy results of Macklin et al. (1985) using field data. He found a curvilinear relationship between readability and Starch recall (a field-testing measure of the percentage of people who actually read an ad in a particular magazine). Ads with both lowest and highest grade-level scores (i.e., Gunning Readability Index) had higher Starch scores than ads with moderate readability scores. Wesson suggested these results may have been due to greater attention allocated toward and greater cognitive involvement with the higher complexity texts. Chebat et al. (2003) also found evidence that low readability mitigates argument strength, regardless of the reader's level of involvement, and suggested that a reader's linguistic ability was the crucial factor in determining language-level effects.

In a procedure similar to that of Wesson (1989), Chamblee, Gilmore, Thomas, and Soldow (1993) looked more specifically at local complexity and found that "type-token ratio" scores (a text difficulty measure that takes into account the uniqueness of words within a text) were significantly correlated with Starch readership scores in a study looking at ad readership in *Time* magazine and *Reader's Digest*. Similarly, Hunt, Kernan, and Bonfield (1992) found that ad texts that presented atypical (compared to typical) arguments resulted in deeper processing of the overall advertising message.

More recently, Phillips (2000) advanced another perspective on the idea that there are benefits to creating ads that require readers to expend some mental effort. She found that headlines that give clues to the meanings of visual metaphors had both high levels of comprehension and liking; ads in which the headlines fully explained the metaphors, however, (and thus required no effort to process) were not well liked.

We extended the work by R. E. Anderson and Jolson (1980) and found that when technical language in advertisements was not accompanied by explanatory context (i.e., making the ad more difficult to read), message comprehension and support arguing suffered compared to when such context was provided (Bradley & Meeds, 2004). This did not directly translate to attitudes, however, but was moderated by need for cognition (NFC; Cacioppo & Petty, 1982). For high-NFC individuals, the comprehensibility of technical language had no effect on attitudes. However, for low-NFC participants, attitudes suffered when no context was provided to make ads more comprehensible and were enhanced when context was provided. Additionally, Meeds (2004) found that how consumer knowledge is operationalized affects consumer ratings of technical ads, with consumers high in objective product knowledge being a better predictor of product attribute perceptions such as durability and difficulty of use, whereas self-assessed knowledge was a better predictor of general cognitive responses and attitudinal evaluations. Given that these studies controlled copy block length, these important local differences in copy are likely to have been missed by a global complexity measure such as Flesch or Gunning. That is, the sentence length and average number of syllables were equivalent, however, the semantic content within that similar structure differed markedly at key points.

A more recent field testing measure found that increasing complexity in broadcast ad copy hurt ad recall (Lowrey, 2006). This contrasts with Wesson's (1989) curvilinear results with magazine ad readability. Particularly interesting with the Lowrey data is that the field study was paired with a laboratory experiment that replicated the initial results. However, the laboratory study found a moderating role of involvement. Complexity negatively affected recall memory only for those participants low in product involvement (Lowrey, 2006). Although product involvement and need for cognition are distinct concepts, these results echo that of Bradley and Meeds (2004): When there is not some supplemental reason for consumers to plod through a less readable or comprehensible ad, memory and attitudes will suffer.

Lexical Effects

Text-level factors often interact with other consumer-level variables in the advertising language research as well. Heller and Areni (2004) found that conditional indicatives (i.e., words such as "because," "since," "however," and "but," that are used as relational cues to link clauses, sentences, and arguments) had a negative effect on comprehension and acceptance when they were used in propositions that contradicted consumers' preexisting beliefs about product attributes. Similarly, Luna's (2005) research indicates that repetition of verbal as well as pictorial cues help establish referents and continuity among different elements of an ad to enhance comprehension.

Syntactic Effects

Two relevant studies have looked at the persuasive effects of syntactic manipulations in advertising copy. For broadcast ads, Lowrey (1998) found that syntactic complexity adversely affected memory measures, but did not affect attitudinal measures. In a follow-up experiment using print stimuli, however, effects of syntactic complexity were moderated by motivation to process. Bradley and Meeds (2002), in an experiment involving low, medium, and high syntactic complexity in ad slogans, found no differences for recognition memory, but higher recall and attitudes for moderately complex slogans.

Levels of Analysis

These studies demonstrate that the relationship between an advertisement's linguistic structure and subsequent memory and attitude change is neither simple nor linear. And even within this inconsistent literature, when a result is replicated within (e.g., Lowrey, 2006) or across studies (e.g., Bradley & Meeds, 2004; Meeds, 1999), the effect sizes (when reported) are generally small, with percentages of variance explained for readability or comprehensibility measures typically ranging from about 3% to about 15%.

In general, however, main effects across this body of consumer research are consistent with the general findings of psycholinguistic research—that more readable text is better remembered and understood. This would seem to support the traditional "simpler is better" approach to marketing communications copy. But, there are also many notable exceptions in the extant literature. Several are due to consumer-level variables such as involvement, motivation to process, need for cognition, or consumer knowledge (e.g., R. E. Anderson & Jolson, 1980; Bradley & Meeds, 2004; Chebat et al., 2003; Lowrey, in press; Meeds, 2004). Others, however, are reported as main effects, with some level of complexity producing more favorable persuasive effects (e.g., Bradley & Meeds, 2002; Chamblee et al., 1993; Hunt, Kernan, & Bonfield, 1992; Phillips, 2000). And, in a few others (e.g., Bradley & Meeds, 2002; Wesson, 1989), the curvilinear relationships suggested by the results actually arc in opposite curves.

One plausible explanation for the contradictory findings is that the differences in results across studies could be due to differences in the level at which complexity is operationalized. Specifically, results appear to be more inconsistent at broader levels of analysis. At the global level, if curvilinear relationships between complexity and comprehension are real and not artifacts of measurement, differential results may be influenced by where different researchers have opted to place their operationalizations of complexity along the high-to-low complexity continuum. Alternatively, and perhaps compellingly, findings at the syntactic (or within-sentence level) appear somewhat more consistent.

In any event, explaining language complexity effects in marketing communications is turning out to be a complex process in itself. Both the scholar and practitioner are left with a series of somewhat confusing studies that fail to make clear and reliable predictions for copywriting. Given the variety of approaches investigators have used to examine the role of language in advertising and marketing communications, and the different levels of analysis that have been explored, we lack the operational and methodological consistency to draw firm conclusions about how consumers process these persuasive messages.

However, these studies, along with our past work, suggest that both local and global properties of copy, as well as consumer-level variables, have substantial psycholinguistic effects. It seems clear then, that advertising copy testing procedures that investigate how advertisements are processed and determine which specific points are important to different consumers (in addition to gathering attitudinal and behavioral outcomes) are needed if investigators are interested in further isolating and ultimately explaining these kinds of interactions between consumers and the language contained in the advertisements they read. Given the somewhat more consistent findings of studies investigating within-sentence (as opposed to global) effects, and the lack of marketing communications research investigating language effects from a propositional framework, it appears that more extensive research using sentence-level approaches in particular is warranted.

SENTENCE IMPORTANCE RATINGS

Although much of the aforementioned discussion on advertising copy complexity research has focused on varying levels of analysis for independent variables (e.g., global copy level vs. syntactic level), we have paid less attention to levels of analysis for dependent variables. However, dependent variables in marketing communications also follow a hierarchy that meshes with independent variable levels of analyses. In particular, we tend to measure dependent variables along a micro- to macro-continuum, ranging from lower order variables (e.g., attention, perception, and memory) to midlevel variables (e.g., cognitive responses and sales point registration) to higher order variables (e.g., attitudes and purchase intent). Our contention is that traditional persuasion measures (e.g., attitude toward the ad, attitude toward the brand, and purchase intent) are most appropriate for research using global copy approaches.

Conversely, although some lower level memory measures are conceptually appropriate for lexical, syntactic, and sentence-level analyses, recognition measures are prone to ceiling effects in immediate posttests, and recall measures are prone to floor effects in delayed posttests. And, given the implications of propositionally focused pyscholinguistic models of comprehension, measuring what people remember from a communication seems less important than measuring what they understand or infer.

The sentence importance ratings task provides a direct measure of the parts of a persuasive text that readers find most important or salient. A practical advantage of the sentence importance rating data collection protocol is its simplicity. After an initial reading of a text, readers are given a pencil-and-paper questionnaire with the sentences of that text presented in random order, which asks the readers to provide a rank-order rating of each sentence's relative importance in the text. Such importance ratings have predicted recall in general texts (Isakson & Spyridakis, 2003), and contextual sentences in ads have been rated as more important than noncontextual sentences (Meeds, 1998). Although originally used to determine how well readers could identify macropropositional or gist sentences (Kieras, 1985), the instructions of the protocol can be easily adapted to focus readers' evaluations on benefits, product features, main sales points, or themes.

Primarily, we see sentence-importance ratings as a useful ancillary copy testing technique, not a replacement for traditional measures. Even though we believe sentence importance ratings are a promising tool for propositional level testing, they do not measure persuasion, attitudes, or even readability. They may also be prone to confounds due to sentence length (i.e., long sentences might intuitively seem to be more important to readers). Despite these limitations, however, they provide a parsimonious way for determining if key communication points are perceived as intended.

AN EXPLORATORY TEST FOR SENTENCE IMPORTANCE RATINGS AND IMPLICATIONS FOR FUTURE RESEARCH

In an ongoing study empirically investigating sentence importance ratings, we prepared advertisements for three product categories (tooth whitening paste, renter's insurance, and an MP3 player; Meeds & Bradley, 2005). Each ad had a 9-sentence copy block. Each copy block was written with a most important benefit sentence and a most important feature sentence. After reading the ads and completing a distraction task, participants were given a list of the sentences for each ad presented in random order. They were then asked to rate the importance of each sentence from highest to lowest (see Appendix A). As predicted, participants rated the most important benefit and feature sentences as significantly more important than the other sentences in the copy block.

This initial test provides evidence that there is some psychological reality to sentence importance in the minds of consumers. Global measures of advertising comprehension and recall have proven effective in predicting memory for advertisements. However, these measures usually predict a relatively small portion of variance in recall or recognition memory, suggesting that other measures of copy testing can help to predict the field effectiveness of an advertisement.

SUMMARY AND IMPLICATIONS

Although a given copy block may contain many sentences, there is almost certainly a central focus or thesis of the advertisement as a whole. That is, there is a key point—or gist—to the advertisement. It is difficult or impossible to evenly spread a key point across an entire copy block. Instead, particular sentences are likely to be the most important enumerations of key features and benefits. A campaign almost assuredly emphasizes key points. A recent trade magazine used the example of the upstart Federal Express trying to position itself as an "overnight" service in contrast to the U.S. Postal Service® (Reis, 2005). FedEx® captured that position with the slogan, "When it absolutely, positively has to be there overnight." However, the copywriter intending for that slogan to be important a priori could not guarantee that it would end up being important in the minds of consumers. That is, an advertiser intending to convey a particular message hardly guarantees that the given message will be perceived. And we argue that this possible misconception is most dangerous with the most important features and benefits to be conveyed. If these points fail to register as important in the minds of consumers, then the entire point of the ad is likely to be missed, and the ad is likely to fail. Sentence importance ratings offer a simple, time-efficient test of how well the message received corresponds with the message that was sent (e.g., Shannon, 1948).

Words convey concepts, and entire ads convey multiple ideas. But, much of the work of communicating ideas happens at the sentence level. Salient points are communicated—or fail to be—at the sentence level. During the strategy process, marketers identify specific ideas to be conveyed in the ad. We convey these ideas at the sentence level. Concepts alone are insufficient. As we illustrated with the driving directions example, encoding and comprehending the concepts of "turn," "left," and "street" are crucial. However, if the meaningful relations between these concepts are insufficiently encoded, then the reader walks away with an incomplete and inadequate message. Psycholinguistic research into advertising has yielded an interesting, yet inconsistent, body of work. These inconsistencies largely preclude any normative guidelines for copywriting. By conceptualizing the sentence as the key conveyer of meaning, we argue that a program of research will help clear up these inconsistencies and clarify an easy-to-use copy testing tool that allows advertisers not only to gauge the potential effectiveness of an ad but provides a fine-tuned diagnostic tool that both identifies problems in ad language and identifies the precise location of the problem.

REFERENCES

Abruzzini, P. (1967). Measuring language difficulty in advertising copy. *Journal of Marketing, 31*, 22–25.

Anderson, J. R., Budiu, R., & Reder, L. M. (2001). A theory of sentence memory as part of a general theory of memory. *Journal of Memory and Language, 45,* 337–367.

Anderson, R. E., & Jolson, M. A. (1980). Technical wording in advertising: Implications for market segmentation. *Journal of Marketing, 44,* 57–66.

Bradley, S. D., & Meeds, R. (2002). Surface-structure transformations and advertising slogans: The case for moderate syntactic complexity. *Psychology and Marketing, 19,* 595–619.

Bradley, S. D., & Meeds, R. (2004). The effects of sentence-level context, prior word knowledge, and need for cognition on information processing of technical language in print ads. *Journal of Consumer Psychology, 14,* 291–302.

Cacioppo, J. T., & Petty, R. E. (1982). The need for cognition. *Journal of Personality and Social Psychology, 42,* 116–131.

Caplan, D., & Waters, G. S. (1999). Verbal working memory and sentence comprehension. *Behavioral and Brain Sciences, 22,* 77–126.

Chamblee, R., Gilmore, R., Thomas, G., & Soldow, G. (1993). When copy complexity can help ad readership. *Journal of Advertising, 33,* 23–28.

Chebat, J. C., Gelinas-Chebat, C., Hombourger, S., & Woodside, A.G. (2003). Testing consumers' motivation and linguistic ability as moderators of advertising readability. *Psychology and Marketing, 20,* 599–624.

Chomsky, N. (1957). *Syntactic structures.* The Hague: Mouton.

Chomsky, N. (1959). Review of verbal behavior by B. F. Skinner. *Language, 35,* 26–58.

Fiebach, C. J., Schlesewsky, M., & Friederici, A. D. (2001). Syntactic working memory and establishment of filler-gap dependencies: Insights from ERPs and fMRI. *Journal of Psycholinguistic Research, 30,* 321–338.

Gordon, P. C., Hendrick, R., & Johnson, M. (2001). Memory interference during language processing. *Journal of Experimental Psychology: Learning, Memory and Cognition, 27,* 1411–1423.

Graesser, A. C., & Riha, J. R. (1984). An application of multiple regression techniques to sentence reading times. In D. E. Kieras & M. A. Just (Eds.), *New methods in reading comprehension research* (pp. 183–218). Hillsdale, NJ: Lawrence Erlbaum Associates.

Haley, R. I., & Baldinger, A. L. (1991). The ARF copy research validity project. *Journal of Advertising Research, 21,* 11–32.

Haviland, S. E., & Clark, H. H. (1974). What's new? Acquiring new information as a process in comprehension. *Journal of Verbal Learning and Verbal Behavior, 13,* 512–521.

Heller, E., & Areni, C. S. (2004). The effects of conditional indicative language on the comprehension and acceptance of advertising claims. *Journal of Marketing Communications, 10,* 229–240.

Huang, W., Schrank, H., & Dubinsky, A. J. (2004). Effect of brand name on consumers' risk perceptions of online shopping. *Journal of Consumer Behaviour, 4,* 40–50.

Hunt, J. M., Kernan, J. B., & Bonfield, E. H. (1992). Memory structure in the processing of advertising messages: How is unusual information represented? *Journal of Psychology: Interdisciplinary and Applied, 126,* 343–356.

Inhoff, A. W., & Fleming, K. (1989). Probe-detection times during the reading of easy and difficult text. *Journal of Experimental Psychology: Learning, Memory, and Cognition, 15,* 339–351.

Isakson, C. S., & Spyridakis, J. H. (2003). The influence of semantics and syntax on what readers remember. *Technical Communication, 50,* 538–553.

Isen, A. M., Labroo, A. A., & Durlach, P. (2004). The influence of product and brand name on positive affect: Implicit and explicit measures. *Motivation and Emotion, 28,* 48–63.

Kieras, D. E. (1985). Thematic processes in the comprehension of technical prose. In B. K. Britton & J. B. Black (Eds.), *Understanding expository text: A theoretical and practical handbook for analyzing explanatory text* (pp. 89–107). Hillsdale, NJ: Lawrence Erlbaum Associates.

Kintsch, W. (1988). The role of knowledge in discourse comprehension: A construction-integration model. *Psychological Review, 95,* 163–182.

Kintsch, W. (2002). On the notions of theme and topic in psychological process models of text comprehension. In M. Louwerse & W. van Peer (Eds.), *Thematics: Interdisciplinary studies* (pp. 157–170). Amsterdam: Benjamins.

Kintsch, W., Kozminsky, E., Streby, W. J., McKoon, G., & Keenan, J. M. (1975). Comprehension and recall of text as a function of content variables. *Journal of Verbal Learning and Verbal Behavior,* 14, 196–214.

Kintsch, W., & van Dijk, T. A. (1978). Toward a model of text comprehension and production. *Psychological Review,* 85, 363–394.

Kintsch, W., & Vipond, D. (1979). Reading comprehension and readability in educational practice and psychological theory. In L. G. Nillson (Ed.), *Perspectives on memory research* (pp. 329–365). Hillsdale, NJ: Lawrence Erlbaum Associates.

Lowrey, T. M. (1998). The effects of syntactic complexity on advertising persuasiveness. *Journal of Consumer Psychology, 7,* 187–206.

Lowrey, T. M. (2006). The relation between script complexity and commercial memorability. *Journal of Advertising, 35*(3), 7–15.

Lowrey, T. M., Shrum, L. J., & Dubitsky, T. M. (2003). The relation between brand-name linguistic characteristics and brand-name memory. *Journal of Advertising, 32*(3), 7–17.

Luna, D. (2005). Integrating ad information: A text-processing perspective. *Journal of Consumer Psychology, 15,* 38–51.

Macklin, M. C., Bruvold, N. T., & Shea, C. L. (1985). Is it always as simple as "keep it simple!"? *Journal of Advertising, 14*(4), 28–35.

Malaviya, P., Kisielius, J., & Sternthal, B. (1996). The effect of type of elaboration on advertisement processing and judgment. *Journal of Marketing Research, 33*(4), 410–421.

McClelland, J. L., & Rogers, T. T. (2003). The parallel distributed processing approach to semantic cognition. *Nature Neuroscience, 4,* 310–322.

Meeds, R. (1998, August). *Using sentence importance ratings for investigating effectiveness of advertising copy blocks: A preliminary test.* Paper presented at the annual meeting of the Association for Education in Journalism and Mass Communication, Baltimore, MD.

Meeds, R. (1999, March). *The effects of technical language and sentence-level context on consumers' processing of ad copy for high-tech products.* Paper presented at the meeting of the American Academy of Advertising, Albuquerque, NM.

Meeds, R. (2004). Cognitive and attitudinal effects of technical advertising copy: The roles of gender, self-assessed and objective consumer knowledge. *International Journal of Advertising, 23,* 309–336.

Meeds, R., & Bradley, S. D. (2005). [Semantic differential sentence importance ratings]. Unpublished raw data.

Phillips, B. (2000). The impact of verbal anchoring on consumer response to image ads. *Journal of Advertising, 29*(1), 15–24.

Pollatsek, A., & Rayner, K. (1989). Reading. In M. Posner (Ed.), *Foundations of cognitive science* (pp. 401–436). Cambridge, MA: MIT Press.

Raney, G. E. (1993). Monitoring changes in cognitive load during reading: An event-related brain potential and reaction-time analysis. *Journal of Experimental Psychology: Learning, Memory, and Cognition, 19,* 51–69.

Rayner, K., & Pollatsek, A. (1989). *The psychology of reading.* Englewood Cliffs, NJ: Prentice-Hall.

Reis, A. (2005, July 11). Recipe for branding success: One word, wrapped in bacon. *Advertising Age, 76,* 16.

Sanford, A. J., & Sturt, P. (2002). Depth of processing in language comprehension: Not noticing the evidence. *Trends in Cognitive Sciences, 6,* 382–386.

Sanford, A. J. S., Sanford, A. J., Filik, R., & Molle, J. (2005). Depth of lexical-semantic processing and sentential load. *Journal of Memory and Language 53*, 378–396.

Shannon, C. E. (1948). A mathematical theory of communication. *The Bell System Technical Journal, 27*, 379–423, 623–656.

Sturt, P., Sanford, A. J., Stewart, A., & Dawdiak, E. (2004). Linguistic focus and good-enough representations: An application of the change-detection paradigm. *Psychonomic Bulletin and Review, 11*, 882–888.

Tabor, W., & Tanenhaus, M. K. (1999). Dynamical models of sentence processing. *Cognitive Science, 23*, 491–515.

Thorson, E., & Snyder, R. (1984). Viewer recall of television commercials: Prediction for the propositional structure of commercial scripts. *Journal of Marketing Research, 21*, 127–136.

Townsend, D. J., & Bever, T. G. (2001). *Sentence comprehension: The integration of habits and rules.* Cambridge, MA: MIT Press.

van Dijk, T. A., & Kintsch, W. (1983). *Strategies of discourse comprehension.* New York: Academic Press.

Van Orden, G. C., Johnston, J. C., & Hale, B. L. (1988). Word identification in reading proceeds from spelling to sound to meaning. *Journal of Experimental Psychology: Learning, Memory, and Cognition, 14*, 371–386.

Vosse, T., & Kempen, G. (2000). Syntactic structure assembly in human parsing: A computational model based on competitive inhibition and a lexicalist grammar. *Cognition, 75*, 105–143.

Warren, T., & Gibson, E. (2002). The influence of referential processing on sentence complexity. *Cognition, 85*, 79–112.

Wells, W., Burnett, J., & Moriarty, S. (1995). *Advertising principles and practice* (3rd. ed.). Englewood Cliffs, NJ: Prentice-Hall.

Wesson, D. A. (1989). Readability as a factor in magazine ad copy recall. *Journalism Quarterly, 66*, 715–718.

APPENDIX A:
SAMPLE AD AND SENTENCE IMPORTANCE RATING
QUESTIONNAIRE

Smile ... with
Dentabrite Tooth Whitening Strips.

Your smile is one of the first things people notice about you. Dentabrite Strips will help you get that bright, confident smile you want people to see. Dentists agree that Dentabrite Strips are easy to use and effective over a short period of time. Whitening toothpastes only touch surface stains, but Dentabrite Strips hold their enamel-safe, powerful whitening gel next to your teeth, giving them time to erase even deep-down stains. Plus, while they take the time to work, they don't take your time. Going to the dentist to get your teeth whitened is time consuming and expensive. But you can apply Dentabrite Strips almost anywhere. Dentabrite Strips—they're something to smile about.

Below you will find, in random order, the eight sentences that appeared in the copy block portion of the Dentabrite Tooth Whitening Strips ad you just read. Please rank each sentence twice.

In the first column, rank each sentence in terms of how important it was for you in understanding the main benefit of the product being advertised. The main benefit is something that communicates what the product will do for you or how it will help you. Rank the most important sentence as #1 and the least important sentence as #8. Please use each rank only once.

In the second column, rank each sentence in terms of how important it was for you in understanding the main product feature of the product being advertised. The main product feature is something that communicates what the product does or how it works. Rank the most important sentence as #1 and the least important sentence as #8. Please use each rank only once.

	Main benefit rank	Main feature rank
Plus, while they take the time to work, they don't take your time.	_____	_____
But you can apply Dentabrite Strips almost anywhere.	_____	_____
Your smile is one of the first things people notice about you.	_____	_____
Going to the dentist to get your teeth whitened is time consuming and expensive.	_____	_____
Whitening toothpastes only touch surface stains, but Dentabrite Strips hold their enamel-safe, powerful whitening gel next to your teeth, giving them time to erase even deep-down stains.	_____	_____
Dentabrite Strips–they're something to smile about.	_____	_____
Dentists agree that Dentabrite Strips are easy to use and effective over a short period of time.	_____	_____
Dentabrite Strips will help you get that bright, confident smile you want people to see.	_____	_____

CHAPTER 7

The Use and Abuse of Polysemy in Marketing Communications

Claudiu V. Dimofte
Georgetown University

Richard F. Yalch
University of Washington

This chapter assesses the practice of using polysemous advertising slogans and words in marketing communications. *Polysemy* is the property of having multiple meanings. For example, Michelin's slogan argues that their brand should be your choice "Because so much is riding on your tires," thus communicating the literal statement that tires must support the weight of an automobile but also a figurative statement that the driver and passengers' physical safety depends on the reliability of the tires, a fact that is critical when these passengers are your children (as in the company's ads). We argue that this multiplicity of meanings makes communications employing polysemous language more complex, thereby potentially more risky as well as more effective. Conceptual frameworks from cognitive psychology, linguistics, pragmatics, and marketing theory are discussed toward enhancing our understanding of how consumers comprehend marketing communications (in particular brand slogans) that have multiple meanings (i.e., are polysemous).

This review begins with a look at current communications practices to determine the motivation and prevalence of polysemous slogans. Next, relevant literature regarding consumer processing of ambiguous language is reviewed to identify message, context, and audience characteristics that explain and predict what meaning(s) will be taken from such messages. This discussion serves as the basis for a new perspective on consumers' processing of polysemous advertising slogans that includes the development of an individual difference measure for assessing one's ability to access more than one meaning. The chapter ends with recommendations regarding what marketers should consider when using polysemous slogans and words in their communications.

POLYSEMY AND MARKETING

As the most powerful linguistic cue associated with its brand name, a brand's advertising slogan represents a priming device that conveys information and occupies a central place in the consumer's memory space. The fact that the mere announcement of a novel slogan has a direct positive impact on company ROI (Mathur & Mathur, 1995) confirms the critical importance of these promotional vehicles.[1] Besides being useful as mnemonic devices, the expressions or sentences making up a slogan often constitute positioning statements that allow marketers to succinctly communicate critical and distinct product benefits. At issue is whether the benefits marketers intend to communicate are the same as the benefits received by consumers when the slogans have both literal and figurative meanings.

Effective communications between individuals rely on a shared understanding of the meaning of the words being uttered (Grice, 1975). Marketers often develop their messages by testing them with the intended audience to ascertain that the intended meaning is in fact what is being inferred. In such a framework, one would expect that literal wording would be favored because it is less likely to be misinterpreted than figurative wording. However, it is nowadays a common marketplace occurrence to observe brand advertising that makes use of linguistic artifices or rhetorical devices (e.g., anaphora, metaphor, analogy, and antithesis), many employing figurative language. For example, Leigh (1994) examined the headlines of 2,183 print advertisements and reported that about three fourths used one or more figures of speech (pun, irony, paradox, hyperbole, etc.). Although he did not break out the number that could be considered polysemous, he found that puns, which usually take advantage of a polysemous quality, were one of the most frequently used forms of figurative language—observed in 17% of the headlines.

Our own examination of the advertising slogans used by the top 100 global brands, as identified in *Business Week,* revealed that numerous brands used a polysemous statement.[2] Examples include GE®'s "We Bring Good Things to Life" (recently changed to "Imagination at Work") and Oracle's "Information Driven." Polysemy is also a popular technique for advertisers who are not among the world's largest. Table 7.1 provides many recent examples with descriptions of the literal and figurative meanings that can be derived from each one. What explains polysemy's popularity with marketing communicators?

Rejecting popular interpretations of Grice's shared understanding theories that favor unambiguous language, Kittay (1987) advocated "purposive ambiguity" as a communications strategy. Polysemy is an example of ambiguity that reinforces se-

---

[1]Another testament to their power is that the protection of brand slogans has become increasingly important. Accordingly, "the user of the slogan should keep detailed records and notes as well as copies of all uses of the slogan in order to document claims of 'secondary meaning,' both for purposes of federal registration as well as its claims under unfair competition and common law trademark laws" (Hoffman, 2001).

[2]Among Business Week's top 100 most valuable brands in the United States, 15% of the top 35 employ polysemous slogans, compared to only 3% of the remaining 65 brands.

TABLE 7.1

Examples of Polysemous Advertising Slogans and Their Meanings

BRAND	SLOGAN	BENEFITS IMPLIED
3M Post-It®	Ideas that stick.	Innovative products that dominate their market. (F) Jot down your ideas and stick the note anywhere. (L)
Ambien® Sleeping Pills	Works like a dream.	Very effective medicine. (F) It provides you with a natural, dreaming sleep. (L)
America's Best™ Eyewear	The lowest price in sight!	No better deal in vision services. (F) The best offer in the industry. (L)
Crest® SpinBrush	A better spin on clean!	Get clean teeth in a new way. (F) The brush bristles now have spinning action. (L)
Folgers® Coffee	It's uncanny.	Extraordinary quality. (F) Now comes in new plastic container. (L)
French's® Mustard	Nothing cuts the mustard like French's	Best product in its category. (F) New packaging reduces spills. (L)
Fujifilm™	Get the picture.	Understand why quality film is important. (F) Finally take that difficult, fully detailed photo. (L)
Hoover® Vacuums	Deep down, you want Hoover.	This is the brand you personally prefer. (F) It is the best for deep carpet dirt. (L)
Michelin® Tires	Because so much is riding on your tires.	The tires you have make a big difference. (F) You carry a lot of precious things in your car. (L)

Note.   L = literal meaning, F = figurative meaning.

mantic links between associations in one's network of relevant thoughts, creates a social bond between the communicator and audience, and/or provides a transition to another line of thought. With regard to advertising, Kittay (1987) noted that "an utterance in which a single meaning cannot be specified ... draws attention to itself and thereby captures our attention" (p. 80). For the advertiser, there is the added benefit of being seen as creative and clever, not merely a huckster mindlessly reciting the desirable characteristics of the sponsor's product. This view is consistent with McQuarrie and Mick's (1999) definition of a rhetorical figure as "an artful deviation in the form taken by a statement." Their prior content analysis of 154 print ads from 3 issues of *People* magazine found that 86% used some form of figure of speech (McQuarrie & Mick, 1992). The advertising copywriter's rewards for using figurative language often extend beyond entertained consumers and a satisfied client to professional acclaim. For example, Shirley Polykoff's intentionally ambiguous 1956 slogan for Clairol®'s hair coloring products, "Does She or Doesn't She?"

was judged the key factor in the ninth greatest advertising campaign in the 20th century ("The top 100 advertising campaigns," 1999). Note that, in conceptual terms, polysemy is a relatively broad phenomenon that includes multiple meaning statements that are not merely plays on words (e.g., puns) or vehicles for comparisons (as in analogies), but manage to accommodate a variety of possible meanings (actual or inferred, positive or negative, humorous or not).

Beyond being generally more attention getting, entertaining, and professionally rewarding than plain language, what else do marketers know about polysemy and figurative language? Surprisingly, marketing practitioners and academic researchers have said little with few exceptions (e.g., Toncar & Munch, 2001). This is likely to change, as MacInnis (2004; among others, e.g., Zaltman, 2003) powerfully argued that bringing metaphoric thinking out into consciousness is an innovative way of expanding dimensional thinking. She further noted that relationships between constructs and the hypotheses developed from them are often well captured by conceptual models whose domains map perfectly onto intuitive and expressive metaphors (see Lakoff, 1995, for an extended discussion). Productivity as the "fruit" of hard work and customer relationship management as a way to "nurture" customer satisfaction are examples of language use that is both suggestive and easy to grasp (MacInnis, 2004), although in theoretical terms they describe different types of metaphor (see Phillips & McQuarrie, chap. 8 in this volume, for a more detailed discussion of conceptual and individual metaphor). As metaphoric thinking in general provides great insights, it is reasonable to explore its use by advertisers to aid consumers in understanding and learning about products and their features.

Although the use of polysemy in marketing appears to match its frequent occurrence in daily discourse, little research addressing literal polysemy resides in the consumer psychology literature. In general, perception and cognition research on the topic is restricted to the consideration of words as the quintessential units of scientific interest, whereas lexical ambiguity in broader terms (e.g., multiple meaning sentences addressed herein) is less commonly researched. The few relevant consumer studies have awarded more attention to visual metaphor, or other delivery-related issues (see Phillips & McQuarrie, 2004), whereas the present chapter looks at the theoretically novel case of how consumers comprehend polysemous brand slogans' multiple meanings, and the moderating role of the context for the advertisement. Because of the deficits in the scientific literature, this chapter draws heavily on the many studies (several unpublished) of polysemy that we have conducted over the past few years. They represent the most direct and extensive investigation of polysemy in marketing communications currently available.

THEORETICAL LITERATURE REVIEW

As an ambiguous form of communication, the meaning ascribed to a polysemous phrase is somewhat indeterminate. What factors affect the specific meaning or meanings, and in the case of multiple meanings, the order of meaning extraction?

Research on lexical and syntactic ambiguity resolution highlights the essential roles played by base frequency and context in individuals' selective access to meanings. In addition, recently completed work by Dimofte and Yalch (in press-b) identifies stable differences across individuals in their ability to access secondary meanings. Each factor is discussed next.

Frequency of Meaning

A major factor in determining what meaning is accessed or (in the case of multiple meanings) which is accessed first, is the base frequency with which a meaning is commonly used (Simpson, 1984). For example, in developing test phrases for one study, Dimofte (2004) presented subjects with several polysemous phrases without a context. Subjects were asked to list their first interpretation. The results showed clear differences across the polysemous phrases. For the phrase, "No One Comes Close," 76% first listed the figurative meaning of "not being as good as," whereas only 24% listed the literal meaning of "not being physically near." On the other hand, for the phrase, "Play With Fire," 78% listed the literal meaning of "avoiding handling a fire" first and only 22% listed the figurative meaning of "being involved with undesirable activities." For a third phrase, "Walk on Thin Ice," the results were nearly equivalent with 46% providing the literal meaning of not "going out on frozen water" and 54% the figurative meaning of "being careful of risky situations." The biased interpretation results can be seen as consequences of prior exposures, because individuals are more likely to have been exposed to the phrase "No One Comes Close" in boastful figurative advertisements and the phrase "Play With Fire" in parental literal warnings about matches and campfires.

Context

The reality of exposure to marketing uses of polysemy is that they do not occur in isolation but rather in a context. Thus, the Jackson Hewitt Tax Preparation slogan, "Get More in Return," is most likely to first trigger thoughts related to tax returns and only after some additional thinking be understood to also mean that the client will get more service in exchange for their fees. This will occur even though most persons (i.e., those who are not tax accountants) think of return in the more general sense of coming back rather than the specific sense of a tax return. In Dimofte's (2004) research of the three polysemous slogans mentioned earlier, he was able to influence their inferred meaning by pairing them with pictures that provided a context suggesting either the figurative or literal meaning. For example, the equibiased slogan, "With us, you're not playing with fire," was paired with a picture of someone using a gas barbeque rather than a charcoal one to suggest the literal meaning of avoiding starting real fires. For the figurative meaning, the slogan was paired with pictures of inferior competing products to suggest that one was taking less of a risk by choosing the sponsor's product.

Although we have used Dimofte's (2004) study to illustrate how either a figurative or literal meaning may be first accessed in exposure to a polysemous slogan (referred to as the primary meaning), the study was actually concerned with the effects of the secondary meanings on consumers' attitudes. The process by which individuals access more than one meaning remains unresolved. Swinney (1979) showed that in cases of equibiased ambiguous words (wherein each possible meaning has the same base frequency of use) lexical access makes available all the meanings, independent of context. Further, even in the case of contextual bias, Duffy, Morris, and Rayner (1988) found that a context that supports the less frequent meaning of a biased word only promotes that meaning to a limited extent. The context aids access to the low base frequency meaning but the high base frequency of the other meaning facilitates its retrieval. Based on this and other research, we concur with MacDonald, Pearlmutter, and Seidenberg's (1994) three conclusions: Frequency of meaning impacts word processing, contextual information can promote the activation of a specific meaning, but context does not eliminate the frequency effect.

In discussing the critical importance of context in understanding metaphor, Gildea and Glucksberg (1983) proposed that relatively little semantic input is required from the adjacent text in order for metaphor processing to be automatically initiated. The broader context often makes the figurative meaning salient to the individual with no immediate personal control over the comprehension process. However, if the message context strongly suggests the meaning intended by the advertiser but one counter to base frequencies, then two aspects come to mind. On the one hand, research suggests that the advertiser should not encounter too much difficulty manipulating consumers to interpret the promotional message in a way that makes a specific meaning more salient, and this should be particularly easy when there is equibiased ambiguity. On the other hand, as memory is constructive (see Loftus, 1996), it is conceptually possible that consumers might have an experience consistent with a sleeper effect. Over time, a potential interchange of the meanings might occur, whereby the out-of-context, high base frequency meaning might become better recalled than the in-context, low base frequency meaning. If so, this might substantially alter the consumer's delayed product judgments.

Individual Differences in Meaning Access

Individual differences across consumers play an important role in their ability to understand polysemy in general and to access one or more of the possible ad slogan meanings in particular. Physiological support for this is found in a recent report on stroke victims. Neuroscientists found that individuals who injured a discrete region on the left side of their brain were unable to understand or explain the figurative meaning of proverbs and metaphorical statements. Instead, they interpreted metaphorical statements such as "the grass is greener on the other side" as the literal judgment of the color of grass in two different locations (McGough, 2005). In studying how consumers comprehend ad messages depending on metaphor type (abstract vs. concrete) and brain hemispheric processing, Morgan and Reichert (1999) further illustrate how individual differences in verbal ability to comprehend and evaluate metaphorical language are important.

What is the process by which individuals determine the meaning of polysemous phrases? The dominant perspective on what has been termed the incoherence view of the metaphor considers that metaphors are "defective" if taken literally (Cacciari & Glucksberg, 1994). The earliest conceptual account of metaphorical speech processing and meaning access along these lines adopted a multistage view that essentially proposed that individuals invariably access the literal meaning first (Searle, 1979). A subsequent matching of this meaning against context in a search for appropriateness results in either acquisition of the meaning or its rejection followed by supplementary search for a match (see Fig. 7.1). After numerous empirical studies failed to support this rather tedious process, Verbrugge (1977) articulated the distinct view that it was erroneous to believe that the literal meaning is the first to be accessed merely because of its supposed cognitive simplicity, and that other factors (most importantly context) play a significant role as well. Glucksberg, Gildea, and Bookin (1982) were even more direct, proposing that the comprehension of metaphors is automatic and need not be mediated by literal meaning access.

Among the applied studies on the topic, McQuarrie and Mick (1999) examined the impact of several specific stylistic elements in advertising: rhyme, antithesis, metaphor, and pun. These elements were addressed in the form of visual rhetorical figures paralleling those found in language, and appeared both to produce more elaboration and to lead to more favorable attitudes toward the ad, without being

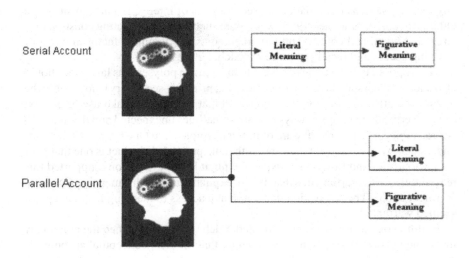

Figure 7.1.   Schematic view of meaning access debate.

more difficult to comprehend. However, these effects significantly diminished or even disappeared for those subjects lacking the capacity required to adequately appreciate the contemporary American ads under review, leading the authors to postulate cultural competency as an important mediating variable.

Roehm and Sternthal (2001) addressed the persuasive impact of analogies as promotional vehicles for novel products. Along a series of studies that proposed expertise and mood as moderating variables, the authors found analogies to be persuasive to the extent that consumers possessed the ability and the resources to map attributes of the base product onto the novel brand.

The apparent theme of these diverse studies of figurative language processing is that moderating variables addressing some sort of consumer proficiency ("cultural competency," "expertise," "attribute-mapping ability," etc.) are needed within any apt explanatory account on the topic.

NEW INSIGHTS IN POLYSEMY RESEARCH

Building on psychological research, Dimofte and Yalch (2003) addressed the role of meaning base frequency and context in terms of consumer reactions to polysemous advertising slogans. Balancing dominant meaning (literal–figurative dominant or equibiased) and contextual support, the following ad slogans were used: "No One Comes Close" referred to a Guardian home alarm system. "Stop Walking on Thin Ice" ads referred to a Kawasaki snowmobile, and finally "With Us, You're Not Playing With Fire" ads referred to a Pro-Chef® barbecue grill. Literal slogan meanings lead to improved attitudes and persuasion, suggesting that the use of figurative language may not necessarily benefit brand advertising. Personally relevant slogans (i.e., that addressed domains of interest to participants—see Ottati, Rhoads, & Graesser, 1999) were more successful in attracting consumer interest and favor, and context support emerged as the dominant factor in terms of meaning access and recall (Dimofte & Yalch, 2003).

We proposed that the issue of access to meaning in polysemous language should also address the issue of base frequencies (i.e., primary–secondary), not simply the literal–figurative dichotomy. We also found that consumers make use of context (i.e., advertisement copy) in ways that are sometimes unexpected and this may occur for subjects that were unaware of it. For example, "No One Comes Close" was understood by some subjects to express that the promoted product is one that people try to avoid, and [lower] subsequent explicit brand evaluations supported this reasoning even for participants that did not explicitly access this meaning (Dimofte & Yalch, 2003). The suggestion that automatic access to meaning may take place seemed warranted.

Building on these results, Dimofte and Yalch (in press-a) joined the previously mentioned debate in psychology by arguing that the rival conceptual accounts of meaning access (serial vs. parallel) could be accommodated into a joint framework with issues of implicit access to meaning at its core. Just and Carpenter (1992) proposed a particular theory of the way working memory capacity constrains comprehension. They argued that both processing and storage are mediated by activation, with total available amount in working memory varying across individuals. The larger capacity of some individuals allows them to cope better in cases of ambiguity, because it apparently permits them to access and maintain multiple interpretations. Dimofte and Yalch (in press-b), therefore, proposed that automatic access to meaning occurs for those individuals with benefit of such high capacity, but not for others. To pursue this account, Dimofte and Yalch (in press-b) developed and validated a novel measure of consumer access to meaning. This measure (SMAART – Secondary Meaning Access via the Automatic Route Test) looks at the occurrence of automatic access and has the advantage of capturing the cognitive processes involved as they happen, without relying on postexposure, recall-based inferences.[3]

The results of several subsequent experiments found empirical support for a novel theoretical account of meaning access that posits high-SMAARTS consumers to have immediate implicit access to multiple meanings of a polysemous expression. It was found that these individuals showed a proposed subtractive effect of dual meaning slogans with a negative secondary meaning, although this secondary meaning was not explicitly acknowledged (Dimofte & Yalch, in press-b). Thus automatic processing happens and—more importantly—measures of implicit processing/association are better equipped to capture and explain it. Moreover, this account posits that low-SMAARTS consumers engage in an affect-driven response to such expressions that lacks adequate understanding of meaning, and support was found for this hypothesis as well.

In one particular study, we provided participants with two versions of the same ad: One that had a literal slogan and one that had a figurative paraphrase thereof (with potentially positive–negative secondary meaning). Thus, participants viewed Minute Maid ads claiming to be "The Obvious Choice" / "The Natural Choice" and Mercedes-Benz ads with the slogans "Unlike Any Other" / "No One Comes Close." Results showed that a slogan with a positive secondary meaning (e.g., "The Natural Choice") provides a cumulative effect that improves consumer attitudes, whereas one that has even unintended, context-driven negative meanings ("No One Comes Close") leads to a subtractive effect that is detrimental to the brand. More interestingly, the automatic meaning access account for high-SMAART consumers was supported by these individuals' newly formed implicit associations (captured via the Implicit Associations Test; Greenwald, McGhee, & Schwartz, 1998), despite their lack of explicit awareness of having accessed the secondary meaning.

---

[3]This sentence verification procedure is designed to see if the availability of metaphorical meanings interferes with literal false decisions. In the procedure, subjects are requested to verify the literal truth of sentences of the type "Some X are Y." During the test block, response latencies (accurate to the millisecond) are measured for both random target sentences such as "Some cars are snails" (literally false but figuratively true) and random filler sentences such as "Some flowers are roses" (literally true) and "Some insects are roses" (literally false). The difference between latencies on metaphor and filler sentences ("incremental response time") is measured and used as a proxy for automatic comprehension.

In Dimofte (2004), one of the present authors provided participants with a brief essay that addressed the topic of regulating the labels of bottled water brands. The title of the article and its last line were "Reading between the lines of bottled water labels." Whereas the primary meaning of this tag line addressed the need to go beyond appearances when evaluating product quality, a secondary, literal meaning suggests the actual search for letters in between the rows of the writing. The ability to perform this is obviously dependent on the paragraph spacing of the article, which was set at about 1.5 lines (exactly 15 points). Consistent with expectations, low-SMAARTS generally showed higher liking for the article than high-SMAARTS individuals, whereas the post hoc assessment of paragraph spacing showed that high-SMAARTS participants engaged in significant overestimation. It is apparent that low-SMAARTS consumers engaged in an appreciation without comprehension process (see Gerrig & Healy, 1983) that led to indiscriminant, positive attitudes that produced what has been termed *experiential processing* (Meyers-Levy & Malaviya, 1999). At the same time, high-SMAARTS individuals accessed the secondary meaning of the tag line, and the new meaning access measure managed to tap into implicit route processing.

Finally, another study by Dimofte and Yalch (in press-a) showed that, when prompted and allowed extra processing time, low-SMAARTS consumers are generally able to access more than one meaning, just as predicted by the working memory constraint explanation of Just and Carpenter (1992). The insights from all these studies suggest that a new model of polysemy processing is warranted (see Fig. 7.2). According to this model, secondary meanings are often processed automatically or at a low level of conscious awareness by high- but not low-SMAARTS indi-

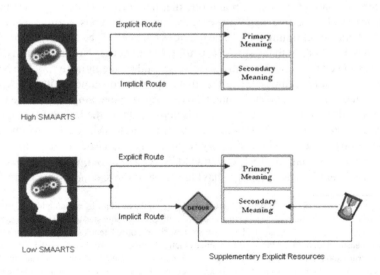

Figure 7.2.   Schematic view of novel meaning access account.

viduals. However, comprehension of polysemy is not completely out of reach even for the later group of consumers, who simply require supplementing the amount of explicit cognitive resources devoted to processing.

RECOMMENDATIONS

The choice to use a polysemous phrase or word in marketing communications can both enhance and undermine the marketer's objectives, depending on the specific meanings of these polysemous words and phrases. One issue is the difficulty in limiting which meanings are likely to be taken from the message. The discussion of the effect of base frequency showed that messages can be tested and selected using the base frequencies to avoid those with high numbers selecting the unintended meanings. Further, context can be developed to lead consumers to the intended meaning. However, there is no guarantee that all consumers will derive the intended and only the intended meaning(s) even if it is (they are) the most frequent and most implied by the context. Of course, even nonpolysemous messages may be misunderstood (Jacoby & Hoyer, 1982).

In many cases, several meanings may be consistent with what the advertiser wants consumers to remember about the brand. For example, Ambien sleeping pills are advertised as "Working Like a Dream." Both meanings (helps you sleep better as do dreams and works as perfectly as you would like it to) are consistent with a desirable sleeping aid. On the other hand, in some cases, the secondary meanings may not be desirable. For example, research by Dimofte and Yalch (in press-b) showed that, when associated with a luxury automobile, the slogan "No One Comes Close" was interpreted by some consumers to mean that the product was so expensive as to be unaffordable. Consequently, they had little interest in the product's features. We recommend that marketers test their polysemous slogans for all meanings and not assume that only the primary meaning will affect consumers' reactions to the message.

As noted in the introduction, polysemy and other forms of figurative speech are valued by copywriters in part because they demonstrate a superior command of the language. However, there is little evidence that consumers often consider this important in their brand evaluations. For example, Toncar and Munch (2001) found that print ads using figurative speech were more persuasive and better remembered but only in low involvement situations. Apparently, an interesting figure of speech might attract the attention of otherwise disinterested consumers. However, disinterested consumers are not necessarily likely to be good prospects. Thus, we recommend that marketers resist using advertising slogans that are very clever but not necessarily effective in communicating the intended message. On the other hand, consistent with Kittay's advocacy of "purposive ambiguity," one should not underestimate the potential bonding that can occur between a marketer and consumer because both "get" the intended ambiguity. The popularity of bumper slogans with the double entendre statements such as "Librarians Do It By the Book," and "Marketers Do It on Commission" (see http://www.dkgoodman.com/doita-f.html for numerous other examples) illustrates how polysemy can tie members to a group much as Shirley Polykoff's Clairol slogan linked natural and artificially colored blondes.

CONCLUSIONS

This chapter has addressed the issue of individuals' access to meaning in polysemous marketing communications, specifically the impact of polysemous brand slogans on consumer attitudes and purchase intentions. We first looked at the antecedents of meaning access. Extant cognitive psychology and linguistic research proposed that two factors are essential in this process: the base frequency of each possible meaning and the context during exposure to the polysemous message. As suggested by several articles from consumer research, work by Dimofte and Yalch (2003) found that consumers' ability to access meaning was an important moderator of these effects, a fact that hinted at the need to adequately capture individual differences in meaning access.

Building on these results, more recent work by the same authors suggested that some consumers were able to automatically access all meanings of a polysemous brand slogan, regardless of base frequencies or exposure context. Other consumers, however, were unable to access more than a single, immediately available meaning. A novel measure of automatic access to secondary meaning was developed and validated. Furthermore, this novel theoretical account contributes to our understanding of consumer reactions to ads that make use of polysemous slogans, and expanding these findings to metaphoric delivery techniques beyond the slogan is a clear possibility for future research. This conceptual account also suggests that the related debate in psychology and linguistics can be attenuated once we (a) perceive the issue as also dealing with primary–secondary issues instead of simply literal–figurative access and (b) we account for individuals' differential abilities to access meaning at implicit levels.

Another finding of the present research addresses the power of context in visual advertising. It is thus important that marketers pay close attention to the context in which they make use of polysemy. Ad placement (e.g., in the context of TV programming, surrounding material in print media, etc.) truly matters, as inadvertent priming with undesirable secondary meanings is a recipe for trouble. Furthermore, the research also indicates the power of figurative speech in affecting both advertising and brand attitudes: In the cited experiments, not only was a relatively minor brand such as Minute Maid helped beyond the mere impact of a literal slogan, but an established and strong brand like Mercedes was hurt by a careless choice of polysemy in its slogans. Advertising agencies everywhere would be well advised to test the SMAARTS of their writers.

REFERENCES

Cacciari, C., & Glucksberg, S. (1994). Understanding figurative language. In M. A. Gernsbacher (Ed.), *Handbook of psycholinguistics* (pp. 447–477). San Diego, CA: Academic Press.

Dimofte, C. V. (2004). *Consumer response to polysemous marketing communications: The antecedents, measurement, and attitudinal consequences of slogan meaning access.* Unpublished doctoral dissertation, University of Washington, Seattle.

Dimofte, C. V., & Yalch, R. F. (2003). The role of advertisement copy in prompting consumer access to slogan meaning. In P. A. Keller & D. W. Rook (Eds.), *Advances in consumer research* (Vol. 30, p. 382). Provo, UT: Association for Consumer Research.

Dimofte, C. V., & Yalch, R. F. (in press-a). Consumer response to polysemous brand slogans. *Journal of Consumer Research.*

Dimofte, C. V. & Yalck, R. F. (in press-b). The SMAART scale: A measure of individuals' automatic access to secondary meanings in polysemous statements. *Journal of Consumer Psychology.*

Duffy, S. A., Morris, R. K., & Rayner, K. (1988). Lexical ambiguity and fixation times in reading. *Journal of Memory and Language, 27*(4), 429–446.

Gerrig, R. J., & Healy, A. F. (1983). Dual processes in metaphor understanding: Comprehension and appreciation. *Journal of Experimental Psychology: Learning, Memory, and Cognition, 9*(4), 667–675.

Gildea, P., & Glucksberg, S. (1983). On understanding metaphor: The role of context. *Journal of Verbal Learning and Verbal Behavior, 22,* 577–590.

Glucksberg, S., Gildea, P., & Bookin, H. B. (1982). On understanding nonliteral speech: Can people ignore metaphors? *Journal of Verbal Learning and Verbal Behavior, 21,* 85–98.

Greenwald, A. G., McGhee, D. E., & Schwartz, J. L. K. (1998). Measuring individual differences in implicit cognition: The implicit association test. *Journal of Personality and Social Psychology, 74*(6), 1464–1480.

Grice, H. (1975). Logic and conversation. In P. Cole & J. L. Morgan (Eds.), *Syntax and semantics* (Vol. 3, pp. 41–58). New York: Academic Press.

Hoffman, I. (2001). Retrieved July 22, 2005, from http://www.adslogans.com/ww/prvwis18.htm

Jacoby, J., & Hoyer, W. (1982). On the miscomprehension of television communications: Selected findings. *Journal of Marketing, 46*(4), 12–26.

Just, M. A., & Carpenter, P. A. (1992). A capacity theory of comprehension: Individual differences in working memory. *Psychological Review, 99*(1), 122–149.

Kittay, E. (1987). *Metaphor: Its cognitive force and linguistic structure.* Oxford, England: Clarendon.

Lakoff, G. (1995). *The neurocognitive self in the science of the mind.* Oxford, England: Oxford University Press.

Leigh, J. H. (1994). The use of figures of speech in print ad headlines. *Journal of Advertising, 23*(2), 17–35.

Loftus, E. F. (1996). The myth of repressed memory and the realities of science. *Clinical Psychology-Science and Practice, 3*(4), 356–362.

MacDonald, M. C., Pearlmutter, N. J., & Seidenberg, M. S. (1994). Lexical nature of syntactic ambiguity resolution. *Psychological Review, 101*(4), 676–703.

MacInnis, D. (2004, Winter). Crystal clear concepts: Using metaphors to expand dimensional thinking. *ACR News,* 1–4.

Mathur, L. K., & Mathur, I. (1995). The effect of advertising slogan changes on the market values of firms. *Journal of Advertising Research, 35,* 59–65.

McGough, R. (2005, May 31). Scientists track stroke victims' inability to understand proverbs. *Wall Street Journal,* p. d6.

McQuarrie, E. F., & Mick, D. G. (1992). On resonance: A critical pluralistic inquiry into advertising rhetoric. *Journal of Consumer Research, 19,* 180–197.

McQuarrie, E. F., & Mick, D. G. (1999). Visual rhetoric in advertising: Text-interpretive, experimental, and reader-response analyses. *Journal of Consumer Research, 26,* 37–55.

Meyers-Levy, J., & Malaviya, P. (1999). Consumers' processing of persuasive advertisements: An integrative framework of persuasion theories. *Journal of Marketing, 63,* 45–60.

Morgan, S. E., & Reichert, T. (1999). The message is in the metaphor: Assessing the comprehension of metaphors in advertisements. *Journal of Advertising, 28*(4), 1–12.

Ottati, V., Rhoads, S., & Graesser, A. C. (1999). The effect of metaphor on processing style in a persuasion task: A motivational resonance model. *Journal of Personality and Social Psychology, 77*(4), 688–697.

Phillips, B. J., & McQuarrie, E. F. (2004). Beyond visual metaphor: A new typology of visual rhetoric in advertising. *Marketing Theory, 4*(1–2), 111–134.

Roehm, M., & Sternthal, B. (2001). The moderating effect of knowledge and resources on the persuasive impact of analogies. *Journal of Consumer Research, 28,* 257–272.

Searle, J. R. (1979). Metaphor. In A. Ortony (Ed.), *Metaphor and thought* (pp. 92–123). Cambridge, MA: Cambridge University Press.

Simpson, G. B. (1984). Lexical ambiguity and its role in models of word recognition. *Psychological Bulletin, 96*(2), 316–340.

Swinney, D. A. (1979). Lexical access during sentence comprehension: (Re)consideration of context effects. *Journal of Verbal Learning and Verbal Behavior, 18*(6), 645–659.

The top 100 advertising campaigns (1999). The advertising century [Special issue]. *Advertising Age,* p. 20.

Toncar, M., & Munch, J. (2001). Consumer responses to tropes in print advertising. *Journal of Advertising, 30*(1), 55–64.

Verbrugge, R. R. (1977). Resemblances in language and perception. In R. Shaw & J. Bransford (Eds.), *Perceiving, acting, and knowing: Toward an ecological psychology* (pp. 365–389). Hillsdale, NJ: Lawrence Erlbaum Associates.

Zaltman, G. (2003). *How customers think: Essential insights into the mind of the market.* Boston: Harvard Business School Press.

CHAPTER 8

Road Map or Secret Weapon?
The Role of Conceptual Metaphor in Shaping
Marketing Communications About Exercise

Barbara J. Phillips
University of Saskatchewan

Edward F. McQuarrie
Santa Clara University

An ad for an exercise supplement displayed in a men's fitness magazine appears unremarkable on the surface: We see a picture of a muscular man posed in a gym topped by the headline, "Win the fight." We might initially be inclined to classify the ad as a straightforward, direct claim far removed from the flights of fancy typically studied by those interested in stylistic devices in marketing communication (e.g., Dimofte & Yalch, 2002; McQuarrie & Mick, 1996; Mothersbaugh, Huhmann, & Franke, 2002; Phillips, 1997). On closer examination, however, the ad in question and many other ads like it rely on conceptual metaphor, a subtle yet powerful stylistic device that has the potential to make salient certain aspects of a concept while masking other aspects. Interestingly, the influence of this rhetorical device on the attitudes and behaviors of consumers is, for the most part, unexamined both by consumers themselves and by consumer researchers.

In the previous ad example, "Win the fight" draws on the conceptual metaphor *exercise is combat*. A conceptual metaphor comprises a family of systematically related metaphorical comparisons. We contend that conceptual metaphor is a persuasive tool that has been overlooked in consumer behavior research. This chapter introduces conceptual metaphor by explaining why it is important to understanding marketing communications directed to consumers, presents an extended example of the use of conceptual metaphor within the consumer behavior domain of exercise, and provides evidence that different conceptual metaphors in marketing communications messages compete to influence how consumers think and act within that domain.

WHAT IS CONCEPTUAL METAPHOR?

The rhetorical figure of metaphor compares two objects through analogy by suggesting that one object is figuratively like another even though on the surface they appear to be quite different (Stern, 1990; Ward & Gaidis, 1990). The essence of metaphor is understanding one thing in terms of another (Lakoff & Johnson, 1980, p. 5) through cross-domain association (Lakoff & Johnson, 1999, p. 46). This analogous comparison is sparked by artful deviations in the style of the communication, which suggests the comparison is not to be taken literally (McQuarrie & Mick, 1996). For example, an article in a fitness magazine uses a metaphor when it states that a specific exercise is an important "ingredient" in one's "fitness recipe." Metaphors such as these invite consumers to compare exercise routines to recipes to infer what the two concepts have in common (McQuarrie & Phillips, 2005). This inference can draw on the "fuzzy set" of attributes that the two concepts share or elicit in the consumer's mind (MacCormac, 1985). In our example, exercise routines are like recipes because they combine specific individual ingredients (e.g., exercises for different body parts or different kinds of foods) to produce a successful and desired outcome (e.g., optimal fitness level or delicious dinner).

To date, most research on advertising metaphor has concentrated on specific or individual metaphors, such as "fitness recipe" (for a review, see Phillips, 2003). It is only recently that researchers in consumer behavior have been drawn to *conceptual metaphor*—a family of metaphors organized around a common implicit theme (Ritchie, 2003). For example, *exercise is construction* is a conceptual metaphor that organizes the ad statements, "build muscle," "give your body the building blocks for muscle mass," and "lay the foundation for lasting fitness." Conceptual metaphor allows us to understand vague, abstract domains of knowledge (e.g., exercise and fitness) in terms of more specific, concrete, and familiar domains (e.g., building a house; Gibbs, 1998). Conceptual metaphors also are often used to help individuals understand and explain their emotional states (Cacciari, 1998). Thus, conceptual metaphors are useful wherever we seek to understand abstract, intangible, or multivalent ideas that might otherwise be difficult to capture in a straightforward declaration.

Conceptual metaphors can be identified by examining recurrent usages in natural language (Boers, 2003). For example, exhortations found throughout exercise magazines to "turn up the heat" so one can "burn more calories" and "help melt the fat away," come together to form the conceptual metaphor *exercise is heat*. It need not be the case that all metaphorical expressions in ads are part of larger conceptual metaphors. "Washboard abs," for example, does not cohere with other exercise expressions into a general metaphorical principle. Instead, it stands alone as an idiosyncratic, unsystematic, and isolated metaphor based on similarity of form (Lakoff & Johnson, 1980, p. 55), sometimes called an "image" metaphor (Gibbs, 1994, p. 258). In this example, abdominal muscles are like washboards only in appearance and shape—hard and rippled. Unlike image metaphors, conceptual metaphors are based on individual metaphors that rely on a common system of relations that are mapped from base to target (Gentner, Bowdle, Wolff, & Baronat, 2001). Since the seminal work of Lakoff and Johnson (1980), researchers in psychology and linguistics have found support for the systematic and hierarchical nature of conceptual metaphors by showing that conceptual metaphors can prime related individual metaphors (Gibbs, 1994, p. 256) and that people can extend conceptual metaphors to understand novel individual metaphors (Gentner et al., 2001).

Recent papers have argued that two types of conceptual metaphors can be distinguished: primary and complex (Boers, 2003). Primary conceptual metaphors are learned through general physical experience and map sensory and bodily realities onto abstract concepts (e.g., *happy is up*; *strong desire is hunger*, etc.). Joy and Sherry (2003) provide a good example of primary conceptual metaphors in their study of consumers' embodied responses to art, such as *touching is knowing* and *attraction is being pulled*. Complex conceptual metaphors are based on particular embedded cultural meanings, such as those found in sports metaphors. Many cultures use sports metaphors but the sports they target differ. Thus, whereas many cricket and boating metaphors circulate in the United Kingdom (e.g., "that exam was a sticky wicket;" "the government is being blown off course"), baseball metaphors are common in the United States and Canada (e.g., "the courts now follow a 'three strikes and you're out' rule"). This chapter focuses on complex conceptual metaphors as a little-understood influence on consumer behavior. Although a few recent papers in consumer research have mentioned complex conceptual metaphor as a way to understand general opinions of advertising and marketing (Coulter, Zaltmann, & Coulter, 2001; MacInnis, 2004), the persuasive power of complex conceptual metaphor to highlight and mask specific aspects of consumer experience, and thus shape individual consumer response, has yet to receive specific attention.

WHY IS CONCEPTUAL METAPHOR IMPORTANT?

Conceptual metaphors are shared within a culture because they are based on commonalities and because they are reinforced in everyday conversation (Ritchie, 2003). Complex conceptual metaphors are frequently found in the discourse of politics, science, law, and journalism (Dunbar, 2001); researchers estimate that six individual metaphors are used per minute of ordinary discourse (Gibbs, 1994, p. 121). This ubiquity makes metaphorical language almost invisible; people process it without noticing (Gentner et al., 2001). Although metaphors often go unnoticed, this does not rob the underlying conceptual metaphor of its power. On the contrary, because we are hardly conscious of the underlying system of relations being brought to bear, a regularly proffered conceptual metaphor gets internalized as normal and expected (Lakoff & Johnson, 1980). Consequently, the relationships underlying the conceptual metaphor come to define and structure the way we think and reason about a situation.

Because the essence of a metaphor is that one domain is like another, the relationship that allows the two domains to be joined also functions to highlight the similarities between the two concepts and mask the differences. Through conceptual metaphor, the characteristics of the situation that match the metaphor are made salient and, at the same time and in the same process, characteristics that do not match the situation become less salient, are not brought to mind, and are essentially masked. For example, Lakoff and Johnson (1980) argue that because Western culture commonly asserts that *argument is war*, we understand that to argue is to "attack" our opponent's position, to "defend" our own, and to try to "gain ground." This conceptual metaphor highlights the goal of "winning" the argument and masks other options, such as compromise. A competing conceptual metaphor, such as *argument is dance*, would make salient the ideas of cooperation and compromise and the ideas of winning and losing would lose salience and be masked.

The potential of conceptual metaphor to highlight and mask has a powerful impact in shaping knowledge and belief. Kokinov and Petrov (2001) illustrate this by describing how human memory can be explained using two competing conceptual metaphors. The classical metaphor for our memory system is a library—a physical space where items are initially stored, subsequently searched, and finally retrieved. This metaphor structures our understanding of how memory might fail (e.g., a book may be lost). An alternative metaphor asserts that human memory is like a paleontologist who uses bone fragments and general knowledge to construct a dinosaur. This metaphor easily makes salient the idea that because the paleontologist reconstructs the dinosaur, it may be quite different from reality; similarly, human memory can be altered through its reconstruction. The library metaphor masks this possibility—books in a library are not rewritten when they are taken off the shelf and read.

Beyond knowledge and beliefs, the highlighting and masking effects of conceptual metaphor have been shown to affect actual behavior. In education research, students who were taught that *electricity is a stream* (i.e., thinking of electrical circuits as dams that let in water) performed better at questions that fit the salient elements of their learned metaphor than students who were taught *electricity is a crowd of people* (i.e., thinking about electrical circuits as gates that let in people), and vice versa (Gibbs, 1994, p. 162). In a hypothetical military crisis situation, U.S. participants presented with subtle analogy cues that made World War II associations salient (e.g., refugees fleeing in boxcars) were more likely to recommend military intervention than those presented with analogy cues that made Vietnam associations salient (e.g., refugees fleeing in small boats; Holyoak & Thagard, 1995, p. 103). Again, the choice of metaphor influenced behavior.

Although the influence of conceptual metaphor on consumer behavior has yet to be determined, research in related areas provides hints concerning its persuasiveness. For example, Markman and Moreau (2001) examined consumer response to a (nonmetaphorical) analogy drawn between a digital camera and either a regular camera or a scanner. These researchers found that the analogy presented placed constraints on the options considered by consumers and on how the options were evaluated. Interestingly, the participants in the study did not recognize the extent of the influence of the analogy presented. These results suggest that *metaphorical* analogy may also turn out to be a powerful tool in a consumer domain.

For the most part in consumer behavior research, analogous thinking has been viewed as an effortful type of processing that requires ample cognitive resources, motivation, and training (Gregan-Paxton & Roedder John, 1997; Roehm & Sternthal, 2001). In education, analogies have long been a staple of the SAT and other attempts to measure academic aptitude (e.g., the Miller Analogies Test). Although analogies may very well require effort and motivation in certain situations, the ubiquity and subtlety of conceptual metaphor suggests it may be processed with less effort and conscious awareness than other types of analogous thinking. If this proposition holds, then conceptual metaphor may be particularly suited for directing and perhaps even misdirecting the thoughts of consumers toward a desired conclusion.

The directive potential of conceptual metaphor stems, in part, from the fact that more than one conceptual metaphor may exist in the culture for any particular concept. Gibbs (1994) gives as examples: *love is a nutrient* and *love is magic*. From a rhetorical standpoint, the availability of alternative conceptual metaphors gives marketers an opportunity to decide how they want consumers to conceptualize a brand or consumption situation. The marketer who succeeds in diffusing a particular conceptual metaphor among a target audience may gain considerable power. As Holyoak and Thagard (1995, p. 180) assert, "Accepting the analogy is tantamount to accepting a prescription for action."

Based on the previous discussion, the purpose of the following research is to show that multiple complex conceptual metaphors can be shown to exist within a consumer behavior domain, and these conceptual metaphors compete in that domain because marketers select conceptual metaphors for their marketing communications that highlight and mask different aspects of consumer experience. For these purposes, we sought a consumer behavior domain that was sufficiently abstract and emotion provoking to allow for conceptual metaphor to emerge as a culturally constituted way of explaining it; was sufficiently broad to allow for multiple conceptual metaphors to emerge, if they existed; and was a familiar part of many consumers' everyday lives. The domain selected was exercise and fitness.

The Centers for Disease Control (CDC, 2004) report that 61% of American adults engage in some leisure-time physical activity, with 31% of adults meeting the minimum requirements of physical activity recommended by the CDC. In addition, these adults have boosted the sales of exercise equipment, apparel, and footwear to $68.2 billion in 2002 (SGMA International, 2003). Conversely, it is increasingly recognized that individuals who do not exercise are at risk for obesity and serious diseases such as diabetes, heart disease, and cancer (CDC, 1996). Consequently, understanding persuasive messages about exercise and fitness has practical as well as theoretical importance. Because we focus on a consumer domain that includes, but is not limited to, consumption (i.e., exercise), our exploration of complex conceptual metaphors goes beyond any one narrow product or service category (e.g., athletic shoes or gym memberships). Our focus on exercise is analogous to a focus on photography rather than cameras, celebrations instead of champagne, or home decorating as opposed to the purchase of carpet. Thus, we approach exercise as a life project that affords multiple and diverse opportunities for consumption, no one of which is definitive of the domain.

The paucity of prior work on conceptual metaphors for exercise argues for the use of an exploratory methodology. To augment the validity of the initial findings, we selected two quite different exploratory techniques. Specifically, we combined a content assessment with multidimensional scaling (MDS) analysis. Content assessment relies on "extensive reading of great quantities of [publications], using the historian's method of reading, sifting, weighing, comparing, and analyzing the evidence in order to tell the story" (Marzolf, 1978, p. 15). A key advantage of content assessment is that it allows for an integrated and holistic approach to data as a result of an extended period of immersion. In addition, content assessment serves as a discovery procedure, revealing unexplored aspects of cultural phenomena. In contrast, multidimensional scaling relies on statistical measures of distance between concepts. Its strength is in portraying the differences between ideas and uncovering underlying dimensions that organize these differences. Study 1 uses content assessment to identify common conceptual metaphors of exercise that recur in discussions and representations of exercise; Study 2 uses MDS analysis to distinguish the dimensions along which these conceptual metaphors vary. Both methods work together to illuminate what is highlighted and what is masked by common conceptual metaphors of exercise.

STUDY I: CONTENT ASSESSMENT TO IDENTIFY CONCEPTUAL METAPHORS OF EXERCISE

A content assessment of the conceptual metaphors commonly used in North American culture to describe exercise and fitness was conducted. To begin, the most popular exercise and fitness magazines in the United States were identified: *Men's Fitness* and *Men's Health* (targeting a primarily male audience) and *Fitness* and *Shape* (targeting a primarily female audience). The circulation of these magazines is presented in Table 8.1. Two current issues of each magazine were selected for examination. The first researcher examined every ad and article in the magazine of at least one-page size or greater, looking for metaphorical statements in both the pictures and the words. These individual metaphors were collected as examples of metaphors of exercise disseminated by cultural intermediaries (Coulter, Price, & Feick, 2003). Each of the four magazines also had a Web site where consumers themselves could post messages, questions, and responses regarding exercise and fitness. Three of these forum communities were active in posting and responding to many exercise-related messages every day, with an archive of between 35,000 to

TABLE 8.1

Magazine Circulation and Web Posting Information

Magazine	Readership		Number of Web Postings
	Women[a]	Men[a]	
Fitness	7,021,000	NA	3,328[b]
Shape	4,868,000	NA	72,654
Men's Health	NA	6,864,000	405,006
Men's Fitness	NA	4,889,000	35,100

[a]Doublebase Mediamark Research Inc., 2001.

[b]The *Fitness Community* Web site counts only initial postings (1,664), not responses. Very few responses were received for each initial posting, so we estimated the number of postings by assuming one response per posting.

405,000 postings available for viewing on *Men's Fitness Forum, Men's Health Forum,* and *Shape Forum* (see Table 8.1). The first researcher examined every fitness and exercise-related posting on these sites for one week. *Fitness Community* had far fewer postings, so the researcher examined a month of postings at this Web site. The individual metaphors taken from the Web sites were collected as examples of metaphors of exercise disseminated by consumers themselves.

Based on the advice for identifying conceptual metaphors provided by Low (2003), individual metaphors were grouped into conceptual metaphors separately by both researchers. The conceptual metaphors were allowed to emerge from the data in a grounded theory approach to the individual metaphors (Strauss & Corbin, 1998) as the analysis moved back and forth between the individual metaphors, the emerging conceptual metaphors, and the judgments of each researcher. No systematic differences existed between the metaphors used by cultural intermediaries and those used by consumers themselves; consequently, metaphors from both sources were combined for analysis.

Results

Several distinct conceptual metaphors were uncovered that seemed to cluster around related themes. Ritchie (2003) has hypothesized that conceptual metaphors often emerge from a field of interrelated concepts; for example, metaphors that emerge from the related activities of friendly competitive games, fisticuffs, and full-scale war cluster around the themes of competition and conflict. Our conceptual metaphors seemed to cluster around themes that explained their underlying nature. Consequently, we retained the clustering themes in our data as part of the results of the content assessment. The initial list of complex conceptual metaphors is presented in Table 8.2, along with the clustering themes and examples of individual metaphors from which they were identified. The six conceptual metaphors

TABLE 8.2

Conceptual Metaphors of Exercise

Clustering Theme	Conceptual Metaphors	Individual Metaphor Examples
Exercise is a process of small steps over a long time	Exercise is a journey (J1)	Exercise provides the roadmap for my life.(J2)
		With exercise, I can take my health in a new direction. (J3)
		With exercise, I can take my body a long way. (J4)
		Exercise is a step in the right direction. (J5)
	Exercise is work for pay (W1)	Exercise provides the job training for my life. (W2)
		With exercise, I earn my way to health. (W3)
		With exercise, I invest in my body. (W4)
		Exercise is a matter of putting in the time. (W5)
Exercise is a production process that transforms inputs to outputs	Exercise is construction (B1)	Exercise provides the blueprint for my life. (B2)
		With exercise, I can build up my health. (B3)
		With exercise, I can design the body of my dreams. (B4)
		Exercise is the foundation for good health. (B5)
	Exercise is sculpting (S1)	Exercise provides the mold for my life. (S2)
		With exercise, I can shape my health. (S3)
		With exercise, I can chisel my body. (S4)
		Exercise is a way to carve my body. (S5)
Exercise is a process that occurs in relation to another force	Exercise is combat (C1)	Exercise provides the battle plan for my life. (C2)
		Exercise arms me for health. (C3)
		With exercise, I can attack body fat. (C4)
		Exercise is the secret weapon for health. (C5)
	Exercise is heat (H1)	Exercise provides the chimney for the fire of my life. (H2)
		With exercise, I get fired up for health. (H3)
		With exercise, I can burn body fat. (H4)
		Exercise is a way to turn up the heat. (H5)

identified include: *exercise is a journey, exercise is work for pay, exercise is construction, exercise is sculpting, exercise is combat,* and *exercise is heat.* Although these do not exhaust the population of metaphors identified in the content assessment, these represent all the conceptual metaphors that were (a) manifest in multiple individual metaphorical statements, (b) present in the discourse of both intermediaries and consumers, and (c) agreed on by both researchers as constituting a cohesive family of individual metaphorical statements. These complex conceptual metaphors appear to comprise the most common ways that individual consumers and cultural intermediaries think about and express their thoughts about exercise.

Next, we examined how these conceptual metaphors could best be distinguished and, more generally, attempted to identify underlying systematic relations that grouped or differentiated these metaphors. The goal of this examination was to identify maximally different and maximally similar conceptual metaphors. Ultimately, we wanted to find out the extent to which the identified conceptual metaphors could serve to highlight and mask different or similar aspects of the exercise domain.

STUDY 2: MDS OF INDIVIDUAL METAPHORICAL STATEMENTS

Design and Materials

Five metaphor statements, derived from the individual metaphors collected during the content assessment, were selected for each of the six conceptual metaphors. The first statement attempts to capture the conceptual metaphor in so far as it is possible for a single statement to do so (e.g., "exercise is a journey"). The second statement lists a tangible metaphorical object that might be used for guidance within the metaphor's specific domain (e.g., "exercise provides the roadmap for my life"). The third metaphorical statement refers explicitly to health (e.g., "with exercise, I can take my health in a new direction") and the fourth refers to the body (e.g., "with exercise, I can take my body a long way"). The fifth statement restates the metaphor (e.g., "exercise is a step in the right direction"). All five statements for each conceptual metaphor are presented in Table 8.2. In addition, the design included a sixth statement, developed by the researchers, that referred to the start or initiation of the process featured in each conceptual metaphor (e.g., "exercise is the first step of my day"). We included these statements to see if consumers would accept researcher-generated extensions of the conceptual metaphor in addition to naturally occurring metaphors. The sixth statements did not cluster with the other five for any of the conceptual metaphors and, hence, are not presented in the results; the set of discarded sixth statements is presented in Appendix A.

The 36 statements generated allow for $(n^2 - n)/2 = 630$ unique pairwise comparisons. We did not believe it would be feasible for a single subject to make this many judgments. Hence, we created six unique subsets (each $n = 105$) of these pairwise comparisons, and randomly assigned subjects to receive one of these subsets. Because the six statements within each conceptual metaphor were themselves generated in accordance with a consistent pattern as already explained, we did not use a random procedure to divide the 630 statements into subsets. Instead, a partially balanced incomplete block design was applied, so that statements drawn from different conceptual metaphors, and also different kinds of statements within conceptual metaphors (e.g., statements summarizing a metaphor vs. statements referring to health) were balanced across subsets. Similarly, comparisons within a conceptual metaphor and comparisons across different conceptual metaphors were balanced across subsets.

Participants and Procedure

Seventy-six students enrolled at a large North American university who had no special training in exercise, fitness, or marketing participated in the study. Participants were instructed that, in a metaphor, one thing is described in terms of something else, such as "rumours are weeds," and that people often use metaphors to describe exercise. These introductory instructions were followed by one of six subsets of pairwise comparisons as described earlier, with each participant making 105 judgments of similarity, using an 11-point scale with end points anchored by "very different meanings" and "very similar meanings." To partially control for order effects, each of the six subsets was printed in two versions, with the order of comparisons inverted in the second version.

Analysis

Each of the 630 unique pairwise comparisons was judged by 13 participants (on average). A mean of these ratings was computed for each comparison, and these means were compiled to make a lower triangular distance matrix suitable for multidimensional scaling analysis. The ALSCAL procedure in SPSS 11.5 was used to conduct a nonmetric MDS analysis using a model of Euclidean distances. A two-dimensional solution was computed first, with Kruskal's stress = .298 and an RSQ value of .512. Next, a three-dimensional solution was examined. This decreased the stress value to .215 and improved the RSQ to .631. Given these results, it seems worthwhile to discuss both the two-dimensional and three-dimensional solutions. The accessibility and interpretability of a two-dimensional solution is advantageous in light of the abstractness of the dimensions to be discussed, and we begin with it. The three-dimensional solution is then introduced to clarify the meaning of the second and third dimensions.

Recall that the purpose of conducting the MDS analysis was to identify the oppositional aspects of exercise that are differentially masked or highlighted across the conceptual metaphors identified. We interpret the dimensions revealed by the

MDS analysis in light of this goal. A conceptual metaphor whose statements lie toward one end of a dimension may be said to highlight that pole and to mask the pole corresponding to the other end of the dimension. In other words, to highlight strife is to mask peace and to highlight quiet is to mask noise.

In addition, a strength of combining two different exploratory methods to study stylistic devices in advertising is that the insights gained from the content assessment can be pressed into service in interpreting the dimensions of the MDS analysis. Because the content assessment studied the use of conceptual metaphor in situ, it is possible to choose among alternative interpretations of a given dimension in the MDS solution, in a way that might not be possible otherwise. Thus, we gravitated toward interpretations of the dimensions that were most consistent with how these conceptual metaphors were actually used by consumers and cultural intermediaries, as ascertained in the content assessment.

Results

The first dimension in the two-dimensional solution (see Fig. 8.1) separates *exercise is combat* and *exercise is heat* from the remaining four conceptual metaphors: *exercise is a journey, exercise is work for pay, exercise is sculpting,* and *exercise is*

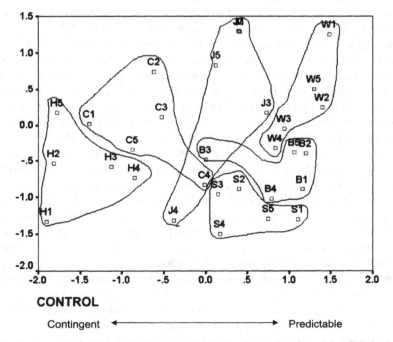

Figure 8.1. Multidimensional scaling maps of conceptual metaphors in exercise: Solution in two dimensions.

construction. This dimension might be interpreted as *degree of control* over the exercise process. It suggests an oppositional continuum ranging from "contingent" to "predictable"; that is, whether exercise and its outcomes are contingent on the actions of someone or something else or whether they are under the control of an individual. Frank (1991) was one of the first sociologists to use the idea of a "continuum of control" in his theory of the body; it has since been applied to exercise and fitness behavior (for a review, see Phillips, 2005). The first dimension separates metaphors that highlight individual control of exercise—*journey, work, sculpting* and *construction*—from those in which exercise is viewed as a process that is not under the direct control of one individual—*combat* and *heat*. In the case of the latter two metaphors, exercise occurs in relation to either a competing force (*combat*) or a force of nature (*heat*).

The first dimension might be interpreted in several alternative ways—as a contrast between "hot" and "cool" emotions, for example. The content assessment is particularly helpful here in supporting an interpretation in terms of degree of control. An examination of the contexts in which heat and combat metaphors appear indicates that these metaphors are used to highlight the idea that exercise outcomes are not under the complete control of the individual but are contingent on other forces; this contingency is expressed in phrases such as "fat can be defeated" (*combat*) and "[product] helps melt the fat away" (*heat*).

Note that within each conceptual metaphor cluster, all but two of the individual metaphors given in verb form and that also name "health" or "body" as a predicate (3 and 4) tend to lie at a distance from the remaining three statements. A cluster analysis performed alongside the MDS also showed this failure to associate with the core metaphor. Although participants were asked to ignore such factors as verb format versus noun format in making their similarity judgments, it appears that they were unable to do so, and the MDS analysis picks up this aspect of subject response. Consequently, on our interpretations of the conceptual metaphors, we place greatest weight on the positions of metaphor statements 1, 2, and 5. These can be observed to form relatively tight clusters that are, in most cases, thin in one dimension (e.g., H1, H2, and H5 in Fig. 8.1). The thinness of the clusters reflects the fact that all these statements have similar coordinates on the first dimension.

Examining the second dimension in the two-dimensional graph (Fig. 8.1), it appears to distinguish *journey* and *work* metaphors from *construction* and especially *sculpting* metaphors. Although a few plausible labels can be attached to this dimension to some extent, none seems to fit the evidence from the content assessment to the same extent as *control* fits the first dimension.

These difficulties in interpretation argue for an examination of the three-dimensional MDS solution. When a distance matrix is best scaled in three dimensions, the second dimension in the restricted two-dimensional solution often represents an amalgam of the "true" second and third dimensions. We turn now to the three-dimensional solution, reproduced graphically in the form of three pairings of dimensions, in Figures 8.2a, 8.2b, and 8.2c. We focus on Figure 8.2b, where Dimensions

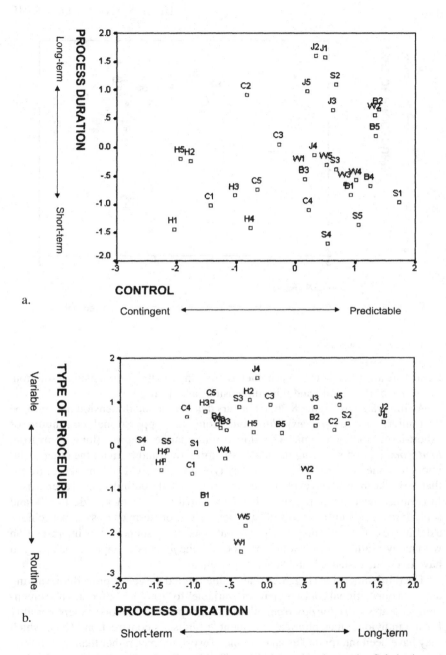

Figure 8.2.   Multidimensional scaling maps of conceptual metaphors in exercise: Solution in three dimensions. (a) Dimensions 1 and 2. (b) Dimensions 2 and 3. (c) Dimensions 1 and 3. (continued)

147

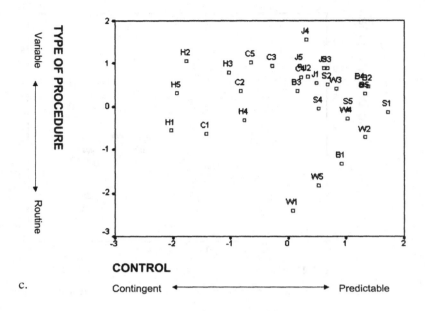

Figure 8.2.   (continued)

2 and 3 are arrayed against one another. By moving to a three-dimensional solution, meanings of the second and third dimensions are clarified.

As illustrated by Figure 8.2b, it appears that the second dimension may now be best interpreted as *process duration*, along the oppositional continuum of "short-term" to "long-term." This dimension separates *journey* (long term) from *heat, combat,* and *sculpting* particularly (short term), and from all the other meta-phors to some degree. That is, a journey typically represents a long-term process that may take months or years to reach a desired goal, if a definitive goal even exists. In contrast, heat (e.g., "fire up," "burn"), combat (e.g., "attack," "destroy"), and sculpting (e.g., "whittle," "chisel") are viewed as short-term processes that achieve a definitive end, often quickly. The content assessment supports this interpretation with many examples of the long-term focus of the *journey* metaphor, such as "you have to go the distance," and "over the long haul."

The third dimension (Fig. 8.2b) can be interpreted as type of procedure, varying along an oppositional continuum from "variable" to "routine" or fixed. This dimen-sion separates *work for pay* from all other conceptual metaphors, except possibly for the individual metaphorical statement "exercise is construction" (B1), which may have been interpreted as an example of work for pay, rather than as building, for some of the young male respondents. Unforeseen obstacles may be encountered during a journey, and sculpture relies on creative thinking, but only work is charac-terized by its habitual routine. An alternative interpretation of the third dimension we considered was "boring vs. exciting" tasks; however, the content assessment did not reveal *work* to be presented as uninteresting, but rather as an important and necessary routine (e.g., "your heart works overtime before most people get out of bed" and "get to work").

DISCUSSION

As discussed previously, arguments for the persuasive power of conceptual metaphor in a consumer domain rest on the idea that conceptual metaphors can highlight some aspects of exercise while masking others. Study 1 and Study 2 present evidence that multiple conceptual metaphors exist in a consumer domain and these metaphors differ along key oppositional dimensions. Most importantly, the pattern of conceptual metaphor use uncovered by the content assessment supports the idea that different conceptual metaphors are used by cultural intermediaries in order to highlight and mask different aspects of exercise.

Specifically, the conceptual metaphors *exercise is a journey* and *exercise is work for pay* are commonly found in the articles in fitness magazines, but less often in the ads. As demonstrated through the MDS analysis, these conceptual metaphors make salient the idea that exercise is both a long-term process and under an individual's control. A magazine publisher who wants consumers to subscribe to his magazine regularly month after month might favor these metaphors because they highlight the need for the magazine's guidance during this step-by-step process. In addition, these metaphors reassure consumers that the achievement of their goals is under their control; ongoing effort over time (e.g., by performing the exercise routines suggested in the magazine) will lead to desired results.

In contrast, *exercise is combat* and *exercise is sculpting* appear more often in ads for exercise products (directed at men and women, respectively) than in exercise articles. Advertisers, as opposed to publishers, might favor these metaphors because they focus on processes that are shorter term and more variable than journeys or jobs; the salience of achieving desired results more quickly may spur consumers to buy the brand offered. Implicit in both metaphors is the idea that tools (e.g., weapons, sculpting tools) are needed in order to succeed; such metaphors are particularly appropriate when one is selling a "solution" in the form of exercise equipment or supplements.

In addition to the competing conceptual metaphors offered by articles and ads, advertisers offer different conceptual metaphors to men (*combat*) and women (*sculpting*). An ad for Met-Rx® protein bars, found in *Men's Fitness*, typifies the *exercise is combat* metaphor offered to male exercisers. The product is presented as a "secret weapon in the fight against small muscles" and "the only ammunition your body will ever need." Because the outcome of armed combat is not solely under an individual's control, technological superiority can provide an advantage; consequently, the product in this ad is offered as "the latest scientific advancement in sports nutrition."

Although the *exercise is combat* metaphor is ubiquitous in men's exercise ads, it rarely appears in woman's ads. For example, an ad for a nutritional supplement in *Fitness* magazine pictures a woman boxing, a realistic (nonmetaphorical) depiction of a popular exercise activity. Yet, instead of making a natural connection to the combat metaphor through pictures or words, *exercise is sculpting* is one of the key conceptual metaphors presented. The product helps the model "cut fat" and "resculpt her body"; it "changes the shape of your life." The sculpting metaphor presents exercise as a transforming process that can occur in the short term; the aesthetic associations of sculpting neatly play into women's beauty ideals while the product puts those outcomes within reach.

In summary, the content assessment supports the idea that a small number of complex conceptual metaphors are likely to structure the discourse in any particular consumer behavior domain. In addition, the MDS analysis provides a sense that these conceptual metaphors are distinct from each other on several dimensions of importance to the domain. By using both methods to assign meaning to the dimensions underlying the conceptual metaphors of exercise, the ideas that those metaphors highlight or mask become clear. Finally, the content assessment suggests that these distinctions between metaphors are, in fact, used systematically by marketers to focus consumers' attention on some aspects of exercise behavior and consumption and mask other undesired aspects.

FUTURE RESEARCH

In addition to exploring conceptual metaphor in different consumer behavior domains, future research might investigate whether exposure to a conceptual metaphor through marketing communications can actually influence consumers' attitudes by making selected beliefs salient and masking others. In addition, conceptual metaphor could be tested for its ability to influence actual behavior that corresponds to the assumptions and implications of each metaphor.

Such research will need to consider an individual's preexisting and preferred conceptual metaphors. In a study of gender stereotyping, Johar, Moreau, and Schwartz (2003) found that ads that stereotype women as housewives increased the accessibility of that stereotypical construct, causing attitudes, judgments, and behaviors to become more stereotypical. However, this assimilation effect was strongest in those consumers who had a low inherent tendency to stereotype women; those who chronically stereotyped women were not affected by the contextual cue because their stereotypical attitudes were accessible anyway. Given this finding, we would expect those consumers who strongly favor a particular conceptual metaphor to be unaffected by further exposure to the same metaphor; instead, the greatest belief change may occur when consumers are presented with less preferred (and, therefore, less accessible) competing metaphors.

Contrasting expectations, however, come from a study examining the use of sports metaphors (Ottati, Rhoads, & Graesser, 1999). For those participants who liked sports, using sports metaphors increased their interest and elaboration in the communication message; those who did not like sports were less interested and less motivated. These results suggest that ads that present a matching conceptual metaphor may be most effective in influencing beliefs and behaviors. Future research will have to incorporate consumers' preexisting beliefs in an attempt to resolve these contradictory predictions with respect to the impact of conceptual metaphor on consumer judgments.

Based on the findings of the content assessment, it is likely that competing conceptual metaphors exist in the marketplace. In their study of analogy using digital camera ads, Markman and Moreau (2001) found that after the initial analogy was presented, subsequent analogies were likely to be rejected; providing another ad with a different analogy did not change the initial attitudes developed. These findings suggest that there would be no benefit to marketers in using different conceptual metaphors for the same brand. However, consumers who are exposed to related but distinct attribute claims (e.g., air bags, anti-lock brakes, traction control) for a product are more likely to rate a general claim (e.g., automobile safety) as true than consumers who are exposed to one attribute claim repeatedly (Hawkins, Hoch, & Meyers-Levy, 2001). Therefore, there may be benefits to presenting different but related metaphors (e.g., *exercise is sculpting* and *exercise is construction*) in a series of conceptual metaphor ads. Alternatively, the most effective approach might be to present different individual metaphor statements, all of which invoke the same conceptual metaphor, as opposed to hammering a single individual metaphor in ad after ad. Once again, these competing propositions of how conceptual metaphor works in a consumer domain can only be resolved through future empirical testing.

Finally, the ability of conceptual metaphor ads to mislead consumers needs to be addressed. Misleading advertising can be defined as a "discrepancy between the factual performance of a product and the consumer's beliefs generated by the advertisement" (Gaeth & Heath, 1987, p. 43). Because conceptual metaphors are largely unexamined and viewed as "normal" by consumers, they have the potential to be powerfully persuasive as they highlight certain ideas and mask others. This is important when identifying misleading messages about particular brands; for example, does the use of a *combat* metaphor for a brand of protein bar imply technological superiority where none exists? Questions of persuasion at the brand level, however, are quickly eclipsed by the social implications of the repeated use of a small number of conceptual metaphors in any one consumer domain. For example, what are the social and cultural implications of reliance on the *combat* metaphor of exercise, where one's own body is viewed as "the enemy" and fun and pleasure in sport is hidden? Similarly, what are the long-term consequences of the *sculpting* metaphor, where women are assured that their bodies are infinitely malleable, and even carvable, with the right "tools"? These types of questions, which move from empirical evidence of persuasiveness at the brand level to the larger social and cultural influence of undue concentration on a particular conceptual metaphor, reinforce the relevance of this rhetorical concept with respect to understanding consumer behavior.

REFERENCES

Boers, F. (2003). Applied linguistics perspectives on cross-cultural variation in conceptual metaphor. *Metaphor and Symbol, 18*(4), 231–238.

Cacciari, C. (1998). Why do we speak metaphorically? Reflections on the functions of metaphor in discourse and reasoning. In A. N. Katz, C. Cacciari, R. W. Gibbs, Jr., & M. Turner (Eds.), *Figurative language and thought* (pp. 119–157). New York: Oxford University Press.

Centers for Disease Control and Prevention (1996). *Physical activity and health: A report of the surgeon general.* Atlanta, GA: U.S. Department of Health and Human Services.

Centers for Disease Control and Prevention (2004). *Health behavior of adults: United States, 1999–2001.* Atlanta, GA: U.S. Department of Health and Human Services.

Coulter, R. A., Price, L. L., & Feick, L. (2003). Rethinking the origins of involvement and brand commitment: Insights from postsocialist central Europe. *Journal of Consumer Research, 30,* 151–169.

Coulter, R. A., Zaltman, G., & Coulter, K. S. (2001). Interpreting consumer perceptions of advertising: An application of the Zaltman metaphor elicitation technique. *Journal of Advertising, 30*(4), 1–21.

Dimofte, C. V., & Yalch, R. F. (2002). The role of advertising copy in prompting consumer access to slogan meaning. In P. A. Keller & D. W. Rook (Eds.), *Advances in consumer research* (Vol. 30, p. 382). Provo, UT: Association for Consumer Research.

Dunbar, K. (2001). The analogical paradox: Why analogy is so easy in naturalistic settings, yet so difficult in the psychological laboratory. In D. Gentner, K. J. Holyoak, & B. N. Kokinov (Eds.), *The analogical mind: Perspectives from cognitive science* (pp. 313–334). Cambridge, MA: MIT Press.

Frank, A. W. (1991). For a sociology of the body: An analytical review. In M. Featherstone, M. Hepworth, & B. S. Turner (Eds.), *The body: Social process and cultural theory* (pp. 36–102). Newbury Park, CA: Sage Publications.

Gaeth, G. J., & Heath, T. B., (1987). The cognitive processing of misleading advertising in young and old adults: Assessment and training. *Journal of Consumer Research, 14,* 43–54.

Gentner, D., Bowdle, B. F., Wolff, P., & Boronat, C., (2001). Metaphor is like analogy. In D. Gentner, K. J. Holyoak, & B. N. Kokinov (Eds.), *The analogical mind: Perspectives from cognitive science* (pp. 199–253). Cambridge, MA: MIT Press.

Gibbs, R. W., Jr. (1994). *The poetics of mind: Figurative thought, language, and understanding.* Cambridge, England: Cambridge University Press.

Gibbs, R. W., Jr. (1998). The fight over metaphor in thought and language. In A. N. Katz, C. Cacciari, R. W. Gibbs, Jr., & M. Turner (Eds.), *Figurative language and thought* (pp. 88–118). New York: Oxford University Press.

Gregan-Paxton, J., & Roedder John, D. (1997). Consumer learning by analogy: A model of internal knowledge transfer. *Journal of Consumer Research, 24,* 266–284.

Hawkins, S. A., Hoch, S. J., & Meyers-Levy, J. (2001). Low-involvement learning: Repetition and coherence in familiarity and belief. *Journal of Consumer Psychology, 11,* 1–11.

Holyoak, K. J., & Thagard, P. (1995). *Mental leaps: Analogy in creative thought.* Cambridge, England: MIT Press.

Johar, G. V., Moreau, C. P., & Schwartz, N. (2003). Gender-typed advertisements and impression formation: The role of chronic and temporal accessibility. *Journal of Consumer Psychology, 13,* 220–229.

Joy, A., & Sherry, J. F., Jr. (2003). Speaking of art as an embodied imagination: A multisensory approach to understanding aesthetic experience. *Journal of Consumer Research, 30,* 259–282.

Kokinov, B. N., & Petrov, A. A. (2001). Integrating memory and reasoning in analogy-making: The AMBR model. In D. Gentner, K. J. Holyoak, & B. N. Kokinov (Eds.), *The analogical mind: Perspectives from cognitive science* (pp. 59–124). Cambridge, MA: MIT Press.

Lakoff, G., & Johnson, M. (1980). *Metaphors we live by.* Chicago: University of Chicago Press.

Lakoff, G., & Johnson, M. (1999). *Philosophy in the flesh: The embodied mind and its challenge to Western thought.* New York: Basic Books.

Low, G. (2003). Validating metaphoric models in applied linguistics. *Metaphor and Symbol, 18*(4), 239–254.

MacCormac, E. R. (1985). *A cognitive theory of metaphor.* Cambridge, MA: MIT Press.

MacInnis, D. (2004, Winter). Crystal clear concepts: Using metaphors to expand dimensional thinking. *ACR Newsletter,* 1–4.

Markman, A. B., & Moreau, C. P. (2001). Analogy and analogical comparison in choice. In D. Gentner, K. J. Holyoak, & B. N. Kokinov (Eds.), *The analogical mind: Perspectives from cognitive science* (pp. 363–399). Cambridge, MA: MIT Press.

Marzolf, M. (1978). American studies—ideas for media historians? *Journalism History, 5*(1), 13–16.

McQuarrie, E. F., & Mick, D. G. (1996). Figures of rhetoric in advertising language. *Journal of Consumer Research, 22,* 424–438.

McQuarrie, E. F., & Phillips, B. J. (2005). Indirect persuasion in advertising: How consumers process metaphors presented in pictures and words. *Journal of Advertising, 34*(2), 7–20.

Mothersbaugh, D. L., Huhmann, B. A., & Franke, G. R. (2002). Combinatory and separative effects of rhetorical figures on consumers' efforts and focus in ad processing. *Journal of Consumer Research, 28,* 589–602.

Ottati, V., Rhoads, S., & Graesser, A. C. (1999). The effect of metaphor on processing style in a persuasion task: A motivational resonance model. *Journal of Personality and Social Psychology, 77*(4), 688–697.

Phillips, B. J. (1997). Thinking into it: Consumer interpretation of complex advertising images. *Journal of Advertising, 26*(2), 77–87.

Phillips, B. J. (2003). Understanding visual metaphor in advertising. In L. M. Scott & R. Batra (Eds.), *Persuasive imagery: A consumer response perspective* (pp. 297–310). Mahwah, NJ: Lawrence Erlbaum Associates.

Phillips, B. J. (2005). Working out: Consumers and the culture of exercise. *Journal of Popular Culture, 38*(3), 525–551.

Ritchie, D. (2003). ARGUMENT IS WAR—or is it a game of chess? Multiple meanings in the analysis of implicit metaphors. *Metaphor and Symbol, 18*(2), 125–146.

Roehm, M. L., & Sternthal, B. (2001). The moderating effect of knowledge and resources on the persuasive impact of analogies. *Journal of Consumer Research, 28,* 257–272.

SGMA International (2003). *Recreation market report.* Retrieved May 22, 2003, from http://www.sgma.com

Stern, B. B. (1990). Beauty and joy in metaphorical advertising: The poetic dimension. In M. E. Goldberg, G. Gorn, & R. W. Pollay (Eds.), *Advances in consumer research* (Vol. 17, pp. 71–77). Provo, UT: Association for Consumer Research.

Strauss, A., & Corbin, J. (1998). *Basics of qualitative research: Techniques and procedures for developing grounded theory* (2nd ed.). Thousand Oaks, CA: Sage Publications.

Ward, J., & Gaidis, W. (1990). Metaphor in promotional communication: A review of research on metaphor comprehension and quality. In M. E. Goldberg, G. Gorn, & R. W. Pollay (Eds.), *Advances in consumer research* (Vol. 17, pp. 636–642). Provo, UT: Association for Consumer Research.

Appendix A
Researcher-Generated Statements for Each Conceptual Metaphor of Exercise

Conceptual Metaphors	Statement
Exercise is a journey (J1)	Exercise is the first step in my day.(J6)
Exercise is work for pay (W1)	Exercise punches the time clock of my day. (W6)
Exercise is construction (B1)	Exercise allows me to break new ground in my day. (B6)
Exercise is sculpting (S1)	Exercise is the first cut in my day. (S6)
Exercise is combat (C1)	Exercise is the call to battle in my day. (C6)
Exercise is heat (H1)	Exercise is like striking a match in my day. (H6)

Note. These statements, which were included in the original MDS calculations, are omitted from Figures 8.1 and 8.2 because they did not cluster with the other statements belonging to their respective conceptual metaphors.

PART III

Stringing Sentences Together—Text and Narrative Analyses

CHAPTER 9

Narrative Structure: Plot
and Emotional Responses

Jennifer Edson Escalas
Vanderbilt University

Barbara B. Stern
Rutgers Business School

First we look for story—events sequentially related (possessing, shall we say, an ir-reducible minimum of "connexity"). And sequence goes nowhere without his doppelganger or shadow, causality.

—Kermode (in Martin, 1986, pp. 79–80)

The purpose of this chapter is to examine consumption narratives in advertisements to ascertain the relationship between chronology and causality, the basic elements of narrative structure, and affective responses (McQuarrie & Mick, 1996; Stern, 1998). Narrative advertisements are able to absorb consumers into an ad and generate favorable emotional responses to the ad and, in turn, to the brand (Brown, Homer, & Inman, 1998; Edell & Burke, 1987; Holbrook & Batra, 1987; Stayman & Aaker, 1988). We begin with a general discussion of narrative structure, drawing from literary criticism, social psychology, and consumer behavior research. Next, we examine sympathy and empathy as emotional responses that lead to other feeling responses such as upbeat and warm feelings (Goodstein, Edell, & Moore, 1990; Stayman & Aaker, 1988). We then present the findings from an experiment designed to shed light on the relationships between advertising narratives and emotional responses. Finally, we identify directions for future research.

INTERDISCIPLINARY PERSPECTIVE
ON NARRATIVE STRUCTURE

Narrative Meaning: Chronology and Causality

Literary Theory: Plot and Character.   Narratives were first studied by literary critics, who in the 20th century developed "narratology," a branch of literary theory that focuses on the relationship between textual structure and content (Martin, 1986; Prince, 1987). Narratologists view plot as the essence of narrative, for plot alone contains both "stories" (a series of events in time) and causality (the reasons for the events). Plot is the distinctive feature that sets narratives apart from stories, which are merely a set of events that occur in time without any explanation of their relationship (Forster, 1927/1954). In the consumer behavior context, whereas a consumption story says that a shopper went to Staples first and Office Depot next, a narrative says that a shopper went to both stores to get the best price on office supplies. Plots satisfy the narrative urge that stems from a deep-seated human desire to answer two questions: "What happened next?" and "Why?" Chronological sequences are habitual means of imposing order on events, and causal relationships are so fundamental to making sense out of the events (Richardson, in Martin, 1986) that individuals have been found to invent narratives spontaneously to explain the random movement of colored rectangles (Michotte, 1963, in Hermans, 1996). Advertisements are but the newest and by now probably the largest repository of a textual form that dates back to "the origins of literature, before reading was discovered" (Forster 1927/1954, p. 40).

In addition to plot, narratives from ancient times to the present all share the common attribute of a narrative presence who presents the plot, defined by Aristotle (c. 5 BC/1991) as "characters in action." The difference between narratives and dramas, also a plotted genre, is that the latter have no narrator and the actions are performed by the characters, whereas the former has a narrator whose perspective governs information about the characters in action. Research on advertising plot structure grounded in literary theory (Deighton, Romer, & McQueen, 1989; Stern, 1994; Wells, 1989) and especially narratology (Stern, 1998) emphasizes the centrality of the narrator—explicit or implicit—from whose "point of view" (Bruner, 1990; Stern, 1994) the narrative gets told. Note that even though narratives differ from dramas, both contain the same structural elements of coherent temporal progression and causality, differing only in the presence of a narrator who tells the plot versus characters who perform it.

Social Science: Chronology and Causality.   The social sciences applied the study of narratives to a wider context than that of literature, because they viewed them as organizing frameworks that help individuals understand life events, impose order on them, and evaluate them. Research on narrative in psychology shifted from aspects of the stimulus text to effects on the responder, especially in terms of narrative comprehension and representation of event sequences in memory (e.g., Bransford, Barclay, & Franks, 1972; Schank & Abelson, 1995; Wyer & Radvansky, 1999). In social psychology, research focused primarily on the role of narrative reasoning in the construction of meaning, where "particular connections between events" (Richardson, p. 118, in Berger, 1997) were said to absorb perceivers and influence persuasion (Bruner, 1986, 1990; Green & Brock, 2000; Kerby, 1991). The social sciences in general expanded the study of narratives in all areas of human life based on its capacity to present coherent accounts of particular experiences that are temporally ordered, context sensitive, and governed by causality (Baumeister & Newman, 1994). From this perspective, chronological sequencing is viewed as the primary dimension of human existence (Polkinghorne, 1991), with progression toward closure considered fundamental to the way that human events are understood (Kerby, 1991).[1] Whereas real time is undifferentiated and chaotic, narrative time is chronologically structured such that it presents an orderly progression of beginning, middle, and end (Bruner, 1986, 1990). However, despite general agreement about the basic structural elements of chronology and causality, terminological inconsistency across disparate fields has prevented threaded discourse.

In psychology, for example, Bruner (1990) identifies four essential narrative elements that correspond to chronology and causality, but are defined somewhat differently. The first is that narratives must contain agents engaged in actions undertaken to achieve goals (causality); the second is that sequential order must be established and maintained (chronology); the third is that narratives must be canonical and conform to general rules, because no matter how unusual the events, the goal is to explain them in a rational way (causality or "narrative reasoning"); and the fourth is that narratives always emanate from a narrator's perspective, which corresponds to narratological "point of view" (Martin, 1986). Mandler (1984) also referenced chronology and causality in his description of narrative elements as stages of temporal progression including a beginning stage, a middle one that presents reactions to the beginning one and goal-setting for the final stage, in which achievement of the goal signifies the ending. The rhetorician Burke's (1969) "pentad" of questions represents similar elements, the familiar journalistic "w's and an h":

1. What was done? (the action).
2. When or where was it done? (the scene).
3. Who did it? (the actor).
4. How did the actor do it? (the instrument or agency).
5. Why? (the purpose or intention).

Burke's ideas resurface in linguistics in the study of "story grammars," based on the premise that just as languages have rules of grammatical form and function, so

---

[1] However, there is variation across cultures, such that the sequence need not always be linear and closure can be accomplished in a variety of ways (see Hoegg & Alba, chap. 1 in this volume).

too do stories, which can be examined on the same dimensions to identify the rules (Brewer & Lichtenstein, 1981). Pennington and Hastie's "episode schema" (1986), like Burke's pentad, organizes events in the narrative according to the causal and intentional relationships among them, with temporal progression facilitating the causal inferencing necessary to explain changing relationships. But whereas early story grammarians such as Propp (1928) had analyzed narrative structure in terms of decomposing Russian folktales into a series of episodes, later ones such as Mick (1987) used similar methods to analyze ads, followed by Lowrey and Otnes (2003), who did the same in an analysis of Christmas rituals. The chronology and causality elements of these research streams are summarized in Table 9.1.

EMOTIONAL RESPONSES TO NARRATIVES

Given the abundance of literary and social science research on narratives, we adopt a multidisciplinary perspective to examine the relationship between an advertisement's narrative structure and positive affective responses (upbeat and warm feelings). Narratives inform emotional responses by playing two main roles in emotion appraisal (Shweder, 1994), the first of which is to function as a precursor of emotion by providing an interpretive scheme to organize one's relationship to the world and to assess the self-relevancy of events (Lazarus, 1991). Some scholars assert that emotions have different "plots" that are matched to current situations, leading to different emotional responses (Shweder, 1994). Second, narratives help people understand, evaluate, and cope with emotions, making them meaningful by locating them in the context of an individual's personal history and goals (Averill, 1994). Indeed, some researchers claim that emotional responses are based on narrative understanding (Clore, 1994), even going so far as to state that emotion itself cannot be intelligible unless it is a constituent of a recognizable narrative (Gergen & Gergen, 1988). Bruner (1986) spells out the means whereby two dimensions of narratives

TABLE 9.1

Chronology and Causality Across Research Streams

Research Stream	Elements of Chronology	Elements of Causality
Bruner's Essential Narrative Elements (1986)	Sequential order	Agents engaged in actions to achieve goals
Story Grammars Mandler (1984)	Beginning, middle, final stages in each episode	Characters set goals that are achieved in the final stage
Burke's Pentad (1969)	What? (action)	• Who? (actor)
		• Why? (intention)
Pennington and Hastie's Episode Schema (1986)	Initiating event leads to action and consequences	• Initiating event leads to physical and psychological state in actor
		• In response, actors develop goals to guide actions

can evoke emotion: One is the landscape of action, defined as the chronological sequence of events visible to the observer, which is embedded in all narrative structure; and the other is the landscape of consciousness, defined as the degree to which viewers are made aware of the character's psychological state. Consciousness is the landscape that allows viewers to "get inside" the characters' head and learn about their thoughts and feelings, attitudes, motivations, goals, and personal development. When it is well-developed, it has been shown to make a narrative more compelling and to evoke emotional responses by stimulating audiences to make more inferences and exert greater effort in interpretation (Feldman, Bruner, Renderer, & Spitzer, 1990). Thus, researchers agree that narratives not only help people to organize and understand events, but also to respond emotionally by providing the temporal and relational structure necessary for people to make sense of the self, their own and others' feelings, their place in the world, and—in advertisements—the products they use.

Prior research indicates that emotional responses to a narrative ad are enhanced by an interesting and relevant plot, a familiar setting, and/or characters with whom the viewer can relate; and that plots engender different emotions in accordance with the specific narrative organization of events and people's relationship to them (Lazarus, 1999; Shweder, 1994). Specific emotion plots are likely to evoke corresponding feelings in the viewer: For example, a happiness-joy narrative (Lazarus, 1999) seems able to stimulate viewers to relive similar joyful emotional experiences. Consumer researchers have extended the idea that emotional responses in real life are triggered by people or events to advertising representations, for narratives also contain characters and situations that can stimulate viewers to experience the emotions they see on screen (Aaker, Stayman, & Hagerty, 1986). Higher quality narratives are likely to elicit stronger emotional responses in that the "better" ones contain more complete development, more compelling characters, and more interesting actions (Mick, 1987; Wells, 1989). When Escalas, Moore, and Britton (2004) tested affective responses to narrative ads, they found that those with a high degree of chronology and causality in their structure positively affect viewers' affective responses. The ability of structural elements such as characters, situations, and emotional plots to generate positive affective responses is enhanced by the extent to which the ad presents a narrative. Therefore, we expect that an increase in the narrative structure of an advertisement will be positively related to warm and upbeat feelings. We now turn our attention to the progression from narrative to emotion, a progression that begins with recognition and proceeds to absorption.

Empathy and Sympathy as Mediators

Many researchers have found a positive relationship between plot and viewer absorption into advertisements (also referred to as immersion, vicarious participation, transportation, and "being hooked"). Deighton, Romer, and McQueen (1989) operationalized Wells's proposition that drama plots draw people in by asking ad viewers whether they "felt drawn into the commercial, whether the actions depicted seemed authentic, whether the commercial had portrayed feelings the subject could relate to and had made the subject want to join the action" (pp. 338–339). In a following study, Deighton and Hoch (1993) found that ad plots were effective in stimulating consumers to comprehend and/or vicariously participate (Wells, 1989). Green and Brock's "immersion into a text," defined as the extent to which individuals become lost in a narrative (2000, p. 702), is similar to the concept of vicarious participation. Most recently, Escalas et al. (2004) termed the in-drawing situation the narrative "hook" and found that well-developed narratives were better able to hook viewers into an ad and evoke emotional responses.

Thus, most researchers agree on the role of plot in absorption. Nonetheless, the construct was viewed as a monolithic construct, which we considered too simplistic to capture the complex emotional response that literary critics and psychologists have been studying since the 1700s (Escalas & Stern, 2003). We conducted a study in which the monolith of absorption was decomposed as a two-dimensional emotional response system consisting of sympathy and empathy, and found that the plotted structure of classical dramas evoked both responses in a two-stage process. Individuals first experience sympathy by recognition of the characters' emotions, and then empathy, the stronger response, by absorption into the emotions themselves (Delacroix, 1927/1953). We will now review the historical development of these two constructs.

Even though the constructs of sympathy and empathy appear to be distinct, the terms have become so enmeshed in a semantic muddle that no two researchers necessarily define or measure them in the same way (Langfeld, 1920/1967). Confusion is traceable to a long and multiperspectival research heritage from fields as disparate as psychology, metaphysics, theology, biology, aesthetics, literary criticism, and moral philosophy or ethics (Morrison, 1988). To clarify the discussion, we must first differentiate between responses to real-life situations and to aesthetic creations, specifying definitions of sympathy and empathy limited to media responses (Eisenberg, Fabes, Schaller, & Miller, 1989). This calls for a leap backward to the late 19th- century work of "psychological aestheticians" (Vivas & Krieger, 1953, p. 277) and their sources—moral philosophy (now called ethics) and Aristotelian aesthetics. The rationale is that responses to advertising stimuli occur in the domain of created media representations rather than that of real-life events. That is, responses to advertisements are influenced by their aesthetic attributes (formal structure), as well as by individual predilections, in contrast to responses to naturally occurring events, influenced solely by the individual and the event. The transition from real life to media representation can be seen as follows: Whereas someone might react with terror to the experience of viewing a sinking ship, that same person might react with enjoyment to the cinematic spectacle of the Titanic going under.

Sympathy: Cognition and Recognition.   Sympathy derives from the Greek *sympatheia* (with suffering), and the term entered psychology via ethics, a branch of philosophical inquiry into (wo)man's moral nature, studied in terms of appropriate responses to real-life situations. Hume's *A Treatise of Human Nature* (1739/1968) is generally considered the earliest modern introduction of the concept in the behavioral sciences (Wispé, 1986). Hume's moral philosophy establishes the logic of sympathy—"A sympathizes 'with' B about some circumstances of B or 'in' some of B's feelings" (Mercer, 1972, p. 4). Sympathy is considered to be cognitively determined, emanating from an understanding of "the difference between the one sympathizing and the object of sympathy ... always somewhat present in consciousness" (Langfeld, 1920/1967, p. 138). That is, sympathy is an other-oriented response to "the other person's state of mind and his circumstances" (Mercer, 1972, p. 5). The "heightened awareness of the suffering of another person as something to be alleviated" (Wispé, 1986, p. 318) stems from understanding the other's misfortune. Note that the etymological derivation limits the kind of stimuli able to evoke sympathy to those that are negatively valenced: depictions of suffering, misfortune, victimization, and so forth (Macfie, 1959). But, insofar as advertisements do not ordinarily aim at achieving these responses, we focused on the definition of sympathy as a cognitive process, emphasizing that ad sympathizers can recognize all emotions, positive as well as negative (Escalas & Stern, 2003). Thus, we follow their definition of ad sympathy responses as cognitively determined, emanating from individuals' predilection to distinguish between another's experience and their own, and demonstrated by individuals' comprehension of the other's state or circumstances.

Empathy: Merging and Mysticism. In contrast, an empathy response is involuntary, un-self-conscious, and affective insofar as the self merges with another person or object. As a response to a created work, empathy refers to a person's capacity to feel within or in an object outside of the self (Langfeld, 1920/1967), and it occurs involuntarily in response to representations that may or may not be negatively valenced—scenes of joy are as likely stimuli as scenes of sorrow. Most researchers now consider its core attribute the vicarious sharing of affect. Eisenberg and Strayer (1987) note the current "cross-disciplinary agreement that affect is a central component of empathy [and] that empathy is the act of 'feeling into' another's affective experience" (p. 391).

This definition accords with the term's historical and etymological roots in the pagan mystic phrase, "I am you and you are I" (see Buber, 1937/1970, pp. 133–134), usually shortened to "I am you." It originally referred to the mystical union between humans and pagan spirits, first appearing in Egyptian theology as "an occult formula or incantation expressing unity of the initiates with their gods" (Morrison, 1988, p. 4). Early classical secular works reinforced this meaning, for in the *Republic* (Plato, c. 5 BC/1991, VI, 508–509), Plato "taught that, like the eye, the soul became what it saw" (Morrison, 1988, p. 17), and Aristotle (1991) described a friend as another I. When the phrase entered Christian theology in the second century AD (Morrison, 1988), it was redefined to mean the union of worshipers with

Christ, symbolized by the sacramental rites of Holy Communion. From the 12th century on, Neoplatonism and Aristotelianism fueled the introduction of "I am you" into western European mysticism, which by the 19th century had entered into German pre-Romantic and Romantic aesthetics and philosophy. From about 1800 onward, the phrase appeared in German philosophy, with Herder being the first to use the word "einfühlung" (1800, pp. 85–86) to express the Romantic belief in a mystical union of humans with external objects described as the "subjective, animate relationship that we maintain with the phenomenal world."

However, when the 19th-century German aesthetic psychologists (Fogle, 1949/1962) discussed this relationship in terms of responses to art and literature, they did not use Herder's term. For example, Scherner's work on dreams (1861), an influential source of Freudian theory, describes "I am you" as a state "in which our whole personality (consciously or unconsciously) merges with the object" (p. 25) and philosopher Friedrich Theodor Vischer (1807–1887), the founder of a new scientific aesthetics—the science of the beautiful—declares that "I am You" is the source of aesthetic appreciation—the "pantheistic impulse to merge our spirit with the sensuous world" (1846–1857/1994, p. 20), but neither uses the term "einfühling." Friedrich's son, Robert Vischer, was mistakenly given credit for inventing "einfühling" in 1873 (1994) to express a pantheistic union. The credit for translation into English goes to Edward Bradford Titchener, who in 1909 coined the word "empathy" to express the difference between "einfühlung" (in-feeling) and another of Robert Vischer's terms, "mitgefühlung" (with-feeling; 1873/1994, "already in the English lexicon as 'sympathy'" (Wispé, 1987, p. 18). We follow Titchener (1909a, 1909b), who followed Vischer (1873/1994), in defining empathy in accordance with the mystic tradition as the merging of the self with another.

The tradition shapes empathic responses to aesthetic stimuli, in which individuals so closely identify "with a particular character in a film, book, or play" (Mercer, 1972, p. 15) that they completely forget their own personal existence in experiencing "the feelings of the characters" (Delacroix, 1927, p. 281). Thus, whereas sympathy stems from the perspective of an observer aware of the self as different from another, empathy stems from the perspective of a participant caught up in the dramatic world. The response is said to be spontaneous and involuntary rather than something that the individual can control (Strayer & Eisenberg, 1987). To summarize the sympathy–empathy distinction in the philosophical, aesthetic, and psychological literatures, empathy is a vicarious emotional reaction to a performance (movie, play, advertisement; Eisenberg et al., 1989) in which the empathizer experiences an involuntary rush of emotional fusion triggered by a unified linear plot leading toward a resolution, causality, and characters who interact and change (Stern, 1994). Based on the premise that advertising narratives possess the same plot elements, we propose that they will engender an increase in sympathy, the recognition of emotions, and empathy, the vicarious sharing of emotions.

Sympathy–Empathy Responses and Positive Feelings

Sympathy and empathy responses are likely to be associated with positive feelings flowing from both understanding characters and sharing their emotions (see Lazarus, 1991, for a review). That is, sympathy generates upbeat or warm feelings and when viewers recognize these feelings in a character, it is a pleasant experience that evokes positive feelings; viewers may also experience personal feelings similar to those recognized via the characters and plot, without losing consciousness of themselves. On the other hand, in empathy, viewers lose their self-awareness and share in the emotional responses perceived to be felt by the characters in the narrative ad. Insofar as viewers are able to lose themselves in an ad, empathy is predicted to mediate emotional responses. Thus, we propose a sequence of emotional responses, where the narrative structure of advertisements brings about sympathy, then perhaps empathy, which in turn produces upbeat and warm feeling responses. Our findings indicate that sympathy is likely to have both a direct effect on emotional response and an indirect effect via empathy, which may not be experienced by some viewers (Escalas & Stern, 2003; see Fig. 9.1).

Response Strength

Finally, we propose that empathy responses will have a stronger effect than sympathy responses on the positive feelings generated by the advertising narrative. Aesthetic psychologists considered empathy the only "correct aesthetic attitude," with correctness defined as a positive affective response in which the perceiver is motivated "to live in the character" (Langfeld, 1920/1967, p. 137). Audience sympathy was deemed a weaker response to created works because viewers remained too detached and too self-aware to experience strong emotions (Langfeld, 1920/1967). Advertising research (Deighton et al., 1988) confirmed the literary assumption, with "good" drama found to induce more empathy than "bad" drama. We follow this research in predicting that empathy will induce stronger warm and upbeat feelings in viewers and that sympathy will induce milder feelings.

Figure 9.1 summarizes the relationships proposed thus far: Advertising narratives are able to evoke the desired positive feelings by providing the context necessary for consumers to recognize (sympathy) and vicariously experience (empathy) the characters' emotions, leading directly to upbeat and warm feelings that have a favorable direct effect on ad attitudes and, via the latter, a favorable indirect effect on brand attitudes.

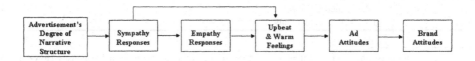

Figure 9.1.   Feelings response progression proposed for advertising narratives.

ADVERTISING NARRATIVE EXPERIMENT

In our study, six ads were shown to 154 participants. The ads were selected from award winning Clio ads in 1999 and 2000 (see Table 9.2); all six commercials tell a story, in varying degrees, to test the relationships highlighted in Figure 9.1.[2] Each ad was coded using a six-item scale developed to measure the degree to which an advertisement has the structural elements identified previously as being indicative of narratives (Escalas, 2004; see Table 9.3). After viewing each ad, participants rated the extent to which they experienced upbeat (19 items, e.g., cheerful, energetic, happy, $\alpha = .91$) and warm feelings (9 items, e.g., affectionate, moved, sentimental, $\alpha = .88$; adapted from Goodstein et al., 1990). This was followed with measures of ad and brand attitudes (each with 3-item scales, $\alpha = .96$ and .97, respectively), and the degree of empathy and sympathy evoked by each advertisement (Escalas & Stern, 2003, see Table 9.4).

Results

The prediction that advertising narratives will lead to positive affective responses is supported. Our study finds that narrative structure has a positive effect on both up-

TABLE 9.2

Stimulus Advertisements for Experiment

Brand	Description of the Ad	Narrative Structure Score	Mean Sympathy Response	Mean Empathy Response
Pepsi®	Cute girl lectures bar owner about American freedom to choose soda brands	3.67	4.90	2.45
Milk	Lover leaving a home turns out to be the milkman	3.83	4.51	2.76
Finesse®	Men's support group recite bad love poems for their wives	3.33	4.25	1.94
E*trade®	Man hospitalized for having money "coming out the wazoo"	3.67	4.75	2.22
E-Campus	Student pretends to be kidnapped to get money from his parents	3.83	5.15	2.81
Kuoni Vacations	Returning vacationers are so lost in their experience they forget to greet their awaiting family	3.67	5.62	2.41

[2]Clearly, there are idiosyncratic differences in these ads that contribute to emotional responses. However, when one combines the results from our study here with the emerging body of work that examines the effect of narrative structure on emotional responses (e.g., Escalas et al., 2004; Escalas & Stern, 2003), the consistent pattern becomes quite compelling.

TABLE 9.3

Narrative Structure Coding Scale Items (Escalas, 2004; $\alpha = .94$)

1. To what extent does this ad consist of actors engaged in actions to achieve goals?

2. To what extent does this ad let you know what the actors are thinking and feeling?

3. To what extent does this ad provide you with insight about the personal evolution or change in the life of a character?

4. To what extent does this ad explain why things happen, that is, what caused things to happen?

5. To what extent does this ad have a well delineated beginning (initial event), middle (crisis or turning point), and ending (conclusion)?

6. To what extent does this ad focus on specific, particular events rather than on generalizations or abstractions?

Note. These items are measured on 5-point scales, anchored by not at all (1) and very much so (5).

TABLE 9.4

Ad Response Sympathy and Empathy Scale Items (Escalas & Stern, 2003)

ARS Items ($\alpha = .78$)	*ARE Items ($\alpha = .93$)*
1. Based on what was happening in the commercial, I understood what the characters were feeling.	1. While watching the ad, I experienced feeling as if the events were really happening to me.
2. Based on what was happening in the commercial, I understood what was bothering the characters.	2. While watching the ad, I felt as though I were one of the characters.
3. While watching the ad, I tried to understand the events as they occurred.	3. While watching the ad, I felt as though the events in the ad were happening to me.
4. While watching the ad, I tried to understand the characters' motivation.	4. While watching the commercial, I experienced many of the same feelings that the characters portrayed.
5. I was able to recognize the problems that the characters in the ad had.	5. While watching the commercial, I felt as if the characters' feelings were my own.

beat and warm feelings (see Table 9.5). Thus, ads that tell better stories are able to evoke more upbeat and warm feelings in ad viewers. Warm feelings in particular have a strong, positive relationship with narrative structure, which is consistent with the theorizing of Stayman and Aaker (1988): Well-developed stories provide meaning for the characters and events these authors state are necessary in ads to evoke warm feelings. However, we propose a specific progression from recognition to absorption in order to better understand the relationship between narrative structure and emotional responses, which we test next.

The prediction that advertising narratives will lead to sympathy and empathy responses is also supported. Narrative structure has a positive effect on both ad re-

TABLE 9.5

Experimental Results

Independent Variable	Dependent Variable	Relationship
Narrative Structure	Upbeat Feelings	β = 64*
	Warm Feelings	β = 1.35***
	Sympathy	β = 1.01*
	Empathy	β = 1.75***
Sympathy	Upbeat Feelings	β = .09**
	Warm Feelings	β = .07*
	Ad Attitudes	β = .16*
Empathy	Upbeat Feelings	β = .23***
	Warm Feelings	β = .23***
	Ad Attitudes	β = .24***
Upbeat Feelings	Ad Attitudes	β = 1.33***
	Brand Attitudes	β = .54***
Warm Feelings	Ad Attitudes	β = .40***
	Brand Attitudes	β = .51***
Ad Attitudes	Brand Attitudes	β = .43***

$*p < .10, **p < .05, ***p < .01.$

sponse sympathy and empathy (see Table 9.5). Thus, ads that tell better stories allow consumers to recognize the emotions portrayed in the ad (sympathy) and also vicariously experience them (empathy), although the overall level of empathy was lower than that of sympathy, consistent with previous research (Escalas & Stern, 2003; see Table 9.2 for means). Our theory predicts a sequential relationship between sympathy, empathy, and positive feelings responses. To test this sequence, we performed a series of mediation tests to explore the relationships found in Table 9.5. First, sympathy should mediate the effect of narrative structure on empathy. We find that the effect of narrative structure on empathy is marginally reduced, $F(1, 146) = 5.35, p = .02; Z = 1.46, p < .10$, when sympathy is added to the model, whereas the effect of sympathy on empathy remains significant, $F(1, 146) = 3.96, p < .01$, indicating partial mediation (see Fig. 9.2 for a graphical summary of our mediation test results).

Next in the sequence, the effect of sympathy on feelings should be mediated by empathy. In the case of warm feelings, sympathy is fully mediated by empathy: Sympathy becomes insignificant, $F(1, 146) = 2.11, p = .15; Z = 2.76, p < .01$, whereas empathy remains significant $F(1, 146) = 30.25, p < .01$. In the case of upbeat feelings, the effect of sympathy is partially mediated by empathy—sympathy:

$F(1, 146) = 3.92, p = .05; Z = 2.73, p < .01$; empathy: $F(1, 146) = 30.79, p < .01$. The partial mediation findings for upbeat feelings are consistent with Escalas and Stern (2003), whereas our findings for warm feelings showing full mediation provide new insight.

Based on previous advertising research (Aaker & Stayman, 1989; Escalas et al., 2004), we would expect empathy to play a stronger role in the generation of warm feelings. Warm feelings include such items as hopeful, kind, and warmhearted. Typically, an individual feels affectionate or moved as a reaction to characters or events. Thus, evoking extensive warm feelings requires a deep connection between the viewer and the ad's characters and plot; such absorption is the purview of empathy. On the other hand, upbeat feelings may not require the same degree of empathic response. Upbeat feelings may be evoked by fast-paced music or graphics in addition to arising as a result of the plot. Thus, not all positive feelings behave in the same way as responses to narrative advertisements.

We also predict that empathy will generate stronger positive feelings than sympathy. Within the models exploring the relationship between narrative structure and upbeat feelings and warm feelings (see Table 9.5), we compared the coefficients of empathy and sympathy to see if there is a significant difference and in each case there is (upbeat feelings: empathy $\beta = .23$, sympathy $\beta = .09$, $t = 1.93$, $p < .05$, one-tailed; warm feelings: empathy $\beta = .23$, sympathy $\beta = .07$, $t = 2.25$, $p < .05$, one-tailed). Empathy responses have a significantly more powerful effect than sympathy responses on both warm and upbeat feelings. Thus, although it appears to be more difficult to elicit an empathy response, compared to a sympathy response (see Table 9.2), even relatively low levels of empathy have a powerful effect on positive feelings responses.

Consistent with previous consumer research, our findings reveal that upbeat and warm feelings have a positive effect on ad attitudes, as do sympathy and empathy

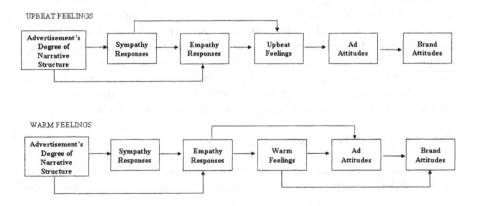

Figure 9.2.   Feelings response progression results.

(see Table 9.5). Upbeat feelings fully mediate the effect of both sympathy—sympathy: $F(1, 146) < 1.0$, ns, $Z = 3.16$, $p < .01$; upbeat: $F(1, 146) = 69.17$, $p < .01$—and empathy on ad attitudes —empathy: $F(1, 146) < 1.0$, ns, $Z = 5.23$, $p < .01$; upbeat: $F(1, 146) = 59.37$, $p < .01$. Warm feelings partially mediate the effect of empathy on ad attitudes—empathy: $F(1, 146) = 5.09$, $p < .05$, $Z = 2.79$, $p < .01$; warm: $F(1, 146) = 10.47$, $p < .01$; there is no need to test for sympathy, because empathy fully mediates the effect of sympathy on warm feelings.[3] This finding is consistent with narrative transportation, where absorption into a story leads to strong affective responses that influence persuasion (Green & Brock, 2000).

Finally, ad attitudes have a positive effect on brand attitudes (see Table 9.5). In terms of the sequence proposed in this chapter, ad attitudes fully mediate the effect of upbeat feelings on brand attitudes (upbeat: $F(1, 146) < 1.0$, ns, $Z = 5.04$, $p < .01$; ad attitudes: $F(1, 146) = 21.04$, $p < .01$). However, in the case of warm feelings, ad attitudes only partially mediate the effect on brand attitudes (warm: $F(1, 146) = 6.80$, $p < .01$, $Z = 2.76$, $p < .01$; ad attitudes: $F(1, 146) = 30.60$, $p < .01$). This result for warm feelings is consistent with both our findings thus far and our theoretical framework. First, we continue to find that not all positive feelings behave in the same manner. Second, there appears to be something powerful about ads that evoke empathy and warm feelings on the downstream responses in our Figure 9.1. This is consistent with the premise of our chapter, which predicts that becoming absorbed in a narrative ad and sharing in the emotions experienced by the characters produces strong effects.

CONCLUSIONS

In summary, our experimental results confirm that ads that tell stories evoke more positive feelings, which favorably impact ad and brand attitudes. How does this happen? Advertising narratives provide the structure necessary to recognize and relive emotions. The chronology and causality of narrative structure gives rise to sympathy and empathy responses to advertisements. Advertisers can set the stage for positive feelings reactions by creating advertising narratives. These narratives show characters engaged in actions to achieve their goals. Good narratives will include characters and plotlines that consumers can sympathize with (in the sense of recognizing the emotions that are portrayed) and empathize with (as in vicariously experiencing the same feelings). Empathy, although more difficult to achieve, is the stronger of the two responses, leading to higher levels of both upbeat and warm feelings.

Future Research Directions

Narrative Structure and Transformation. Future researchers can benefit from more detailed exploration of the effects of variations in the narrative structure

---

[3]More detailed mediation test results may be obtained from the lead author of this chapter.

of advertisements. Aspects of advertising structure available for further examination include the brand as a minor prop versus a central feature, the use of different dramatic plots (comic, romantic; Stern, 1995) to evoke various types of feelings, variation in the degrees of character development, and the influence of surprise (plot twists) and suspense (cliff-hanger endings). One open question is whether ads with narrative imbalance are inherently more interesting and provocative than ads with balance, which may come across as too mechanistic. Another is whether formulaic ads versus novel ones elicit more favorable responses, with some researchers finding that overly formulaic scriptlike narratives score poorly (Brewer & Lichtenstein, 1981), and others stating that overly novel narratives risk being incomprehensible (Mandler, 1984) in a 30–60 second advertisement. The cards are also still out on research claims that narrative ads have the power to guide consumption experiences such as Puto and Wells' claim (1984) that one type of ad is able to "transform" product usage experiences, and Scott's claim (1994) that narratives are better able than exhortation to change beliefs. Deighton's (1984) proposition that advertising narratives affect consumption by presenting viewers with a hypothetical experience that sets up a confirmatory bias also requires further investigation to discover whether consumer decisions confirm the hypothetical scenario.

Advertiser Versus Consumer Manipulation of Responses: Automaticity and Control.   Advertisers are often considered manipulators of consumer responses, but it may be that consumers are able to control emotional responses rather than being victims of external manipulation. Hodges and Wegner (1997) proposed a theory of automatic versus controlled responses based on the premise that control, as an "intentional, conscious, controllable, or effortful" response (our sympathy), is on one pole of an emotional response continuum in which automaticity (our empathy), an "unintentional, outside of awareness, [and] uncontrollable" response, is on the other. That is, the automaticity–control spectrum spans a response range from automatic merging of self–other to learned awareness that one's own mental states are different from those of others. The theory grows out of developmental research findings that the purely automatic emotional responses of infancy give way to the learned responses of adults. Following motor mimicry theory (Hoffman, 1977), Hodges and Wegner posit infants as "veritable emotional sponges, automatically experiencing the emotions of everyone they encounter as a result of basic processes of imitation" (1997, p. 316), in contrast to adults who learn to control their emotions. The research assumption is that adults are motivated to establish voluntary control by morality (altruism, doing the right thing), intellectual curiosity (discovering reasons for people's behavior), self-curiosity (discovering reasons for personal behavior), and desire for external rewards. Advertisers are particularly practiced in figuring "out how others feel in order to manipulate their behavior ... to win dates, sales, and lots of other good stuff" (1997, p. 321), and even adults who can control responses can also be susceptible to "emotional contagion" if "seeing and mirroring the emotional expressions of physical states of others" becomes an automatic pathway to empathy (1997, p. 16). Nonetheless, consumers can fight back and manipulate their exposure to stimuli such that an automatic response is precluded by the control mechanisms of "initialization" (Hodges & Wegner, 1997, p. 318), a conscious decision to avoid absorption in a character (Bargh, Chen, & Burrows, 1996), or "perspective suppression" to suppress thoughts that encourage empathy. It is possible that advertising objectification can generate these mechanisms because stereotyping characters as members of a class, rather than as individuals, may block absorption. At present, research on emotional effects of narratives is at so early a stage that it is ripe for future study. According to Pasco (1994), "The genre has a central, identifiable set of characteristics which each age and each author deploys in different ways and with different variables. The result is generally recognizable ... but specific to the author, age, and culture" (p. 115). What researchers can be sure of is that advertising narratives are merely the newest branch of an old tree and they will continue to evolve just as they have for millennia.

ACKNOWLEDGMENTS

We thank Tina M. Lowrey and Rashmi Adaval for their thoughtful comments on this chapter.

REFERENCES

Aaker, D. A, & Stayman, D. M. (1989). What mediates the emotional response to advertising? The case of warmth. In P. Cafferata & A. M. Tybout (Eds.), *Cognitive and affective responses to advertising* (pp. 287–303). Lexington, MA: Lexington Books.

Aaker, D. A., Stayman, D. M., & Hagerty, M. R. (1986). Warmth in advertising: Measurement, impact, and sequence effects. *Journal of Consumer Research, 12*, 365–381.

Aristotle. (1991). *Rhetoric* (G. A. Kennedy, Trans.). New York: Oxford University Press.

Averill, J. R. (1994). I feel, therefore I am—I think. In P. Edman & R. J. Davidson (Eds.), *The nature of emotion: Fundamental questions* (pp. 379–385). New York: Oxford University Press.

Bargh, J. A., Chen, M., & Burrows, L. (1996). Automaticity of social behavior: Direct effects of trait construct and stereotype activation on action. *Journal of Personality and Social Psychology, 71*, 230–244.

Baumeister, R. F., & Newman, L. S. (1994). How stories make sense of personal experiences: Motives that shape autobiographical narratives. *Personality and Social Psychology Bulletin, 20*(6), 676–690.

Berger, A. A. (1997). *Narratives in popular culture, media, and everyday life*. Thousand Oaks, CA: Sage Publications.

Bransford, J. D., Barclay, J. R., & Franks, J. J. (1972). Sentence memory: A constructive versus interpretive approach. *Cognitive Psychology, 3*, 193–209.

Brewer, W. F., & Lichtenstein, E. H. (1981). Event schemas, story schemas, and story grammars. In J. Long & A. Baddeley (Eds.), *Attention and performance* (Vol. 9, pp. 363–379). Hillsdale, NJ: Lawrence Erlbaum Associates.

Brown, S. P., Homer, P. M., & Inman, J. J. (1998). A meta-analysis of relationships between ad-evoked feelings and advertising responses. *Journal of Marketing Research, 35*, 114–126.

Bruner, J. (1986). *Actual minds, possible worlds*, Cambridge, MA: Harvard University Press.

Bruner, J. (1990). *Acts of meaning*, Cambridge, MA: Harvard University Press.

Buber, M. (1970). *I and thou* (W. Kaufmann, Trans.). New York: Scribner's. (Original work published 1937)

Burke, K. (1969). *A grammar of motives*. Berkeley, CA: University of California Press.

Clore, G. L. (1994). Why emotions require cognition. In P. Ekman & R. J. Davidson (Eds.), *The nature of emotion: Fundamental questions* (pp. 181–191). New York: Oxford University Press.

Deighton, J. (1984). The interaction of advertising and evidence. *Journal of Consumer Research, 11*, 763–770.

Deighton, J., & Hoch, S. J. (1993). Teaching emotion with drama advertising. In A. A. Mitchell (Ed.), *Advertising exposure, memory, and choice* (pp. 261–282). Hillsdale, NJ: Lawrence Erlbaum Associates.

Deighton, J., Romer, D., & McQueen, J. (1989). Using drama to persuade. *Journal of Consumer Research, 16*, 335–343.

Delacroix, H. (1953). Varieties of aesthetic experience. In E. Vivas & M. Krieger (Eds.), *The problems of aesthetics* (pp. 279–284). New York: Holt, Rinehart & Winston. (Original work published 1927)

Edell, J. A., & Burke, M. C. (1987). The power of feelings in understanding advertising effects. *Journal of Consumer Research, 14*, 421–433.

Eisenberg, N., Fabes, R. A., Schaller, M., & Miller, P. A. (1989). Sympathy and personal distress: Development, gender differences, and interrelations of indexes. In N. Eisenberg (Ed.), *Empathy and related emotional responses* (pp. 107–127). San Francisco: Jossey-Bass.

Eisenberg, N., & Strayer, J. (1987). Critical issues in the study of empathy. In N. Eisenberg & J. Strayer (Eds.), *Empathy and its development* (pp. 3–16). Cambridge, MA: Cambridge University Press.

Escalas, J. E. (2004). Narrative processing: Building consumer connections to brands. *Journal of Consumer Psychology, 14*, 168–179.

Escalas, J. E., Moore, M. C., & Britton, J. E. (2004). Fishing for feelings: A hook helps! *Journal of Consumer Psychology, 14*, 105–113.

Escalas, J. E., & Stern, B. B. (2003). Sympathy and empathy: Emotional responses to advertising dramas. *Journal of Consumer Research, 29*, 566–578.

Feldman, C. F., Bruner, J., Renderer, B., & Spitzer, S. (1990). Narrative comprehension. In B. K. Britton & A. D. Pelligrini (Eds.), *Narrative thought and narrative language* (pp. 1–78). Hillsdale, NJ: Lawrence Erlbaum Associates.

Fogle, R. H. (1962). *The imagery of Keats and Shelley: A comparative study*. Chapel Hill, NC: University of North Carolina Press. (Original work published 1949)

Forster, E. M. (1954). *Aspects of the novel*. New York: Harcourt, Brace & World. (Original work published 1927)

Gergen, K. J., & Gergen, M. M. (1988). Narrative and the self as relationship. *Advances in Experimental Social Psychology, 21*, 17–56.

Goodstein, R. C., Edell, J. A., & Moore, M. C. (1990). When are feelings generated? Assessing the presence and reliability of feelings based on storyboards and animatics. In S. J. Agres, J. A. Edell, & T. M. Dubitsky (Eds.), *Emotion in advertising: Theoretical and practical explorations* (pp. 175–193). Westport, CT: Quorum Books.

Green, M. C., & Brock, T. C. (2000). The role of transportation in the persuasiveness of public narratives. *Journal of Personality and Social Psychology, 79*(5), 701–721.

Herder, J. G. (1800). Kalligone. In B. Suphan (Ed.), *Herders samtliche werke* [The complete works of Herde] (Vol. 22, pp. 85–86). Berlin: Weidmann'sche Buchhandlung.

Hermans, H. M. (1996). Voicing the self: From information processing to dialogical inter-change. *Journal of Personality and Social Psychology, 119*(1), 31–50.

Hodges, S. D., & Wegner, D. M. (1997). Automatic and controlled empathy. In W. Ickes (Ed.), *Empathic accuracy* (pp. 311–340). New York: Guilford.

Hoffman, M. L. (1977). Empathy, its development, and prosocial implications. In *Nebraska symposium on motivation* (Vol. 25, pp. 169–217). Lincoln, NE: University of Nebraska Press.

Holbrook, M. B., & Batra, R. (1987). Assessing the role of emotions as mediators of con-sumer responses to advertising. *Journal of Consumer Research, 14*, 404–420.

Hume, D. (1968). *A treatise on human nature* (L. Shelby-Bigge, Ed.). London: Oxford Uni-versity Press. (Original work published 1739)

Kerby, A. P. (1991). *Narrative and the self.* Bloomington, IN: Indiana University Press.

Langfeld, H. S. (1967). *The aesthetic attitude.* Port Washington, NY: Kennikat Press. (Origi-nal work published 1920)

Lazarus, R. S. (1991). Progress on a cognitive-motivational-relational theory of emotion. *American Psychologist, 46*, 819–834.

Lazarus, R. S. (1999). *Stress and emotion: A new synthesis.* New York: Springer.

Lowrey, T. M., & Otnes, C. C. (2003). Consumer fairy tales of the perfect Christmas: Villains and other *dramatis personae.* In C. C. Otnes & T. M. Lowrey (Eds.), *Contemporary con-sumption rituals: A research anthology* (pp. 99–122). Mahwah, NJ: Lawrence Erlbaum Associates.

Macfie, A. L. (1959). Adam Smith's moral sentiments as a foundation for his Wealth of Na-tions. *Oxford Economic Papers, 11*, 209–228.

Mandler, J. M. (1984). *Stories, scripts, and scenes: Aspects of schema theory.* Hillsdale, NJ: Lawrence Erlbaum Associates.

Martin, W. (1986). *Recent theories of narrative.* Ithaca, NY: Cornell University Press.

McQuarrie, E. F., & Mick, D. G. (1996). Figures of rhetoric in advertising language. *Journal of Consumer Research, 22*, 420–434.

Mercer, P. (1972). *Sympathy and ethics: A study of the relationship between sympathy and morality with special reference to Hume's Treatise.* Oxford, England: Clarendon.

Mick, D. G. (1987). Toward a semiotic of advertising story grammars. In J. Umiker-Sebeok (Ed.), *Marketing and semiotics: New directions in the study of signs for sale* (pp. 249–278). Berlin: de Gruyter.

Morrison, K. F. (1988). *"I am you": The hermeneutics of empathy in Western literature, the-ology, and art.* Princeton, NJ: Princeton University Press.

Pasco, A. H. (1994). On defining short stories. In C. E. May (Ed.), *The new short story theo-ries* (pp. 114–130). Athens, OH: Ohio University Press.

Pennington, N., & Hastie, R. (1986). Evidence evaluation in complex decision making. *Journal of Personality and Social Psychology, 51*(2), 242–258.

Plato. (1991). *The republic* (2nd ed.; A. Bloom, Trans.). New York: Basic Books. (Original work published c. 5 BC)

Polkinghorne, D. E. (1991). Narrative and self-concept. *Journal of Narrative and Life His-tory, 1*(2–3), 135–153.

Prince, G. (1987). *A dictionary of narratology.* Lincoln, NE: University of Nebraska Press.

Propp, V. (1958/1968). *Morfologiia skazki* [Morphology of the folktale] (2nd ed.; L. Scott, Trans.; L. A. Wagner, Ed.). Austin, TX: University of Texas Press. (Original work pub-lished 1928)

Puto, C. P., & Wells, W. D. (1984). Informational and transformational advertising: The dif-ferential effects of time. In T. C. Kinnear (Ed.), *Advances in consumer research* (Vol. 11, pp. 572–576). Provo, UT: Association for Consumer Research.

Schank, R. C., & Abelson, R. P. (1995). Knowledge and memory: The real story. In R. S. Wyer, Jr. (Ed.), *Knowledge and memory: The real story* (pp. 1–85). Hillsdale, NJ: Lawrence Erlbaum Associates.

Scherner, K. A. (1861). *Das leben des traumes* [The life of dreams]. Berlin: Heinrich Schindler.

Scott, L. M. (1994). The bridge from text to mind: Adapting reader-response theory to consumer research. *Journal of Consumer Research, 21*, 461–480.

Shweder, R. A. (1994). "You're not sick: You're just in love:" Emotion as an interpretive system. In P. Ekman & R. J. Davidson (Eds.), *The nature of emotion: Fundamental questions* (pp. 32–44). New York: Oxford University Press.

Stayman, D. M., & Aaker, D. A. (1988). Are all the effects of ad-induced feelings mediated by A_{Ad}? *Journal of Consumer Research, 15*, 368–373.

Stern, B. B. (1994). Classical and vignette television advertising dramas: Structural models, formal analysis, and consumer effects. *Journal of Consumer Research, 20*, 601–615.

Stern, B. B. (1995). Consumer myths, Frye's taxonomy, and the structural analysis of consumption text. *Journal of Consumer Research, 22*, 165–185.

Stern, B. B. (1998). Narratological analysis of consumer voices in postmodern research accounts. In B. B. Stern (Ed.), *Representing consumers: Voices, views and visions* (pp. 55–82). London: Routledge.

Strayer, J., & Eisenberg, N. (1987). Empathy viewed in context. In N. Eisenberg & J. Strayer (Eds.), *Empathy and its development* (pp. 389–398). Cambridge, England: Cambridge University Press.

Titchener, E. B. (1909a). *A text book of psychology*. New York: Macmillan.

Titchener, E. B. (1909b). *Elementary psychology of the thought processes*. New York: Macmillan.

Vischer, F. T. (1846–1857). *Ästhetik, oder Wissenschaft des Schönen* [Aesthetics: Or the science of beauty]. Reutlingen und Leipzig: C. Macken.

Vischer, R. (1994). On the optical sense of form: A contribution to aesthetics. In H. F. Mallgrave & E. Ikonomou (Trans.), *Empathy, form, and space: Problems in German aesthetics, 1873–1893* (pp. 98–173). Chicago: University of Chicago Press. (Original work published 1873)

Vivas, E., & Krieger, M. (1953). Section 5: The aesthetic experience. In E. Vivas & M. Krieger (Eds.), *The problems of aesthetics* (pp. 277–279). New York: Holt, Rinehart & Winston.

Wells, W. D. (1989). Lectures and dramas. In P. Cafferata & A. M. Tybout (Eds.), *Cognitive and affective responses to advertising* (pp. 13–20). Lexington, MA: Lexington Books.

Wispé, L. (1986). The distinction between sympathy and empathy: To call forth a concept, a word is needed. *Journal of Personality and Social Psychology, 50*, 314–321.

Wispé, L. (1987). History of the concept of empathy. In N. E. Eisenberg & J. Strayer (Eds.), *Empathy and its development* (pp. 17–37). Cambridge, England: Cambridge University Press.

Wyer, R. S., & Radvansky, G. A. (1999). The comprehension and validation of social information. *Psychological Review, 106*, 89–118.

CHAPTER 10

The Role of Language and Images in the Creation and Use of Advertising Myths

Rashmi Adaval
Hong Kong University of Science and Technology

On Christmas Eve, thousands of children across North America snuggle into bed, comforted by the belief that Santa will come down the chimney and leave behind wonderful gifts if they have been good (or perhaps even if they have been a little bad). The myth of Santa Claus is one of the many that have persisted for generations. Although myths have traditionally involved gods and heroes, they can also refer to a belief or a set of beliefs (often unproven) that have accrued around a person, an object, a phenomenon, or an institution. The study of myths is rooted in literature and sociology and few attempts, if any, have been made to understand the psychology behind how these unsubstantiated beliefs are formed, their integration into our knowledge base, and the myriad ways in which they can influence our behavior.

DEFINING A "MYTH"

Defining a "myth" poses a challenge. When a construct taken from one discipline is discussed using psychological theories from another, its definition takes on particular importance because not only should the definition be one that is parsimonious with the psychological theories that will be used to discuss it, but it should also be acceptable to the disciplines that have traditionally studied it.

Historically, the word "myth" comes from the Greek word "mythos," which means "speech" or "discourse." Over time, however, the word took on multiple meanings. It is sometimes used to refer to a fable or legend that explained the mysteries of creation and nature. These mythical stories were not necessarily thought of as untrue. In many cases, their validity was taken for granted by cultures and was passed down from one generation to the next. Myths can also refer to ill-founded beliefs in support of current practices that are accepted by members of a group or culture and are not open to question. The multiplicity of meanings makes it difficult to come up with a definition that is acceptable. However, for the purposes of this chapter, a myth will be defined as a belief or set of beliefs that is propagated culturally but is not verified, either because it is not possible to do so or because it exists at a level at which we do not question it. Thus, "myths" are not necessarily falsehoods. They are merely beliefs that have not been questioned and verified.

All beliefs can be categorized as verifiable or not verifiable. Among beliefs that are potentially verifiable, some have been verified and found to be true (or untrue). For example, the belief that most people pay their bill after eating a meal at a restaurant is one that we all have acquired through exposure to restaurant behavior. It is not only potentially verifiable but has been verified as "true" through numerous experiences at restaurants. Thus, it would not fall into the category of a myth. The Santa "myth" provides an interesting example. According to the definition adopted in this chapter, it is categorized as myth because from a child's perspective, it is a belief that has not yet been questioned or verified as true or false. From the perspective of an adult, it is not a myth because it has been questioned and found to be false (i.e., a portly figure does not descend down the chimney on Christmas Eve). Other types of beliefs that tend to persist in several cultures such as "a woman's place is in the home" are, for two reasons, typically not verifiable. First, in cultures where they persist, they are not even open to question. Second, even if they were open to scrutiny, it would often require a massive social experiment to demonstrate their validity (e.g., show that women were more proficient in the home than at any other task outside the home). The lack of scrutiny coupled with the inability to really prove or disprove a belief leads to its persistence over the years. Thus, the definition of a myth is not based on whether a belief is "true" or "false." Rather, it is based on the tacit acceptance of a belief (without verification) and its propagation culturally.

This somewhat broad definition of "myths" allows us to examine a wide variety of beliefs (concrete and abstract) that guide our consumption behavior. Many of these myths find their origins in the language and images used by advertising. By a process that is relatively ambiguous, the images and words portrayed on television become myths and take on the appearance of "universal truths" that are often not questioned and are taken for granted within a particular culture. As a result of this "taken for granted' quality, they form the bedrock of tacit knowledge that we have about the world in which we live.

Myths can exist at several different levels of complexity. At a more concrete level, they are manifest in language, signs, and stereotypes. For example, simple words and objects are imbued with similar meaning that is shared by members of a culture. Barthes (1972) illustrates how we see a difference between various types of cleaning agents like "chlorinating fluids" and "detergents." Chlorinating fluids are seen as "liquid fire" whose use should be limited lest they have a mutilating and abrasive action, whereas soap powders and detergents are seen as "liberators" and separating agents where dirt is forced out and not killed. Beliefs that exist at this level are often not articulated and we are perhaps not even aware of them. Nonetheless, they do influence our behavior, as is apparent in our choice of harsh, chlorinating fluids to beat out stubborn stains and our choice of gentler detergents for baby clothes.

Similarly, a gift can also convey either symbolic or iconic meaning and can communicate the gift-giver's intent (Mick, 1986). Such communication would not be possible if there were no culturally shared beliefs about the objects. Other concrete beliefs can also be detected in the shared meaning that is conveyed through a sign that inadvertently propagates a cultural stereotype. For example, Aunt Jemima and Frito Bandito were two such signs developed in advertising that portrayed minorities in stereotypical ways reflecting the majority's perception of the subgroup (Wilson & Gutierrez, 1985).

Myths can also take a relatively abstract form and might be detected at the level of general beliefs that cultures or subgroups share. For example, the myth that "Spending is good for the economic health of a nation" suggests that unrestrained consumption activities are good. Similarly, the belief that it is important to make a favorable first impression is also an abstract myth that is prevalent in many cultures.

The objective of this chapter is to identify how images and language from advertising combine to form myths of different sorts and the impact they have on our behavior. In addressing these issues, myths that exist at the concrete level of language (e.g., our belief that roses signify passion, or that detergents liberate dirt) and those that exist at a more abstract level (e.g., "spending is good for the economy") will be considered. Research from social and cognitive psychology will be used to identify: (a) how myths at these different levels are formed from images and language in the media and (b) how they can impact our behavior without conscious awareness of either their existence *or* the nature of their influence. The chapter is organized into four sections. The first identifies different types of myths that have emerged from past and contemporary advertising (both concrete and relatively abstract) and the processes that might be involved in their formation. The next section identifies frameworks in social and cognitive psychology that help one understand how real-world information is processed and how images and language in advertising might be represented in memory. The third section then uses these theories to show how myths are constructed and the various ways in which they influence our beliefs and behaviors. The final section discusses how myths acquire the status of "common sense" or "truth" and the forces that lead to their reinforcement, rejection, or change.

MYTHS FROM PAST AND CONTEMPORARY ADVERTISING

As described earlier, myths can exist at varying levels of abstractness. Advertising myths are no exception and a few examples of both concrete and abstract myths will be helpful.

Concrete Myths

Consider myths that originate with the use of language. These types of myths represent beliefs about language (i.e., what words and symbols signify). Thus, a person might believe that a rose signifies romance and a tomahawk chop signifies aggression in sports. These concepts might be communicated either visually or verbally. An understanding of how the mind comprehends not only the literal meaning of these signs but also what they signify (without conscious awareness of how these associations are formed) is important in understanding the impact of myths.

Formation of Associations and Meaning.   According to Saussure (1915), any linguistic sign represents a diadic relationship between two components: (a) the "signifier," which is the sound image or the psychological impression that the sound makes; and (b) the "signified," or the concept that the sign represents. Thus, when one sees the letters "ROSE" or sees a picture of a rose, two things happen. In comprehending the sign, a sound image (or signifier) is elicited. This is similar to the psychological impression that is made when one says the word "rose" to oneself. The signifier will obviously vary with the language spoken (e.g., a "rose" is called "gulab" in Hindi and "rosa" in Spanish and speakers of these languages might silently utter the appropriate sound image in their language upon encountering the sign). This sound impression (signifier) is associated with a concept, which is called the "signified." The "signified" is merely the referent of the sign (in this case, a type of flower).

Any sign, therefore, is the union of the signifier and the signified and has certain important characteristics. First, the bond between the signifier and the signified is arbitrary. Thus, a rose can be called by another name in a different language. In this case, the signifier (or sound impression) is different even though the concept it represents is the same. Second, it is also possible to change the relationship between them. Thus, the impression that the word "rose" makes could also be associated with several different concepts (e.g., "love," "Valentine's Day," "hot house plant") allowing for ambiguity and multiplicity of meaning.

Peirce (1931–1958) distinguishes between three types of signs: icons, indexes, and symbols. The difference between them depends on the nature of the relationship between the sign and its referent (i.e., the "signified"). Thus, an iconic sign is one whose meaning is based on its similarity in appearance or function to an object. For example, the icon of a folder on the computer desktop makes sense to computer users because we recognize the similarity in function between a real folder and the desktop folder. An index's referential meaning is based on a causal relationship. For example, customer satisfaction is an indexical sign in marketing linked to the idea that the product has satisfied a customer need (see Mick, 1986). Finally, a symbolic sign relates to its referent on the basis of cultural norms or convention. Thus, according to Mick (1986), advertising material that shows a couple lounging by the fireplace with a bottle of wine might represent either the good life or love, depending on the person who is interpreting the sign. It is important to note that for icons and indexical signs, the pairing of the sign with the referential meaning is not arbitrary. However, symbols derive their referential meaning from arbitrary pairings of the symbols and what they signify, allowing for multiplicity of meaning. (Thus, roses could be associated not only with passion, romance, and Valentine's Day, but also with hot house plants.)

Advertising signs are often not chosen arbitrarily. The communicator often takes into account the addressee's background, even in one-way communications like television advertisements (Fussell & Krauss, 1992; Krauss & Fussell, 1991; Lau, Chiu, & Hong, 2001). Referential meaning and associations are typically formed through advertising and marketing that shows the consumer the relationships that exist between these symbols and their personal and emotional needs. Thus, the repeated co-occurrence of roses and romantic occasions might make one person believe that roses signify romance and could account for the nebulous feeling of dissatisfaction that results when that person does not receive roses on Valentine's Day. Another person, who sees roses in the context of gardening (e.g., in a home and garden catalog), might end up with the belief that a rose is a hot house plant and signifies "high maintenance."

Consider another example of a concrete myth: signs developed in advertising based on stereotypical views of a subgroup. Advertising has conveyed certain ethnic and gender stereotypes through visual images and names that have now fallen out of favor. Nonetheless, in their time, ads for certain companies reinforced myths about the behavior of specific ethnic groups. Wilson and Gutierrez (1985) discuss the existence of Frito Bandito, the lovable Mexican bandit with an oversized mustache, sombrero, and guns, who was introduced by Frito Lay to sell corn chips. Although popular with other cultural groups, it drew the ire of Latino and Chicano activists because it reinforced a negative stereotype of Mexicans as mustachioed thieves. It is interesting to note that the myth that was perpetuated was based on a sign that consisted of a label "Frito Bandito" and an image of a small man with a big mustache wearing a sombrero and carrying guns. The pairing of the word Frito with Bandito not only suggested Mexican origins of the chips but also, by association, linked Mexicans to bandits. Similarly, the visual image perpetrated certain stereotypical images of Mexicans. Thus, the visual image, the semantic label, and the behavior of the character in the different situations depicted in the ads could lead to the formation of associations without one being aware of their various ramifications.

Inference Making and Beliefs.   The previous example of Frito Bandito shows how constant exposure to certain types of verbal information as well as nonverbal cues can lead to the formation of certain associations. Peirce (1931–1958) suggests that meaning is derived through signs by processes involving deduction, induction, or abduction. Mick (1986) provides clear examples of these processes. The two most relevant (induction and abduction) are described here to illustrate how certain beliefs that exist at the level of language (e.g., roses–passion; roses–Valentine's Day) are formed.

Advertising often shows positive stereotypes (attractive models, super moms, wealthy families, etc.). Suppose one observes a positive stereotype (e.g., an attractive man) in a television ad. One would immediately categorize him as a good role model based on his attractiveness. If he is seen engaging in a certain behavior (e.g., giving roses to his partner on Valentine's Day) then, by an inductive process, one can infer a rule (or a belief) that suggests that "Men like him give their partners roses on Valentine's Day. They have successful relationships." The process of abduction suggests a somewhat different process. In this case, one notices the behavior first, not the model. Thus, if one observes the same behavior (giving roses), one might then come up with the rule (men who give their partners roses on Valentine's Day have successful relationships) and then conclude that the person is a good role model. Thus, in both cases, simple associations might be formed between the person involved in the action, the behavior, and the conclusion ("roses–Valentine's Day–successful relationship–good partner"), and the sign "rose" might come to mean something more than just a flower.

Abstract Myths

Myths that are relatively more abstract (e.g., general beliefs about consumption activities) are not necessarily formed in the same way. Their existence at a more abstract level suggests that they perhaps require a higher level of thinking and the consumer makes inferences based on a series of very different events without being aware of having done so. Several of these more abstract myths were identified by Marchand (1985). In his analysis of early 20th-century advertising, he uncovers certain "parables" that have guided consumption behavior for decades. He calls these common themes in advertising "parables" (practical, moral lessons that can be learned from incidents in everyday life). Many of these parables reflect deep-seated beliefs (myths) that have acquired a veneer of truth and are often acted on without much questioning.

Exposure to Common Themes in Advertising.   The first parable that Marchand identified in the early 20th-century advertising was called the "parable of first impressions." He suggested that in a society that was increasingly mobile and consisted of a number of interpersonal interactions, the importance that advertising placed on first impressions helped explain and justify why some people succeeded and why others did not. Susman (1979) and Rodgers (1978) also note a shift in the 20th-century advice manuals where there was a move from the "culture of character" that was important in the 19th century to the "culture of personality." This was accompanied by changes in advertising that often promised success and popularity because of a winning first smile that could be attained by using the specified toothpaste. Similar shifts can be seen in ads for clothing, soap, shaving creams, and so on.

A second parable pertained to the impact of mass production and distribution on society. As a result of industrialization, every person in society could enjoy the convenience of mass produced goods. Labeling this parable the "democracy of goods," Marchand noted how advertising reminded people that "any woman can buy" or "every home can afford" the advertised product. Thus, equal access to consumer products was used to implicitly define democracy. For example, Ivory soap assured women that even though they could not afford an expensive maid, using Ivory would help them to have hands as nice as a lady who had such a maid. In contrast, the "democracy of afflictions" suggested that even the rich and the famous were not immune from attacks of halitosis and Listerine could help them overcome this problem. Thus, advertising endorsed this myth of equality through consumption.

Other advertising myths are reflected in the "parable of civilization redeemed" and the "parable of the captivated child." The former was based on the idea that in his attempt to master the environment, man had been led astray and only a return to things that were "natural" could set things right. The return to nature could be accomplished only through his use of "natural" products. Brands such as Squibb's vitamin products, Post's bran flakes, and Fleishman's yeast allowed him to take that path to redemption. The latter myth about the captivated child reflected an increased attention to childrearing in which the mother was shown as the only person who could guide her child's tastes by using the indispensable advertised products. Several of these parables have been categorized as myths because they were all guided by the same underlying beliefs that were shared within a culture. Further, people were not aware of how they were created and did not question them.

Extraction of Underlying Principles.   The abstract myths described earlier were created through the observation of several different situations that have at their heart a common theme even though they pertain to different products and represent different situations. The extraction of the underlying principle (and how this happens) is at the heart of how these myths are formed. For instance, assume that people see several different commercials of the form: Problem X (dandruff) can be solved by using Product A; Problem Y (falling hair) can be solved by using Product B; Problem Z (greasy hair) can be solved using Product C. The repetition of these commercials can lead them to acquire the rule, IF (problem) THEN (product), rather than an equally plausible rule, IF (problem) THEN (take care of nutrition and health). These types of propositions are learned through frequent exposure to several different types of situations that share a common theme and are called implicit theories (Wyer, 2004; Wyer & Carlston, 1979, 1994). The formation of such implicit theories and their impact on behavior will be discussed in greater detail later. However, it is sufficient at this point to note that a high degree of exposure to similar themes in advertising is necessary for the formation of such propositions. Further, the propositions are extracted from several different types of situations, unlike the simpler inference making processes that govern the creation of concrete myths.

Myths as "Truth"

Regardless of whether a myth is concrete or abstract, for it to become universal, it must take on the aura of "truth." That is, it must become something that is not questioned and is taken for granted. Barthes (1972) likens these shared meaning systems to an "anonymous ideology" that exists at the level of "normal common sense"—a place where beliefs are most firmly entrenched. Hall (1977) suggests that it is at this level of "common sense" that any ideology is very hard to refute because its spontaneous quality, transparency, and naturalness make one instantly recognize it and accept it as true without questioning the premises on which it is based.

For example, an advertisement that uses a war metaphor to describe a consumer's battle with pests at home frames the situation as a battleground and the advertised product as an entity that possesses all the attributes of a weapon (see also Phillips & McQuarrie, chap. 8 in this volume). The ads spontaneously create the idea that the modern home is a fort that has to be defended from the invading hordes of insects with the weapons (brands) that are advertised. People within a culture often share this myth and one scarcely questions it because it is very "natural" or "normal" to deal with insects in this way. Thus, the consumer's reaction to the offending pest appears normal and one does not question the idea that a small insect needs to be destroyed with such lethal force. The myth of the home as a fortress, and the consumer's battle with the elements and outside invaders, is continued in other advertising episodes where the same basic narrative (a story skeleton or prototype; see Schank & Abelson, 1995) is used to advertise products that protect the home (e.g., traps, burglar alarms, protective wood finishes, etc.) This preoccupation with protecting the home might appear strange to a person from Southeast Asia where the boundaries between the home and the outdoors are less well defined and creatures come in and out of houses more freely. It is only when a member of an out-group reflects, "Why are you killing it? Just open the window and let it fly out" does one begin to question the behavior and one's beliefs.

In a similar vein, Lakoff (2002) argues that common sense is unconscious even though it has conceptual structure. Commonsense reasoning is unconscious because we think and talk too fast and at a level that we have little awareness of and control over. Lakoff's work on metaphorical common sense illustrates how the use of metaphors in communications elicits commonsense reasoning, making the message easy to understand and unlikely to be questioned (see also Glucksberg, 2001). Lakoff discusses how a newspaper article described a district with a budget shortfall in terms of a metaphor of a poor but compassionate mother with a credit card. In the article, the local government was likened to the mother who wants to do what is good for her child. However, because she does not have the money to do so, she uses her credit card indiscriminately. The metaphor could also be interpreted to mean that the government is like an overindulgent and impractical mother who needs to learn self-discipline and self-denial to become a good mother. Lakoff says that most readers understand such rhetoric very easily because it appeals to their common sense. People rarely question the myth that is being perpetrated by the language used and demand a more responsible discussion of economic policy.

Understanding Advertising Myths
From a Psychological Perspective

To understand how myths are formed, how they take on this aura of truth, and how they impact our behavior, we must consider how the communications that we receive in verbal and nonverbal form get internalized into beliefs and why these beliefs are not questioned and consequently influence behavior (either consciously or without much cognitive deliberation).

The existence of these two levels of advertising myths suggests that they might be created at different levels of cognitive activity. That is, they could be created in the course of passively observing events that occur in one's natural surroundings or in the mass media without much cognitive effort. Or, they might be formed via a more deliberative process. To better understand how signs and symbols in advertising take on meaning and form the basis of our beliefs, it is useful to blend findings from the areas of semiotics and psycholinguistics with research in other areas of social and cognitive psychology. The preceding discussion has focused on three major points. First, myths can exist at various levels of abstractness. Second, the processes that lead to the formation of myths at these two levels of abstractness could be quite different. Third, they are formed not only via language but also through our observation of events that consist of both verbal and visual information, and it is their closeness to real-life experience that might give them an aura of truth. The following discussion addresses how this might happen.

The next section will identify frameworks in social and cognitive psychology that can be used to show how images and language in advertising might be represented in memory, and identify different dual process theories that help understand how real-world information is processed. The section that follows then uses these frameworks to show how these myths are formed and the ways in which they can influence our beliefs and behaviors. The final section will discuss how myths acquire this status of "commonsense" or "truth" and the forces that lead to their reinforcement, rejection, or change.

COMPREHENSION AND PROCESSING OF VERBAL
AND NONVERBAL INFORMATION

Advertising typically consists of verbal (linguistic) and nonverbal information (music and images). To identify how advertising reinforces certain myths through images and language, one must confront the issue of how these two types of information are represented in memory in the course of comprehending the commercials. Several theories in cognitive and social psychology have attempted to provide a conceptualization of how stimuli of the sort encountered in everyday life are represented in memory (Wyer, 2004; Wyer & Radvansky, 1999). Many of these theories suggest that, in the course of comprehending stimuli (e.g., an event shown in an ad or a sentence from the copy), a mental representation or simulation of it is created. This representation has sometimes been conceptualized as a mental model (Johnson-Laird, 1983, 1989) or a situation model (Wyer & Radvansky, 1999). It is formed in the course of comprehending both sentences (Johnson-Laird, 1983; Kintsch, 1998; Zwann & Radvansky, 1998) and observed events (Adaval & Wyer, 2004; Magliano, Dijkstra, & Zwann, 1996).

Nature of Representational Forms

Wyer and Radvansky (1999) suggest that in the course of comprehending an event that is temporally and spatially localized, a mental simulation of it is formed. This simulation (an event or situation model) is similar to a mental image and might reflect the spatial relationships between the various objects and entities composing the situation. Thus, its contents might be coded both visually and acoustically.

Empirical work by Radvansky and Zacks (1991; see also Radvansky, Wyer, Curiel, & Lutz, 1997) validates the fact that one or more event models are formed depending on the information. For example, Radvansky and Zacks (1991) show that one situation model is formed in the course of learning statements such as "the book is on the table," "the cup is on the table," and "the pen is on the table," because all three objects can be represented as lying on one table. On the other hand, statements such as "the book is on the table," "the book is on the chair," and "the book is on the floor" lead to the creation of multiple models.

Wyer and Radvansky (1999) suggest that an event model can consist of both the mental image and the linguistically coded description of the event. Further, if the event information is conveyed verbally, images might be spontaneously generated in the course of comprehending it. Glenberg, Meyer, and Lindem (1987) provide evidence for this assumption. Participants in their study read a story about a protagonist who went jogging. In one condition, the protagonist at the beginning of the story put on a sweatshirt and went jogging. In the other condition, he took off his sweatshirt and went jogging. After participants had read the story, their recognition for specific features of the story was assessed. Participants took less time to identify "sweatshirt" in the first condition (when he went jogging with it) than in the second. This presumably occurred because in the first condition, the mental image that was initially constructed of him with his sweatshirt on persisted throughout the story, and therefore was more salient at the time of judgment. Other studies by Bower, Black, and Turner (1979) also attest to the fact that mental images might be formed in the course of comprehension. Further, the comprehension of events is quite different if they are described verbally than if they are conveyed pictorially (Wyer, Adaval, & Colcombe, 2002). That is, verbal descriptions of events spontaneously generate images. Consequently, they can later be identified equally well on the basis of a picture as they can on the basis of a verbal label. In contrast, events that are conveyed pictorially do not necessarily elicit linguistic or verbal labels (unless the pursuit of a specific goal forces them to generate this label). As a result, they are less likely to be identified later when a verbal label is presented.

This stream of research suggests that when people view advertising (particularly on television) they are likely to form a representation of the events depicted in the course of comprehending the commercial. Adaval and Wyer's (2004) work suggests that these representations contain much of the original detail of the scenes they represent. Their work also suggests that although these representations are formed spontaneously in the course of comprehension, additional linguistic representations might be formed by goals that arise after the event sequence has been viewed. Thus, individuals whose goal is to form an impression of the product or describe the ad to someone else might form a more generalized representation of the event (e.g., "that was a sexist commercial and showed the woman in a very traditional role"). This generalized representation might consist largely of semantic concepts that are applied in the course of thinking about the commercial and, therefore, might contain fewer images and details than the original representation. Both representations might then be available for use by the individual and the relative accessibility of each might depend on the type of information that has most recently been accessed. If the commercial is viewed again, the original representation might be more accessible. If the viewer is engaged in a discussion about certain types of commercials (e.g., their portrayal of women), then the generalized representation might be more accessible.

A myth could therefore be formed either in the course of comprehension or in the course of more goal-directed activity that involves thinking back about the information that has been viewed. However, note that people are often not aware of the myths that influence them. Therefore, even if the myths are formed in the course of pursuing goal-directed activity, they must by definition exist beneath one's conscious awareness. Other dual-process theories that focus specifically on how real-world information is processed (Lieberman, Gaunt, Gilbert, & Trope, 2002; Strack & Deutch, 2004) help identify what aspects of the information are processed automatically and without much cognitive deliberation.

Processing Mechanisms

To reiterate, different types of representations might be created in the course of comprehension versus goal-directed activity (Adaval & Wyer, 2004). This possibility is corroborated by several dual process theories that suggest the existence of both automatic and controlled processing. A conceptualization by Lieberman et al. (2002) postulates the existence of two systems—the *reflexive* (X-system) and the *reflective* (C-system)—that describe how information might be processed. The X-system is largely automatic and takes in information in its original form without any additional cognitive work. In many ways, the experience of the information is like one's stream of consciousness. The information is not challenged, questioned, or thought about in any great detail. If goals necessitate greater attention to the information, the C-system kicks into operation and greater cognitive work might go into evaluating the information.

Lieberman et al. (2002) describe the X-system as part of the brain that automatically provides the stream of conscious experience. It spans one's entire visual field and objects in the stream and the stream are one and the same. In contrast, reflective awareness is consciousness of a specific object in the stream that happens to draw one's attention and is reflected on. The output of these systems may be similar to the event models postulated by Wyer and Radvansky (1999) and Adaval and Wyer (2004).

The X-system is largely responsible for the processing and categorization of visual information. Evidence from cognitive neuroscience studies appears to be consistent with the idea that visual images are processed differently and consist of answers to the "where" (the spatial location of the object) and "what" (the identity of the object) questions (Mishkin, Ungerleider, & Macko, 1983). This allows one to recognize situations (e.g., a date, a funeral, a dark alley, etc.). The identity and category membership of the objects and persons involved in the event are determined in the inferotemporal cortex (ITC), which performs a pattern-matching function (Lieberman et al., 2002). The neurons in the *posterior* ITC represent complete objects. In response to the presentation of a face, each of these neurons provides its own view of the face. It is only when the information is transmitted to the *anterior* ITC that a more abstract "common" view is obtained (Wang, Tanaka, & Tanifuji, 1996). Neuroimaging studies show that this part of the ITC (the anterior part) is responsible for automatic, semantic categorization and implicit learning (Boucart et al., 2000; Posner & Keele, 1968).

Although this part of the X-system allows one to identify and categorize objects (e.g., a gun or a dark alley), implicit learning requires the understanding of dynamic behavior—not merely a categorization of situations, persons, and objects. One of the more interesting aspects of the X-system surrounds the identification of behavior. That is, it allows one to notice the dynamic aspects of a behavioral action (e.g., "the man in the dark alley is pointing the gun at me," as opposed to "the man with a gun is part of a studio setting for filming a commercial"). The pathway responsible for the behavior identification lies along the superior temporal sulcus (STS) and neurons in this region respond to intentional action. Allison, Puce, and McCarthy (2000) show that the same neurons are activated when people look directly at you than when they have their face in profile and have turned their head to look at you (suggesting that in any situation, the person's intent toward oneself is noted by the superior temporal sulcus). The automatic categorization of situations, objects, and persons (described earlier) and the detection of dynamic behavior allows one to understand how an event or episode in real life (or on television) can be processed automatically without conscious awareness of any specific object—almost as if it is part of one's stream of consciousness.

This discussion is relevant to the creation of myths or beliefs about language. These myths consist of object-attribute associations (e.g., "roses–passion," "funeral–black"). Although this issue will be discussed in greater detail later,

Lieberman et al.'s (2002) framework suggests that the X-system can process objects, individuals, and behavior (e.g., funerals are associated with tombstones, black clothes, crying, and sadness) leading to the formation of associations between signs. Their model would suggest that the co-occurrence of various features (e.g., in a funeral situation) might be sufficient to create associations over time. Thus, if funerals, black clothes, and crying always co-occur, the presence of one feature might automatically elicit the other. This could happen without invoking any sort of causal relationship between the two concepts (e.g., wearing black clothes does not necessarily mean that one is going to a funeral even though most people wear black clothes to a funeral). The idea that associations might be formed via a reflexive system (X-system) is also echoed in other dual process approaches (Sloman, 1996; Strack & Deutsch, 2004). However, the notion of causality (e.g., funerals *make* people cry) falls into the domain of the reflective system (C-system). This system comes into play in the course of problem solving (e.g., How did he die? What kind of flowers should I take to the funeral? How do I get there?), involves symbolic logic (if–then statements), is subject to capacity constraints, and is usually triggered in response to an alarm (i.e., a situation that requires attention). These processes are discussed in greater detail in the following section.

HOW ARE DIFFERENT TYPES OF MYTHS CREATED AND HOW DO THEY IMPACT OUR BEHAVIOR?

An intuitive answer to the question, "how do these myths come into being?" is that they are formed as a result of constant exposure to information that perpetuates the basic idea underlying them. Thus, if one's father gives one's mother roses on an anniversary, and one sees roses on Valentine's Day, then an association between roses and romance might be formed. However, the creation of abstract myths (e.g., the myths behind the various parables that Marchand identifies, or the myth that the home is a fortress that has to be protected) might be formed through a different process. Thus, repetition and frequency of exposure may be necessary, but not sufficient, for their creation. Further, the cognitive work that is presumably involved in the creation of these higher order myths seems almost paradoxical to the idea that people are not aware of these myths.

Acquisition of Concrete Myths

Consider myths that exist at the level of language: for example, the meaning associated with soap powders and detergents as described by Barthes (1972). If this meaning was acquired through advertising that used language to describe how the soap powders "lifted" out the dirt and visual imagery that showed bubbles floating away with the dirt, then based on Wyer and Radvansky's (1999) theory, one would expect that such advertising scenes are represented in terms of a single event model (a mental simulation of the event involving the use of this detergent). The co-occurrence of detergents with other features of the situation, such as stubborn stains, detergent, and bubbles floating away with dirt (present in this event model) could lead to the formation of associations between these various features by the X-system, without any inference of causality (Lieberman et al., 2002). Thus, associations between the various features depicted in the advertisement can be created automatically. All that is needed is that they co-occur as in the funeral example given in the previous section. Note that at this stage, the person does not make any causal inferences (e.g., "to remove stains, I must use detergents"). All that happens at this stage is the creation of the association between the three ideas—"detergents–lift out–stains"—allowing the sign "detergent" to be associated with "lifting out stains." A similar process might underlie the meaning generation for chlorinating fluids leading to the formation of the language myth or belief that Barthes (1972) discusses when he makes a distinction between detergents and chlorinating fluids.

Similar processes could also explain how stereotypical beliefs are acquired through advertising. In the example given earlier, Frito Bandito was a character created to sell corn chips. According to Wyer and Radvansky (1999), an event model would be constructed in the course of comprehending commercials involving this character. The presence of the mustache, sombrero, and pistols, as well as the actions of this cartoon character coupled with the knowledge of his Mexican origins, might lead to the association between Frito corn chips and Mexico as well as Mexicans and bandits. Because much of this information is processed reflexively (Lieberman et al., 2002), it forms part of one's stream of consciousness. Over time and with repeated exposure, one might come to believe that most Mexican males have mustaches and/or are associated with unsavory activities.

It is worth noting that the similarity between the information seen in television ads with that occurring in real-life situations might make it difficult to invalidate the advertising information being presented. Real-world information is processed reflexively and is spontaneously thought of as "valid." Lieberman et al. (2002) suggest that information processed by the X-system is usually not invalidated. Information can only be invalidated by the C-system that kicks in when something does not seem quite right and deviates from the pattern one expects (see also Strack & Deutch, 2004). Causal inferences fall in the domain of the C-system and might be triggered by unusual images, humor, and so forth. However, this type of reflective processing is not necessarily very deep, particularly because it is not very self-relevant. Thus, the likelihood that one would spontaneously notice the stereotype being perpetuated by Frito Bandito is remote (despite the fact that his antics are funny).

Acquisition of Abstract Myths

Not all myths can be explained via simple associative mechanisms. As noted earlier, some myths can take the form of parables of the sort identified by Marchand (1985). To account for these myths, suppose that the repetition of certain types of events in advertising leads people to extract common principles from them. Then, these common principles might form the basis of a story skeleton or an event proto-type. It is important to note that not all event prototypes are myths. For example, the prototype of what goes on in a restaurant is not a myth because it has been verified on the basis of restaurant visits. However, a prototype created after viewing several different ads that show people trying to make a favorable first impression could lead to the formation of a myth about how one's future might depend on making a good first impression.

The existence of such prototypes (Colcombe & Wyer, 2002; Trafimow & Wyer, 1993) or schemata (Graesser & Nakamura, 1982) is widely discussed in research on prose comprehension (Bower et al., 1979; Graesser, 1981; Schank & Abelson, 1995). Once these prototypes are formed from actual events that are observed, they might be used to comprehend new experiences. Colcombe and Wyer (2002) showed that when participants read five different exemplars of a problem situation, they extracted the common principle that was used to solve the problem and applied it to a different target exemplar. This occurred only when they had been exposed to a large number of similar stories. A single exemplar story, however, was insufficient to lead to the extraction of a prototype. Further, a specific goal (e.g., comprehension, problem solving, etc.) that required the comparison of different exemplars might be necessary to lead to the extraction of a common principle. However, such a goal could be activated unconsciously (Chartrand & Bargh, 1999; see Chartrand, 2005, for a summary), making it possible for these types of abstract myths to be formed without awareness.

Myths and Their Influence on Behavior

A skeptic would argue that the mere existence of associations does not necessarily mean that one believes in their validity or that they influence behavior. For instance, one might know that Mexicans are associated with something unsavory but one might not necessarily believe that this negative stereotype is true. Further, one might not necessarily avoid them in a dark alley. However, according to the preceding discussion, if much of the advertising information is processed reflexively (Lieberman et al., 2002) and does not elicit much cognitive deliberation, it might be retained in memory in the form of a situation model that closely resembles the original information conveyed (Adaval & Wyer, 2004). When a similar situation is encountered in real life, the perceptual similarities between it and the situation model stored in memory might be sufficient to elicit an automated conditioned response.

Conditioned responses can be acquired by the mere co-occurrence of two stimuli. Work by Clark and Squire (1998, 1999) and Clark, Manns, and Squire (2001, 2002) on eye-blink conditioning (where a neutral conditioned stimulus, like a tone, is associated with the unconditioned stimulus—a puff of air) shows that when the conditioned and unconditioned stimuli overlap, the conditioned response (the eye blink) is acquired without awareness of the contingency between the two. When the two stimuli do not overlap, however, it is more difficult for the observer to determine the connection between the conditioned and unconditioned stimuli. In such a case, people acquire the conditioned response only when they realize that the presence of one is contingent on the other. This type of contingency awareness might be facilitated by frequent repetition of the information or the salience of the conditioned stimulus (Galli, Brendl, & Chattopadhyay, 2005). Advertising typically uses these strategies by frequently repeating the information and making the conditioned stimulus salient through popular or creative symbols. Thus, "Frito Bandito" was a salient sign (conditioned stimulus) associated with corn chips (unconditioned stimulus) and elicited an eating–buying impulse (conditioned response).

Contingency awareness might also be facilitated by information in the form of an event or a sequence of events. When advertising consists of a sequence of events that are temporally and spatially connected (e.g., an advertising narrative), single events might be represented in memory as "event models" that preserve all the verbal and nonverbal information shown in the ad. Further, multiple events shown in the ad are also stored together as a longer "episode model" that preserves the temporal connections between the various individual events (Wyer, 2004; Wyer & Radvansky, 1999). Such representations that are temporally and thematically connected can obviously facilitate the detection of contingency awareness, leading to the production of a conditioned response. This response could be cognitive, affective, or behavioral and could occur without our conscious awareness of the factors that led to its generation.

The link between myths and our own behavioral response is an intriguing one. By definition, myths are often not recognized unless they are called to one's attention. Their existence as tacit knowledge suggests that any influence they exert on behavior should occur automatically. Once they have been acquired, they could serve as a backdrop and moderate the link between our perception of new situations and our behavior in these situations. Their moderating impact could occur without our being aware of either the myth or the nature of its influence. Several researchers (Bargh, 1994; Dijksterhuis & Bargh, 2001; Dijksterhuis, Smith, van Baaren, & Wigboldus, 2005) have suggested that behavior can be unconsciously influenced by three possible mechanisms: activation of a production system (or procedural knowledge), mimicry, and the activation of a trait, concept, or goal.

Cognitive Productions.   Behavior can be automatically elicited by the activation of a cognitive production (Anderson, 1982, 1983; see also Smith, 1990). These cognitive productions are very similar to the conditioned responses described earlier. Essentially, they consist of rules that take the form "If [X], then [Y]." In these rules, [X] is typically a configuration of perceptual and cognitive stimulus features and [Y] is a sequence of actions that are elicited automatically. These productions are learned and strengthened by repetition. A simple example of a cognitive production is one that is elicited while starting a car. As Bargh (1997) noted, many of our behaviors in everyday life resemble productions. Such productions could also be elicited when we learn certain styles of responding to problems based on the myths we hold.

In the context of advertising, let us see how a situation portrayed in a commercial might elicit a cognitive production. Imagine a commercial that shows a cockroach daring to defile a kitchen and being exterminated with the help of "Raid®." This commercial might be stored in memory in the form of an event model with all its perceptual and spatial features intact (Wyer & Radvansky, 1999). When the viewer encounters a similar situation in real life, the similarity in features between the real-life situation and the ad might make the event model of the ad more accessible (Adaval & Wyer, 2004) and might elicit a cognitive production that makes them reach for that can of Raid and treat the offending bug with the same degree of ruthlessness as that shown in the ad.

If several commercials of the sort described here (e.g. for pest control products) are seen, then a linguistic representation of it (a prototype) might be created. This prototype or abstract myth might then serve as a prime that activates procedural knowledge (or a "production system") in much the same way that Anderson (1983) and Wyer (2004) postulate. Again, the individual might not be consciously aware that these processes are being initiated and acted on. However, this abstract myth might determine whether or not the behavior is appropriate. In this context, a study by Aarts and Dijksterhuis (2003) is noteworthy. In this research, people were primed by merely asking them to look at a visual image of a library (or restaurant). If participants were led to believe that they would visit the location, they started engaging in behavior consistent with these locations. For example, they automatically started whispering in the library condition. These findings suggest that the visual cue presumably elicited a simulation of going to the library and primed a pattern of responding very similar to a cognitive production. The prototypical myth about how one behaves in a library might have guided this behavior, even though respondents were not in the library.

Mimicry.   Many behavioral responses to advertising myths can be explained using mimicry. However, most responses that have been studied under mimicry are lower level behaviors (like smiling, foot shaking, and nose rubbing) and pertain to gestures, facial expressions, postures, and speech. Chartrand and Bargh (1999), for example, showed how participants in an experiment mimicked another participant (a confederate) who was either rubbing her nose or shaking her foot. Similarly, a waitress who repeated the customer's order verbatim was likely to receive more tips, whereas a waitress who paraphrased the order received smaller tips. In recent research, Knippenberg (2003) also noted that behavioral mimicry increases when the interdependent self is primed and decreases when the independent self is primed, suggesting that shared beliefs (characteristic of interdependent selves) might actually facilitate mimicry.

It is important to note that we rarely mimic unfavorable stereotypes (Johnston, 2002). This suggests that there is some degree of volition in the process. In an interesting study, Johnston (2002) showed that participants who were asked to participate in a taste test for ice cream usually followed a confederate and helped themselves to more ice cream if the confederate did the same. Although this behavior appeared to be based on a simple environmental cue (watching the actions of a confederate), it was also contingent on the weight of the confederate. Specifically, the effects did not occur when the confederate was overweight. This raises some interesting questions for advertising. Will one mimic only attractive models eating ice cream? Will viewers always respond only to favorable stereotypes in advertising? Or, are people likely to mimic any behavior if it is shown often enough?

One can explain Johnston's (2002) findings using two processes. First, if we assume that advertising typically shows attractive (slim) models eating ice cream, then the representation of this behavior that exists in memory should contain features of these types of persons engaging in the behavior (i.e., attractive people enjoying ice cream) rather than people of all weights and sizes enjoying ice cream. Thus, if a confederate in the experiment is a slim person (rather than an overweight person), then the situation bears closer resemblance to the representation that exists in memory and it should elicit a mimicry response. A second possibility is that respondents can have different prior beliefs about ice cream consumption. For example, some people might believe that ice cream is to be enjoyed whenever available and/or ice cream should be avoided because it leads to weight gain. Which of these myths (or beliefs) is salient is likely to depend on what external cues are perceived. When non-obese confederates help themselves to more ice cream, mimicry might be initiated. However, perception of the overweight confederate engaging in the same action might make the belief about weight gain more salient and might moderate the link between perception of the situation (observation of the actor's/confederate's behavior) and one's own behavior.

Trait and Concept Activation. Behavioral responses can also be elicited through the activation of certain concepts. For example, Bargh, Chen, and Burrows (1996) showed that participants who were primed with "rudeness" through a scrambled sentence construction task tended to interrupt people more often at a later point in time relative to those primed with "politeness." In a second experiment, participants primed with the concept "elderly" took relatively longer to walk to the nearest elevator. In the advertising context, environmental cues might prime specific traits, stereotypes, and concepts that can then exert an influence on behavior. Billboards (or ads) that juxtapose "fun times" with "cigarettes" could lead to the creation of an association between the two. This association (as discussed earlier) could be formed without conscious awareness. At a later point in time, the presence of cigarettes in one's environment (e.g., a person smoking at a party) might make the concept "enjoyment" more accessible in memory and might lead one to be more tolerant of the behavior. On the other hand, if one has been exposed to a lot of antismoking ads, the associations formed might not be that favorable and cigarettes might be associated with cancer. In this case, the presence of cigarettes might elicit the concept "cancer" and lead to a more negative response toward the smoker.

Much of the research on automaticity shows how cues in the environment are unconsciously picked up and influence our behavior. This preceding discussion merely outlines how advertising myths (beliefs at varying levels of abstractness) moderate the perception of a daily-life situation and our behavioral response to it. Their existence as knowledge structures of which we are not aware allows their influence to be fairly pervasive and gives our behavioral responses the aura of "being perfectly normal."

REINFORCEMENT OF MYTHS AND CHANGE OVER TIME

Although some have argued that advertising shapes society, others claim that it merely mirrors the values that society finds favorable. The signs, symbols, and themes used in advertising are clearly chosen with a target group in mind. Yet, the people who choose these signs are themselves part of society and consider only those signs with which the viewer can identify. However, advertising appears to have its greatest influence not necessarily through the specific signs and themes that are chosen, but because of its frequency and ubiquitous nature. Given that different myths become more or less popular over time, it is useful to understand some of the processes that underlie how myths are reinforced and changed at both the micro- and macrolevels.

Advertising myths obviously result from repeated exposure to certain types of ads. The overrepresentation of certain types of models in advertising can influence our values and beliefs about how things are or ought to be. Sometimes such overrepresentations play on the consumer's feeling of inadequacy or fear. For instance, a large proportion of commercials in Hong Kong show that fair skin is a desirable attribute for women. Some even go as far as to suggest that melanin in the skin is undesirable and should be removed. These commercials obviously fail to mention that melanin protects us against the sun's ultra violet rays. Consequently, the myth of beauty that is created is one of an anorexic, pale woman. Young girls who view these commercials often feel inadequate if they perceive themselves as different from the models shown in the advertising, and rush to purchase fairness creams and other herbal remedies that might help restore their "ideal self." The products that they seek in the marketplace arrive there already laden with significance through the packaging and symbols they use (Hebdige, 1984). Thus, not only are the consumers primed and ready to accept the symbolic meaning these products present, but actually seek them.

Myths: Frequency of Exposure

The frequency of exposure to a certain type of ad message obviously plays an important role in the acquisition of knowledge unconsciously. Cultivation research by Shrum, Wyer, and O'Guinn (1998) has already shown the impact of heavy television viewing on peoples' perceptions of social reality. They show, for example, that frequent viewers of television soap operas tend to overestimate the number of people who have swimming pools or are lawyers. Consider this finding in the context of the discussion of myths. The frequency of advertisements that advertise a drug directly to the consumer ("Ask your doctor about ———") is on the increase. The high frequency of these ads can create the myth that doctors will not give you what is best for you unless you ask them for it. Over a period of time, the overrepresentation of this type of message in the media can lead to hypervigilance and suspicion of medical professionals.

The creation of myths through passive viewing gives the impression that the consumer is putty in the hands of media. However, there are clearly instances when the consumer is an active participant. Consider for example, the "myth" that Japanese products are of high quality or that a woman's place is in the home. Both notions are fairly well represented in the media. Nonetheless, there are many U.S. consumers who would not buy a foreign-made car and many women who reject the myth about women as homebodies. What leads to these group differences?

Let us start with the assumption made earlier that myths are essentially meaning systems and beliefs that are shared within a culture. Although several definitions for culture abound, according to Brumann (1999), culture can be considered as a cluster of common concepts, emotions, and practices arising when people interact. In a similar vein, Chiu and Chen (2004) use the term *culture* to designate a network of knowledge that is produced, distributed, and reproduced among a network of interconnected people. Thus, myths are merely knowledge structures at varying levels of abstractness that are shared by a group of interconnected people. Chiu and Chen (2004) also argue that people are carriers of a culture just as songs, mass media, icons, advertising, and social policies are other carriers. It is therefore possible for one carrier of culture (e.g., mass media advertising) to influence another carrier (people). Further, it is also likely that at any given point in time, different groups of people will have different knowledge structures (even myths) more or less accessible in memory. The relative accessibility of these knowledge structures might influence both their interpretation of different ideas that are being communicated in advertising and the extent to which they are persuaded by it, as described next.

Interpretation. In his discussion of differences in how liberals and conservatives think, Lakoff (2002) suggests that these differences actually stem from the different moral systems (or beliefs about morality) that these individuals have. These different beliefs are used to interpret the various issues. The metaphors that Lakoff uses to describe these alternate moral systems are those of a "strict father" (for conservatives) and a "nurturant parent" (for liberals). The different belief systems held by the two groups lead to different discourse forms, different choices of words, and different reasoning. People who believe in the "strict father" model, for instance, are usually known to be very helpful when their communities are affected by disasters. However, their willingness to help does not always extend to situations in which individuals are responsible for their own suffering because the morality dictates that people have to learn to face the consequences of their actions. People who believe in the "nurturant parent" model might, on the other hand, not show these differences.

Persuasion.   Lakoff also suggests that framing a message to appeal to these belief systems is likely to lead to greater acceptance of the message. In a similar vein, Ottati, Rhoads, and Graesser (1999) showed that the use of sports metaphors in a persuasive communication increased the motivation to process this information when the readers were people who liked sports. Thus, when these individuals were given a persuasive message containing either weak or strong arguments, they were better able to distinguish between them because of the increased motivation to process information. Ottati et al.'s work does not show that the mere use of the sports metaphor makes people who like sports agree with the message. Rather, it shows that they are better able to discriminate between good and bad arguments. However, if the message is framed not only in terms of metaphors that the individual can resonate with but also contains arguments consistent with one's ideological beliefs, then greater acceptance is likely to follow (see Phillips & McQuarrie, chap. 8 in this volume, for a more detailed discussion of metaphors).

Thus, group differences in the acceptance of various myths and in the extent to which these myths impact behavior result from the differences in the accesibility of these myths in memory. Their relative accessibility can influence not only the way people interpret a situation and behave in it, but also the extent to which they are persuaded by advertising messages.

Myths: Changes Over Time

For a myth to be questioned or challenged, something has to threaten it. Consider for example, a past lifestyle myth (the belief that men should have their hair cropped short, wear pin striped suits, work for a big corporation, have a wife, two kids, and a home in the suburbs). What could shake this myth? Hebdige (1984) argues that it has to be an object so extreme that it threatens one's fabric of existence. He points out how punk groups threatened the existence of the dominant culture and the lifestyle myth. When these subcultures first appeared, they were seen as "noise" or interference in the orderly sequence. As a result, they were objects of curiosity and were given a large amount of attention by the media. He argues that one's own identity is so deeply ingrained in consciousness that a challenge to it is fairly startling and one is bound to find it threatening. It is this kind of threat that elicits a greater amount of reflection. A punk hairdo might make one at least wonder if all men should have their hair cropped short.

Barthes (1972; see also Hebdige, 1984) notes that society has two ways of dealing with this threat. First, the "other" that represents the threat can be transformed into exotica, a spectacle, or a clown. In this case, the difference is consigned to a place where further analysis and contemplation is not necessary. Second, the "other" can be trivialized, domesticated, or naturalized. In this case, the "otherness" is reduced to "sameness" through (a) the conversion of the subculture's signs (dress, music, etc.) into mass-produced objects (in the case of punks, we had punk jewelry, hair color, etc.), and (b) the relabeling and redefinition of the group's deviant behavior by the majority (e.g., "they are just a harmless group of kids"). The commoditization of the punk culture and its relabeling brought it into the mainstream and rendered its presence in society less threatening.

This conceptualization suggests that consumers do play a role in shaping and interacting with the myths that exist in society. Many myths that exist today do not exist in the same form as they did originally. Consumers interact with and shape these myths when they are drawn to their attention. Thus, when a cultural stereotype is questioned by a subculture, when feminists protest about the portrayal of women, or when linguists analyze the rhetoric put forth by the government or the media, they challenge our tacit knowledge and commonsense approach to thinking. This reflection is what eventually forces us to be sensitive to the many myths that we buy into.

CONCLUSIONS

This chapter has drawn attention to the diversity of myths that pervade our world and thrive beneath our consciousness. Myths have been defined broadly so as to discuss a variety of knowledge structures that have an impact on our behavior in unknown ways. The literature that is discussed is varied and is not restricted to any one discipline or area in the hope that it will provide "talking points" and a very broad framework within which one can examine these phenomena. The importance of verbal and nonverbal information in the creation of these myths is incontrovertible. A greater understanding of how this information is processed, how it enters into our behavioral decisions, and more broadly, how it shapes our cultural values and societies is of interest to not just a host of academicians but also people from all walks of life. As stated earlier, advertising myths form and reflect the bedrock of our tacit knowledge and the beliefs we have about the world in which we live. Their influence on our consumption behavior and way of thinking is something that we need to understand more fully.

ACKNOWLEDGMENTS

The writing of this chapter was supported by Grant No. HKUST 6192/04H from the Research Grants Council of the Hong Kong Special Administrative Region, China. The author wishes to thank C-y. Chiu, Ying Yi Hong, Bob Wyer, Tina Lowrey, and an anonymous reviewer for their helpful and insightful comments. The chapter benefited greatly from the insights provided by these experts.

REFERENCES

Aarts, H., & Dijksterhuis, A. (2003). The silence of the library: Environment, situational norm, and social behavior. *Journal of Personality and Social Psychology, 84*, 18–28.

Adaval, R., & Wyer, R. S. (2004). Communicating about a social interaction: Effects on memory for protagonists' statements and nonverbal behaviors. *Journal of Experimental Social Psychology, 40*, 450–465.

Allison, T., Puce, A., & McCarthy, G. (2000). Social perception from visual cues: Role of the STS region. *Trends in Cognitive Sciences, 4*, 267–278.

Anderson, J. R. (1982). Acquisition of cognitive skill. *Psychological Review, 89*, 369–406.

Anderson, J. R. (1983). *The architecture of cognition*. Cambridge, MA: Harvard University Press.

Bargh, J. A. (1994). The four horsemen of automaticity: Awareness, intention, efficiency and control in social cognition. In R. S. Wyer, Jr. & T. K. Srull (Eds.), *The handbook of social cognition* (Vol. 2, pp. 1–40), Hillsdale, NJ: Lawrence Erlbaum Associates.

Bargh, J. A. (1997). The automaticity of everyday life. In R. S. Wyer (Ed.), *Advances in social cognition* (pp. 1–62). Mahwah, NJ: Lawrence Erlbaum Associates.

Bargh, J. A., Chen, M., & Burrows, L. (1996). Automaticity of social behavior: Direct effects of trait construct and stereotype activation on action. *Journal of Personality and Social Psychology, 71*, 230–244.

Barthes, R. (1972). *Mythologies* (Annette Lavers, Trans.). New York: Hill & Wang.

Boucart, M., Meyer, M. E., Pins, D., Humphreys, G. W., Scheiber, C., Gounod, D., & Foucher, J. (2000). Automatic object identification: An fMRI study. *Neuroreport: An International Journal for the Rapid Communication of Research in Neuroscience, 11*, 2379–2383.

Bower, G. H., Black, J. B., & Turner, T. J. (1979). Scripts in memory for texts. *Cognitive Psychology, 11*, 177–220.

Brumann, C. (1999). Writing for culture: Why successful concepts should not be discarded. *Current Anthropology, 40*, 1–27.

Chartrand, T. L. (2005). The role of conscious awareness in consumer behavior. *Journal of Consumer Psychology, 15*, 203–210.

Chartrand, T. L., & Bargh, J. A. (1999). The chameleon effect: The perception-behavior link and social interaction. *Journal of Personality and Social Psychology, 76*, 893–910.

Chiu, C-y., & Chen, J. (2004). Symbols and interactions: Application of the CCC model to culture, language, and social identity. In S-H. Ng, C. Candlin, & C. Chiu (Eds.), *Language matters: Communication, culture, and social identity* (pp. 152–182). Hong Kong: City University of Hong Kong Press.

Clark, R. E., Manns, J. R., & Squire L. R. (2001). Classical conditioning, awareness, and brain systems. *Trends in Cognitive Science, 6*(12), 524–531.

Clark, R. E., Manns, J. R., & Squire L. R. (2002). Trace and delay eyeblink conditioning: Contrasting phenomena of declarative and nondeclarative memory. *Psychological Science, 12*(4), 304–308.

Clark, R. E., & Squire, L. R. (1998). Classical conditioning and brain systems: The role of awareness. *Science, 280*(5360), 77–81.

Clark, R. E., & Squire, L. R. (1999). Human eyeblink classical conditioning: Effects of manipulating awareness of the stimulus contingencies. *Psychological Science, 10*(1), 14–18.

Colcombe, S. J., & Wyer, R. S. (2002). The role of prototypes in the mental representation of temporally-related events. *Cognitive Psychology, 44*, 67–103.

Dijksterhuis, A., & Bargh, J. A. (2001). The perception-behavior expressway: the automatic effects of social perception on social behavior. In M. P. Zanna (Ed.), *Advances in experimental social psychology* (Vol. 33, pp. 1–40), San Diego: Academic Press.

Dijksterhuis, A., Smith, P. K., van Baaren, R. B., & Wigboldus, D. H. J. (2005). The unconscious consumer: Effects of environment on consumer behavior. *Journal of Consumer Psychology, 15*, 193–202.

Fussell, S. R., & Krauss, R. M. (1992) Coordination of knowledge in communication: Effects of speakers' assumptions about others' knowledge. *Journal of Personality and Social Psychology, 62,* 378–391.

Galli, M., Brendl, C. M., & Chattopadhyay, A. (2005). *Persuasion via associative mechanisms: Are we in control?* Working paper, Hong Kong University of Science and Technology.

Glenberg, A. M., Meyer, M., & Lindem, K. (1987). Mental models contribute to foregrounding during text comprehension. *Journal of Memory and Language, 26,* 69–83.

Glucksberg, S. (2001). *Understanding figurative language: From metaphors to idioms.* New York: Oxford University Press.

Graesser, A. C. (1981). *Prose comprehension beyond the word.* New York: Springer-Verlag.

Graesser, A. C., & Nakamura, G. V. (1982). The impact of a schema on comprehension and memory. In G. H. Bower (Ed.), *The psychology of learning and motivation: Advances in research and theory* (Vol. 16, pp. 66–109), New York: Academic Press.

Hall, S. (1977). Culture, the media and "the ideological effect." In J. Curran, M. Gurevitch, & J. Woollacott (Eds.), *Mass communication and society* (pp. 315–348). London: Edward Arnold.

Hebdige, D. (1984). *Subculture—The meaning of style.* London: Methuen.

Johnson-Laird, P. N. (1983). *Mental models: Towards a cognitive science of language, inference and consciousness.* Cambridge, MA: Harvard University Press.

Johnson-Laird, P. N. (1989). Mental models. In M. I. Posner (Ed.), *Foundations of cognitive science* (pp. 469–500). Cambridge, MA: MIT Press.

Johnston, L. (2002). Behavioral mimicry and stigmatization. *Social Cognition, 20,* 18–35.

Kintsch, W. (1998). *Comprehension: A paradigm for cognition.* Cambridge, England: Cambridge University Press.

Knippenberg, A. (2003). It takes two to mimic: Behavioral consequences of self-construals. *Journal of Personality and Social Psychology, 84,* 1093–1102.

Krauss, R. M., & Fussell, S. R. (1991). Perspective-taking in communication: Representations of others' knowledge in reference. *Social Cognition, 9,* 2–24.

Lakoff, G. (2002). *Moral politics: How liberals and conservatives think.* Chicago: University of Chicago Press.

Lau, I. Y-m., Chiu C-y., & Hong, Y-y. (2001). I know what you know: Assumptions about others' knowledge and their effects on message construction. *Social Cognition, 19,* 587–600.

Lieberman, M. D., Gaunt, R., Gilbert, D. T., & Trope, Y. (2002). Reflexion and reflection: A social cognitive neuroscience approach to attributional inference. In M. P. Zanna (Ed.), *Advances in experimental social psychology* (Vol. 34, pp. 199–250). San Diego: Academic Press.

Magliano, J. P., Dijkstra, K., & Zwann R. A. (1996). Generating predictive inferences while viewing a movie. *Discourse Processes, 22,* 199–224.

Marchand, R. (1985). *Advertising the American dream: Making way for modernity, 1920–1940.* Berkeley, CA: University of California Press.

Mick, D. G. (1986). Consumer research and semiotics: Exploring the morphology of signs, symbols, and significance. *Journal of Consumer Research, 13,* 196–213.

Mishkin, M., Ungerleider, L. G., & Macko, K. A. (1983). Object vision and spatial vision: Two cortical pathways. *Trends in Neuroscience, 6,* 414–417.

Ottati, V., Rhoads, S., & Graesser, A. C. (1999). The effect of metaphor on processing style in a persuasion task: A motivational resonance model. *Journal of Personality and Social Psychology, 77*(4), 688–697.

Peirce, C. S. (1931–1958). *Collected papers* (C. Hartshorne, P. Weiss, & A. W. Burks, Eds.). Cambridge, MA: Harvard University Press.

Posner, M. I., & Keele, S. W. (1968). On the genesis of abstract ideas. *Journal of Experimental Psychology, 77,* 353–363.

Radvansky, G. A., Wyer, R. S., Curiel, J. M., & Lutz, M. F. (1997). Mental models and abstract relations. *Journal of Experimental Psychology: Learning, Memory and Cognition, 23,* 1233–1246.

Radvansky, G. A., & Zacks, R. T. (1991). Mental models and the fan effect. *Journal of Experimental Psychology: Learning, Memory and Cognition, 17,* 940–953.

Rodgers, D. (1978). *The work ethic in industrial America, 1850–1920.* Chicago: University of Chicago Press.

Saussure, F. (1915/1966). *Curso de linguistica generale* [Course in general linguistics] (W. Baskin, Trans.). New York: McGraw-Hill.

Schank, R. C., & Abelson, R. P. (1995). Knowledge and memory: The real story. In R. S. Wyer (Ed.), *Advances in social cognition* (Vol. 8, pp. 1–85). Hillsdale, NJ: Lawrence Erlbaum Associates.

Shrum, L. J., Wyer, R. S., & O'Guinn, T. (1998). The effects of watching television on perceptions of social reality. *Journal of Consumer Research, 24,* 447–458.

Sloman, S. A. (1996). The empirical case for two systems of reasoning. *Psychological Bulletin, 119,* 3–22.

Smith, E. R. (1990). Content and process specificity in the effects of prior experiences. In T. K. Srull & R. S. Wyer, Jr. (Eds.), *Advances in social cognition* (Vol. 3, pp. 1–59). Hillsdale, NJ: Lawrence Erlbaum Associates.

Strack, F., & Deutsch, R. (2004). Reflective and impulsive determinants of social behavior. *Personality and Social Psychology Review, 8*(3), 220–247.

Susman, W. I. (1979). "Personality" and the making of twentieth-century culture. In J. Higham & P. K. Conkin (Eds.), *New directions in American intellectual history* (pp. 214–216). Baltimore: Conkin.

Trafimow, D. A., & Wyer, R. S. (1993). Cognitive representiaton of mundane social events. *Journal of Personality and Social Psychology, 64,* 365–376.

Wang, G., Tanaka, K., & Tanifuji, M. (1996). Optical imaging of functional organization in the monkey inferotemporal cortex. *Science, 272,* 1665–1668.

Wilson, C. C., & Gutierrez, F. (1985). *Minorities and media.* Newbury Park, CA: Sage Publications.

Wyer, R. S. (2004). *Social comprehension and judgment: The role of situation models, narratives, and implicit theories.* Hillsdale, NJ: Lawrence Erlbaum Associates.

Wyer, R. S., Adaval, R., & Colcombe, S. J. (2002). Narrative-based representations of social knowledge: Their construction and use in comprehension, memory and judgment. In M. P. Zanna (Ed.), *Advances in experimental social psychology* (Vol. 34, pp. 131–197). San Diego: Academic Press.

Wyer, R. S., & Carlston, D. E. (1979). *Social cognition, inference and attribution.* Hillsdale, NJ: Lawrence Erlbaum Associates.

Wyer, R. S., & Carlston, D. E. (1994). The cognitive representations of persons and events. In R. S. Wyer & T. K. Srull (Eds.), *Handbook of social cognition* (2nd ed., Vol. 1, pp. 41–98). Hillsdale, NJ: Lawrence Erlbaum Associates.

Wyer, R. S., & Radvansky, G. A. (1999). The comprehension and validation of social information. *Psychological Review, 106,* 89–118.

Zwann, R. A., & Radvansky, G. A. (1998). Situation models in language comprehension and memory. *Psychological Bulletin, 123,* 162–185.

Indexical and Linguistic Channels in Speech Perception: Some Effects of Voiceovers on Advertising Outcomes

Susannah V. Levi
David B. Pisoni
Indiana University

Marshall McLuhan wrote "the medium is the message." That is, not only is the content of the message itself important in conveying information, but so too is the medium, or the way in which the intended message is conveyed to an audience. When people perceive spoken language, information about the content of the message is transmitted to the listener, along with information about the specific person who produced the message. Because these two sources of information are ineluctably bound together in the speech stream, both channels of information contribute to the final product of perception and both should be considered by advertisers when developing voiceovers.

Speech is a complex, multimodal time-varying pattern. Although both auditory and visual cues function in speech perception, we focus only on the auditory portion. Spoken language encodes two different sources of information. First, it carries linguistic information about the symbolic content of the talker's intended message. This content contains several levels of linguistic information: phonological (sounds), morphological (units that form words), syntactic (combining words into sentences), and semantic (meaning of an utterance). Taken together, this linguistic information provides the content of an utterance.

The second type of information carried in the speech stream is often termed *paralinguistic, extralinguistic,* or *indexical.* Indexical information can be thought of as the "medium" through which the message is conveyed. Abercrombie (1967) wrote that "[s]uch 'extra-linguistic' properties of the medium ... may fulfil other functions which may sometimes even be more important than linguistic communication, and which can never be completely ignored" (p. 5). Abercrombie divided the indexical properties of speech into three sets: (a) those properties that indicate group membership (e.g., regional, dialectal, and social aspects of speech), (b) those that characterize the individual (e.g., age, gender, and size and shape of the vocal tract), and (c) those that reveal changing states of the speaker (e.g., affective properties such as fatigue, excitement, amusement, anger, suspicion, health, speaking rate). Indexical and linguistic information in speech correspond to what cognitive psychologists often refer to as source and item information, respectively (see Hilford, Glanzer, Kim, & DeCarlo, 2002).

What makes speech a complex signal is that these two properties are carried simultaneously in a single acoustic waveform that is at first produced by an individual speaker and then perceived by a listener who can extract both sources of information. Speech is generated by a speaker's larynx and supralaryngeal vocal tract. The vocal tract, which extends from the larynx through the throat and mouth to the lips, acts as an acoustic filter, enhancing certain resonance frequencies (formants) and attenuating others. When speakers produce different sounds in a language, they constrict their vocal tract at different locations. Which frequencies are enhanced or attenuated in the vocal tract is determined both by its length and by the location of the constriction. In the productions of sounds, the *relative frequencies* provide the linguistic information about the place of constriction of sounds. In contrast, the *absolute frequencies* that resonate in a particular person's vocal tract are dependent on the length of that person's vocal tract and thus provide talker-specific information. The sound spectrogram in Figure 11.1 provides a specific example of the integration of linguistic and indexical properties of speech in the

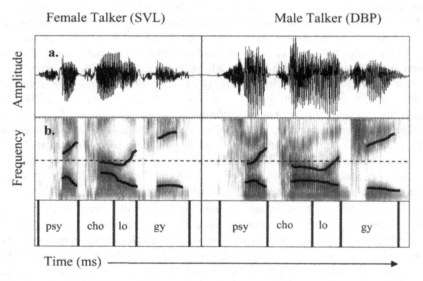

Figure 11.1.   Waveform (a) and spectrogram (b) of the word "psychology" produced by the first author (SVL) and the second author (DBP). Dark lines in the spectrogram represent the first formant (lower curve) and second formant (upper curve).

production of speech. The formant values produced by the female speaker (first author) are higher than those produced by the male speaker (second author), showing one indexical difference resulting from differences in vocal tract length. The overall movement and relative locations of the formants, on the other hand, provide linguistic information and indicate that the speakers are saying the same utterance. Thus, the same vocal mechanisms produce both linguistic and indexical information simultaneously and both sources of information are encoded and carried in the same signal.

The perception of these two different aspects of speech is illustrated in Figure 11.2. The basilar membrane (bottom of Fig. 11.2) is situated in the cochlea in the inner ear and allows a listener to segregate frequencies. The left path in Figure 11.2 shows the absolute frequencies that are heard by the listener and provide indexical information about an individual talker. The right path represents the relative frequencies that provide linguistic information about the intended message. In this way, both the linguistic and the indexical properties of the speech signal can be perceived and encoded by the listener.

The remainder of this chapter is organized into three sections. The first reviews several lines of neurolinguistic and psycholinguistic research on the perception of indexical properties of speech. The findings discussed in this section confirm that two distinct channels of information are carried in the speech signal. Moreover, the results suggest that the processing of one set of properties affects the processing of the other. The second section considers research from the advertising and marketing literature that examines which voices are the most suitable for voiceovers, whether speech rate compression is advisable, and in what contexts selecting the appropriate voice is most important. The last section integrates these two separate bodies of literature in order to determine what kinds of voices should be used for the most effective advertising.

THE SCIENCE OF VOICE PROCESSING

Behavioral and neural studies on the perceptual processing of speech illustrate its bipartite nature. By asking listeners to attend to either the linguistic or the indexical (voice) properties of speech, neuroscientists have shown that these two aspects of speech are processed differently in the brain. Despite this difference in neural processing, behavioral studies show that the two are in fact closely linked and that voice (indexical) characteristics affect linguistic processing of speech.

Neural Processing of Voices

Neural studies of voice identification and discrimination reveal that characteristics of the voice are processed in brain areas that are distinct from those that process the linguistic properties of the speech signal. In an early study of hemispheric specialization, Landis, Buttet, Assal, and Graves (1982) found that whereas both hemispheres

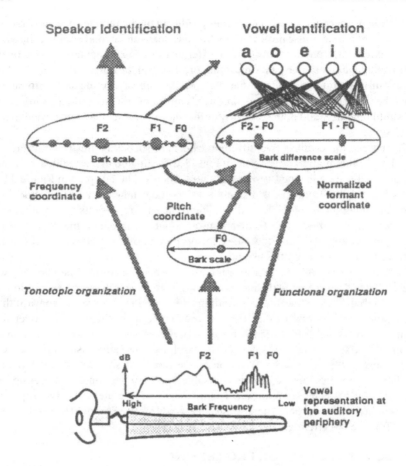

Figure 11.2.   Representation of auditory perception of both indexical and linguistic properties of speech. The absolute frequencies (left side) provide speaker identification, while the relative frequencies (right side) provide vowel identification. From "The effect of F0 on vowel identification," by T. Hirahara and H. Kato, 1992, in Y. Tohkura, E. Vatikiotis-Bateson, and Y. Sagisaka (Eds.), *Speech perception, production, and lingusitic structure*, pp. 89–112. Copyright © 1992 by Ohmsha Publishing, Tokyo. Reprinted with permission.

can be utilized in voice recognition, there was a distinct advantage of the left hemisphere for linguistic tasks. Landis et al. (1982) played monosyllabic consonant-vowel words into either the right or the left ear. In the linguistic task, listeners were asked to press a button every time they heard a specific target word. Listeners' reaction times showed a clear right-ear advantage (REA), responding faster when the target word was presented to the right ear than the left. Because the two hemispheres control contralateral body functions, showing a preference for the right ear indicates that the left hemisphere dominates in the linguistic task. In a second experiment, listeners were asked to push a button when they heard a particular male or female voice. In this study, female voices elicited a REA, but male voices resulted in a left-ear advantage (LEA). Landis et al. interpreted these results by remarking that higher frequencies have been shown to elicit a REA and female voices, with their higher pitch and formants, may therefore also be processed with a REA. The major finding of this study was the demonstration that both hemispheres are involved in voice recognition, whereas word recognition displays left hemisphere dominance.

Kreiman and Van Lancker (1988) found similar results using a dichotic listening paradigm. In a dichotic listening task, listeners hear different words presented simultaneously in both ears and are asked to attend only to the stimuli that are played in either the right or the left ear. Using a set of 50 famous male voices, they asked listeners to write down both the word (linguistic task) and the person who said the word (indexical task). As expected, they found a clear REA in the word recognition task. The results of the voice identification task were less conclusive. Listeners showed no ear advantage for the voice recognition task, consistent with the earlier results of Landis et al. (1982). They did, however, find a *relative* left-ear advantage; that is, relative to the word recognition task, listeners showed a greater advantage for the left ear.

More recent studies have been able to isolate voice processing to more specific brain regions. Glisky, Polster, and Routhieaux (1995) tested elderly listeners' ability to recall either the content or the voice of previously heard sentences. They found that listeners with high frontal lobe function outperformed those with poor frontal lobe function on the voice task, but showed no difference in their performance on the sentence recall task. Conversely, listeners with high medial temporal lobe function outperformed listeners with low function in the sentence recall task, but did not differ on the voice task. These results confirm that the processing of voice information is independent of linguistic processing.

More recently, using functional magnetic resonance imaging (fMRI), Stevens (2004) reported distinct brain regions for voice- and word-discrimination tasks. Listeners were asked to determine whether two talkers were the same or whether two words were the same. Stevens found that attending to either the word or the voice altered the functional activity of the brain. In particular, the voice comparison task produced activation in the right fronto-parietal area, whereas lexical processing was associated with increased activation in the left frontal and bilateral parietal areas.

Other studies have shown that voice processing can be further subdivided; familiar voices are processed differently than unfamiliar voices. In these studies, familiarity refers to people who were personally known to the listeners.[1] Using fMRI,

---

[1] In several studies, Van Lancker, Kreiman, and colleagues (Van Lancker, Cummings, Kreiman, & Dobkin, 1988; Van Lancker & Kreiman, 1987; Van Lancker, Kreiman, & Cummings, 1989) showed that recognizing famous voices and discriminating between unfamiliar voices engaged different brain areas. It is not possible to conclude from these studies that famous and unfamiliar voices themselves are processed differently because the two tasks were fundamentally different. In the famous voice recognition task, listeners were asked to name the famous voice and to draw on long term memory. In the unknown voice discrimination task, listeners compared two unknown voices that were presented one following the other.

Shah et al. (2001) found that familiarity of voices and faces resulted in increased activity in the posterior cingulate cortex as compared to unfamiliar voice and face processing. Nakamura et al. (2001) also found different brain areas involved in familiar versus unknown voice processing using positron emission tomography (PET).

Taken together, these studies of the neural processing of speech demonstrate that the indexical (source) properties are indeed distinct from the linguistic (symbolic) properties of speech, despite the fact that they are carried simultaneously in the same speech waveform. When listeners are asked to attend to voice characteristics of the speaker, they utilize different areas of the brain than when they process the linguistic information in the signal.

Interactions of Indexical (Voice) and Linguistic Processing

Although the studies reviewed in the previous section revealed that distinct brain areas are involved in voice perception and linguistic processing, results of behavioral studies indicate that these two properties of the speech signal are closely coupled functionally. Properties of the voice affect the processing of linguistic information. Most important for the concerns of advertisers are the incidental or indirect effects of voice information on the processing of the content of the message, which show that consistency and familiarity of the voice facilitates linguistic processing of the message.

Evidence from a variety of behavioral studies shows that consistency of the voice is an important aspect of linguistic processing. Using a speeded classification task, Mullennix and Pisoni (1990) asked listeners to categorize a set of spoken words that differed on two perceptual dimensions: the linguistic dimension in which the initial sound of the words varied between "p" and "b" and the indexical/gender dimension in which words were spoken by either a male or a female talker. In the control conditions, a single talker produced all words, thereby holding the indexical dimension constant. In the orthogonal conditions, the two dimensions varied randomly so there was no consistency between the two dimensions. Listeners were asked to classify words using each dimension separately, ignoring possible variation along the other dimension. Mullennix and Pisoni found that reaction times were slower in the orthogonal conditions than in the control conditions, indicating that listeners were not able to "filter out" the indexical variation while performing the linguistic task and that variation of the voice inhibits listeners' performance. They also found that increasing the number of talkers from 2 to 16 had an even greater effect of slowing down classification times. This study revealed that the indexical properties of speech are not processed independently of linguistic content of the signal and irrelevant variation in a non-attended perceptual dimension (in this case, the indexical dimension) is not discarded when performing such a task, but is instead processed in an integral manner.

Schacter and Church (1992) found a similar same-voice advantage in a stem completion task. In the study phase, listeners heard a series of words and rated either the pleasantness of the word or the pitch of the voice. In the test phase, listeners heard a series of syllables mixed with noise and were asked to write down the first word that came to mind. Schacter and Church found that when voices of the study words and the test syllables matched, a greater priming effect was observed than when the voices were switched. In other words, listeners were more likely to respond with a word they had heard during the study phase of the experiment if that studied word was spoken in the same voice as the syllable heard during the test phase.

In another study, Goldinger (1996) showed that listeners exhibit a same-voice advantage in recognition memory when performing a linguistic task. Listeners were asked to type the word they heard when it was presented in noise. Test words that were spoken by the same talker were recognized more often than words spoken by a different talker. Perhaps even more striking was the finding that the same-voice advantage did not decline significantly across different delays between study and test. Listeners who returned after a week showed the same voice advantage as those who returned after only a 5-minute delay, indicating that listeners encode and store information about a voice for an extended period of time, even when the demands of the task do not consciously ask listeners to do so. The lack of an effect of delay suggests that the voice effect does not disappear rapidly, but is available and stored in memory for an extended period of time. In a separate voice-recognition task, Goldinger (1996) found that listeners' ability to explicitly remember voices did decline with an increased delay. Together, these two sets of results suggest that although listeners may lose their ability to explicitly remember the voice, attributes of a voice remain in memory and have effects on language processing for an extended period of time.

Using a list recall task, Goldinger, Pisoni, and Logan (1991) also found an advantage for voice consistency in learning and memory. In this study, listeners first heard 10 words and were subsequently asked to recall the list. Goldinger et al. varied the number of voices that were used to present the list of words and the rate at which the stimuli were presented. The authors found that at fast presentation rates, lists of words produced by multiple talkers were recalled less accurately than lists that were spoken by only a single talker. In contrast, at slow presentation rates, lists produced by multiple talkers were actually remembered more accurately than single-talker lists. Lightfoot (1989) conducted a follow-up study using this same methodology. The difference in Lightfoot's study was that lists were spoken by voices that were familiar to the listeners. Interestingly, voice familiarity caused the advantage of voice consistency to disappear.

In a continuous recognition memory experiment using spoken words, Palmeri, Goldinger, and Pisoni (1993) played long lists of words to listeners and asked them to determine whether each word was "old" (one that had been previously heard) or "new" (one that had not been previously heard). In order to assess the effects of voice on recognition memory, half of the old words were repeated in the same voice and half were repeated in a different voice. As in the previous studies, listeners responded more quickly and more accurately when old words were repeated in the same voice. Palmeri et al. also found that the lag (i.e., the number of words intervening between the first and second presentation of a word) did not interact with the same-voice advantage, indicating that the facilatory effect of maintaining the same voice is robust over time.

In addition to consistency of voices, familiarity with voices facilitates recall and recognition of spoken language. Several studies have shown that familiarity with a set of talkers allows for faster and more accurate linguistic processing. For example, Nygaard, Sommers, and Pisoni (1994) trained listeners to identify 10 unfamiliar talkers by name over a period of 10 days. During the test phase on the last day, listeners were presented with novel words mixed in noise that were spoken either by the now familiar talkers or by unknown talkers. Subjects were simply asked to identify words and were not required to respond to the voice of the talker. The results indicated that listeners identified novel words in noise better when the words were spoken by familiar talkers, than when the words were spoken by unfamiliar talkers. In a follow-up study, Nygaard and Pisoni (1998) showed that the advantage of talker familiarity extends to sentence-length utterances as well.

The behavioral studies reviewed in this section suggest that the linguistic and indexical channels of speech are closely coupled. In linguistic tasks (e.g., word recognition and phoneme discrimination), which on the surface do not appear to rely on indexical or voice properties, a strong effect of voice is reliably observed. Both familiarity with the voice and consistency of the voice facilitate processing of the linguistic (symbolic) content of the message.

ADVERTISING/MARKETING

Advertising messages using spoken language contain meaningful information (the intended message text), visual information (in the case of television advertising), and voice information. It has been shown that when both audio and visual information are present, the auditory information has attentional priority over the visual modality and can mask otherwise distracting information in the visual signal. Drew and Cadwell (1985) varied the angle and zoom of jump cuts in an informational video. They found that when an audio signal accompanied the video, there were no negative effects on viewers' attitudes toward the video, showing the importance of an audio stream for maintaining coherence and sufficiently masking distracting visual cues. Because audio information is clearly relevant in both radio and television advertising, selecting an appropriate voice to accompany the product of the advertisement is important and may have significant effects on a wide range of outcome measures. This section considers some factors that are relevant for selecting an appropriate voice for an advertising campaign. It also discusses under what conditions voice characteristics are likely to affect listeners' attitudes toward and memory for the product.

Picking the Right Voice

Several decisions must be made when selecting the right voice to accompany an ad. For instance, should the voice of a famous person be used? What gender voice is appropriate for a given product? Does the accent or nativeness of the talker's voice play a role in listeners' understanding, attitude, and memory for the product?

A first question pertains to whether the spokesperson for a product should be famous. It may be the case that famous actors are better able to read the script of an ad (Alsop, 1987). Not surprisingly, it is also important to be sure that if celebrities are used in an ad, they must match the product in such a way that credibility of the product is enhanced (Misra & Beatty, 1990; Plapler, 1974).

While using a celebrity voice in advertising is more expensive, it may be the case that a celebrity is actually better at selling a product than an unknown person. Leung and Kee (1999) conducted an experiment to test whether celebrity spokespeople were better than unknown actors in selling a product. They took a recent television commercial that used two well-known DJs in Hong Kong as the voiceovers for the ad and recorded the same ad with two trained but not well-known actors. Viewers who saw the ad with the celebrity voiceover had higher brand recall and encoded more product brand information, although there was no significant difference in viewers' intent to buy the product.

Finding the right talker for a voiceover also includes deciding on the appropriate gender of the speaker. Although male voices dominate the world of voiceovers (Bartsch, Burnett, Diller, & Rankin-Williams, 2000), several studies indicate that female voices may be a better choice under some circumstances and that the gender of the voice interacts with the product. Whipple and McManamon (2002) tested listeners' attitudes toward male-gendered, female-gendered, and neutral-gendered products that differed in the voice of the spokesperson. Their results indicated that the gender of the spokesperson does not have an effect on gender-neutral or male-gendered products. However, for female-gendered products, a female voice elicited a more positive attitude toward the ad. The only scenario where a male voice was preferred was for the female-gendered product when men were the target audience (e.g., for men purchasing the product as a gift). Thus, Whipple and McManamon conclude that female voices are at least as effective, if not more, than male voices.

In examining the gender of spokes-characters (non-human animated characters), Peirce (2001) found that the likelihood that a viewer would buy the product was increased when the gender of the spokes-character matched that of the product (golf balls vs. vacuum cleaners, in the case of this study). Conversely, the gender-neutral spokes-character was not the most effective for the gender-neutral product; instead, the female spokes-character was preferred for the gender-neutral product (coffee). These studies demonstrate that there is little basis to continue to prefer male-gendered voices or spokespeople in advertising.

LEVI AND PISONI

A third consideration in selecting the voice for an ad is the nativeness of the talker. Although there may be other considerations, such as the intended audience or product congruity (e.g., using an Italian-accented voice for pasta), several studies have shown that foreign-accented voices are less intelligible than native voices. In a study examining the effects of voice on listeners' ability to comprehend and retain information from a short narrative, Mayer, Sobko, and Mautone (2003) found that listeners performed better on both a retention task and a transfer task when the speaker was a native speaker of English as compared to when the speaker was a second-language learner of English with a Russian accent. They also found that the native speaker received higher positive ratings scores than the nonnative speaker. Foreign-accented speech has also been found to be less intelligible when mixed with noise (Lane, 1963; Munro, 1998) and requires more effort to process (Munro & Derwing, 1995).

In the advertising literature, foreign-accented voices have also been shown to elicit less favorable responses and lower purchase intentions. Tsalikis, DeShields, and LaTour (1991) found that Greek-accented English voices received lower scores on 15 bipolar adjectives than native English voices for a hypothetical commercial for a VCR. In a similar study, DeShields, Kara, and Kaynak (1996) tested listeners' attitudes toward native English and Spanish-accented speech when presented with an ad for car insurance. They found that the intent to buy was significantly higher when the speaker was native than for the Spanish-accented speakers. DeShields and de los Santos (2000) found that the impact of accent depends on the relationship between the source of the accent and the listeners. In accordance with previous work, they found that U.S. listeners perceived the native English speaker more positively than the Spanish-accented speaker in an ad for car insurance. Mexican listeners, however, did not rate the native Spanish salesperson differently than the English-accented Spanish-speaking salesperson. DeShields and de los Santos hypothesized that this may be due to the influence the United States has on Mexican culture.

Time Is Money

Speaking rate is another indexical property that can be manipulated and controlled by advertisers. Because advertising time is expensive, a reasonable question to ask is whether the fast presentation of information, which allows more information to be transmitted in a shorter period of time, has any deleterious effects on listeners' attitudes toward the message, their ability to remember the product, or their intention to buy. Unfortunately, the studies examining the effects of speech rate are not conclusive, although the majority suggest that a faster rate is not problematic.

In some cases, faster rates of speech have been shown to be preferred by listeners. Miller, Maruyama, Beaber, and Valone (1976) conducted two experiments in order to test the effects of speech rate on listeners' attitudes toward the speaker. In the first experiment, groups of listeners heard a passage about the dangers of coffee at two different speaking rates. In addition to varying rate, they also varied the credibility of the speaker by telling listeners that the speaker was either a locksmith or a biochemist. In a second experiment, listeners heard a passage about hydroponically grown vegetables at two speaking rates and at two levels of message complexity. Listeners answered a series of questions designed to determine their attitude toward the speaker. The results showed that listeners judged the speaker of the faster rate to be more knowledgeable, more persuasive, more objective, and also to have greater intelligence. The effects of speech rate were robust; the faster rate elicited more positive responses in all conditions, regardless of the credibility of the speaker or the complexity of the message. One limitation of this study, however, was that the speaker was asked to vary his speech rate, thus it is very likely that other aspects of the voice were altered as well, such as pitch and amplitude.

LaBarbera and MacLachlan (1979), however, avoided these possible confounds by electronically compressing the speech rate. First, they conducted a series of experiments to test listeners' preference for different speech rates. They compressed and expanded the speech rate without altering the pitch of the voice and asked listeners in a paired-comparison task to select which speech sample they preferred. The results of these studies indicated that listeners preferred a faster than normal speaking rate. In a follow-up study, LaBarbera and MacLachlan tested listeners' attitudes and recall of six radio commercials at both normal and fast speech rates. They found that, in all cases, the faster commercial was rated as more interesting and elicited higher brand recall after a 2-hour delay. Thus, the faster rate was both preferred by listeners and also resulted in higher retention.

MacLachlan (1982) also reported positive effects of faster speech rates. Four radio commercials were used either in their normal or compressed versions, and listeners rated the speaker along four dimensions: friendliness, knowledge, enthusiasm, and energy. The fast commercials were either rated the same as the normal version or more positively. In this study, then, increasing the speech rate had no negative effects on listeners' attitudes about the speaker.

Other studies have shown mixed effects of altering the speech rate. Schlinger, Alwitt, McCarthy, and Green (1983) found that time compression can sometimes interfere with encoding the content in television commercials. Viewers in this study expressed fewer ideas about one of the two commercials in their study when it was presented at the faster rate, but no significant difference was found for the second commercial. As for listeners' attitudes, 6 of 52 response statements showed the noncompressed version as receiving more positive responses, although the remaining 46 statements showed no difference. Furthermore, the results showed no significant difference in buying intentions for the normal and time-compressed versions of the commercials. Thus, listeners may encode less information and may have fewer positive responses for some response statements, but this does not seem to affect the likelihood that they will actually purchase the product.

More recently, Megehee, Dobie, and Grant (2003) found mixed results for faster rates of speech. They created five versions of a message about the benefits of using a "SmartCard" (an identification card that also functions as a debit card): normal, time-compressed, pause-compressed, time-expanded, and pause-expanded. Thus, three rates (normal, fast, slow) and two methods of rate alteration were studied. Time-adjusted speech changes the overall rate of the message by compressing or expanding all portions equally, but the tempo remains the same. In pause-adjusted speech, the pauses themselves are either shortened or lengthened; thus, the actual presentation rate of the words remains the same, but the tempo of the utterance is altered. When comparing the main effect of rate, Megehee et al. found no difference in the attitude toward the product, message, or speaker, although the faster rate did have more affective responses, whereas the slower rate had more cognitive responses. The authors also found that at faster rates, time compression produced more affective responses and a more favorable attitude toward the speaker than did the pause-compressed version.

Chattopadhyay, Dahl, Ritchie, and Shahin (2003) found different results for the method of rate adjustment. They varied both syllable speed (compression of the actual speech forms) and interphrase pause duration and found that reducing the interphrase pause time had little effect on the way listeners processed the message, suggesting that this might be the preferred method of time compression. Increasing syllable speed, on the other hand, did affect the way listeners processed the message, as revealed by measures of attention and recall. They found, however, that increasing syllable rate can increase persuasion, implying that this might be the preferred method of rate compression.

Although a few results from these studies show that increasing the speech rate has some negative consequences (e.g., fewer cognitive responses), the overwhelming conclusion is that faster rates are not problematic and are in some cases preferred. The best method of compression, however, is less obvious. Megehee et al. showed a clear advantage of overall time compression, whereas Chattopadhyay et al. showed some superiority for pause compression. Whatever the method of compression, increases in speech rate appear to be well-tolerated by listeners.

When Voice Characteristics Matter Most

The impact of voice characteristics varies depending on how much involvement and interest the listener has with the message. Gelinas-Chebat and Chebat (2001) conducted a study to examine the contribution of voice characteristics on listeners' attitudes toward an ad by varying the level of involvement. Listeners, who were all university students, heard either a low involvement ad, which invited them to visit the local bank to acquire an ATM card, or a high involvement ad, which invited them to visit the local bank to learn about student loans. The assumption was that students would be more interested in learning about student loans because it could directly affect their financial situation. In addition to varying the level of involvement, voice characteristics were varied orthogonally along two dimensions (intensity and intonation) with two levels each, creating four versions of each message.

As predicted, the high involvement message increased the acceptance of the arguments of the message. Additionally, changes in voice characteristics did not have an impact on listeners' attitudes in the high-involvement message. However, in the low-involvement message where listeners did not have an a priori interest in the message, the peripheral characteristics of the message (i.e., the changes in voice characteristics) did have an effect on their attitude toward the message. In other words, when listeners do not have a particular interest in the product or message, the quality of the voice used has an effect on listeners' attitudes.

Further support for effects of voice on processing and memory comes from another study by Goldinger (1996). He varied the level of processing (LOP) in order to determine whether the focus of listeners' attention would interact with changes in a speaker's voice. In the study phase, listeners encoded 150 words in terms of the gender of the speaker (shallowest LOP), their initial sound, or their syntactic class—namely, noun, verb, or adjective (deepest LOP). In the test phase, listeners were given a set of 300 words and were asked to classify words as old or new depending on whether they had been heard in the initial part of the study. Half of the old words were repeated in the same voice and half in a different voice. The strongest effect of voice change was found at the shallowest LOP where words repeated in the same voice received more accurate responses. This result suggests that when listeners' attention is directed toward the deeper symbolic content of the message, they are less disrupted by changes in voice in later recognition tasks. On the other hand, if listeners are not encoding the meaning of the words, but instead are processing them in a shallower manner, inconsistencies in the voice have a significant effect on their recognition accuracy. Thus, the initial level of encoding of the spoken words determines how much of an impact the voice will have on memory tasks following acquisition.

INTEGRATING PSYCHOLINGUISTIC AND ADVERTISING RESEARCH

The ultimate goals of advertising are to increase brand recall, instill confidence in the brand, and finally to sell a product. Because much advertising relies on auditory input using spoken language to transfer information about the product to the target audience, the effects of the speech input must be carefully considered. Based on a number of studies in psycholinguistics, speech perception, and marketing research, several general conclusions can be drawn concerning how to best control for and manipulate the effects of voice on listeners' attitudes toward and memory for a product.

A natural first question to ask is whether it is important to be selective when choosing a voice for an ad. Two factors related to the encoding of speech make it clear that voice characteristics are crucial for advertising. First, advertising frequently targets a listener's implicit memory for voices because potential consumers are not generally asked to make explicit, direct judgments about the speaker when confronted with a television or radio commercial. Psycholinguistic research demonstrates that voice information that is encoded implicitly lasts at least up to a week in memory. Because advertising tends to target a listener's implicit memory for voices, voice changes and voice characteristics may have both short-term and long-term effects on the success or failure of a marketing campaign.

The second factor that illustrates the importance of voice characteristics in advertising relates to the level of processing. If listeners already have a vested interest in the product, then differences in the voice may not affect listeners' perceptions very much. However, when listeners are not personally invested in the content of the message, the vocal characteristics of the talker have significant effects on their attitudes toward the message. Similarly, when listeners encode stimuli in a shallow manner, voice effects are most apparent. Because advertisers are interested in both retaining current consumers and gaining new ones, they cannot guarantee that the listener will have a prior interest in the product. Therefore, voice characteristics are likely to influence the initial encoding of the message and carryover to the buying intentions of potential consumers.

The research reviewed in this chapter establishes a reliable benefit of voice consistency, revealed by a same-voice advantage. Listeners are faster and more accurate when performing linguistic and memory tasks if the voice of the speaker remains constant. Thus, in advertising, it would be advantageous to use a consistent mapping between a voice and a set of ads for a given product. In addition to consistency, familiarity with voices provides a facilitatory effect on a range of language processing tasks. Psycholinguistic research reveals that the intelligibility of a talker's voice in noise is better when listeners are familiar with the speaker. This finding is directly relevant for advertising because many commercials are likely to contain music or may be heard in noisy environments (e.g., in a car). Thus, if the listening environment is not ideal and contains conditions that make perceiving the speech more difficult, having a familiar voice can mitigate these factors. Advertising research shows that brand recall is higher when the voice is a celebrity, and therefore familiar to the listener. Finally, the voice of the spokesperson should of course be highly intelligible. Research has shown that nonnative speakers are less intelligible than native speakers and are thus likely to make less ideal candidates for voice advertising, unless other factors, such as product congruity, are relevant.

A practical concern for advertisers is the cost of air time. A realistic concern is whether speech rate can be increased without causing negative effects on listeners' attitudes and memory for the product. In this area, the evidence is promising. Studies of the effects of speech rate on listeners' attitudes and memory suggest that, in general, increasing the rate has no negative effects and may in fact be preferred. However, considerations of speech rate are not independent of other concerns of voice and linguistic processing. If advertisers elect to use a faster rate of speech, then they must be aware of the possible consequences on the behavior of the intended audience. The psycholinguistic research reviewed here shows that at fast presentation rates, consistency of the voice is more important than at slower rates.

Thus, if advertisers use a fast rate, then they should be sure to use only a small number of voices. Additional research shows that consistency of the voice is less important if listeners are familiar with the speakers. Thus, if advertisers use well-known "celebrity voices," then it may be possible to use more or varied voices in the ad.

CONCLUSIONS

Advertisers have a great deal of control over both the linguistic information of an advertising campaign, as well as the indexical information encoded in the speech signal. Evidence from psycholinguistic studies indicates that voice characteristics have an effect on the processing (encoding, storage, retrieval, and transfer) of linguistic information in the message. Thus, it is not only important that advertisers display care when selecting the particular words and content of the message, but also when choosing a voice to represent a specific marketing campaign. If possible, the voice should remain constant across repetitions of an ad, be familiar (either famous or familiar as the result of repetition), and be produced by a native speaker of the language. It is not surprising that these aspects of a speaker's voice affect language processing; these findings are consistent with psychological research on human factors and ergonomics, which shows that response consistency, repetition, and familiarity are important for learning and retention. The rate of speech of an ad may be increased without deleterious effects, although in this case, it is even more important that the voice remain consistent. Because consumers of advertising may only be passively attending to a particular ad, selection of the right voice is even more important in these cases where the effects of voice quality have been found to be most apparent.

ACKNOWLEDGMENTS

Preparation of this chapter was supported by grants from the National Institutes of Health to Indiana University (NIH-NIDCD T32 Training Grant DC-00012 and NIH-NIDCD Research Grant R01 DC-00111). We wish to thank Luis Hernandez and Darla Sallee for technical assistance and help with this manuscript.

REFERENCES

Abercrombie, D. (1967). *Elements of general phonetics*. Chicago: Aldine.
Alsop, R. (1987, October 22). Listen closely: These TV ads might have a familiar ring [Electronic version]. *Wall Street Journal*.
Bartsch, R. A., Burnett, T., Diller, T. R., & Rankin-Williams, E. (2000). Gender representation in television commercials: Updating an update. *Sex Roles, 43*, 735–743.
Chattopadhyay, A., Dahl, D. W., Ritchie, R. J. B., & Shahin, K. N. (2003). Hearing voices: The impact of announcer speech characteristics on consumer response to broadcast advertising. *Journal of Consumer Psychology, 13*, 198–204.
DeShields, O. W., Jr., & de los Santos, G. (2000). Salesperson's accent as a globalization issue. *Thunderbird International Business Review, 42*, 29–46.

DeShields, O. W., Jr., Kara, A., & Kaynak, E. (1996). Source effects in purchase decisions: The impact of physical attractiveness and accent of salesperson. *International Journal of Research in Marketing, 13*, 89–101.

Drew, D. G., & Cadwell, R. (1985). Some effects of video editing on perceptions of television news. *Journalism Quarterly, 62*, 828–831, 849.

Gelinas-Chebat, C., & Chebat, J.-C. (2001). Effects of two voice characteristics on the attitudes toward advertising messages. *Journal of Social Psychology, 132*, 447–459.

Glisky, E. L., Polster, M. R., & Routhieaux, B. C. (1995). Double dissociation between item and source memory. *Neuropsychology, 9*, 229–235.

Goldinger, S. D. (1996). Words and voices: Episodic traces in spoken word identification and recognition memory. *Journal of Experimental Psychology: Learning, Memory, and Cognition, 22*, 1166–1183.

Goldinger, S. D., Pisoni, D. B., & Logan, J. S. (1991). On the nature of talker variability effects on recall of spoken word lists. *Journal of Experimental Psychology: Learning, Memory, and Cognition, 17*, 152–162.

Hilford, A., Glanzer, M., Kim, K., & DeCarlo, L. T. (2002). Regularities of source recognition: ROC analysis. *Journal of Experimental Psychology: General, 131*, 494–510.

Hirahara, T., & Kato, H. (1992). The effect of F0 on vowel identification. In Y. Tohkura, E. Vatikiotis-Bateson & Y. Sagisaka (Eds.), *Speech perception, production and linguistic structure* (pp. 89–112). Tokyo: Ohmsha Publishing.

Kreiman, J., & Van Lancker, D. (1988). Hemispheric specialization for voice recognition: Evidence from dichotic listening. *Brain and Language, 34*, 246–252.

LaBarbera, P., & MacLachlan, J. (1979). Time-compressed speech in radio advertising. *Journal of Marketing, 43*, 30–36.

Landis, T., Buttet, J., Assal, G., & Graves, R. (1982). Dissociation of ear preference in monaural word and voice recognition. *Neuropsychologia, 20*, 501–504.

Lane, H. (1963). Foreign accent and speech distortion. *Journal of the Acoustical Society of America, 35*, 451–453.

Leung, L., & Kee, O. K. (1999). The effects of male celebrity voice-over and gender on product brand name recall, comprehension, and purchase intention. *New Jersey Journal of Communication, 7*, 81–92.

Lightfoot, N. (1989). Effects of talker familiarity on serial recall of spoken word lists. *Research on speech perception, progress report No. 15*. Bloomington, IN: Indiana University.

MacLachlan, J. (1982). Listener perception of time-compressed spokespersons. *Journal of Advertising Research, 22*, 47–51.

Mayer, R. E., Sobko, K., & Mautone, P. D. (2003). Social cues in multimedia learning: Role of speaker's voice. *Journal of Educational Psychology, 95*, 419–425.

Megehee, C. M., Dobie, K., & Grant, J. (2003). Time versus pause manipulation in communications directed to the young adult population: Does it matter? *Journal of Advertising Research, 43*, 281–292.

Miller, N., Maruyama, G., Beaber, R. J., & Valone, K. (1976). Speed of speech and persuasion. *Journal of Personality and Social Psychology, 34*, 615–624.

Misra, S., & Beatty, S. E. (1990). Celebrity spokesperson and brand congruence: An assessment of recall and affect. *Journal of Business Research, 21*, 159–173.

Mullennix, J. W., & Pisoni, D. B. (1990). Stimulus variability and processing dependencies in speech perception. *Perception and Psychophysics, 47*, 379–390.

Munro, M. J. (1998). The effects of noise on the intelligibility of foreign-accented speech. *Studies in Second Language Acquisition, 20*, 139–154.

Munro, M. J., & Derwing, T. M. (1995). Processing time, accent, and comprehensibility in the perception of native and foreign-accented speech. *Language and Speech, 38,* 289–306.

Nakamura, K., Kawashima, R., Sugiura, M., Kato, T., Nakamura, A., Hatano, K., Nagumo, S., Kubota, K., Fukuda, H., Ito, K., & Kojima, S. (2001). Neural substrates for recognition of familiar voices: A PET study. *Neuropsychologia, 39,* 1047–1054.

Nygaard, L. C., & Pisoni, D. B. (1998). Talker-specific learning in speech perception. *Perception and Psychophysics, 60,* 355–376.

Nygaard, L. C., Sommers, M. S., & Pisoni, D. B. (1994). Speech perception as a talker-contingent process. *Psychological Science, 5,* 42–46.

Palmeri, T. J., Goldinger, S. D., & Pisoni, D. B. (1993). Episodic encoding of voice attributes and recognition memory for spoken words. *Journal of Experimental Psychology: Learning, Memory, and Cognition, 19,* 309–328.

Peirce, K. (2001). What if the Energizer Bunny were female?: Importance of gender in perceptions of advertising spokes-character effectiveness. *Sex Roles, 45,* 845–858.

Plapler, L. (1974, April 15). Some famous spokesmen—and how to use them in ads. *Advertising Age,* p. 38.

Schacter, D. L., & Church, B. A. (1992). Auditory priming: Implicit and explicit memory for words and voices. *Journal of Experimental Psychology: Learning, Memory, and Cognition, 18,* 915–930.

Schlinger, M. J. R., Alwitt, L. F., McCarthy, K. E., & Green, L. (1983). Effects of time compression on attitudes and information processing. *Journal of Marketing, 47,* 79–85.

Shah, N. J., Marshall, J. C., Zafiris, O., Schwab, A., Zilles, K., Markowitsch, H. J., & Fink, G. R. (2001). The neural correlates of person familiarity: A functional magnetic resonance imaging study with clinical implications. *Brain, 124,* 804–815.

Stevens, A. A. (2004). Dissociating the cortical basis of memory for voices, words and tones. *Cognitive Brain Research, 18,* 162–171.

Tsalikis, J., DeShields, O. W., Jr., & LaTour, M. S. (1991). The role of accent on the credibility and effectiveness of the salesperson. *Journal of Personal Selling and Sales Management, 11,* 31–41.

Van Lancker, D. R., Cummings, J. L., Kreiman, J., & Dobkin, B. H. (1988). Phonagnosia: A dissociation between familiar and unfamiliar voices. *Cortex, 24,* 195–209.

Van Lancker, D. R., & Kreiman, J. (1987). Voice discrimination and recognition are separate abilities. *Neuropsychologia, 25,* 829–834.

Van Lancker, D. R., Kreiman, J., & Cummings, J. (1989). Voice perception deficits: Neuroanatomical correlates of phonagnosia. *Journal of Clinical and Experimental Neuropsychology, 11,* 665–674.

Whipple, T. W., & McManamon, M. K. (2002). Implications of using male and female voices in commercials: An exploratory study. *Journal of Advertising, 31,* 79–91.

CHAPTER 12

Dual Language Processing of Marketing Communications

Ryall Carroll
David Luna
Baruch College

Laura A. Peracchio
University of Wisconsin–Milwaukee

If you talk to a man in a language he understands, that goes to his head. If you talk to him in his language, that goes to his heart.

—Nelson Rolihlahla Mandela

The growth of the Internet and the expanding reaches of open markets have created an increasingly multicultural world marketplace. With the borders between countries and markets being blurred, marketers and consumers are becoming increasingly multilingual in their communications. In countries around the world, the increased exposure to multiple languages has created a multilingual environment that is becoming more prevalent in everyday life, as well as in consumer-based interactions. In the United States, for example, over 42% of children from age 5 to 17 in the state of California are bilingual (University of California Linguistic Minority Research Institute [UC LMRI], 2003), and 72% of all Hispanics speak both English and Spanish (Levey, 1999). Currently, Hispanic purchasing power is nearly $700 billion per year and is projected to reach $1 trillion by 2010 (*Hispanic Business Research*, 2004). Businesses, as well as the media, are becoming more aware of the growth and economic power of Hispanics and are trying to understand the implications of this growing bilingual environment. To assist in this pursuit, there has been a surge in bilingual and multicultural studies in marketing journals over the past decade. This chapter reviews some of that research.

The examination of how language influences the perception and interpretation of marketing communications is the one common underlying theme in recent bilingual and multicultural research. In essence, language choice has a major influence

221

on the perceived meaning of what is said. In a metaphoric sense, language can be viewed much in the same way as the barrel in which wine is stored. The barrel has an influence over the taste and smell of the wine. If wine is stored in an oak barrel, then it will have a much different taste than if the same wine is stored in a stainless steel tank, and French oak will produce a different wine than American oak. In other words, language can be viewed as the container or packaging in which the meaning of a message is stored, but this packaging also influences the perceived message meaning.

Surprisingly, much of the past research in marketing communications has focused on one language or on monolinguals and how they process information (Usunier, 1996), generally ignoring the language of the communication. Hence, consumer research has not fully explored the impact that different languages can have on message perception. The goal of this chapter is to further understand how language choices and multilanguage situations impact the process and the social perception of a message. Although consumer research in this area is still in its infancy, three main areas of research have emerged, as pictured in Figure 12.1. The three streams of research are unique language processing, bilingual cognitive processing, and bilingual-bicultural processing. As language and communication does not take place in a vacuum, overlap between these research streams does exist. The present research examines some of the factors that determine the way in which people process and interpret messages and suggests future research directions.

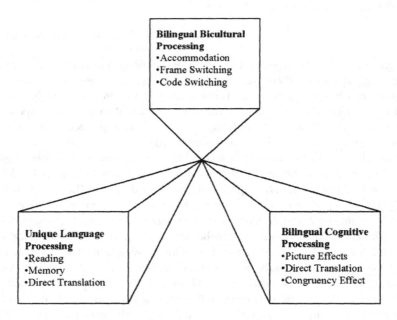

Figure 12.1.   Language processing issues.

UNIQUE LANGUAGE PROCESSING

The concept of "unique language" is another way of saying that every language is different. When dealing with different languages, it would be erroneous to assume that all languages are processed in the same manner. Language processing can differ in several ways, from obvious differences such as the direction in which the lexicon is read (e.g., left to right vs. right to left) to more complex mental processes (e.g., the way verbal information is encoded in memory). These language differences exist, despite the fact that many modern languages descend from the same ancient languages. The research reviewed in this section focuses on the differences between unique languages. Without an understanding of how each language is uniquely processed, it is difficult to develop an understanding of bilingual processing. For instance, knowledge of how each unique language is processed is vital for understanding the potential complications that bilinguals face due to the different ways in which different languages are processed. These complications may also arise because, for bilinguals, processing a language is partly a matter of activating the correct language, but also a matter of suppressing the other language (Green, 1986). This need for language activation and suppression could lead to a higher processing difficulty compared to monolingual individuals.

Visual Versus Verbal Processing

One of the basic differences found between languages is the way in which language is read. When reading alphabetic languages, such as English, the reader relies on a sound-based, or phonological, process. This differs from logographic languages, such as Chinese, where the reader relies on a more visual process. English readers' reliance on an alphabetic script in which letters represent sounds causes readers of English to subvocalize written words (McCusker, Hillinger, & Bias, 1981). This subvocalization of English words is then processed through a subsystem of short-term memory known as the phonological loop (Baddeley, 1986; Paivio, 1986). This subvocalization, in turn, forces the processor to rely more heavily on auditory memory processing and rely less on visual short-term memory (Gathercole & Baddeley, 1993). For readers of languages with logographic scripts, the process is quite different. In logographic languages, each logograph represents a different meaning, and a reader can mentally access concepts without the use of the phonological loop (Perfetti & Zhang, 1991; Spinks, Liu, Perfetti, & Tan, 2000). Reading a logographic language does not appear to be dominated by sound-based processes and appears instead to rely to a greater degree on visual processes (Hung & Tzeng, 1981; Schmitt, Pan, & Tavassoli, 1994; Zhou & Marslen-Wilson, 1999). It has been speculated that, in logographic languages like Chinese, the abundance of homophones—words that sound the same but have different meanings and are spelled differently, such as "die" and "dye," or "sea" and "see,"—may be the main reason for the need to process language in a visual manner. The multitude of homophones makes sound an ambiguous mental code, and Chinese speakers may supplement the ambiguous code with visual information for which meaning is less ambiguous (Tavassoli & Lee, 2003).

Because languages are processed differently, it is no surprise that the way in which verbal information is encoded in memory is different as well. In a brand recall study, it was shown that because English readers rely heavily on the phonological process, the interaction of memory mode and language on unaided recall is based on the ability to access the phonological trace rather than a visual trace. Individuals that have a logographic language background are more likely to recall information when the visual memory is accessed (Schmitt et al., 1994). As mental representations of verbal information in logographic languages are coded primarily in a visual manner, marketers should concentrate their efforts on brand names and logos that facilitate visual encoding. Conversely, marketers targeting individuals that have an alphabetic language background should attempt to facilitate the phonological process by using brand names that are more sound focused (Schmitt et al., 1994).

Tavassoli and Lee (2003) continued this stream of research by showing the impact that these language differences can have in advertising recall, attitudes, and customer interest. In three different studies, Tavassoli and Lee manipulated audio and visual stimuli to show that auditory stimuli interfered more than nonverbal visual stimuli when an advertisement was processed in an alphabetic (English) language, then when an advertisement was processed in a logographic (Chinese) language. When English readers were exposed to distracting audio levels, they had a difficult time processing the information, causing recall, attitude, and interest in the advertisement to be lower. Conversely, those measures were lower for those reading logographic languages when given visually distracting stimuli. Interestingly, Tavassoli and Lee also found that the same audio or visual interference stimuli could actually increase recall if the levels of stimuli are at an appropriate level. The increased level of recall results validated Tavassoli and Han's (2002) finding that relational memory is effectively encoded between words and visual brand logos in Chinese, whereas words and auditory brand identifiers, or jingles, are more effectively encoded in English.

These studies are examples of how understanding the way different languages are processed can further our understanding of bilinguals and their dual language processing. The respondents in most of the studies reviewed so far were bilingual individuals, reinforcing the notion that the simple difference of the language in which a message is presented and that language's unique processing will have a tremendous impact on the perception of the message for a bilingual individual. Because a bilingual must, at least initially, process messages in the language it is presented, the same message can be processed by the same individual in different ways and can result in different interpretations. In the Tavassoli and Han (2002) study, for example, when bilinguals were presented with a message in a logographic language and the overwhelming environmental stimuli were of a visual nature, the result was an increased difficulty in processing, whereas when the same bilingual was presented with the same message with the same visual interfering environmental stimuli but in an alphabetic language, the environment had little to no effect on processing.

Despite the processing differences of unique languages, it is important to note that the majority of constructs and processes in the psychology of advertising for monolinguals also apply to bilinguals. Constructs such as processing motivation, ability to process information, opportunity to process information, and simple exposure to information (MacInnis & Jaworski, 1989) all play a role in a bilinguals' processing and the consequences of that processing. As shown in the preceding example, when visual distractors are presented to a logographic reader, ability to process information, a construct typically considered in monolingual research, becomes important in advertising processing (Tavassoli & Han, 2002).

Other Script Processing Differences

Another factor that may be important in unique language reading is the direction in which languages are written and read. Surprisingly, the effects of reading pattern differences in unique languages have not been fully researched. The effects of these differences could add significantly to current marketing research. For example, the Greek alphabet and many of its Western successors settled on a left-to-right pattern, from top to bottom of the page. However, other scripts, such as many East Asian scripts (e.g., Chinese and Japanese), are written top-to-bottom, from the right to the left of the page (Garry & Rubino, 2001). Marketing research has not investigated to what extent these unique reading patterns influence the visual processing of advertisements. Advertisers will many times attempt to manipulate the visual context of an ad to mimic the anticipated movement of consumers' eyes when reading. The placement of visual elements helps shape and direct the readers' advertisement experience (Scott, 1994), so the impact of unique language patterns of reading may have an impact on the advertisement message. Will advertising elements suggested by previous monolingual research, such as the effect of increasing text size in a marketing communication to produce the perception of a larger discounted sale (Scott, 1994), still hold true even with different reading patterns? As these visual advertising elements have only been researched in languages that are read left to right and top-down, it remains to be seen whether or not these concepts still hold true in other languages.

Another issue that the marketing literature has not fully explored is the use of vowels and consonants in different languages. For instance, biblical Hebrew has an alphabet that contains 22 letters with no vowels. Although biblical Hebrew is no longer used, the current Hebrew alphabet still follows much of traditional guidelines, in which vowels are normally not indicated. Instead of formal letters, vowels are usually inferred from the combination of letters or from the context of the written passage. It is possible for vowels to be marked in a word, and where vowels are marked, it is usually a result of weak consonant combinations with a previous vowel causing the vowel to become silent (Garry & Rubino, 2001). This phenomenon is also true of the Arabic language: In the Arabic language, short vowels are generally not written. Occasionally, short vowels are marked where the word would otherwise be ambiguous and cannot be resolved simply from context (Garry & Rubino, 2001). Because the context and surroundings of the word play a vital role in word meaning and word interpretation, a larger emphasis must be placed on the surrounding context. This effect might change the use of graphics and pictures used in advertising.

Also, languages like Hebrew and Arabic have such a strong dependence on the surrounding context that the use of certain visual rhetoric in advertising may not be advisable in these types of language situations. Visual rhetorical figures such as puns, metaphors, antithesis, and rhyme have been shown to produce more elaboration and more favorable attitudes toward ads in experiments with English monolinguals (McQuarrie & Mick, 1999). McQuarrie and Mick (1999) noted that these positive effects all but disappear in the absence of the ability required to adequately comprehend the visual rhetoric placed in an advertisement. In the case of languages such as Arabic and Hebrew, because these visual rhetorical figures may produce more confusion, the resultant attitudes toward the advertisement may be less favorable.

Research has shown how the use of language influences the type of processing undertaken by the viewer. As research shows that the same communication in different languages can result in multiple interpretations, customizing marketing messages for each language may be an important part of marketing efforts in multiple language settings.

Brand Processing

Recently, Yorkston and De Mello (2005) raised an important issue with regard to brand names in multilanguage settings. In their research, Yorkston and De Mello (2005) looked at linguistic gender agreement and brand names across different languages. In linguistics, gender can be defined as "classes of nouns reflected in the behavior of associated words" (Hockett, 1958, p. 231). Therefore, in linguistic terms, gender markers assign nouns, and the objects they designate, to classes. Nouns are assigned to gender by the use of two different types of gender marking rules: *formal* or *semantic*. In formal language systems such as Spanish, the use of gender markings is generally based on the structure of the word and the gender is independent of the object it represents. So, a "floating vessel" can be masculine (e.g., in the Spanish word for "boat"—"el barco,") or feminine (e.g., in the Spanish word for "small canoe"—"la chalupa"). This gender assignment can be based on the sound of the word or the spelling of the word. In a semantic language system like English, gender markings are generally assigned based on the underlying object they represent, so that a "floating vessel" is always feminine whether it is a "small canoe" or a "boat" (Yorkston & De Mello, 2005).

Although some formal languages like Spanish can have both masculine and feminine names in a particular class, established product classes usually have deeply embedded semantic meanings as well. For example, despite some technology-based products having feminine names, the technology product class is predominantly associated with the masculine. In Yorkston and De Mello's (2005) study, they took the product classes of shoes and alcoholic beverages, which contain products that are either semantically masculine or semantically feminine and then paired these products with brand names that follow the formal language system. These brand names were either congruent or incongruent in semantic gender agreement to the product in question. The results of the study showed that respondents had higher recall and higher brand evaluations for those products that had congruent brand names as compared to those products that had incongruent brand names. For example, according to Yorkston and De Mello (2005), white wine is typically associated with the female user, so when the brand name was formally considered feminine, recall and evaluations were high versus when the brand name was formally considered masculine.

Yorkston and De Mello's (2005) study exemplifies the complications that can arise in the brand naming process. Most of the current marketing research has focused on brand names in one language and the moderating effects that language devices such as the use of unusual spellings of words (Lukatela, Frost, & Turvey, 1998), the fit between the brand name and product attributes (Keller, Heckler, & Houston, 1998), or the use of puns or word play (McQuarrie & Mick, 1992) can have on memory for the brand names (Lowrey, Shrum, & Dubitsky, 2003). This research has relied on the basic premise that the brand names are going to be exclusively read and processed in one language. When dealing with brands that have the potential to be bought and sold in multilanguage settings, language issues arise that may force companies to rethink how brand names are created.

Brand naming in multilanguage settings has not been fully explored, thus there is ample work that still needs to be done. Marketers are continually expanding worldwide into countries that differ in languages, so it is of great necessity that this research be further explored to provide tested solutions with practical application. For example, an analysis of the current brand naming practices used by companies in multilingual settings may reveal important brand naming solutions and thwart potential naming disasters. Linguistically based brand name research could analyze the wisdom of Proctor & Gamble's use of the brand Safeguard in North America and other regions of the world, while calling the same product Escudo ("shield" in Spanish) in Latin America (P&G, 2005). What is the reasoning behind translating a brand name in some languages but not in others? Answers to questions like these may reveal important solutions to multilingual brand naming research.

BILINGUAL COGNITIVE PROCESSING

One of the keys to comprehending language processing is to first understand how language is stored. An overview of how individuals cognitively store language will help provide a more comprehensive explanation of how language is learned, processed, and later used. This section first discusses the encoding process for language and non-language.

According to dual coding theory, memory is split into two separate systems, one for verbal and one for non-verbal information. These systems can work independently or jointly. These systems are independent of one another, so each time they are used together, recall should increase due to the activation of not one, but two memory systems. Paivio and Csapo (1973) tested this theory by using tasks in which the respondents were asked to either read a word that was shown by itself, or read a word linked to a picture. The results indicated that, for the verbally encoded pictures, recall was double that of the recall when words were presented by themselves. These results demonstrate the impact that pictures can have on memory and processing, as well as illustrate how activating two memory systems can strengthen recall.

With dual coding theory in mind, Paivio and Lambert (1981) looked at the coding of multiple languages to see how these separate languages would fit into the dual coding framework. According to the bilingual coding model, there are two separate processing and memory stores for each language. Following the dual coding theory framework, dual language theory postulates that memory recall should be greater for a translation task than for a simple recall task because the translation task involves multiple processing systems. Because visual memory storage is considerably stronger than verbal memory stores, recall of the stimuli involved in a translation task should result in a memory score that falls between the visual and verbal encoding task. In a test of this theory, Paivio and Lambert (1981) asked bilingual respondents to look at 51 different stimuli and then perform a simple task that tested the bilingual coding theory. The stimuli and tasks were split into three types. Respondents were to either write down the English word associated with a picture, write down the English translation to a French word, or just copy an English word. After the respondents went through all stimuli and tasks, they were unexpectedly asked to write down all of the items they could recall. The results showed that the recall scores were highest (47.4%) for pictures linked with words, midrange (31.3%) for translated words, and lowest (17.7%) for recall of words that were just repeated. The higher recall score for the translation stimuli over the repeated word stimuli showed that the translation task must have involved multiple processing systems. Because the process involved multiple processing systems, it was concluded that each language is contained within its own processing system, at least at the lexical (word) level.

With the understanding that different language systems are stored separately in a bilingual's mind, we can now focus our attention on how these two language systems interact with one another. A widely accepted model of language storage is the revised hierarchical model (RHM; Kroll & Stewart, 1994). This model helps explain the varying stages in processing that take place for bilinguals. The model is also useful for showing how early learners, as well as advanced bilinguals, process language. See Figure 12.2 for a graphic representation of the RHM model. The model is adapted to include picture–text congruity as a moderator, as discussed later in this section.

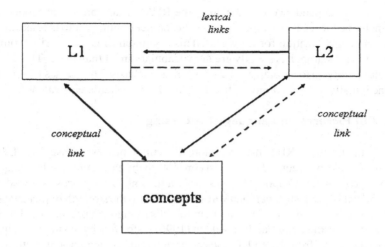

Figure 12.2.   Adapted version of the revised hierarchical model (RHM). Conceptual links between L2 and concepts: The solid arrow represents the conceptual link, which has increased strength with picture text congruity or L2 fluency. The dotted arrow represents the conceptual link, which has decreased strength with picture text incongruity or lack of L2 fluency. Reprinted from *Journal of Memory and Language, 33*, J. F. Kroll and E. Stewart, "Category Interference in Translation and Picture Naming: Evidence for Asymmetric Connections Between Bilingual Memory Representations," pp. 149–174, copyright © 1994, with permission from Elsevier.

According to the RHM, the lower the level of fluency, the stronger the link will be from the least-proficient language (L2) to the primary language (L1). This link between L1 and L2 is much stronger than the link from L2 to the semantic (meaning) concepts that the words represent. The difference in link strength between the different languages and concepts occurs due to the way in which a second language is learned. In learning a second language, individuals depend on their native language in the early stages to help understand the second language's concepts. This process will continue during the learning stages until the speaker can function without the need for the primary language as a crutch. An example of this process is that when an individual is asked to name a picture, the time required by an L2 learner will be greater than if the L2 learner is asked to perform a direct translation (Chen & Lueng, 1989; Kroll & Curley, 1988). This extra time required in the picture-naming task is the result of the weak link between the L2 and conceptual processing. The weak or nonexistent link to the object's mental representation forces the object to first be conceptualized via L1 and then translated to L2. In the direct word translation, the processing of the L1 word is simply translated to L2 and no conceptualization is needed. With increased fluency, the link between L2 and conceptual processing grows stronger, allowing individuals that are fluent in L2 to process objects directly in L2 without involving L1 in the process.

The strong dependence on L1 makes the RHM an asymmetrical model. The asymmetry occurs because the early language learner requires L1 to mediate the access to conceptualization for L2 words. This asymmetry may also arise from the fact that the L2 learner has a vastly greater vocabulary in L1 than in L2. This creates difficulties early on to verbalize in L2 on a consistent basis. This causes L1 words to be conceptually processed more often than the L2 translation equivalent.

Effects of Pictures on Language Processing

The asymmetry in the RHM makes it more difficult to process messages in L2 due to the weak links between L2 words and concepts in the early stages of language acquisition. Paivio and Csapo's (1973) study on the encoding process showed how picture recall is much stronger than verbal recall due to the strength of pictorial processing. The use of visual cues may help facilitate language processing. La Heij, Hooglander, Kerling, and Van Der Velden (1996) tested this by asking participants to translate words from L2 to L1 when congruent and noncongruent pictures accompanied the L2 words. Their studies showed that, with congruent pictures, the time respondents required to translate from L2 to L1 was less then the time required when the respondents were shown incongruent pictures (La Heij et al., 1996).

The use of picture congruity in advertising is not new to monolingual research. The spreading activation paradigm suggests that advertisement pictures activate a conceptual node, which then becomes closely associated with the concept described by the advertisement. The strength of this association will then be moderated by the amount of picture–text congruity (Anderson, 1983). With pictorial congruency helping language processing and memory, the probability of a concept being retrieved is higher when the concept is more closely associated with a picture (Unnava & Burnkrant, 1991).

Luna and Peracchio (2001) tested the impact of picture–text congruency in L1 versus L2 in advertising. In one study, picture–text congruency and interactivity of the product brand name with the picture were manipulated in advertisements. Picture–text congruency was manipulated by whether the product attribute described in the ad claim was congruent with the ad picture. Brand name interactivity was manipulated by whether or not it was consistent with the ad's picture. The hypothesis of this study was that the higher congruity levels would result in stronger links in memory between pictorial and verbal concepts. These strong links would then help facilitate processing and increase the likelihood that the ad claims would be remembered (Lippman & Shanahan, 1973). According to the RHM framework, recall for ads in L1 should always be superior because L1 has a unique asymmetry over L2. Surprisingly, the results from this study actually found that L2 ads can have very similar levels of memory to L1 ads when the ads' picture and text are congruent. These results are consistent with the findings of Paivio and Lambert (1981), who found that translated words were recalled better than L1 words that were only read and not translated. When the ad's picture and text are not congruent, the results suggest a strong support for the RHM model because L1 recall was superior to L2 re-call. The marketing implications of this study are that the level of congruity between the picture and the text of an ad may enhance the effectiveness of ads in English targeting bilingual consumers such as linguistic minorities in the United States.

To further test the impact of picture–text congruency in L1 versus L2 in advertis-ing, Luna and Peracchio (2001) manipulated respondents' processing motivation. Processing motivation is a factor that generally prompts higher levels of elabora-tion and memory (Unnava & Burnkrant, 1991). The findings of the second study in-dicate that the manipulation of the processing motivation did not affect L2 recall. The inability for processing motivation to affect L2 recall provides further support for the RHM's claim that L2 conceptual processing is more difficult than L1 con-ceptual processing. Because the L2 ads do not provide an adequate processing op-portunity, bilingual individuals are less likely to process L2 messages conceptually unless they contain high levels of picture–text congruity or similarly facilitative cues, regardless of increased processing motivation. In subsequent research, how-ever, Luna and Peracchio (2002b) found that, under very high levels of motivation, and provided bilinguals are fairly proficient in both languages, L2 recall can increase to a level similar to L1.

Effects of Language and Cultural Frames on Concepts

The RHM is a model of the links between languages and concepts, thus it is of inter-est to understand how other constructs, such as cultural frames, fit into the model. Cultural frames are further investigated in the bilingual-bicultural section of this chapter, but they are also relevant in the current discussion of the RHM. Because the RHM does not make any detailed claims about the structure of lexical and concep-tual information, but instead focuses on the global connections between informa-tion and the language in which it is processed (Kroll & Dussias, 2002), the model leaves room for speculation as to potential effects of other variables, such as cul-tural frames, on the links and the structures of the model.

Cultural frames have been described as the internalization of a culture, its norms, and values within an individual (Luna, Ringberg, & Peracchio, 2005). When individuals socialize with multiple distinct cultures, they are said to move back and forth between these cultural frames depending on the cultural setting. In order to mesh with the norms of each cultural setting, a multicultural individual is able to switch from operating in a particular cultural frame to another based on cul-tural settings and primes. For example, if Hispanic Americans are immersed in or primed by Anglo cues, then the individual may tend to exhibit more Western pat-terns of speech and behavior in comparison to the same individuals' pattern of speech and behavior when they are immersed or primed by Hispanic cues (Padilla, 1994). In the research by Briley, Morris, and Simonson (2005), the use of language as a cultural prime was found to influence how individuals behave. In Briley et al.'s

(2005) research, respondents (Hong Kong undergraduate students fluent in both Chinese and English) exhibited distinct culturally consistent choices as a result of the language used in the study. It was found that respondents' decisions depended on the language in which the questions were presented. The subject's choices in each case were found to be consistent with the cultural norms of the language in which the choice was presented.

The RHM is used to show the link between the lexicon and concepts, and cultural frames could have an effect on this link, so the precise structure of the way cultural frames fit into the RHM requires further examination. Research has shown that language can be used as a cultural prime that activates cultural frames. In turn, these cultural frames have a mediating effect on conceptual activation and on the decision-making process, so it can be speculated that cultural frames are integrated within the lexical and conceptual structures of the RHM. There is no research in this area, which makes it difficult to state whether cultural frames lie within the conceptual structure or as part of the link between the lexical and the conceptual structures. Regardless of the precise location of the cultural frames in the model, cultural frames must exist at a minimum as a first stage in the conceptual process. At that stage, all messages may be filtered through a cultural frame, resulting in a message that is culturally constrained. This process may precede the conceptualization process of a message. The cultural interpretation will therefore be different for each language and will in turn have an effect on the concepts activated by each message.

An example of this process can be found in Briley et al.'s (2005) research. When respondents were asked questions in Chinese, the question was first filtered through the cultural frame before it could reach conceptualization. After the message was filtered through the cultural frame, the culturally influenced message was then conceptualized. In Briley et al. (2005), the Asian cultural frame affected the conceptualization process and resulted in the respondents' making decisions that were consistent with the prevention-oriented cultural norms of the Asian culture. We can further speculate that, similar to the lexicons, these cultural frames may also have an asymmetric connection with L1 because individuals have more cultural exposure in L1. Therefore, to display the impact that cultural frames have on the RHM, cultural frames are presented as mediating factors that exist as a first stage in the conceptual structure in Figure 12.3.

The Distributed Conceptual Representation Model

The way different languages and concepts are linked has been established, which allows us to focus on the conceptual features that each word has in each language. Every word that an individual knows has its own unique set of conceptual features. These features, or concepts, are language independent and are distributed so that one word is connected to a number of concepts that ultimately define the subjective meaning of the word for each individual (Luna & Peracchio, 2004). As discussed earlier, the difficulty for many second language learners comes from their strong

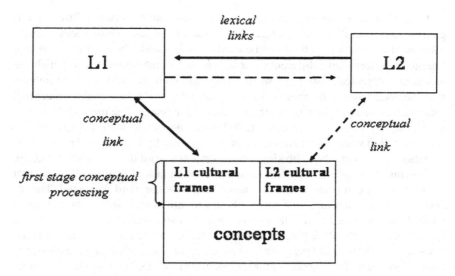

Figure 12.3.   Cultural frames mediate the relationship language concept. Adapted version of the revised hierarchical model (RHM). Reprinted from *Journal of Memory and Language, 33*, J. F. Kroll and E. Stewart, "Category Interference in Translation and Picture Naming: Evidence for Asymmetric Connections Between Bilingual Memory Representations," pp. 149–174, copyright © 1994, with permission from Elsevier.

predisposition to use words from L1 to convey words, pictures, or ideas. A manifestation of this dependency on L1 is that the L2 vocabulary in the early stages of acquisition must be mediated through L1. The process becomes more complex with the notion that not all words in both languages will have direct translations. For cognate words, words that are derived from the same word in an ancestral language (e.g., "addiction" and "addicción"), and concrete words, words that relate to an actual thing or instance (usually nouns), the difficulty in translation, and the speed in which the translation occurs will be reduced compared to other more abstract words. The decrease in difficulty with the cognate and concrete words is due to the direct link of the L2 word to an object or word that exists in L1. This direct link helps facilitate processing of the L2 cognate and concrete words, making the translation easier and faster. In addition, these L1 cognate and concrete words also share the same conceptual features.

For abstract words, words that exist only in the mind because they usually are social constructions, difficulty in translation will be heightened. The difficulty with abstract words is a result of the fact that not all abstract words have identical sets of linked conceptual features. Many abstract words only have partial meaning overlap, so differences in the linguistic and cultural contexts have the greatest influence in determining their meaning (Kroll & Tokowicz, 2001). De Groot (1992) developed a model that illustrates this concept called the distributed conceptual representation model.

In an effort to uncover the divergence in word meanings between different languages, Luna and Peracchio (2002a) developed a word association methodology. This word association method can be used to understand whether the words that bilinguals process have different meanings based on the languages in which the words are presented. Using this word association method, marketers can investigate the divergence in meanings to a bilingual individual based on the conceptual features attached to each word in their marketing message. The methodology recommended by Luna and Peracchio (2002a) for uncovering word association is a free-elicitation word association test that involves multiple sessions. The word association process involves showing the respondent a word in a particular language and having the respondent perform a free-elicitation task of naming all words that the respondent can generate that are associated with the word presented. The respondent then, in a future time period about a month later, is shown the translated equivalent word in a different language, the respondent is again asked to perform a free-elicitation task of naming all words that the respondent can generate that are associated with the word presented. The overlapping words between sessions are then computed, to find the conceptual equivalent to the word that is to be translated. This process can be performed multiple times to ensure reliability of word conceptual convergence.

As discussed earlier in the chapter, motivation can play an important role in the processing of advertisements (MacInnis & Jaworski, 1989). In terms of advertising, motivation can be defined as the desire to process brand or ad information. When motivation or desire is increased, so is the level of processing and focus the individual has toward the information presented (MacInnis & Jaworski, 1989). If the level of processing and focus can be manipulated by the individual's level of motivation, then what effect does motivation have on the distributed conceptual representation model with regard to the conceptual divergence of abstract words? Because there is some basic conceptual overlap between languages when abstract words are presented, the overlapping concepts may be easiest to retrieve for the individual. When the level of processing and focus is low, as found in low motivation circumstances, then this ease of retrieval may cause these shared concepts to be most salient. If low motivation causes shared concepts to be most salient, then these shared concepts will cause abstract words to have the same linked concepts regardless of the language in which the abstract words are presented.

However, when motivation is high, attention levels will also be high. This will then translate into the activation of more divergent conceptual nodes for each language, that is, more divergent concepts activated for each abstract word. The result of this divergence will be that the same abstract words may have very different subjective meanings based on the language in which they are presented. These expectations are only speculative and have yet to be tested, but if these results were found in future studies, the results would indicate that motivation level might moderate the distributed conceptual representation model when dealing with abstract words and their conceptual divergence. This would indicate that an individual's interpretation of the same advertisement in two different languages, when the advertisement contains abstract words, would be more divergent under high motivation conditions. These results would differ from the low motivation condition, because in the low motivation condition only the overlapping concepts would be activated, causing the perception of the advertisement to be more convergent across languages.

An additional potential influence over the distributed conceptual representation model processes is the type of need an individual is attempting to satisfy when processing the information presented. Prior research has deviated in the classifications and definition of individual's different types of needs, but the one thing that the research does converge on is the viewpoint that an individual's need stimulates motivation. The motivation to process and focus attention to specific advertisement message cues has been shown to differ based on the type of need present in the individual (Batra, 1986). Based on the conceptual framework presented by MacInnis and Jaworski (1989), two types of needs have been identified: *utilitarian* and *expressive*. Utilitarian needs are defined as requirements for products that remove or avoid problems, whereas expressive needs are defined as requirements for products that provide social or aesthetic utility (MacInnis & Jaworski, 1989). When consumers have utilitarian needs, they generally focus on the specific attribute information of a product; this attribute information is usually expressed by using concrete words to describe attributes such as the dimensions of the product or its ingredients. When consumers have expressive needs, respondents' decisions depend on the symbolic or expressive value of the product; this symbolic or expressive value is usually expressed by using abstract words to describe the value of the product such as its look or feel (MacInnis & Jaworski, 1989). In other words, when needs are utilitarian, the focus may be on concrete words that describe the product and, according to the distributed conceptual representation model, the perception of the product will be the same, regardless of the advertisement's language. However, when needs are expressive, the focus will be on the abstract words that describe the experiential dimension of the product and, according to the distributed conceptual representation model, the perception will be different due to the differences in the conceptual links that each language has for each abstract word. If these results were found in future studies, they would indicate that the type of need could have an impact over an ad's perception depending on its language. Therefore, to display the potential moderation that motivation and type of need have on the distributed conceptual representation model process, these constructs have been added to the distributed conceptual representation model diagram in Figures 12.4a and 12.4b.

BILINGUAL-BICULTURAL PROCESSING

People around the world are becoming more mobile and increasingly migrating to new countries in search of better opportunities and lives. One of the largest issues and potential barriers to this mobility is the need to adopt a new language. If new language acquisition is needed, then how people utilize and interact with multiple languages and multiple cultures is of great interest.

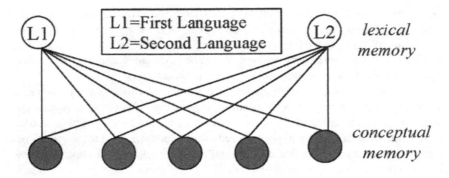

Figure 12.4a Distributed Conceptual Representation Model

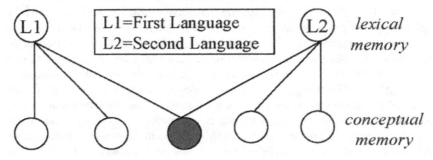

Figure 12.4b Distributed Conceptual Representation Model

Figure 12.4.   Adapted version of the distributed conceptual representation model Note: Figure 12.4a represents the distributed feature model for concrete words, abstract words under low motivation, and situations in which needs are utilitarian based. Figure 12.4b represents the distributed feature model for abstract words under high motivation and situations in which needs are expressive-based. Reprinted from *Orthography, phonology, morphology, and meaning, 1*(1), A. M. B. de Groot, "Bilingual lexical representation: A closer look at conceptual representation," pp. 389–409, copyright © 1992, with permission from Elsevier.

Attitude Toward Languages

Koslow, Shamdasani, and Touchstone's (1994) research evaluates U.S. Hispanics' responses to the use of the Spanish language in advertising. Their research found that the positive effects of Spanish language, or minority subculture language, in advertising could be partially explained by the sociolinguistic theory of accommodation. The theory of accommodation predicts that "the greater the amount of effort in accommodation [using the language of the listener] that a bilingual speaker of one group was perceived to put into this message, the more favorably he would be perceived by listeners from another ethnic group, and also the more effort they in turn would put into accommodating back to" the speaker (Giles, Taylor, & Bourhis,

1973, p.177). Koslow et al. (1994), using the theory of accommodation, found that the use of Spanish language not only has an impact on a Hispanic individuals' message comprehension, but also communicates a message about the advertiser's sensitivity to the Hispanic culture. This sensitivity to the Hispanic culture can result in a significant and positive influence on the individual's attitude toward the advertisement (Koslow et al., 1994).

In addition to their findings on accommodation theory, Koslow et al.'s (1994) study also found a negative attitude toward a fully translated message due to a language-related inferiority complex. This inferiority complex, as described by Rose (1992), is a result of the transitional cultural identity process that individuals adopting a new culture can go through. Cultural transition is the process through which one's original ethnic identity dissipates over time. Typically, theorists have argued that intensity of identification with one's native ethnicity slowly dissipates as one assimilates to the host society's ethnic identity. When an ethnic minority subculture, such as the Hispanic population found in the United States, first moves to a new host society, they may still identify themselves as their native ethnicity living in a foreign land. As generations and time pass, individuals may continue to assimilate, and they may no longer identify with their original ethnicity, but instead consider themselves part of the host society's ethnicity. The more individuals identify themselves with the host society, the more they will feel distanced by messages in their original native language.

The findings of Koslow et al.'s (1994) studies indicate that their Hispanic respondents saw themselves as both Hispanic (their "original" culture) and Anglo (their "host" culture), creating a new Hispanic-Anglo identity. Because the theory of accommodation refers to the advertiser's sensitivity to a culture, accommodation theory only predicts a positive outcome when the message is targeted to the individuals' new Hispanic-Anglo identity. Thus, when the message is presented to a Hispanic-Anglo exclusively in their native language, Spanish, there will be a negative affect toward the message due to the inferiority complex, but when the message is presented in a mixture of languages, there is positive affect toward the message. The results of this study indicate that the sole use of a minority subcultures' language in an advertisement is not advisable.

However, as stated earlier in the chapter, language and language-related issues do not occur in a vacuum, so for each effect, there may be a myriad of potential moderators. One possible moderator for Koslow et al.'s (1994) findings may be found in the results of Deshpande and Stayman's (1994) study on ethnic identification. That study found that when members of minority groups, where minority groups are defined as a group that shares an ethnicity and is not the dominant group in the overall population in question, were shown a print advertisement with a spokesperson of their own ethnic group, the message recipient perceived the advertisement to be more trustworthy. This increased trustworthiness then leads to more positive attitude toward the brand. The level of representation, or the degree to which one is considered a minority in the environment, was found to moderate these findings. The implication here is that minority individuals, whose ethnicity makes up a smaller percentage of their surrounding environment, are more likely to identify themselves in an ethnic manner than individuals from the majority group. This ethnic identification will then translate into a more positive attitude toward the advertisement if it contains a spokesperson of their minority ethnic group because this spokesperson is perceived as more similar. These results show how the intertwining of social issues with language issues creates a complex world in which to research bilingual-bicultural individuals.

Although traditionally researchers had assumed a linear process of assimilation to a host culture, more recent research indicates that this may not be completely accurate. Because each individual's experience, when moving between cultures, is different, the acculturation process for each individual will also be different. This divergence in the acculturation process can be a result of many different factors ranging from individuals' reasons or motivations to move from their native land, to the new environment in which an individual undergoes the acculturation process. The acculturation process has been defined as "those phenomena which result when groups of individuals having different cultures come into continuous first-hand contact, with subsequent changes in the original cultural patterns of either or both groups" (Redfield, Linton, & Herskovits, 1936, p. 149). This acculturation process is said to occur at two different levels: the population (the ecological, cultural, social, and institutional) and the individual (the behaviors and traits of the person) levels (Berry, 1989). An important issue to understand in this definition of acculturation is that the phenomenon is an evolving process not just within the individual, but also with the individual's surroundings. The process will be affected by a great number of factors that may include, but are not limited to, the reason for the interaction of the cultures, length of contact, the permanence of the interaction, the size of both cultures' populations, and the cultural characteristics of both cultures (Berry, 1989). In fact, several possible outcomes are possible in the acculturation process, depending on how individuals feel toward their original culture and their host culture (Berry, 1980). For instance, they could assimilate, as most consumer research to date assumes, so they abandon their original culture and language, favoring their host culture and language, or they could maintain both cultures (Lau-Gesk, 2003), or they could maintain their original culture and resist the host culture. For a complete review of acculturation, see Berry (1989).

In an ethnography study on Hispanic consumers in the United States by Peñaloza (1994), these diverse acculturation variables described by Berry (1989) were shown to have significant effects on Hispanic consumers. In this ethnographic study of Mexican immigrants to the United States, factors such as language proficiency, demographics, recency of arrival to the United States, education, as well as social interaction features (e.g., the influence of cultural assimilation of family and friends,) played major roles in the acculturation of the Hispanic immigrants. These results would again indicate that the process that bicultural-bilingual individuals go through will differ among individuals and will determine a great deal in terms of the individuals' evolving ethnic identity. These factors then will play a large role in how culturally assimilated an individual becomes. We can conclude, then, that when studying bicultural-bilingual issues, caution must be taken not to make overgeneralizations. Multiple moderating factors must be identified in order to place proper perspective on research findings. Different acculturation patterns (Berry, 1980) must be considered and it cannot be assumed that all immigrants will follow a linear assimilation process.

Frame Switching

A previous section defined the concept of frame switching and discussed the cognitive aspects of the phenomenon. This section discusses some social linguistic aspects of frame switching. Consistent with Briley et al.'s (2005) findings, a recent study was conducted that analyzed autobiographical memories retrieved by bilingual-bicultural individuals (Marian & Kaushanskaya, 2004). In that study, the language spoken at the time of retrieval of the autobiographical memories was found to influence participants' sociocultural narratives. The respondents, Russian-English bilinguals, were born in Russia and moved to the United States in their teens to study at an American school. The difference in U.S. and Russian sociocultural orientation is that individuals from the United States behave and score higher on the individualism scale, whereas individuals from Russia behave and score higher on the collectivism scale. Consequently, the study analyzed the autobiographical memories for individualistic versus collectivistic narratives. To analyze the narratives, two measures were used, a linguistic measure and a content measure. The linguistic measure was the number of personal and group pronouns used in respondents' narratives. For the content measure, two separate judges used a 1–5 scale (1 being completely self-oriented and 5 being completely group-oriented in the narrative). The results showed that when the individuals spoke English and told autobiographical memories, they used more personal pronouns and the judges rated the narratives as more self-oriented. The opposite was found for when the individuals spoke Russian, so that both the linguistic and content measures reflected a group orientation. These differences in the individualistic versus collectivistic narratives within respondents indicate a cultural difference in self-construal and cultural value that is primed by the language that the respondent uses in the narrative. The results indicate a significant difference between the narratives within the same respondents across the two languages, which would support the notion that the two cultures are very stable and distinctive from one another.

   In research by Lau-Gesk (2003), the issue of how individuals internalize cultures is further examined. In that study, bilingual Asian American immigrants who consistently spoke the same language within a given cultural context were labeled alternators. The term *alternator* represents an individual who tends to compartmentalize and alternate between two cultures. Alternators prefer the activation of one cultural frame at a time. On the other hand, integrating biculturals were bilingual Asian American immigrants who spoke both languages within a given cultural context, tending to integrate and blend the two cultures. Integrators prefer the activation of both cultural frames at the same time. Various factors, such as fear of losing identification with their native culture, ability to learn a new language, motivation, and opportunity determine whether an individual becomes an integrator or alternator. Based on these factors, immigrants make various language and cultural decisions. The result of these decisions could be to abandon their original culture and language, favoring their host culture and language, or to maintain both cultures, or to maintain their original culture and resist the host culture. In Lau-Gesk's study, alternators rated ads the highest when the appeals were either individualistic or interpersonal in nature—presumably depending on what "mode" alternators were in at the time of exposure. However, integrators preferred the combination of the individualistic and interpersonal appeal.

All of these very different acculturation scenarios occur in the everyday lives of bilinguals and create a society with very dynamic cultural frames among individuals of similar bicultural background. Attitudes toward languages can be very diverse and must be considered when communicating with bilingual-bicultural individuals.

We can conclude, then, that because language is a focal process determining how we interact among others in society, cultural norms are deeply ingrained and embedded in language and therefore language can influence how individuals perceive the world and make decisions.

Code Switching

Another interesting phenomenon in bilingual communities is the combination of two unique languages, or code switching. Code switching is a communication strategy consisting of the mixing of several languages in the same phrase or utterance (Wei, 2004). It has been documented that code switching is used and encountered in a variety of situations by bilinguals on a daily basis (Grosjean, 1982). Recently, code switching has found its way into advertising. For example, in a recent ad in the magazine *Hispanic*, which targets U.S. Latinos, code switching was used when the ad asked, "Twenty million hijas are covered by AFLAC. Is yours?" The word "hija" means daughter in Spanish. It has been hypothesized that the social motivation behind code switching is to emphasize a desired or perceived group membership or interpersonal relationship (Luna & Peracchio, 2005a). Myer-Scotton's (1991, 1993, 1999) markedness model has been used to explain why individuals code switch. In the markedness model, the code-switched element becomes marked because it is in contrast with the language context created by the rest of the phrase or utterance. This markedness can be viewed as analogous to perceptual salience. With perceptual salience, an object becomes more salient because it stands out from its immediate context; the same is true for a marked language element, except the perceived saliency is due to the language context and not the visual context. The markedness of the element will be caused by the individual's prior experience, expectations, or from other foci of attention. (Fiske & Taylor, 1984; Luna & Peracchio 2005a). This salience of the marked element then activates the language schema to which that word belongs, causing an awareness of the social meaning carried by that language (Luna & Peracchio, 2005a).

Code switching can be viewed as a formal language because it has, like any formal language such as English or Spanish, certain structural rules that govern both the production and perception of the language (Luna, Lerman, & Peracchio, 2005; Myer-Scotton, 1993, 1995; Myer-Scotton & Jake, 2000). Luna, Lerman, and Peracchio (2005) found that code-switched ads that followed the structural rules governing the production of code switching were more persuasive than ads that did not follow them. For example, one of the grammatical rules that was manipulated was noun-adjective word order so that some respondents rated an ad in which the noun-adjective word order followed the correct code switching grammar, or rated the same ad slogan but with the incorrect noun-adjective word order.

Luna et al. (2005) found that the type of processing the respondent used moderated the advertisement's persuasion results. When processing an ad message, an individual can use one of two types of processing: data-driven or conceptually driven (Roediger, 1990). Because conceptually driven processing involves semantic elaboration, in which individuals may imagine the action involved in the ad's narrative, this type of processing may lead respondents to "skip" code-switched words, thus overlooking improper code-switched grammar (Altarriba, Kroll, Sholl, & Rayner, 1996). Conversely, data-driven processing is bottom-up processing, in which the processing is triggered directly by external stimuli. Luna et al.'s (2005) study found that, under conceptually driven processing, the improper use of code-switching grammar did not result in any difference in ad persuasion. However, under data-driven processing, the improper use of grammar resulted in a significant decline in a slogan's persuasiveness.

Code-switching behavior is prevalent in bilinguals' everyday lives, so it may be assumed that the behavior is always accepted. However, the response that code-switching activates is based on multiple factors such as the proper use of grammar, the language schema that is activated, the attitude toward code switching, and the context of the code-switched message (Luna & Peracchio, 2005a, 2005b). Language schemas are defined as an individuals' perception about the situation and occasion when a language should be spoken, the kind of people that speak the language, the topics for which the language is best suited, the beliefs about how the language may be perceived by others, and the meaning communicated by use of that language (Luna & Peracchio, 2005b). Certain language schemas will be activated by a code-switched message because, as discussed earlier, code switching makes the code-switched element marked in contrast with the language context created by the rest of the phrase. The language schema corresponding to the marked element is activated. For example, if a message is presented in English and then switches to Spanish, the language schema for Spanish will be activated, because the Spanish language is the marked element.

Luna and Peracchio (2005b) define attitude toward code switching as the extent to which individuals perceive code switching to be a desirable practice. Although attitudes toward code switching are commonly negative, even in bilingual communities where code switching is a wide spread practice (Hidalgo, 1986; Ramirez, Milk, & Sapiens 1983), attitudes toward code switching are most likely moderated by factors such as education and degree of acculturation. This attitude toward code switching does not have to be positive or negative; an individual may also have a neutral attitude toward code switching as well.

The results of Luna and Peracchio (2005a) suggest that the attitude toward a code-switched message is primarily influenced by the individual's attitude toward the language schema the code-switched message has activated. For example, if a respondent has a negative language schema toward the Spanish language and the code-switched message makes the Spanish language marked, this individual will have a more negative attitude toward the message in comparison to the same message where the English language is marked. Additionally, Luna and Peracchio (2005b) found that individuals' attitudes toward code switching also influence their responses to a code-switched message.

Moderating the language schema results, Luna and Peracchio (2005b) found that context effects could offset the negative affect prompted by a language schema. As code switching is used in multiple settings, individuals may develop a belief that a particular switching behavior, such as code switching from English to Spanish, is a widely used practice. This belief then creates a context effect in which the individual perceives this code-switching behavior to be the norm. This belief about code-switching norms will then influence the individual's interpretation of the code-switched message. If an individual is presented with a code-switched message that corresponds to the perceived norm, then the individual will respond more favorably to the code-switched message because of the perceived fit due to the context effect. This means that if an individual perceives a code-switching behavior, such as English to Spanish, as the cultural norm, and the code-switched message is presented in that direction, then the resulting attitude toward the message becomes positive regardless of the language schema one holds for the marked Spanish language (Luna & Peracchio, 2005b).

CONCLUSIONS

This chapter has reviewed the current literature on dual language processing. The literature was divided into three areas: unique language processing, bilingual language processing, and bilingual-bicultural language processing. Throughout, the discussion provided several new directions for research. The chapter attempted to integrate the growing literature in dual language processing in marketing and consumer research. The topic of language processing, and bilingual processing in particular, is of great importance for marketers and consumer researchers because most of the world's population speaks more than one language (Grosjean, 1982).

However, relatively little research is available in this area. With volumes of marketing research dedicated to monolinguals, it is time for marketing researchers to focus their attention on the future and realities of a multilingual, multicultural world and provide practical real-world marketing solutions.

REFERENCES

Altarriba, J., Kroll, J., Sholl, A., & Rayner, K. (1996). The influence of lexical and conceptual constraints on reading mixed-language sentences: Evidence from eye fixation and naming times. *Memory and Cognition, 24*(4), 477–492.

Anderson, J. R. (1983). A spreading activation theory of memory. *Journal of Verbal Learning and Verbal Behavior, 22,* 261–295.

Baddeley, A. D. (1986). *Working memory.* Oxford, England: Clarendon.

Batra, R. (1986). Affective advertising: Role, processes, and measurement. In R. A. Peterson, W. D. Hoyer, & W. R. Wilson (Eds.), *The role of affect in consumer behavior: Emerging theory and applications* (pp. 53–85). Lexington, MA: D. C. Heath.

Berry, J. W. (1980). Acculturation as varieties of adaptation. In A. M. Padilla (Ed.), *Acculturation: Theory, models and some new findings* (pp. 9–25). Boulder, CO: Westview Press.

Berry, J. W. (1989). Psychology of acculturation. *Nebraska Symposium on Motivation, 37,* 201–234.

Briley, D. A., Morris, M. W., & Simonson, I. (2005). Biculturals and shifting strategies: The role of language and audiences in eliciting cultural styles of decision making. *Journal of Consumer Psychology, 15, 351–362.*

Chen, H.-C., & Leung, Y.-S. (1989). Patterns of lexical processing in a non-native language. *Journal of Experimental Psychology: Learning, Memory, and Cognition, 15,* 316–325.

de Groot, A. (1992). Bilingual lexical representation: A closer look at conceptual representations. In R. Frost & L. Katz (Eds.), *Orthography, phonology, morphology, and meaning* (pp. 389–412). Amsterdam: Elsevier.

Deshpande, R., & Stayman, D. M. (1994). A tale of two cities: Distinctiveness theory and advertising effectiveness. *Journal of Marketing Research, 31,* 57–64.

Fiske, S. T., & Taylor, S. (1984). *Social cognition.* New York: McGraw-Hill.

Garry, J., & Rubino, C. (2001). *Facts about the world's languages: An encyclopedia of the world's major languages, past and present.* New York: New England Publishing Associates.

Gathercole, S. E., & Baddeley, A. D. (1993). *Working memory and language.* Hillsdale, NJ: Lawrence Erlbaum Associates.

Giles, H., Taylor, D. M., & Bourhis, R. Y. (1973). Toward a theory of interpersonal accommodation through speech accommodation: Some Canadian data. *Language in Society, 2,* 177–192.

Green, D. W. (1986). Control, activation and resources: A framework and a model for the control of speech in bilinguals. *Brain and Language, 27,* 210–223.

Grosjean, F. (1982). *Life with two languages: An introduction to bilingualism.* Cambridge, MA: Harvard University Press.

Hidalgo, M. (1986). Language contact, language loyalty, and language prejudice on the Mexican border. *Language and Society, 15*(2), 193–220.

Hispanic Business Research (2004). U.S. Hispanic purchasing power growth rate three times the national rate in the last decade. Retrieved July 6, 2005, from http://www.hispanicbusiness.com/news/newsbyid.asp?id=16028

Hockett, C. F. (1958). *A course in modern linguistics.* New York: MacMillan.

Hung, D. L., & Tzeng, O. J. L. (1981). Orthographic variations and visual information processing. *Psychological Bulletin, 90*, 377–414.

Keller, K. L., Heckler, S .E., & Houston, M. J. (1998). The effects of brand name suggestiveness on advertising recall. *Journal of Marketing, 62*, 48–57.

Koslow, S., Shamdasani, P. N., & Touchstone, E. E. (1994, March). Exploring language effects in ethnic advertising: A sociolinguistic perspective. *Journal of Consumer Research, 20*, 575–585.

Kroll, J. F., & Curley, J. (1988). Lexical memory in novice bilinguals: The role of concepts in retrieving second language words. In M. Gruneberg, P. Morris, & R. Sykes (Eds.), *Practical aspects of memory* (Vol. 2, pp. 389–395). London: Wiley.

Kroll, J. F., & Dussias, P. E. (2002). The comprehension of words and sentences in two languages. In T. Bhatia & W. Ritchie (Eds.), *Handbook of bilingualism* (pp. 169–200). Cambridge, MA: Blackwell.

Kroll, J. F., & Stewart, E. (1994). Category interference in translation and picture naming: Evidence for asymmetric connections between bilingual memory representations. *Journal of Memory and Language, 33*, 149–174.

Kroll, J. F., & Tokowicz, N. (2001). The development of conceptual representation for words in a second language. In J. L. Nicol (Ed.), *One mind, two languages: Bilingual language processing* (pp. 49–71). Cambridge, MA: Blackwell.

La Heij, W., Hooglander, A., Kerling, R., & Van Der Velden, E. (1996). Nonverbal context effects in forward and backward translation: Evidence for concept mediation. *Journal of Memory and Language, 35*, 648–665.

Lau-Gesk, L. G. (2003). Activating culture through persuasion appeals: An examination of the bicultural consumer. *Journal of Consumer Psychology, 13*, 301–315.

Levey, R. H. (1999, May 21). Give them some credit. *American Demographics,* 41–43.

Lippman, M. Z., & Shanahan, M. W. (1973). Pictorial facilitation of paired-associate learning: Implications for vocabulary training. *Journal of Educational Psychology, 64*(2), 216–222.

Lowrey, T. M., Shrum, L. J., & Dubitsky, T. M. (2003). The relation between brand-name linguistic characteristics and brand-name memory. *Journal of Advertising, 32*(3), 7–17.

Lukatela, G., Frost, S. J., & Turvey, M. T. (1998). Phonological priming by masked nonword primes in the lexical decision task. *Journal of Memory and Language, 39*, 666–683.

Luna, D., Lerman, D., & Peracchio, L. A. (2005). Structural constraints in codeswitched advertising. *Journal of Consumer Research, 32*, 416–423.

Luna, D., & Peracchio, L. A. (2001). Moderators of language effects in advertising to bilinguals: A psycholinguistics approach. *Journal of Consumer Research, 28*, 284–295.

Luna, D., & Peracchio, L. A. (2002a). Uncovering the cognitive duality of bilinguals through word association. *Psychology and Marketing, 19*, 457–475.

Luna, D., & Peracchio, L. A. (2002b). Where there is a will … : Motivation as a moderator of language processing by bilingual consumers. *Psychology and Marketing, 19*, 573–594.

Luna, D., & Peracchio, L. A. (2004). Language in multicultural advertising: Words and cognitive structure, In J. D. Williams, W. Lee, & C. Haugtvedt (Eds.), *Diversity in advertising* (pp. 153–176). Mahwah, NJ: Lawrence Erlbaum Associates.

Luna, D., & Peracchio, L. A. (2005a). Advertising to bilingual consumers: The impact of code-switching on persuasion. *Journal of Consumer Research, 31*, 760–765.

Luna, D., & Peracchio, L. A. (2005b). Sociolinguistic effects on code-switched ads targeting bilingual consumers. *Journal of Advertising, 34*(2), 43–56.

Luna, D., Ringberg, T., & Peracchio, L. A. (2005). *The influence of language on frame switching among bicultural consumers.* Working Paper.

MacInnis, D. J., & Jaworski, B. J. (1989). Information processing from advertisements: Towards an integrative framework. *Journal of Marketing, 53*, 1–23.

Marian, V., & Kaushanskaya, M. (2004). Self-construal and emotion in bicultural bilinguals. *Journal of Memory and Language, 51*, 190–201.

McCusker, L. X., Hillinger M. L., & Bias, R. G. (1981). Phonological recoding and reading. *Psychological Bulletin, 89*, 217–245.

McQuarrie, E. F., & Mick, D. G. (1992). On resonance: A critical pluralistic inquiry into advertising rhetoric. *Journal of Consumer Research, 19*, 180–197.

McQuarrie, E. F., & Mick D. G. (1999). Visual rhetoric in advertising: Text-interpretive, experimental, and reader-response analyses. *Journal of Consumer Research, 26*, 37–54.

Myer-Scotton, C. (1991). Making ethnicity salient in code-switching. In J. R. Dow (Ed.), *Language and ethnicity* (pp. 95–109). Philadelphia: Benjamins.

Myer-Scotton, C. (1993). *Social motivation for code-switching: Evidence from Africa.* Oxford, England: Oxford University Press.

Myer-Scotton, C. (1995). A lexically based model of code-switching. In L. Milroy & P. Muysken (Eds.), *One speaker, two languages: Cross-disciplinary perspectives in code-switching* (pp. 233–256). Cambridge, England: Cambridge University Press.

Myer-Scotton, C. (1999). Explaining the role of norms and rationality in code-switching. *Journal of Pragmatics, 32*(9), 1259–1271.

Myer-Scotton, C., & Jake, J. L. (2000). Explaining aspects of code-switching and their implications. In J. Nicol (Ed.), *One mind, two languages: Bilingual language processing* (pp. 84–116). Cambridge, England: Blackwell.

P&G. (2005). *Who we are product list.* Retrieved July 27, 2005, from http://www.pg.com/company/who_we_are/global_products.jhtml

Padilla, A. M. (1994). Bicultural development: A theoretical and empirical examination. In R. G. Malgady & O. Rodriguez (Eds.), *Theoretical and conceptual issues in Hispanic mental health* (pp. 20–51). Malabar, FL: Krieger.

Paivio, A. (1986). *Mental representations.* New York: Oxford University Press.

Paivio, A., & Csapo, K. (1973). Picture superiority in free recall: Imagery or dual coding? *Cognitive Psychology, 5*, 176–206.

Paivio, A., & Lambert, W. (1981). Dual coding and bilingual memory. *Journal of Verbal Learning and Verbal Behavior, 20*, 532–539.

Peñaloza, L. (1994). Atravesando fronteras/border crossing: A critical ethnographic exploration of the consumer acculturation of Mexican immigrants. *Journal of Consumer Research, 21*, 32–54.

Perfetti, C. A., & Zhang, S. (1991). Phonological processes in reading Chinese characters. *Journal of Experimental Psychology: Learning, Memory, and Cognition, 17*(4), 633–643.

Ramirez, A. G., Milk, R. H., & Sapiens, A. (1983). Intragroup differences and attitudes towards varieties of Spanish among bilingual pupils from California and Texas. *Hispanic Journal of Behavioral Sciences, 5*(4), 417–429.

Redfield, R., Linton, R., & Herskovits, M. J. (1936). Memorandum on the study of acculturation. *American Anthropologist, 38*, 149–152.

Roediger, H. (1990). Implicit memory: Retention without remembering. *American Psychologist, 45*, 1043–1056.

Rose, P. B. (1992). Hispanic acculturation/assimilation: The need for an emic perspective. In L. N. Reid (Ed.), *Proceedings of the 1992 conference of the American Academy of Advertising* (pp. 1–6). Athens, GA: American Academy of Advertising.

Schmitt, B. H., Pan Y., & Tavassoli, N. T. (1994). Language and consumer memory: The impact of linguistic differences between Chinese and English. *Journal of Consumer Research, 21*, 419–431.

Scott, L. (1994). Images in advertising: The need for a theory of visual rhetoric. *Journal of Consumer Research, 21*, 252–273.

Spinks, J. A., Liu Y., Perfetti, C. A., & Tan, L. H. (2000). Reading Chinese characters for meaning: The role of phonological information. *Cognition, 76*(1), B1–B11.

Tavassoli, N. T., & Han, J. K. (2002). Auditory and visual brand identifiers in Chinese and English. *Journal of International Marketing, 10*(2), 13–28.

Tavassoli, N. T., & Lee, Y. H. (2003). The differential interaction of auditory and visual advertising elements with Chinese and English. *Journal of Marketing Research, 40*, 468–480.

University of California Linguistic Minority Research Institute. (2003). *Percent of population 5–17 years of age who report speaking a language other than English and speaking English with some difficulty, California in U.S., 1990 and 2000.* Retrieved July 6, 2005, from http://lmri.ucsb.edu/resdiss/2/pdf_files/elfacts_number4.pdf

Unnava, H. R., & Burnkrant, R. E. (1991). An imagery-processing view of the role of pictures in print advertisements. *Journal of Marketing Research, 28*, 226–231.

Usunier, J. C. (1996). *Marketing across cultures.* New York: Prentice-Hall.

Wei, L. (2004). *The bilingualism reader.* New York: Routledge Press.

Yorkston, E., & De Mello, G. (2005). Linguistic gender marking and categorization. *Journal of Consumer Research, 31*, 224- 234.

Zhou, X., & Marslen-Wilson, W. (1999). Phonology, orthography, and semantic activation in reading Chinese. *Journal of Memory and Language, 41*, 579–606.

PART IV

Afterword

CHAPTER 13

Comprehension Processes in Advertising: Words, Sentences, and Narratives

Robert S. Wyer, Jr.
Hong Kong University of Science and Technology

The information we receive in advertisements and television commercials is often transmitted simultaneously in several sense modalities. An understanding of how meaning is extracted from these complex configurations of stimulus inputs, and how inferences are made on the basis of this meaning, is obviously a formidable task. The task is rendered even more difficult by virtue of the fact that humans are not passive information processors. The concepts and knowledge that people use to comprehend the information they receive are determined in part by the purpose for which they acquire it. They can depend on whether recipients are motivated to learn about the object or event being described, whether they wish to refute the validity of the information's implications, or whether they are simply trying to understand the information with no other specific objective in mind.

The chapters in this volume discuss many aspects of this general comprehension process. Some chapters focus on the comprehension of single words. Others consider reactions to sentences and still others analyze responses to clusters of sentences of the sort that compose a story. The authors consider information that is conveyed not only linguistically but also visually, acoustically, and through taste, and discuss the manner in which the information that is conveyed through these different sense modalities combines to influence both memory and judgment. Furthermore, they identify individual and situational differences in the type of knowledge that people bring to bear on the meaning they extract from information and the emotional reactions that result from this processing. The present authors, like others (e.g., Childers & Jass, 2002; Doyle & Bottomley, 2006), recognize that paralinguistic features of information (e.g., the font in which the information is presented, the vocal qualities of the speaker, the rate at which the information is transmitted, etc.) can convey meaning in their own right. Furthermore, the meaning extracted from more complex sets of verbal information can depend on whether it is presented in bullet point or in a temporally ordered narrative (Adaval, Isbell, & Wyer, in press; Adaval & Wyer, 1998). Finally, information transmitted in one modality can be mentally transformed into other modalities in the course of comprehending it. Thus, visual features of linguistic information can be assigned semantic meaning (Doyle & Bottomley, 2006) and verbal information can stimulate the construction of mental images (Black, Turner, & Bower, 1979; Garnham, 1981; Glenberg, Meyer, & Lindem, 1987). In short, the medium may not be all of the message, but it is certainly an important part of it (McLuhan, 1967).

Several theoretical formulations are proposed in this volume to explain the phenomena under discussion (e.g., brand name meaning, the impact of metaphors, sentence comprehension, etc.). Although these formulations are not incompatible, a single conceptualization that can effectively integrate and account for all of the phenomena they consider is well beyond the scope of the present chapter. A theory of comprehension proposed by Wyer (2004; Wyer & Radvansky, 1999) may nevertheless help to see how many of the issues raised in previous chapters of this volume might ultimately be integrated into a general formulation of comprehension processes in advertising. The theory is a component of a more general conceptualization of information processing that considers not only comprehension but also other stages of processing (Wyer, 2004; Wyer & Srull, 1989). Although it is complex in detail, its essential features can be conveyed fairly simply. After summarizing aspects of the conceptualization that are particularly useful in the present context and noting a few auxiliary principles that derive from research and theory in social information processing more generally, I will review a number of the issues raised earlier in this book and indicate how they might be conceptualized within this more general framework.

A CONCEPTUAL FRAMEWORK

In the course of comprehending information in terms of previously formed concepts and knowledge, people normally construct a mental representation of its referents and store this representation in memory. The content and form of this representation, however, is rarely identical to that of the information on which it is based (Wyer & Srull, 1989). Wyer and Radvansky (1999) distinguish between two types of information, each of which can elicit a different type of mental representation. One type of information refers to relations among persons, objects, and situations that are unconstrained in time and space (e.g., assertions that honesty is the best policy or that wealthy people own big cars). This information is normally transmitted verbally, and is comprehended in terms of preexisting semantic concepts and knowledge. The mental representations constructed in the course of comprehending this type of information are likely to be coded linguistically (or metalinguistically).

The second type of information refers to events and states of affairs that occur at a specific, although perhaps not specified, time and place. For example, we might be told that George W. Bush gave a speech to the American Legion, that a boy kicked a football, or that Michael Jordan drank a Coca-Cola. If this information is transmitted verbally, it may also be interpreted in terms of semantic concepts and knowledge. In addition, however, this type of information theoretically stimulates the construction of a mental simulation of the event and the persons or objects involved in it. These simulations, or *situation* models, normally include a nonverbal image of the event or situation being described. If several states or events are described in a temporal sequence, they may be integrated to form a multiframe *episode* model.

Visual images are often formed spontaneously in the course of comprehending verbal descriptions of events (e.g., Black et al., 1979; Garnham, 1981; Glenberg et al., 1987; Radvansky, Wyer, Curiel, & Lutz, 1997). Moreover, information that elicits visual images is relatively easier to remember and has more impact on judgments (Reyes, Thompson, & Bower, 1980). Note, however, that visual images, like pictures, depict situations and events that are localized in time and space. Consequently, they are unlikely to be formed spontaneously in response to a verbal description unless the event or situation being described is itself temporally and spatially localized (Wyer & Radvansky, 1999). Thus, "The boy kicked the football" theoretically elicits a mental image in the course of comprehending it, as the event necessarily occurred at a particular point in time. However, "The boy owns a football," or "Honesty is the best policy," would not spontaneously elicit a mental image because the conditions described by the statements are not temporally and situationally constrained.

The preceding discussion is restricted to comprehension processes that occur spontaneously when people are exposed to information with no objective other than to understand it. When people process information for a more specific purpose, however, they may bring specific goal-related concepts to bear on its interpretation and may encode it into memory in a form that is particularly useful for attaining this goal. The distinction between spontaneous and deliberative comprehension processes is not always clear. For ease of communication, however, I will discuss each type of processing separately.

Spontaneous Comprehension Processes

In conceptualizing spontaneous comprehension processes, Wyer and Radvansky (1999; see also Wyer, 2004) distinguish metaphorically between two interacting processing systems. One, linguistic process involves the translation of verbally coded input material into subject-verb-object propositions and the assignment of semantic meaning to these propositions on the basis of previously acquired concepts and knowledge. A second, nonverbal processing system has the capability of constructing nonverbally coded "images." This can be done either by retrieving an existing situation or episode model whose linguistic coding ("caption") is similar to that of the input information to be comprehended, or by extracting nonverbal features of several different representations and combining them to form a new representation in the manner suggested by Barsalou's (1993) formulation of *perceptual symbols*. Thus, for example, a person who is told that Bill Clinton plays the saxophone might construct a mental image of the event by combining a perceptual symbol of his appearance that was formed while watching a newscast with a perceptual symbol of a saxophone player that was formed on the basis of quite different experiences. Similarly, a person who reads that a lion walked into McDonald's and ordered a Big Mac might construct a visual image of this event by combining perceptual symbols of a lion, McDonald's, a hamburger, and a nonverbal image of ordering behavior that are extracted from preexisting models containing these elements. Given these assumptions, the processes that underlie the comprehension of nonverbal and verbal information can be summarized in a series of postulates.

Comprehension of Nonverbal Information.   Although the events that people encounter are experienced as a continuous stream of stimulus input, they are not encoded into memory as such. Rather, as Ebbesen (1980; see also Newtson, 1976) suggests, people extract static frames from the stream, each of which exemplifies a preexisting event concept. Thus, the frames in combination permit the sequence of events to be reconstructed. If successive frames pertain to the same person or situation, then they are combined to form an episode model stored in memory as a unit. If the frames pertain to different situations or protagonists, then separate representations may be formed. To summarize:

> *Postulate 1.* People encode sequences of events they experience or observe as a series of static frames, each corresponding to a different event model. If successive frames are thematically related or pertain to the same individual, they may be organized and stored in memory as a single unit (i.e., an episode model).

A second postulate is based on evidence reported by Newtson (1976):

> *Postulate 2.* Fewer situation models are formed from an observed sequence of events if the events are familiar (i.e., they are similar to preexisting models) than if they are not.

A third postulate, proposed by Wyer and Radvansky (1999) and empirically supported by Wyer, Adaval, and Colcombe (2002), is of particular importance:

> *Postulate 3.* Nonverbal stimulus information is encoded into memory in the modality(ies) in which it is experienced. However, it is not encoded linguistically unless this encoding is necessary in order to attain a specific objective that exists at the time.

Comprehension of Verbal Information.   The comprehension of verbal information requires both a semantic encoding of the information and, in many instances, the construction of a mental image of it as well:

Postulate 4. Each conceptual unit of verbal information is spontaneously transformed into the equivalent of a subject-verb-object proposition. These features independently serve as retrieval cues that stimulate the retrieval of previously formed representations that contain them:

1.   If all three sentence components are contained in the linguistic coding of one or more preexisting representations, these representations are retrieved and used as a basis for constructing a new one.[1] This representation may or may not contain a visual image, depending on whether the retrieved representations have nonverbal features.

2.   If a previously acquired representation containing all three sentence components does not exist, then representations that contain various subsets of the components are retrieved. If these representations are nonverbally coded, perceptual symbols are extracted and used to construct a nonverbal representation of the event(s) described by the new information.

3.   If one or more of the sentence components do *not* cue the retrieval of a representation that contains a nonverbal (image) component, a mental image is not constructed of the information, and a linguistic coding of it alone is stored in memory.

Thus, for example, most Chicago Bulls fans should spontaneously form a mental image when encountering the statement, "Michael Jordan sank a three-pointer," as they are likely to have several previously formed situation models of this event. They may also form a mental image of "Michael Jordan is driving a BMW" because, although they do not have a preexisting model of this event, they can combine perceptual symbols extracted from existing representations of "Michael Jordan," "driving," and "BMW." In contrast, consider the sentence, "Michael Jordan owns a BMW." In this case, "owning" is not spatially and temporally constrained and so it is unlikely to elicit a mental image (for evidence, see Radvansky et al., 1997). In this case, a nonverbal representation would not be formed, and only a linguistic representation of the proposition would be stored in memory.

A fifth postulate concerns the integration of several individual event representations into a single one. It is therefore somewhat analogous to Postulate 1:

Postulate 5. When two or more event descriptions are presented in sequence and refer to the same referents, they are likely to be combined to form a single episode model that is comprehended and stored in memory as a whole.

---

[1]Following Hintzman (1986), Wyer and Radvansky (1999) assume that a stimulus feature retrieves a composite of all existing representations that contain it, and the features associated with it in these representations provide the basis for the new representation that is formed. Thus, "person" is likely to stimulate the retrieval of a very diverse set of representations with few features in common, whereas "Michael Jordan" is likely to stimulate the retrieval of a more specific set. As a result, the subject of an event model that is constructed from a statement about Mr. Jordan will be more detailed than a model constructed from a statement about "a person."

Deliberative Comprehension Processes

The preceding discussion has focused on the comprehension of information that occurs spontaneously at the time the information is encountered. This comprehension is often uncontrollable. (For example, try *not* to understand "The boy kicked the ball.") However, comprehension may also be governed by more conscious attempts to understand the meaning and implications of information. One such condition arises when the spontaneous processes implied by Postulates 1–4 fail. A second, more general condition arises from the need to interpret and organize one's knowledge in a way that facilitates a general understanding of the world in which we live.

In the first case, we noted earlier that certain constraints are imposed on the subject and object of an event or episode model. Thus, an image can be easily formed of "The man pounded a nail into the wall" because "man" and "nail" have attributes that are compatible with those of actors and objects in previously formed models of this action "pounds." In contrast, the statement "The nail pounded a man into the wall" is anomalous on the surface because attributes of the actor and object in the sentence violate constraints imposed by preexisting situation models of the action. Thus, comprehension of the statement requires cognitive deliberation (e.g., the construction of a cartoonlike image of a big nail battering a human being through a piece of plaster board.) In other cases, information may be easy to comprehend in isolation but is difficult to comprehend in the context in which it occurs. For example, "John took off his clothes" is meaningful out of context. However, it would be difficult to comprehend in the context of one's description of a restaurant visit.

Still other information may appear to violate normative rules of communication (Grice, 1975; Higgins, 1981; Wyer & Gruenfeld, 1995). (These rules may constitute implicit theories of the sort described earlier.) That is, communications are assumed to be informative, to convey the truth as the communicator sees it (Grice, 1975), and to be relevant to the topic under discussion (Sperber & Wilson, 1986). In conceptualizing the effects of these rules, Wyer and Radvansky (1999) postulate that people spontaneously recognize that a statement they encounter is totally redundant with previously acquired knowledge, inconsistent with this knowledge, or incompatible with other information conveyed in the same situation. Furthermore, when one of these conditions arises, the recipients are likely to engage in deliberative processing in an attempt to understand why the statement was made. Thus, a statement that is so obviously true as to go without saying, a statement that is patently false ("Bill Clinton is Prime Minister of England"), or a statement that is ostensibly irrelevant to the topic at hand (as in the restaurant example given earlier) is likely to stimulate more extensive processing. To formalize:

Postulate 6. If a mental representation cannot be formed spontaneously on the basis of previously acquired concepts and knowledge, or if the representation formed exceeds the range of values that render it plausible or relevant under the conditions in which it occurs, its meaning and implications are established on the basis of deliberative cognitive processing.

Although this postulate is imprecise, its implications for the comprehension of advertisements and television commercials are worth noting. For example, a statement that "General Motors is producing a new line of automobiles" is easily comprehended in terms of prior knowledge about its components and is likely to fall within an acceptable range of plausibility. To this extent, it may stimulate little additional information processing. On the other hand, the statement, "General Motors is producing a new line of lingerie" is likely to exceed the range of plausibility implied by prior knowledge, and thus to stimulate additional cognitive activity.

Recipients' attempts to make communications both relevant and informative are often exploited by advertisers. For example, customers who read that "Brand X contains no chromatic disconsummate" may have no idea what the ingredient is. In order to make the statement relevant and informative, however, they may infer not only that other products on the market do have the attribute (thus making the claim informative) but also that the attribute is undesirable (thus making it relevant). By the same token, similar considerations would lead them to infer from the statement "Brand X contains chromatic disconsummate" that other products do not have the ingredient and the ingredient is desirable. Postulate 6 also comes into play in the comprehension of metaphors, as will be indicated presently.

The Role of General Knowledge: Implicational Molecules and Implicit Theories

To reiterate, the spontaneous comprehension of a specific experience may stimulate the construction of a complex representation of an event, or sequence of events, that contain visual images as well as linguistic encodings. However, people may be motivated to develop a more general understanding of the world in which they live, and it is often very hard to understand the consequences of these experiences for oneself or others on the basis of situation-specific examples alone. It seems intuitively obvious that in order to simplify one's understanding of the world in which we live, we form more general concepts about the interrelations among events that permit new experiences to be explained and their consequences to be predicted.

This knowledge can pertain to a series of temporally related events that have been frequently observed and function as *implicit theories* about their causal relatedness (Dweck, Chiu, & Hong, 1995; Ross, 1989; Wyer, 2004). Once these theories are formed, they may be applied spontaneously in understanding descriptions of new experiences, inferring the occurrence of events that were not mentioned in these descriptions, and predicting the consequences of the experiences for the future. Thus, if we hear that a person who ordered filet mignon at a restaurant paid $35 for it, then we are likely to infer that the person ate the meal despite the fact that this event had not been mentioned. This is because we have an implicit theory about the events that typically occur in restaurants and their relatedness.

Many theories can be viewed as *implicational molecules* of the sort originally conceived by Abelson and Reich (1969; see Wyer, 2004). Implicational molecules consist of sets of propositions that are logically or psychologically bound together and, in combination, exemplify a generalization about the world at large. For example, the generalization that "people get what they deserve" might be exemplified by the two-proposition molecule:

[P is good (bad); good (bad) things befall P].

Similarly, the generalization that smoking causes lung cancer is exemplified by the molecule:

[P smokes; P has (will get) lung cancer],

and the generalization that people do things for a purpose might be exemplified by:

[P wants Y; X causes Y; P does X].

More complex sets of propositions can exist concerning the temporal and causal relations among people and objects. For example, people might have a theory that individuals who get married at an early age fall out of love and ultimately wind up divorced by age 25, or that economically disadvantaged women whose husbands have left them have children out of wedlock in order to collect welfare benefits. These theories may function similarly to "story skeletons" of the sort postulated by Schank and Abelson (1995).

When the order in which people learn about events does not correspond to the order of their occurrence, implicit theories can be used to organize the events in a way that permits their relations to be understood. Furthermore, they may lead to spontaneous inferences of events that were not explicitly mentioned. Abelson and Reich (1969) assume that this is done according to a *completion principle*. That is, if information about a specific sequence of events exemplifies all but one component of an implicational molecule, then an instantiation of the remaining component is spontaneously inferred. This principle theoretically operates regardless of which components are instantiated by the information and which is missing. Thus, for example, people who have formed the molecule [P is bad; bad things befall P] might infer that a particular person will be punished if he has done something bad. However, they might also infer that individuals who have encountered misfortune are likely to be bad or, for other reasons, to deserve their fate (for evidence, see Lerner, Miller, & Holmes, 1976; Walster, 1966; Wyer, Bodenhausen, & Gorman, 1985).

The role of implicational molecules and implicit theories in comprehension and memory may be particularly evident in responses to advertisements. As suggested by Hung (2005), people often have an implicit theory that ads promote products that solve problems or accomplish some purpose. This molecule could have the form:

[P has a problem; X eliminates the problem; P uses X; P's problem is alleviated].

Thus, suppose an ad conveys information that a person was overweight, she ate Brand A for a week, and she lost 10 pounds. This information instantiates all but one of the propositions that compose the molecule (i.e., the second). According to the completion principle, however, people may spontaneously infer an instantiation of this proposition (i.e., "Brand A produces weight loss") and this inference may stimulate them to make a purchase. Research and theory on misleading advertising (Burke, DeSarbo, Oliver, & Robertson, 1988; Kardes, 1988; Sawyer & Howard, 1991) provide numerous examples that can be conceptualized in this manner.

Other Considerations

The importance of understanding comprehension processes is predicated on the assumption that these processes mediate the impact of stimulus information (e.g., advertisements and television commercials) on consumer judgments and decisions. In understanding this mediating role, two additional assumptions are worth stating more explicitly.

Cognitive Efficiency.   The first assumption is almost universally recognized in research and theory on social information processing. That is, people do not conduct an exhaustive search of memory for all concepts and knowledge that are potentially relevant to a cognitive objective they wish to attain (Chaiken, Liberman, & Eagly, 1989; Taylor & Fiske, 1978; Wyer & Srull, 1989). Rather, they typically apply the first applicable unit of knowledge that comes to mind. In the present context, this means that if information can be interpreted in terms of more than one concept, then the concept that is most easily accessible in memory is most likely to be used and other, equally applicable concepts are often ignored (Förster & Liberman, in press; Higgins, 1996; Wyer, in press).

Several factors can influence knowledge accessibility, including the recency with which it has been acquired and used, the frequency with which it has been applied, and the amount of thought that has been devoted to it in the past (for theoretical formulations of the processes underlying these effects, see Craik & Lockhart, 1972; Higgins, Bargh, & Lombardi, 1985; Wyer, 2004; Wyer & Srull,1989). Thus, concepts and knowledge that recipients have frequently employed in the past become chronically accessible in memory and, therefore, are likely to be applied in the future (Bargh, Bond, Lombardi, & Tota, 1986). However, if specific subsets of knowledge are activated and used a short time before stimulus information is presented, their effects on the interpretation of this information can override the effects of chronically accessible concepts. To summarize:

Postulate 7. When more than one concept or unit of knowledge is applicable for interpreting new information, recipients are most likely to use the concept or knowledge that is most easily accessible in memory at the time. The accessibility of this knowledge is an increasing function of the frequency with which it has been used in the past, the recency with which it has been acquired and used, and the amount of thought that has been previously devoted to it.

Persistence Over Time.   The second assumption might be considered a corollary of the first. That is, once an interpretation of information has been made and a representation of the information has been formed and stored in memory, this representation may be recalled and used as a basis for later decisions independently of the original information on which the interpretation was based (Carlston, 1980; Higgins & Lurie, 1983; Sherman, Ahlm, Berman, & Lynn, 1978; Srull & Wyer, 1980). In Sherman et al.'s (1978) study, for example, people rated recycling as more important in the context of trivial social issues than in the context of very important ones. These ratings were presumably a result of the effect of contextual stimuli on the range of values to which the response scale was apparently relevant (Lynch, Chakravarti, & Mitra, 1991; Ostrom & Upshaw, 1968; Wyer, 1974). Later, however, participants recalled their earlier rating out of context and used it as a basis for deciding to help out on a recycling project, providing more help if they had reported a high rating of the issue than if they had reported a low one.

In the present context, this suggests the following postulate:

Postulate 8. Once information has been interpreted in terms of concepts and knowledge that are accessible in memory at the time, the representation based on this interpretation may be retrieved independently of the information on which it is based and used as a basis for later judgments and decisions.

This postulate is particularly important in light of considerations raised by Postulate 7. That is, if information can be interpreted in many ways, concepts that happen to be accessible in memory may affect the interpretation that is given to it. Once this interpretation is made, it can have persisting effects on judgments and decisions even though the original information can no longer be recalled. Thus, alternative interpretations of the information that have different implications for the judgments are not considered.

Postulate 8 has implications for memory as well. According to Postulates 1–4, events that are observed or directly experienced may be retained in memory in the same modality in which they were encountered. However, if the experience is relevant to a processing objective that is activated later, a new representation may be formed that is less detailed than the original information. This new representation may also be stored in memory and later used as a basis for reconstructing the original experience without consulting the original material.

A study by Adaval and Wyer (2004) confirms this possibility. Participants who had watched a movie were unexpectedly asked either to describe the events that took place or to report their impressions of the characters. After doing so, they were given a recognition memory test. Participants in the course of performing their postinformation writing task apparently formed a new representation that was generally more abstract than the episode models they had formed while watching the movie. Later, they used this abstract representation as a basis for their recognition responses. As a result, their memory was poorer than that of participants who had not performed the post-movie communication task.

Summary

The conceptualization outlined in this section does not pretend to be a complete theoretical formulation of comprehension processes either in the consumer domain or more generally. In fact, several phenomena described in other chapters suggest the need for an elaboration and refinement of the processes captured by Postulates 1–8 and, in some cases, qualify their validity. Nevertheless, the postulates and the conceptualization surrounding them may be useful in seeing how the various issues of concern in this volume might ultimately be incorporated within a broader theoretical framework. For example, the research on word comprehension discussed in the first few chapters can be viewed in terms of the interpretation of subject and object components of a subject-verb-object proposition, and research on sentence comprehension can often be conceptualized in terms of the role of situation models on the interpretation of the verb component. The comprehension of sequences of sentences bears on the construction of episode models and the influence of implicit theories. These areas of research are discussed in the sections that follow.

THE COMPREHENSION OF NOUN CONCEPTS

To reiterate, verbal communications are often comprehended by parsing the statements they contain into subject-verb-object propositions and then searching memory for previously acquired concepts and knowledge about the propositions' components. A considerable amount of prior knowledge may often be available about each of these components. This knowledge not only can be used to give meaning to the component itself but also can influence the interpretation of the sentence as a whole. Numerous demonstrations of this influence are provided by Bransford and his colleagues (e.g., Bransford, Barclay, & Franks, 1972; Bransford & Johnson, 1972). For example, accompanying apparently anomalous sentences (e.g., "the haystack was important because the cloth would rip") by a single word (e.g., "parachute") can substantially increase the recall of the sentence. This is presumably because the word cued the retrieval of a large body of episodic knowledge that permitted a mental representation to be formed of an event to which the sentence was relevant.

Bransford and his colleagues show that a word's meaning can influence the interpretation of its context. However, the influence can be reciprocal. To give an obvious example, the subject of "the man tickled the baby" has quite different associates than the subject of "the man tickled the waitress." This is because "tickled" is represented differently in the event models that are activated in the course of comprehending the two sentences.

These considerations still do not capture the complexity of meaning that words can convey. For one thing, words that have unique referents may elicit images of these referents when the words are encountered. Particularly interesting in this regard is evidence obtained by Gontijo and Zhang (chap. 2 in this volume) that brand names, unlike words in general, stimulate activity in not only the left brain hemisphere (which is associated with semantic information processing), but also the right hemisphere, which is traditionally associated with visual processing. Brand names are typically not encountered in isolation. Rather, they occur in the context of events that are either experienced personally or observed on television. Thus, exposure to brand names apparently activates a complex knowledge representation that contains both linguistic and visual features and, therefore, stimulates visual imagery in much the same way that a picture would. As Gontijo and Zhang point out, however, the visual and acoustic features of the word itself can convey meaning that is independent of the referent of the words. This possibility is discussed in the next section.

The possibility that words elicit visual images and stimulate processing in both modalities is compatible with the conceptualization of comprehension proposed earlier in this chapter. Carroll, Luna, and Peracchio (chap. 12 in this volume) provide a second dual-coding formulation (see also Paivio & Lambert, 1981) and apply it in conceptualizing language comprehension in bilinguals.

Dimensions of Meaning

Information is often processed configurally, and the meaning assigned to it is based on the configuration as a whole. There may nevertheless be general dimensions of meaning along which informational features can be analyzed. These dimensions may apply not only to the denotative meaning of the information but also to its nonverbal, paralinguistic features. Moreover, the meanings of these various features may not always be compatible.

Shrum and Lowrey (chap. 3 in this volume) provide several examples of instances in which the sound of a word conveys meaning independently of its denotative implications (see also Lerman, chap. 5 in this volume). The sounds "uh" and "sl," for example, have a negative connotation. The phonetic and linguistic meanings of a word are often difficult to distinguish. However, people can match antonymic pairs in a foreign language to equivalent pairs in their own language fairly accurately despite having no direct knowledge of the foreign language itself (Brown, Black, & Horowitz, 1955; Tsuru & Fries, 1933). This suggests that meaning can be transmitted separately from the semantic implications of a word. Effects of phonetic meaning have been found when words are heard as well as read. On the other hand, sound symbolism is not evident among deaf people (Johnson, Suzuki, & Olds, 1964). These findings rule out visual cues as reasons for the effect of phonetic similarity.

A major dimension of meaning along which information varies is evaluative. As Shrum and Lowrey's work testifies, however, the evaluative meaning of paralinguistic features of a word is not sufficient to understand its influence when the word is conveyed in the context of a more complex message. Lowrey and Shrum (2005), for example, found that preferences for fictitious brand names that varied phonetically depended on the product category to which the names were assigned. A detailed conceptualization of the interplay of phonetic and semantic features in an analysis of brand name meaning is provided by Lerman (chap. 5 in this volume). She points out that the impact of phonetic features of a brand name on the meaning assigned to it may decrease when its diagnosticity is called to consumers' attention (see Yorkston & Menon, 2004, for evidence). However, its role in the spontaneous comprehension of brand names seems well established.

The effects of nonverbal features in other sense modalities raise similar considerations. Based on normative data, Doyle and Bottomley (2006; see also Childers & Jass, 2002) identified the meaning assigned to different typefaces along the three dimensions proposed by Osgood, Suci, and Tannenbaum (1957): evaluation, potency, and activity. They determined the meaning of brand names, and also the product categories themselves, along the same dimensions. Then, in the main study, participants were exposed to "Yellow Pages" advertisements for products that varied in meaning along each of the three dimensions and were conveyed in typefaces that likewise varied. The likelihood of choosing a product increased with the evaluative meaning of both its brand name and the typeface in which its name was conveyed, and these effects did not depend on the nature of the product itself. However, the effects of brand name and typeface meaning along other dimensions depended on whether this meaning was compatible with that of the type of product being advertised. That is, participants preferred products that were high in activity (or potency) when the typeface and brand name were also high in activity (or potency), and preferred products that were low in activity (or potency) when the brand name and typeface were also low along this dimension.

Lowrey and Shrum's (2005) study could have similar implications. That is, the meaning implied by the acoustic characteristics of the brand also varied along the dimensions identified by Osgood, Suci, and Tannenbaum (1957) and its effects might be analogous to those identified by Doyle and Bottomley (2006). That is, the evaluative meaning assigned to the acoustic quality of the brand names might have effects independently of the characteristics of the brand name itself, whereas the meaning of the brand name's acoustic quality along dimensions of activity and potency may be contingent on its compatibility with the brand name's denotative meaning.

In combination, these studies point out the complexity of the reactions that people can have to a brand name. That is, these reactions not only depend on the denotative meaning of the name itself, but also the typeface in which the name is conveyed, the sound of the name, and the type of product to which the name is assigned. The results obtained by Doyle and Bottomley (2006), Lowrey and Shrum (2005), and others provide some insight into how these meanings interface. It seems unlikely that people respond equally to variation along all dimensions simultaneously, however. The question is what dimensions of meaning exert the predominant influence in any given case.

In this regard, the relative impact of differences along these dimensions may vary over cultures. In the Chinese language, for example, there is little relation between the visual representation of a word and the sound of it (Schmitt, Pan, & Tavassoli, 1994). In Western cultures, however, this relation is much more apparent. (Thus, people can often guess how a word is pronounced from seeing it.) This could indicate a cultural difference in the ease of processing visual versus acoustic meaning, and thus might qualify the conclusions drawn by Doyle and Bottomley (2006) and Lowrey and Shrum (2005).

Persisting Effects of Linguistic and Nonverbal Meaning

The impact of typeface and other nonverbal contributors to meaning might seem to be transitory. However, this may not be true. Postulate 8 asserts that once information has been interpreted and a representation of its referent on the basis of this interpretation has been stored in memory, the interpretation may have an impact on subsequent judgments and behavior independently of the information on which the interpretation was based (Carlston, 1980; Sherman et al., 1978; Srull & Wyer, 1980).

However, the labels to which meaning has been assigned can influence not only behavior decisions but also perceptions of the stimuli themselves. The role of meaning similarity and sound quality in categorization is described by Zhang and Schmitt (chap. 4 in this volume). Hoegg and Alba (chap. 1 in this volume) have also discussed this possibility and have provided an intriguing demonstration of it in the domain of taste perception. Participants were exposed to two pairs of juices. One pair was labeled "Brand A," and the other was denoted "Brand B." The two Brand A juices were low and moderate in sweetness, and the two Brand B juices were moderate and high. Later, participants re-tasted the juices and judged the difference in taste between two juices with the same brand name that differed in taste and two juices with different brand names that were similar in taste. Participants judged the first difference to be less than the second. In other words, the labels assigned to the juices had greater effect on participants' judgments than the actual taste sensations. This difference did not occur when participants had not performed the original taste test, indicating that results were not simply a result of compliance with the experimenter's implicit expectations. Rather, the labels assigned to the juices appeared to have an effect on participants' underlying perceptions.

The implications of these findings are obvious. That is, people are more likely to "remember" that two brands differ simply because they have different brand names, independently of their actual experiences with using the brands. As Allison and Uhl (1964) found, there is little relation between individuals' a priori preferences for different brands of beer and the preferences they report in a blind taste test. These effects might help to explain individuals' tendency to remain loyal to a brand despite evidence that their preference is inconsistent with their actual experience. Hoegg and Alba suggest that cross-cultural differences in categorization processes (Schmitt & Zhang, 1998; see also Zhang & Schmitt, chap. 4 in this volume) might also produce conceptual differences in perception and judgment.

SENTENCE COMPREHENSION

The unit of meaning in a communication is often the sentence. A sentence typically describes an event or, alternatively, the relation between two entities. In a consumer context, for example, a statement might assert that a product has certain desirable attributes or that using the product will have certain desirable consequences. In either case, the comprehension of such a sentence may occur in two stages. First, as noted earlier, sentences that refer to specific events that are spatially or temporally constrained may be comprehended spontaneously by constructing a mental simulation (i.e., a situation model) of the event consisting of both a semantic representation of the sentence and a nonverbal mental image (i.e., a "picture plus caption"; see Abelson, 1976).

In some cases, however, statements are difficult to interpret in terms of prior knowledge. For example, their literal implications may be obviously false, or in some cases, may be incompatible with the implications of other statements that have been made in the same context. Thus, as implied by Postulate 6, people may resort to deliberative information processing (Wyer & Gruenfeld, 1995). In doing so, they may infer that the literal meaning of the information is not the meaning the communicator intends to convey, and may reinterpret it. For example, they may perceive the statement to be ironic or, alternatively, metaphorical.

As DiMofte and Yalch (chap. 7 in this volume), Phillips and McQuarrie (chap. 8 in this volume), and Adaval (chap. 10 in this volume) note, the use of metaphors in advertising and television commercials is pervasive. The question is about how people recognize metaphors as such and how these metaphors are understood. Some verbal metaphors (e.g., "Listerine® fights bad breath") are used so frequently in a given context that they acquire the status of idioms, and so their intended meaning can be extracted nearly as easily as that of their literal counterparts (Verbrugge, 1976). Consequently, as Lakoff (2002; see also Glucksberg, Gildea, & Bookin, 1982) notes, this meaning may often be applied unconsciously in construing the implications of information. In other instances, however, metaphorical statements may only be recognized as such when their literal meaning is either anomalous or inconsistent with the information that accompanies them. Furthermore, when the literal meaning of a metaphor activates a visual image of an event to which it descriptively refers, it may lead to the construction of a mental representation that differs from the representation that would be formed on the basis of its literal equivalent. In these cases, the comprehension of a metaphor is likely to require much more cognitive effort than a statement whose meaning can be taken literally.

This process may be conceptualized in terms of the comprehension processes summarized in Postulates 4–6. To reiterate, people parse a sentence into a subject-verb-object proposition and then search memory for previously formed situation models that contain the proposition's components. If a preexisting representation contains all three components, then the proposition is comprehended quickly. If a previously formed event model is activated by the verb and object and a perceptual symbol of the subject has also been identified, then this symbol may be substituted for the subject of the preexisting model to form a new one.

In the case of a metaphor, however, a previously formed representation of the predicate may not exist. Moreover, features of the subject or object that are extracted from previously formed models could violate the constraints imposed by the verb in much the same way they do in our earlier example of a nail pounding a man into the wall. For simplicity, suppose an ad asserts that "Ajax attacks grease." This particular metaphor is used frequently and, therefore, may be idiomatic, being processed with miminal cognitive activity (Glucksberg et al., 1982; see Phillips & McQuarrie, chap. 8 in this volume). To a naïve reader, however, a previously formed event model of "attacks grease" would not exist, and so the statement would have to be comprehended on the basis of more deliberative processing (Searle, 1979). This processing would presumably require the identification of previously formed event models of "attacking," which presumably depict physical combat. A new event representation might then be constructed on the basis of previously formed representations of the behavior to which the verb "attack" has been applied. This construction might lead a cartoonlike image to be formed of an animated jar of cleaning powder engaged in physical combat with an animated representation of grease. (This processing would be similar to that required to comprehend a nonmetaphorical statement such as "The lion walked into McDonald's®.")

Note, however, that in the construction of such a representation, the features of both the action and the agent are restricted. In our example, certain attributes of the subject that are incompatible with an "attacker" (i.e., kindness, softness, etc.) are precluded. Thus, these features would be excluded from representations of the referent "Ajax®" in the proposition being evaluated. To this extent, the application of a metaphor in comprehending a proposition circumscribes the attributes of the referent in ways that render later characterizations of the subject inappropriate. Thus, these characterizations may be rejected when the referent is thought about at a later point in time. As Markman and Moreau (2001) indicate, the representation formed of the referent of a metaphor may become fixed and may be resistant to change by information that occurs later. (This observation is consistent with Postulate 8.)

Multiple Meanings

As the preceding analysis suggests, metaphors are typically used to focus recipients' attention on a particular meaning that the communicator wishes to convey. When the metaphor being applied is uncommon, the literal meaning of the statement is the first meaning that comes to mind, and the metaphorical meaning may only be identified through cognitive effort once the literal meaning is recognized as anomalous. In some cases, however, both the literal and the figurative meaning of a statement may be equally viable. Dimofte and Yalch (chap. 7 in this volume) provide several examples. In the admonition to use Michelin "because so much is riding on your tires," for example, the literal meaning of "riding" is just as applicable as the figurative one.

When multiple meanings of a statement are not incompatible, recipients may assign it the meaning that comes to mind most quickly and easily (Postulate 7). This meaning may be determined by the recency of its prior application if a short time has elapsed since it was first considered. However, the frequency of prior use may predominate after a period of time has elapsed (Higgins et al., 1985).

Thus, the phrase "riding on" in the previous example has the status of an idiom and so its figurative meaning may normally be applied automatically in the course of comprehending it. In the context of a Michelin ad, the literal meaning of "riding on" may be activated as well, and a mental representation may be formed that contains both meanings. Over time, however, the more frequently emphasized meaning may become dominant, leading to a perception of Michelin as dependable that persists over time.

As Dimofte and Yalch discuss, however, the metaphorical meaning of a phrase may not always be recognized spontaneously. In fact, it might not be discovered at all unless recipients are motivated and able to engage in the cognitive work required to identify it. When people view advertisements and television commercials, their motivation to think much about the material is generally low. In such cases, the meaning could easily be lost.

When the apparently anomalous content of a statement is sufficient to stimulate an attempt to comprehend it, however, the additional cognitive activity required to do so can be beneficial. Toncar and Munch (2001) found that figures of speech were typically more persuasive, and were better recalled, when participants were relatively uninvolved in the situation at hand. These nonliteral descriptions apparently stimulated the interest of individuals who would otherwise be unlikely to pay much attention to the material presented. Thus, contextual features that affect both the ability and motivation to assign alternative meanings to information can play an important role in the effectiveness of this information.

Motivational Considerations

Although the motivation to comprehend a statement's metaphorical meaning is often situationally induced, it can also reflect a chronic desire to engage in cognitive activity. Bradley and Meeds (2004; see Meeds & Bradley, chap. 6 in this volume), for example, found that people with low need for cognition (Petty & Cacioppo, 1986) were less persuaded by advertisements for technical products when explanations of technical terms described in the ads were not provided. In contrast, recipients with high need for cognition were equally persuaded regardless of whether the explanations were given. Lowrey (2006) also reported that the complexity of an ad's content decreased the ad's impact on participants who had little personal interest in the ad material. Involved participants, however, were equally influenced by the ad, regardless of the effort required to comprehend it.

Metaphors and Persuasion

To reiterate, some metaphors are so well learned that they are understood and used with a minimum of cognitive deliberation (Phillips & McQuarrie, chap. 8 in this volume). To this extent, their influence may also be largely unconscious (Lakoff, 1987; Lakoff & Johnson, 1980). As Phillips and McQuarrie note, however, this does not rob metaphors of their power. Reference to a soap product as "attacking grease," for example, might be understood with little difficulty. At the same time, it could activate a body of knowledge about fighting and aggression that goes beyond the particular event to which it is applied. In this regard, the power of metaphors can lie in part from their ability to evoke visual images. Likening a foreign ruler's physical appearance to that of Adolf Hitler, for example, might elicit images of the Holocaust and attempts to conquer the world that are inappropriately associated with the person and might elicit negative feelings toward him.

In addition, the cognitive processes that underlie the comprehension of metaphors can influence attention to other information that accompanies them. In a study by Ottati, Rhoads, and Graesser (1999), for example, participants read a persuasive message containing either strong or weak arguments in support of a thesis requirement. In some conditions, the message employed sports metaphors (e.g., "if students want to play ball with the best ...") and in other conditions, the literal meaning was conveyed ("... if students want to work with the best ..."). When recipients had favorable attitudes toward sports, introducing sports metaphors increased the influence of strong arguments and decreased the influence of weak arguments. When recipients had unfavorable attitudes toward sports, however, metaphors had the opposite effects. Thus, the metaphors stimulated more attention to the communication by the former participants, and so the quality of the arguments contained in it had more impact.

NARRATIVES

The chapters in the last section focus on the comprehension of advertisements and commercials that are conveyed in the form of a narrative, that is, a thematically related sequence of events. Not all advertising material is conveyed in this form, of course, and the impact of other presentation formats may differ. Some television commercials, for example, portray a number of rapidly changing vignettes of unrelated situations in which a product might be used, but have little else in common. Moreover, many print advertisements convey product attributes in bullet point, in an ostensibly unordered list. The process of extracting meaning from the latter type of information may be quite different from the process of comprehending a narrative. Rather than constructing a coherent story and evaluating the implications of the story as a whole, people may construe the implications of each piece individually and integrate these implications mechanistically in a manner similar to that suggested by Anderson (1971).

Research by Adaval and her colleagues (Adaval et al., in press; Adaval & Wyer, 1998) obtained evidence of this difference. They further showed that the effect of accompanying the information with pictures depended on the format in which the information was presented. That is, pictures increased the impact of information that was conveyed in a narrative, presumably because they facilitated the construction of visual images of the protagonist and provided cognitive "glue" that permitted the story to have more coherence. However, pictures interfered with the piecemeal integration of listed information and, therefore, decreased the information's impact.

A study by Hung (2005) provides further insight into the role of pictures in narrative-based processing. Participants read print ads whose segments exemplified components of a "problem–solution" molecule of the sort described earlier in this chapter. That is, they conveyed (a) the problem to which the product was relevant, (b) the nature of the product itself, and (c) the consequences of using the product. However, the first (problem) segment was conveyed either verbally (e.g., "hair loss is a problem for men") or pictorially (a picture of a prematurely bald man). The last (solution) segment was likewise conveyed either verbally or visually. Conveying either the problem or the solution in a picture increased evaluations of the product relative to conditions in which both segments were described verbally. However, conveying both components in a picture decreased participants' evaluations relative to conditions in which only one of the components was pictured. Hung (2005) suggested that when only one of the two components was conveyed in a picture, participants comprehended the verbal component by constructing their own mental image of it in a manner that was consistent with the picture. When both components were pictured, however, flexibility in interpreting the effects of the product was reduced. Consequently, the ad's implications seemed less plausible and so product evaluations were less favorable.

These studies suggest not only that the processing of information in a narrative differs from the processing of information in an unordered list but also that the effectiveness of this processing depends on whether or not the information is conveyed visually. Other ways in which information is presented can also have an impact on its comprehension. Levi and Pisoni (chap. 11 in this volume), for example, discuss the effect of differences in the rate in which information is transmitted on perceptions of the source and, therefore, the implications drawn from it. The attribution processes that mediate the effects of this information are much different from those considered by Adaval and her colleagues. However, the effects strengthen the general conclusion that the literal meaning of narrative information is only one of several factors that influence perceptions of its implications.

As Adaval (chap. 10 in this volume) points out, narrative representations in memory can take many forms. On one hand, they may be episode models of situation-specific events that one has observed or personally experienced. In addition, they include abstract sequences of events (e.g., the events that occur during a restaurant visit) that people might use to comprehend specific sequences of events they encounter, to explain the antecedents of an event, and to predict its consequences. The chapters by Escalas and Stern (chap. 9 in this volume) and Adaval (chap. 10 in this volume) discuss the effects of both types of narrative representations.

Effects of Situation-Specific Event Representations on Comprehension and Judgment

The spontaneous use of generalized event representations to comprehend new information may not be as common as one might expect. According to Postulate 4, this may only occur if the information refers to a specific person or object for which one has a previously formed mental image. Colcombe and Wyer (2002), for example, found evidence that verbal descriptions of routine sequences of events (e.g., the events that occur during a restaurant visit) were comprehended with reference to a prototypic representation of the event sequence when the information pertained to an unknown person. This was not the case, however, when the participants were told to assume that the sequence referred to their best friend.

This possibility has implications for the conditions in which advertisements are likely to be effective. If advertisements portray situations similar to those that viewers have personally experienced or have imagined themselves experiencing, they are likely to comprehend the ads with reference to a preexisting episode model in which they are personally involved as either participants or observers. That is, they may imagine themselves experiencing the situations in which the product being advertised is involved.

Escalas and Stern (chap. 9 in this volume) elaborate this possibility. They argue that advertisements are more effective if they tell a story that elicits emotional reactions. These reactions are more likely to occur if the observers imagine themselves as participants in the situation or, alternatively, are "transported" into the story being communicated (see also Green & Brock, 2000). However, the considerations raised earlier place constraints on the conditions in which this is likely to occur. If, for example, the protagonist in the situation portrayed in the advertisement, or the situation itself, is too far removed from participants' personal experience, a self-representation is unlikely to be retrieved and used to comprehend it. In this case, the ad is less likely to be effective.

Escalas and Stern focus attention on the elicitation of positive feelings. That is, they assume that if people read a narrative that elicits positive emotions, and if these emotions are associated with using the product or service being promoted, then they may experience positive feelings when they encounter the product at a later point in time. However, the story conveyed by an advertisement can elicit negative emotions as well. Fear-arousing communications (Leventhal, 1970) focus on the negative consequences of not performing a behavior rather than the benefits of performing it. Public service advertisements, or warnings of the harmful consequences of smoking or drug addiction, are often of this type. Appeals for charitable donations often portray the severe hardship being encountered by the individuals who are in need of help. Note that a representation formed from these latter appeals is unlikely to be comprehended with reference to a personal experience.

However, the negative emotions that these narratives elicit could have an impact for other reasons. Lerner et al. (1976) postulate that events with negative consequences for innocent people threaten individuals' belief that the world is just and, therefore, may increase their concern that they (admirable people) might also be the victims of misfortune. Consequently, they may try to reinforce their belief in a just world by helping to reduce the consequences of the misfortune and, therefore, decrease the injustice that has occurred. As Miller (1977) showed, however, this behavior will only occur if people perceive that their behavior will actually be effective. (Thus, for example, people are more willing to donate money to help a single family whose house has burned down than to help victims of a famine, because they can imagine their money having greater impact in the former case than the latter.)

The Effect of Perspective on Emotional Reactions. Although an emotion can be elicited by an event description, the nature of this emotion is not foreordained. In particular, the visual representation of an event sequence may be formed from different perspectives (Black et al., 1979), and the emotions the sequence elicits may depend on the features that one focuses on from these perspectives. A Frankenstein movie is likely to elicit fear in someone who views it from the perspective of the potential victims of the monster's destructive acts. If the same movie is viewed from the perspective of the monster, who finds himself in a strange environment in which people misinterpret his behavior and react to him with irrational horror, it may enlist sympathy.

As another example, suppose one reads that an old man has taken his grandson's favorite toy and has sold it for a bottle of Irish whiskey. A person who imagines this scenario from the perspective of the boy and focuses attention on the boy himself may feel sad, whereas a person who takes the boy's perspective and focuses on the grandfather may experience anger. On the other hand, a person who thinks about the grandfather from the grandfather's own perspective may experience happiness, and someone who thinks about the boy from the grandfather's perspective might experience feelings of guilt.

Advertisements and television commercials attempt to stimulate individuals to imagine events from the perspective of someone who is using the product or enjoying the experience that the product ostensibly provides. However, the effectiveness might depend on the extent to which this is accomplished. The perspective from which people view an advertisement may be potentially determined by the purpose for which they view it either at the time they encounter the ad or subsequently. This may determine which aspects of the commercial to which they attend and retain in memory and, therefore, the effects of the commercial on later behavior (Postulate 8).

Myths as Metaphors

Situation-specific episode models may often be constructed in the course of comprehending events that occur in a temporal sequence. However, the sequence may sometimes be comprehended in terms of more general event representations, or implicit theories that convey the relations among the events and specify their antecedents and consequences. As Adaval (chap. 10 in this volume) notes, many of these theories may be applied spontaneously, without clear recognition of the factors that led them to be used. In some cases, the principles may function as cultural truisms and be applied without clear recognition of their existence (Lakoff, 2002). The parables identified by Marchand (1985) are illustrative. For example, the parable that people gain equality from consumption may be applied without consciously verbalizing its content or implications. Rather, the parable may function as an unverbalized principle that guides the acceptance of more specific information that exemplifies it (e.g., advertisements implying that everyone is afflicted by bad breath regardless of social status, or that a brand of dish soap will make everyone's hands as soft as a debutante's; see Adaval, chap. 10 in this volume).

Myths associated with materialism are particularly pervasive, as are those that promote the desirability of being "physically attractive" or "fashionable." Note that the criteria for inferring these latter characteristics are arbitrary. However, once the myths that being "fashionable" or "attractive" are constructed, they take on a life of their own independently of any specific criteria. Consequently, one becomes a victim of advertisers who arbitrarily define the criteria to suit their own ends and then associate their products with the criteria they have chosen.

These dynamics can be conceptualized with reference to Postulate 8. That is, once a concept is acquired and stored in memory, it may later be retrieved and applied independently of the experiences that led to its formation. Thus, suppose individuals learn early in life that it is desirable to be "attractive." They may later apply this principle in making behavioral decisions independently of the factors that led to it being acquired and, for that matter, independently of the referent of "attractive." Thus, new products or fashion styles that are arbitrarily labeled as "attractive" are likely to stimulate purchasing.

One of the more ironic manifestations of materialism-related myths has been identified in research on terror management (Arndt, Solomon, Kasser, & Sheldon, 2004; Kasser & Sheldon, 2000). Individuals whose mortality is called to their attention become more materialistic. Moreover, this materialism is not reflected in a desire for products that will increase longevity. Rather, mortality salience increases preferences for products that enhance self-esteem by increasing social status in the eyes of others. Thus, for example, it increases preferences for suntan lotion rather than sunscreen that guarantees protection against skin cancer (Routledge, Arndt, & Goldenberg, 2004).

Paralinguistic Influences on Complex Information Processing

As noted earlier, paralinguistic features of single words can have a substantial im-pact on the meaning assigned to them (Childers & Jass, 2002; Doyle & Bottomley, 2006; Shrum & Lowrey, chap. 3 in this volume). However, paralinguistic factors can have an impact on the comprehension of complex sets of information as well. Levi and Pisoni (chap. 11 in this volume) note that when information is transmitted orally, the rate at which it is conveyed can influence perceptions of the source's in-telligence and, therefore, can influence the impact of the information independ-ently of other information available about its source. Carroll, Luna, and Peracchio (chap. 12 in this volume) cite evidence that the grammatical structure of ads with semantically similar meaning influenced their persuasibility among persons whose only objective was to comprehend them. These findings, combined with evidence of the effects of pictures on the processing of information in different formats (Adaval et al., in press; Adaval & Wyer, 1998), confirm the conclusion that an anal-ysis of the semantic implications of information is not sufficient to understand the meaning extracted from it.

CONCLUDING REMARKS

Perhaps the main message conveyed by the research and theory summarized in this volume is that the comprehension of the information conveyed in an advertisement or television commercial cannot be inferred from its semantic content alone. Not only the denotative meaning of single words but also the typeface in which the words are presented and their phonetic quality can influence the meaning assigned to them. The meaning extracted from information can depend on the order in which it is presented and whether or not it is accompanied by pictures. Not only speakers' voice quality but also their speaking rate can influence the impact of a message through its mediating influence on attributions about the communicator. In short, as noted at the outset, the medium is a large part of the message.

Considered in their totality, the chapters in this volume provide enormous in-sight into the factors that affect the comprehension of not only single words but also sentences and a message considered as a whole. However, comprehension is only one of the stages of processing that must be taken into account in predicting a mes-sage's impact. As McGuire (1972) recognized many years ago, and more contem-porary theories of persuasion have confirmed (e.g., Chaiken et al., 1989; Petty & Cacioppo, 1986), people's postcomprehension responses to a message (i.e., their elaboration of the message's content, or counterarguments against its validity) must be taken into account as well. McGuire's (1972) formulation, in simplified form, can be conveyed by the equation:

$$I = R(E - CA),$$

where I is an index of the message's influence, R is an index of the reception and comprehension of its implications, and E and CA are indices of the elaboration and counterarguing of these implications. An obvious implication of the conceptualization is that the effect of elaboration and counterarguing is less when comprehension is low than when it is high. On the other hand, the impact of comprehension depends on whether recipients are relatively more disposed to elaborate the message's positive implications or to counterargue. Most current research on persuasion performed in social psychology has focused largely on E and CA. In contrast, the comprehension of the implications of a message along dimensions to which its influence is relevant is no less important. The work cited in the present volume provides fundamental insights into these matters, and thus contributes substantially to an overall conceptual understanding of communication impact.

ACKNOWLEDGMENTS

The writing of this chapter, and some of the research discussed therein, was supported by grants HKUST6053/01H, HKUST6194/04H, and HKUST6192/04H from the Research Grants Council, Hong Kong.

REFERENCES

Abelson, R. P. (1976). Script processing in attitude formation and decision making. In J. S. Carroll & J. W. Payne (Eds.), *Cognition and social behavior* (pp. 33–46). Hillsdale, NJ: Lawrence Erlbaum Associates.

Abelson, R. P., & Reich, C. M. (1969). Implicational molecules: A method for extracting meaning from input sentences. In D. E. Walker & L. M. Norton (Eds.), *Proceedings of the International Joint Conference on Artificial Intelligence* (pp. 641–647). Washington, DC.

Adaval, R., Isbell, L. M., & Wyer, R. S. (in press). The impact of pictures on narrative- and list-based impression formation: A process interference model. *Journal of Experimental Social Psychology.*

Adaval, R., & Wyer, R. S. (1998). The role of narratives in consumer information processing. *Journal of Consumer Psychology, 7,* 207–245.

Adaval, R., & Wyer, R. S. (2004). Communicating about a social interaction: Effects on memory for protagonists' statements and nonverbal behaviors. *Journal of Experimental Social Psychology, 40,* 450–465.

Allison, R. I., & Uhl, K. P. (1964). Influence of beer brand identification on taste perception. *Journal of Marketing Research, 1,* 36–39.

Anderson, N. H. (1971). Integration theory and attitude change. *Psychological Review, 78,* 171–206.

Arndt, J., Solomon, S., Kasser, T., & Sheldon, K. M. (2004). The urge to splurge: A terror management account of materialism and consumer behavior. *Journal of Consumer Psychology, 14,* 198–212.

Bargh, J. A., Bond, R. N., Lombardi, W., & Tota, M. E. (1986). The additive nature of chronic and temporary sources of construct accessibility. *Journal of Personality and Social Psychology, 50,* 869–878.

Barsalou, L. W. (1993). Flexibility, structure, and linguistic vagary in concepts: Manifestations of a compositional system of perceptual symbols. In A. F. Collins, S. E. Gathercole, M. A. Conway, & P. E. Morris (Eds.), *Theories of memory* (pp. 29–102). Hillsdale, NJ: Lawrence Erlbaum Associates.

Black, J. B., Turner, T., & Bower, G. H. (1979). Point of view in narrative comprehension, memory, and production. *Journal of Verbal Learning and Verbal Behavior, 11*, 717–726.

Bradley, S. D., & Meeds, R. (2004). The effects of sentence-level context, prior word knowledge, and need for cognition on information processing of technical language in print ads. *Journal of Consumer Psychology, 14*, 291–302.

Bransford, J. D., Barclay, J. R., & Franks, J. J. (1972). Sentence memory: A constructive versus interpretative approach. *Cognitive Psychology, 3*, 193–209.

Bransford, J. D., & Johnson, M. K. (1972). Contextual prerequisites for understanding: Some investigations of comprehension and recall. *Journal of Verbal Learning and Verbal Behavior, 11*, 717–726.

Brown, R., Black, A. H., & Horowitz, A. E. (1955). Phonetic symbolism in natural languages. *Journal of Abnormal and Social Psychology, 50*, 388–393.

Burke, R. R., DeSarbo, W. S., Oliver, R. L., & Robertson, T. S. (1988). Deception by implication: An experimental investigation. *Journal of Consumer Research, 14*, 483–494.

Carlston, D. E. (1980). Events, inferences and impression formation. In R. Hastie, T. Ostrom, E. Ebbesen, R. Wyer, D. Hamilton, & D. Carlston (Eds.), *Person memory: The cognitive basis of social perception* (pp. 89–119). Hillsdale, NJ: Lawrence Erlbaum Associates.

Chaiken, S., Liberman, A., & Eagly, A. H. (1989). Heuristic and systematic information processing within and beyond the persuasion context. In J. S. Uleman & J. A. Bargh (Eds.), *Unintended thought* (pp. 212–252). New York: Guilford.

Childers, T. L., & Jass, J. (2002). All dressed up with something to say: Effects of typeface semantic associations on brand perceptions and consumer memory. *Journal of Consumer Psychology, 12*, 93–106.

Colcombe, S. J., & Wyer, R. S. (2002). The role of prototypes in the mental representation of temporally related events. *Cognitive Psychology, 44*, 67–103.

Craik, F. I. M., & Lockhart, R. S. (1972). Levels of processing: A framework for memory research. *Journal of Verbal Learning and Verbal Behavior, 11*, 671–684.

Doyle, J. R., & Bottomley, P. A. (2006). Dressed for the occasion: Font-product congruity in the perception of logotype. *Journal of Consumer Psychology, 16*, 112–123.

Dweck, C. S., Chiu, C-y., & Hong, Y-y. (1995). Implicit theories and their role in judgments and reactions: A world from two perspectives. *Psychological Inquiry, 6*, 267–285.

Ebbesen, E. B. (1980). Cognitive processes in understanding ongoing behavior. In R. Hastie, T. Ostrom, E. Ebbesen, R. Wyer, D. Hamilton, & D. Carlston (Eds.), *Person memory: Cognitive basis of social perception* (pp. 179–226). Hillsdale, NJ: Lawrence Erlbaum Associates.

Förster, J., & Liberman, N. (in press). Knowledge activation. In A. Kruglanski & E. T. Higgins (Eds.), *Social psychology: Handbook of basic principles* (2nd ed.). New York: Guilford.

Garnham, A. (1981). Mental models as representations of text. *Memory and Cognition, 9*, 560–565.

Glenberg, A. M., Meyer, M., & Lindem, K. (1987). Mental models contribute to foregrounding during text comprehension. *Journal of Memory and Language, 26*, 69–83.

Glucksberg, S., Gildea, P., & Bookin, H. B. (1982). On understanding nonliteral speech: Can people ignore metaphors? *Journal of Verbal Learning and Verbal Behavior, 21*, 85–98.

Green, M. C., & Brock, T. C. (2000). The role of transportation in the persuasiveness of public narratives. *Journal of Personality and Social Psychology, 79*, 701–721.

Grice, H. P. (1975). Logic and conversation. In P. Cole & J. L. Morgan (Eds.), *Syntax and semantics: Speech acts* (pp. 41–58). New York: Academic Press.

Higgins, E. T. (1981). The "communication game:" Implications for social cognition and persuasion. In E. T. Higgins, C. P. Herman, & M. P. Zanna (Eds.), *Social cognition: The Ontario symposium* (Vol. 1, pp. 342–392). Hillsdale, NJ: Lawrence Erlbaum Associates.

Higgins, E. T. (1996). Knowledge activation: Accessibility, applicability, and salience. In E. T. Higgins & A. Kruglanski (Eds.), *Social psychology: Handbook of basic principles* (pp. 133–168). New York: Guilford.

Higgins, E. T., Bargh, J. A., & Lombardi, W. (1985). The nature of priming effects on categorization. *Journal of Experimental Psychology: Learning, Memory, and Cognition, 11*, 59–69.

Higgins, E. T., & Lurie, L. (1983). Context, categorization and recall: The "change-of-standard" effect. *Cognitive Psychology, 15*, 525–547.

Hintzman, D. L. (1986). "Schema abstraction" in a multiple-trace model. *Psychological Review, 93*, 411–428.

Hung, I. W. P. (2005). *The impact of problem-solution implicational molecules on product memory and evaluation.* Unpublished manuscript, Hong Kong University of Science and Technology.

Johnson, R. C., Suzuki, N. S., & Olds, W. K. (1964). Phonetic symbolism in an artificial language. *Journal of Abnormal and Social Psychology, 69*, 233–236.

Kardes, F. R. (1988). Spontaneous inference processes in advertising: The effects of conclusion omission and involvement on persuasion. *Journal of Consumer Research, 15*, 225–233.

Kasser, T., & Sheldon, K. M. (2000). Of wealth and death: Materialism, mortality salience, and consumption behavior. *Psychological Science, 11*, 348–351.

Lakoff, G. (1987). *Women, fire, and dangerous things: What categories reveal about the mind.* Chicago: University of Chicago Press.

Lakoff, G. (2002). *Moral politics: How liberals and conservatives think.* Chicago: University of Chicago Press.

Lakoff, G., & Johnson, M. (1980). *Metaphors we live by.* Chicago: University of Chicago Press.

Lerner, M. J., Miller, D. T., & Holmes, J. G. (1976). Deserving and the emergence of forms of justice. In L. Berkowitz (Ed.), *Advances in experimental social psychology* (Vol. 9, pp. 133–162). New York: Academic Press.

Leventhal, H. (1970). Findings and theory in the study of fear communications. In L. Berkowitz (Ed.), *Advances in experimental social psychology* (Vol. 5, pp. 119–186). San Diego, CA: Academic Press.

Lowrey, T. M. (2006). The relation between script complexity and commercial memorability. *Journal of Advertising, 35*(3), 7–15.

Lowrey, T. M., & Shrum, L. J. (2005). *Effects of phonetic symbolism on brand name preference.* Unpublished manuscript, University of Texas at San Antonio.

Lynch, J. G., Chakravarti, D., & Mitra, A. (1991). Contrast effects in consumer judgments: Changes in mental representations or in the anchoring of rating scales? *Journal of Consumer Research, 18*, 284–297.

Marchand, R. (1985). *Advertising the American dream: Making way for modernity, 1920–1940.* Berkeley, CA: University of California Press.

Markman, A. B., & Moreau, C. P. (2001). Analogy and analogical comparison in choice. In D. Gentner, K. J. Holyoak, & B. N. Kokinov (Eds.), *The analogical mind: Perspectives from cognitive science* (pp. 363–399). Cambridge, MA: MIT Press.

McGuire, W. J. (1972). Attitude change: An information processing paradigm. In C. G. McClintock (Ed.), *Experimental social psychology* (pp. 108–141). New York: Holt, Rinehart & Winston.

McLuhan, M. (1967). *The medium is the message.* New York: Random House.

Miller, D. T. (1977). Altruism and threat to a belief in a just world. *Journal of Experimental Social Psychology, 13,* 113–124.

Newtson, D. A. (1976). Foundations of attribution: The perception of ongoing behavior. In J. Harvey, W. Ickes, & R. Kidd (Eds.), *New directions in attribution research* (Vol. 1, pp. 223–247). Hillsdale, NJ: Lawrence Erlbaum Associates.

Osgood, C. E., Suci, G. J., & Tannenbaum, P. H. (1957). *The measurement of meaning.* Urbana, IL: University of Illinois Press.

Ostrom, T. M., & Upshaw, H. S. (1968). Psychological perspective and attitude change. In A. G. Greenwald, T. M. Ostrom, & T. C. Brock (Eds.), *Psychological foundations of attitudes* (pp. 217–242). New York: Academic Press.

Ottati, V. C., Rhoads, S., & Graesser, A. C. (1999).The effect of metaphor on processing style in a persuasion task: A motivational resonance model. *Journal of Personality and Social Psychology, 77,* 688–697.

Paivio, A., & Lambert, W. (1981). Dual coding and bilingual memory. *Journal of Verbal Learning and Verbal Behavior, 20,* 532–539.

Petty, R. E., & Cacioppo, J. T. (1986) *Communication and persuasion: Central and peripheral routes to attitude change.* New York: Springer-Verlag.

Radvansky, G. A., Wyer, R. S., Curiel, J. M., & Lutz, M. F. (1997). Mental models and abstract relations. *Journal of Experimental Psychology: Learning, Memory, and Cognition, 23,* 1233–1246.

Reyes, R. M., Thompson, W. C., & Bower, G. H. (1980). Judgmental biases resulting from differing availabilities of arguments. *Journal of Personality and Social Psychology, 39,* 2–12.

Ross, M. (1989). Relation of implicit theories to the construction of personal histories. *Psychological Review, 96,* 341–357.

Routledge, C., Arndt, J., & Goldenberg, J. L. (2004). A time to tan: Proximal and distal effects of mortality salience on sun exposure intentions. *Personality and Social Psychology Bulletin, 30,* 1347–1358.

Sawyer, A. G., & Howard, D. J. (1991). Effects of omitting conclusions in advertisements to involved and uninvolved audiences. *Journal of Marketing Research, 28,* 467–474.

Schank, R. C., & Abelson, R. P. (1995). Knowledge and memory: The real story. In R S. Wyer (Ed.), *Advances in social cognition* (Vol. 8, pp. 1–85). Hillsdale, NJ: Lawrence Erlbaum Associates.

Schmitt, B. H., Pan, Y., & Tavassoli, N. T. (1994). Language and consumer memory: The impact of linguistic differences between Chinese and English. *Journal of Consumer Research, 21,* 419–431.

Schmitt, B. H., & Zhang, S. (1998). Language structure and categorization: A study of classifiers in consumer cognition, judgment, and choice. *Journal of Consumer Research, 25,* 108–122.

Searle, J. R. (1979). Metaphor. In A. Ortony (Ed.), *Metaphor and thought* (pp. 92–123). Cambridge, MA: Cambridge University Press.

Sherman, S. J., Ahlm, K., Berman, L., & Lynn, S. (1978). Contrast effects and the relationship to subsequent behavior. *Journal of Experimental Social Psychology, 14,* 340–350.

Sperber, D., & Wilson, D. (1986). *Relevance: Communication and cognition.* Oxford, England: Blackwell.

Srull, T. K., & Wyer, R. S. (1980). Category accessibility and social perception: Some implications for the study of person memory and interpersonal judgments. *Journal of Personality and Social Psychology, 38*, 841–856.

Taylor, S. E., & Fiske, S. T. (1978). Salience, attention and attribution: Top of the head phenomena. In L. Berkowitz (Ed.), *Advances in experimental social psychology* (Vol. 11, pp. 249–288). New York: Academic Press.

Toncar, M., & Munch, J. (2001). Consumer responses to tropes in print advertising. *Journal of Advertising, 30*, 55–64.

Tsuru, S., & Fries, H. (1933). A problem in meaning. *Journal of General Psychology, 81*, 281–284.

Verbrugge, R. R. (1976). Resemblances in language and perception. In R. Shaw & J. D. Bransford (Eds.), *Perceiving, acting and comprehending: Toward an ecological psychology* (pp. 365–389). Hillsdale, NJ: Lawrence Erlbaum Associates.

Walster, E. (1966). Assignment of responsibility for an accident. *Journal of Personality and Social Psychology, 3*, 73–79.

Wyer, R. S. (1974). *Cognitive organization and change: An information-processing approach*. Hillsdale, NJ: Lawrence Erlbaum Associates.

Wyer, R. S. (2004). *Social comprehension and judgment: The role of situation models, narratives and implicit theories*. Mahwah, NJ: Lawrence Erlbaum Associates.

Wyer, R. S. (in press). The role of knowledge accessibility in cognition and behavior: Implications for consumer information processing. In C. Haugtvedt, F. Kardes, & P. Herr (Eds.), *Handbook of consumer research*. Mahwah, NJ: Lawrence Erlbaum Associates.

Wyer, R. S., Adaval, R., & Colcombe, S. J. (2002). Narrative-based representations of social knowledge: Their construction and use in comprehension, memory and judgment. In M. P. Zanna (Ed.), *Advances in experimental social psychology* (Vol. 34, pp.131–197). San Diego: Academic Press.

Wyer, R. S., Bodenhausen, G. V., & Gorman, T. F. (1985). Cognitive mediators of reactions to rape. *Journal of Personality and Social Psychology, 48*, 324–338.

Wyer, R. S., & Gruenfeld, D. H. (1995). Information processing in social contexts: Implications for social memory and judgment. In M. P. Zanna (Ed.), *Advances in experimental social psychology* (Vol. 27, pp. 49–91). San Diego, CA: Academic Press.

Wyer, R. S., & Radvansky, G. A. (1999). The comprehension and validation of social information. *Psychological Review, 106*, 89–118.

Wyer, R. S., & Srull, T. K. (1989). *Memory and cognition in its social context*. Hillsdale, NJ: Lawrence Erlbaum Associates.

Yorkston, E., & Menon, G. (2004). A sound idea: Phonetic effects of brand names on consumer judgments. *Journal of Consumer Research, 31*, 43–51.

Author Index

Subject Index

A

Abstract myths, 182–183
Accentuation theory, 9–10
Acquisition of abstract and concrete myths, 189–191
Across-boundary exaggeration, 9, 11
Activating brand name meaning, 87–90
Advertising and marketing, 210–215
Advertising myths, 185
Advertising narratives, 166–170
Attribute identifiers, 3
Attribute labels, 7–8

B

Bilingual–bicultural processing, 235
Bilingual cognitive processing, 227–230, *see also* chapter 4 of this volume
Brand discrimination, 18
Brand equity, 6
Brand identifiers, 3
Brand processing, 226–227
Brand names and phonetic symbolism, 47–53, *see also* chapter 5 of this volume

C

Categorization, 3, 5, *see also* chapter 4 of this volume, 262, 263
Code switching, 240–242

Color perception, 4–5, *see also* Shape perception
Comprehension processes in advertising
cognitive efficiency, 257–259
comprehension of noun concepts, 259–260
deliberative comprehension processes, 254–255
dimension of meaning, 260–262
event representations, 268–270
implicational molecules, 255–257
metaphors and persuasion, 266
motivational considerations, 265–266
multiple meanings, 264–265
myths and metaphors, 270
narratives, 266–268
paralinguistic influences, 271
persistence over time, 258–259, 262–263
sentence comprehension, 263–264
spontaneous comprehension processes, 251–2153
verbal and nonverbal information, 185–189
Conceptual categorization, 11
Conceptual metaphor, 135–151 (chapter 8 of this volume), *see also* Metaphor
Concrete myths, 179–182
Consumer predictability, 11–12

289

Printed in the United States
by Baker & Taylor Publisher Services